Smart Transitions in City Regionalism

T0383099

In recent years "smartness" has risen as a buzzword to characterise novel urban policy and development patterns. As a result of this, debates around what "smart" actually means, both theoretically and empirically, have emerged within the interdisciplinary arenas of urban and regional studies. This book explores the changes in discourse, rationality and selected responses of smartness through the theme of "transition."

The concept of transition provides the broader context and points of reference for adopting smartness in reconciling competing interests and agendas in city-regional governance. Using case studies from around the world, including North America, Europe and South Africa, the authors link external regime transition in societal values and goals with internal moves towards smartness. While reflecting the growing integration of overarching themes and analytical concerns, this volume further develops work on smartness, smart growth, transition, city-regionalism, governance and sustainability.

Smart Transitions in City Regionalism explores how smart cities and city regions interact with conventional state structures. It will be of great interest to postgraduates and advanced undergraduates across urban studies, geography, sustainability studies and political science.

Tassilo Herrschel is Reader in Urban and Regional Governance in the Department of Politics and International Relations at the University of Westminster, UK, and Associate Research Fellow at the Brussels Centre for Urban Studies, Vrije Universiteit Brussel, Belgium.

Yonn Dierwechter is Professor in the Urban Studies Program at the University of Washington, Tacoma, USA.

Regions and Cities
Series Editor in Chief
Joan Fitzgerald, *Northeastern University, USA*

Editors
Ron Martin, *University of Cambridge, UK*
Maryann Feldman, *University of North Carolina, USA*
Gernot Grabher, *HafenCity University Hamburg, Germany*
Kieran P. Donaghy, *Cornell University, USA*

In today's globalised, knowledge-driven and networked world, regions and cities have assumed heightened significance as the interconnected nodes of economic, social and cultural production, and as sites of new modes of economic and territorial governance and policy experimentation. This book series brings together incisive and critically engaged international and interdisciplinary research on this resurgence of regions and cities, and should be of interest to geographers, economists, sociologists, political scientists and cultural scholars, as well as to policy-makers involved in regional and urban development.

For more information on the Regional Studies Association visit www.regionalstudies.org

There is a **30% discount** available to RSA members on books in the *Regions and Cities* series, and other subject related Taylor & Francis books and e-books including Routledge titles. To order just e-mail Joanna Swieczkowska, Joanna.Swieczkowska@tandf.co.uk, or phone on +44 (0)20 3377 3369 and declare your RSA membership. You can also visit the series page at www.routledge.com/Regions-and-Cities/book-series/RSA and use the discount code: **RSA0901**

Smart Transitions in City Regionalism

Territory, Politics and the Quest for Competitiveness and Sustainability

**Tassilo Herrschel
and Yonn Dierwechter**

Routledge
Taylor & Francis Group

LONDON AND NEW YORK

First published 2018 by Routledge

2 Park Square, Milton Park, Abingdon, Oxfordshire OX14 4RN

52 Vanderbilt Avenue, New York, NY 10017

Routledge is an imprint of the Taylor & Francis Group, an informa business

First issued in paperback 2020

British Library Cataloguing-in-Publication Data
A catalogue record for this book is available from the British Library

Library of Congress Cataloging-in-Publication Data
Names: Herrschel, Tassilo, 1958– author. | Dierwechter, Yonn, author.
Title: Smart transitions in city regionalism : territory, politics and the quest for competitiveness and sustainability / Tassilo Herrschel and Yonn Dierwechter.
Description: Abingdon, Oxon ; New York, NY : Routledge, 2018. | Series: Regions and cities | Includes bibliographical references and index.
Identifiers: LCCN 2017048664 (print) | LCCN 2017056402 (ebook) | ISBN 9781315696775 (Ebook) | ISBN 9781138903609 (hardback : alk. paper)
Subjects: LCSH: Regional planning. | City planning. | Urban policy. | Regionalism.
Classification: LCC HT391 (ebook) | LCC HT391 .H395 2018 (print) | DDC 307.1/216—dc23
LC record available at https://lccn.loc.gov/2017048664

ISBN: 978-1-138-90360-9 (hbk)
ISBN: 978-0-367-66694-1 (pbk)

Typeset in Bembo
by Book Now Ltd, London

Contents

Illustrations

Figures

Tables

Introduction

Smartness as new rubric

All things "smart" are now all the rage. So debates about what it all actually means are raging as well, not least in the interdisciplinary arenas of urban and regional studies. "Smartness," it now appears, serves increasingly as the expansive rubric under which several related, yet at times antecedent, concepts and policy concerns gather: e.g. smart *growth*, smart *cities*, smart *administration*, smart *specialization*, smart *labour*, smart *objects* and even something some researchers have called *smartization*. Each of these synoptic concepts and analytical concerns – and many others in various fields – has its own intellectual bloodlines, adherents, critics, believers, opportunists and sceptics. Moreover, too often we find in applied practice little more than smart *wash* to make policy documents and agendas simply appear trendy, novel and innovative. Not only is there a gap between practitioners and academics in viewing and utilizing "smart" as an add-on adjective, deeper epistemic cultures among researchers diverge and, sometimes, clash. Political scientists invoke the relevance of institutions; economists, markets; architects, built-environments; geographers, spatialities; anthropologists, subjectivities; and engineers, gadgets.

For observers outside the academy, especially in the business world and in most journalism, smartness probably still evokes "hard" discussions of ICT integration, Big Data, sensors, digital competencies, coding creativity, efficiency and so on. It is this view of smartness that most of us are confronted with in daily life: smart metering, smart payments, smart parking and so on – a brave new (urbanized) world of widgets, digits and apps, producing, so the narrative runs, better-timed traffic lights, lower-energy refrigerators and open parking spaces and thus, in the end, a better quality of life. As one commentator sees it, *smart cities* are:

> communities where technology improves everything from traffic flow and trash collection to snow removal and healthcare services and where an infrastructure of sensors enables public officials to identify and address emergencies more quickly, are surely better than the status quo. Smart cities are for smart citizens who want better living through technology.
>
> (Munro, 2017)

For many questions, too, that is probably quite adequate, especially given the dominance in total research output of large and well-funded fields like electrical and electronic engineering, telecommunications and computer science. "Hard" smartness, following the work of Albino, Berardi and Dangelico (2015) and others, is thus about integrating ICT into city networks, digitizing urbanism, prying open public administration and unleashing social activism in new ways. Smartness here is about more efficient functionality through optimized timing and interconnections between different relations.

This is novel, we acknowledge, but also strangely familiar. Railways changed everything in their day. So did airplanes and cars and more or less at the same time. The predictability, reliability and connectivity these ground-breaking technologies introduced into the world also produced fundamental re-evaluations of time and space and thus perceived opportunities for action and engagement. Radios and telephones further collapsed cultural and economic spaces and created novel connections and once-unimagined efficiencies based on knowledge of developments beyond daily face-to-face routines. Indeed, telephone densities served as reliable indicators of spatial and social connectivities, the delimitation of market areas and centrality of places (Ullman, 1941; Güssefeldt, 1980). While the diffusion of these forms of mobility, connectivity and information changed cities and societies fundamentally, however, the jury is still out on the new dimensions and impacts of socio-political and economic adjustments that information and communication technology (ICT) has occasioned. Much of what we experience as "change" may well be the "repetition" of a longer cycle, perhaps couched only in the language and appearance projected through a new medium, for example, a fresh Kondratieff wave; a social pattern of behaviour that is suddenly given a new tool to regain relevance and influence and seeming novelty. Technological experiences may be new *to us*, but not to socio-historical change.

This all raises many intriguing questions. Is smartness just a more grounded way of talking about established policy agendas and political debates, such as sustainability, for instance? Alternatively, has smartness inadvertently (or perhaps even deliberately) oversimplified sustainability, tritely reducing our biggest global problems to funding, building and managing stylish technologies in the city-as-cyberspace – to the new infrastructures of 'smartization' *per se*? In contrast, as we move well into the 21st century, can we really conceive to implement sustainability and competitiveness – however defined – without the various meso-concepts that now populate the broader rubric of smartness itself? Can we so do without the new, smarter ways of communicating, governing, moving around, learning, assembling land uses, gathering and disseminating data and policy ideas and so on? A good deal of carbon emissions, after all, relate to the simplest of recurrent daily routines: to idling cars, for instance, or even just to circulating (blindly) through cities in search of always scarce parking. This may seem too banal and for many advocates of sustainability the whole point is to get beyond circulating cars *tout court*. Still, big problems often result from small rituals, as the "constitution of society" as a whole results from what Anthony Giddens (1984) – drawing on Hagerstrand – memorably theorized as the repetitive "time-geographies" of everyday life. Giddens captured this as "structuration." And so, if we can make our everyday *agency* smarter, can we also reshape our larger structures as we do so? Is the diffusion of urban smartness in particular *places*, so rendered, part and parcel of the structuration of global sustainability in all its various facets? Is, perhaps, smartness the ability to connect effectively the many different interests to produce a hypothetical win–win situation for all?

Infused with the expansive promises of data technology and with such grand questions in the background, in this book we explore the idea that smartness has become the new paradigm *de rigueur* to characterize urban and regional policies that go beyond the competitiveness agenda, to address also the multifaceted quest for various forms of sustainability. Sustainability, so imagined, drives long-term ambitions to do things differently than before through improved policy balance, institutional integration and renewed democratic legitimacy. Can we really still benefit from globalized, metropolitan-based economies struggling with competitiveness without severely degrading multi-scalar ecosystems or reproducing untenable social divisions and immoral inequalities (Talen, 2012)? Smartness theories suggest that perhaps we can – and, possibly, we already are doing so, at least to some extent, in some respects, in some places, some of the time. And arguably at minimum, the conventional, modernist paradigm of quantitative growth is steadily giving way to a more nuanced, reflective, responsible, qualitative form of (smarter) development. References to "happiness" and the United Nations' annual reports on Human Development Indicators, rather than standard GDP figures, reflect such shifts (Wolfers & Leigh, 2006). Various policy movements within metropolitan regions around urban livability and resilience further represent rejections of modernist-style approaches, *viz.* segregated land-uses, automobile-dependency, low-density development and carbon-intensive urbanism (Evans, 2002; Jonas, 2012a). Smartness is one way – at least as a suggested attempt – to grapple with these multi-scalar and uneven shifts.

Within this context, we seek to explore in the coming chapters select changes in discourse, rationality and suggested responses of smartness through the organizing theme of "transition" (Deakin, 2013). Originally developed in conjunction with regime change as part of post-authoritarian democratization (Herrschel, 2005; Schmitter & O'Donnell, 2013), we suggest here that transition can be applied to the search for sustainability in its wider sense (Smith, Stirling, & Berkhout, 2005). Specifically, we link external *regime transition* in societal values and goals with internal moves toward smartness in policy applications, governing strategies and project practices "on the ground" (Adler and Webster, 1995; Ginsberg, 1996; Kuzio, 2001; Schmitter & O'Donnell, 2013). While the former reflects the "bigger picture" of change at the societal level, then, the latter is more concerned with the design and instrumentalization of governing at the city-regional scale. Such work involves efforts to (try to) reconcile the contradictions between modernist (quantitative) growth models and more post-modernization concerns with a wider range of qualitative parameters, perhaps including "happiness." Transition, we suggest, provides the broader context, situated, so the argument here, at two primary scales – national/global and sub-national/city-regional and points of reference for adopting urban smartness as a way to manage material interests and policy agendas in city-regional governance.

The interrelationships between the wider societal context, especially discourses about the nature of developmental goals, objectives and outcomes and their manifestations in city-regional governance, therefore sit at the centre of this book. We use urban case studies from different parts of the world – North America, Western and Eastern Europe and South Africa – to illustrate the varying empirics of the two main transitions distinguished here: (a) wider societal, political and economic changes and, especially, their interactions with diverse agendas and (b) *modi operandi* in the manifestation of city-regional governance. The analysis on offer seeks, in particular, to integrate discourses of "smart cities," often too heavily focused on ICT themes, with "smart growth," in turn concentrated narrowly on planning. This is attempted in novel ways, while also insisting (with others) on the "city-region" as a key geopolitical and policy space for territorial governance in the global economy that has re-emerged since the early 1990s (Harrison, 2010; Jonas, 2012a; Morandi, Rolando, & Di Vita, 2015). Accordingly, the title of this book, *Smart Transitions in City Regionalism*, reflects the growing integration of these overarching themes and analytical concerns, while further attempting to develop our own earlier work on smartness, smart growth, transition, city-regionalism, governance and sustainability (Dierwechter, 2013, 2014, 2017; Herrschel, 2013, 2014; Herrschel & Dierwechter, 2015; Herrschel & Newman, 2017). As geographers, we are especially eager to emphasize a globalized plurality of *transitions*, of variously situated pathways and differentiations, even as we identity common themes and challenges in smartly rebuilding city-regions for twenty-first century challenges.

Smart city-regionalism, as used here, has striated conceptual origins, or what we shall refer to in Chapter 2 as a complex "genetic coding," that results from the cross-fertilization of various intellectual bloodlines. In brief, the contemporary popularity of the policy term "smart" appears to have North American origins, although no one has conclusively established that. The urban planning concept of "smart growth" emerged influentially in the United States, in general and the Environmental Protection Agency and Maryland, in particular, during the mid-1990s as a novel, if syncretic, regulatory response to ongoing suburban sprawl and fiscal stress, but also as a pragmatic way to operationalize and territorialize somewhat vague global sustainability goals (Brown & Southworth, 2008; Chapin, 2012; Dierwechter, 2014; Krueger & Gibbs, 2008). It soon also appeared just as forcefully across metropolitan Canada, in key city-regions such as Toronto, Calgary and Vancouver. If well-located and properly connected, the concept held, "growth" could be a solution, not only a problem (Arku, 2009; Burchell, Listokin, & Galley, 2000; Daniels, 2001; Downs, 2001, 2005; Goetz, 2005; Hess & Sorensen, 2014; Pozdena, 2002).

Since that time, however, smart growth *stictu sensu* has diffused quite rapidly across global policy space – splintering, morphing and evolving into a now wider label for a new, more reflective and putatively innovative way of doing things beyond just planning/land-use/transportation approaches *per se* (Caragliu, Del Bo, & Nijkamp, 2011). From 2008 or so, as just suggested, the astonishing proliferation of applied work on "smart cities" – advanced by the marketing prowess of IBM, Siemens, Cisco, Microsoft, etc. – has shifted popular and scholarly attention to the presumed role of ICT, big (and open) data and "real-time" monitoring in the more intelligent management of built-environmental and other types of urban-regional systems (Angelidou, 2015; Batty, 2016; Batty et al., 2012; Caragliu et al., 2011; Deakin, 2013; Glasmeier & Christopherson, 2015; Kourtit, Nijkamp, & Arribas, 2012; Townsend, 2013). Researchers are now exploring economic competitiveness, ecological sustainability, energy budgets, administrative efficacy, data integration and coordination, citizen empowerment and, ultimately a more agile, "intelligent," efficient and problem-oriented culture of territorial (e)governance (Allwinkle & Cruickshank, 2011). With such growing trendiness, however, there is obviously a real danger of smartness becoming breezily normative and overly technocratic, with insufficient empirical considerations of *differing* political, economic, cultural and societal milieux as place-specific descriptors. Although smartness also generates commonalities, one main motivation for this book is that such milieux *vary geographically* – not only within the Western world, of course, but also within and especially between, all parts of the globe.

In our view, smartness increasingly signifies a discursive formula to capture variegated changes in the way urban development both can and by growing public consensus should, be directed. Smartness as innovative and also experimental governance seeks to accommodate this broader range of aspirations and agendas (Herrschel, 2013) – including underlying theoretical claims and empirical meanings that vary from place to place and between scholars, but especially with strategic reference to *city-regional* dynamics (Jonas, 2012b). We agree with Shahrokni and Brandt (2013, p. 117), for example, who suggest that a smart city is actually a broader "urban region" where Internet and communication technologies "weave together" physical, social and business infrastructures; such creative handiwork might facilitate "intelligent decision-making and efficient city dynamics in order to realize sustainable development goals through citizen empowerment and participatory democracy." For this is an ambitious conceptualization of global change, touching on and *articulating together*, technocracy, democracy, urbanism and sustainability.

Yet, we also maintain, that the pre-conditions for such change will vary considerably, influencing the propensity for any given "inter-weaving" and its practical manifestations. Recent international smart city-networks like City Protocol, for instance, envision an urban future of "open, collective movement[s] to radically improve the way people around the globe develop, deploy and embrace technologies for the benefit of humanity" (City Protocol, 2014). More generally conceptualized, Deakin (2013, p. 7) sees the recent, sometimes locally self-proclaimed, but still empirically under-explored, emergence of "*smart-er* cities" [and regions] as "people-based, human, socially-inclusive, environmentally sensitive and culturally aware." We wonder how the many components of smartness, whether studied in one city alone or across several, are reconciled and then actually operationalized, to make it into more than a broadly appealing, seemingly obvious, yet still fuzzy, concept enrolled by publicity-conscious mayors and splashed across interactive webpages.

This key research concern requires, in our view, an extended treatment developed through the lens of comparative urbanism, set in the wider framework of political-economic and societal transformation. For smartness increasingly extends to new approaches and does so world-wide, in multi-scalar policy efforts to reconcile contradictory aspirations for urban (economic) and regional (re)development between politically motivated short-term growth agendas and a politically more difficult to drive long-term global sustainability agenda. In consequence, we could interpret the "smart turn" mainly as a post-Keynesian, thoroughly neoliberalized, opportunistically driven and overly techno-utopian adaptation of older forms of territorial and economic governance (Lafferty, 2004), seen mostly from a Western perspective. So read, smart partnerships between governments, corporations, citizen-consumers and NGOs only mask deeper tensions in contemporary global capitalism. Yet, we suggest, the *degree* to which this applies and the *role* public discussions acquire vis-à-vis political structures, adopted governmental practices and capitalist principles, *vary* on the basis of particular circumstances, histories and political-economic milieux.

This geographical concern leads to the book's central argument around seeing the variegated nature of urban smartness through the theoretical lens of a "dual transition."

A "dual transition"?

We suggest and attempt to substantiate through a series of comparative case studies, that smartness might be productively interpreted as an inchoate, contested, politically open and institutionally dynamic effort to find fresh answers to both ideological and practical conundrums. We argue, specifically, that smartness is a political and geographical effort to "square the circle" (Herrschel, 2013) between contending agendas and *modi operandi*. Smartness, in our judgement, seeks a new governance pathway between regulatory state interventions and market-based neo-liberalism – or what we shall discuss here as a (presumably) democratic quest for competitiveness and sustainability beyond a fixation on, for example, Ostrōm-inspired "new public management." Accordingly, we trace the ways in which practitioners and actors are actively negotiating how to balance local, regional and global concerns with ecological (un)sustainability, economic (un)competitiveness and democratic (un)accountability in both policy-making and institution-building (Herrschel, 2014) and their varying spatial manifestations.

Reflecting often-clashing interests by topic, time horizons and geographic (scalar) references, such negotiations are of course deeply political, but we believe increasingly signal emergent empirical changes in contemporary territorial governance across the world. Smartness, we additionally suggest, is about developing and utilizing new forms of networked governance and governmental institutions to address the challenges of established hierarchies and state structures in response to and with the involvement of, respective electorates. We show that the relational, opportunistic and imagined spaces of smartness often fail to coincide with long-term static, yet familiar, state-administrative territorialities of power and public authority. Yet while new forms of smart governance are frequently *ad hoc*, precarious, reversible and unpredictable, this book shows how they are also potentially helping: first, to emancipate and re-energize cities and their economic and political-ecological regions (Scott, 2012; Taylor, 2005) beyond a focus on a few global cities as hypothesized beacons of success; second, to build city-centric networks of various kinds at multiple scales in pursuit of diverse goals, from carbon mitigation, to 'multi-scaled' democracy and the recursive exchange of redevelopment practices (Anderson, 2002; Barber, 2013); and, third, how to construct a platform for examining the potential challenges to state-territorial and democratic-representative cohesion by focusing on urban-centric re-spatializations of the territorial heritage. In particular, we theorize and place at the centre of this book, these key changes as a "dual transition" composed of, respectively, an "internal" transition as well as an "external" transition to the locus of governing city-regions (Herrschel & Dierwechter, 2015).

On the one hand, we explore the general transition to smartness as a new phase in city-regional governance, drawing on recent debates, themes and claims associated with the impacts of city-regionalism (Dierwechter, 2013; Harding, 2007; Harrison, 2007; Harrison & Heley, 2014; Herrschel & Dierwechter, 2015; Herrschel & Newman, 2002; Jonas, 2012a; Scott, 2001; Simmonds, 2000). The turn to smartness represents, we argue, a "transitioned" form of city-regional *governing*, now different from post-Fordist, neo-liberal paradigms – a theme that comports with Alan Scott's (2011) suggestion that we have now likely moved "beyond post-Fordism." At a time when nation-state democracy, the "most successful political philosophy of the 20th century," may be in "deep crisis" (*The Economist*, 2014), new trends in smart city-regionalism foreground potentially far-reaching developments in linking new geographic spaces with older state structures and governing practices. By mobilizing fresh resources, being imaginative about new governance practices and using institutions and less formal collaborative organizations, we aim to show how smart city-regionalism is opening up and pressing for, important new ideas about democratic legitimacy and political inclusion (cf. Barber, 2013).

On the other hand, we also seek to understand how these same dynamics are influenced by wider externalities, such as moments (and places) of major regime change, which alter the points of reference and legitimacy for the criteria used to guide and justify the principles of governance in practice at the city-regional level "emancipating" and re-energizing cities, building new city-centric networks and providing novel platforms of territorial governance. And such highlights urban relationships with "non-urban" areas within the region and state, which include various types of settlements within the city-regional space-economy. This question becomes particularly significant when "gaps" between the core urban nodes widen as part of broader political-economic processes now associated with a more devolved, network-based arrangement for policy-making processes and powers. This whole system of dual transition is in constant flux, as globalization and technological changes continuously redefine societal-economic parameters, values and political agendas, which in turn, redefine what is understood as good practice and efficient and legitimate democratic governance. And learning processes about what works and what does not, add also to the inherent dynamic of the meaning and practice of smartness in city-regional governance.

Conventional state structures and territorialities appear as antidotes to this new dynamic, network-based, city-centric (and city-created) form of seeking to influence and respond to, economic processes; and they do so by continuously evolving into new forms of governing mechanisms and practices (Jonas, 2013). Yet these static structures also offer fixed and reliable points of reference for the location and arrangement of variable network governance, even if their own relative positions and roles are changing in the wider national and international system of relationships, linkages and perceived opportunities and threats. For these shifts, such as during *régime* changes, we examine how city-centric networks develop and operate in their dependency on cities as anchors – albeit themselves potentially repositioning as part of the proposed *dual transition* – and thus paradoxically increasing the likely distance between conventional state structures and urban networks as channels of (relational) power. It is this that sits at the heart of dual regime transition as understood here in relation to changing city-regional practices in governing within a shifting discursive and functional national and international setting. Once again, this book seeks to fuse the concept of *régime* transition within city-regional governance and "smartness" as the mechanism linking the two agendas and practices together.

Contents of book

To develop our argument, the book is divided into two main parts, each containing three main chapters, plus an introduction, interim conclusions for both parts and general conclusions.

The first part of this book consists of three chapters that critically engage and synthesize debates and themes relating to recent research on "smartness" in the politics and governance of city-regions vis-à-vis the discursive and actual changes in the geopolitical economies and societies of globalized urbanism. This leads to the introduction and elaboration of the concept of smartness as "dual transition" in city-regional governance. We trace two concurrent processes of change: one inside cities and city regions as in the form of evolving 'smartness' in governance, shaped by local conditions and one much wider, outside city-regions, providing shifting societal values, discursive priorities and institutional settings as transitioning systemic (values, agendas, practices) frameworks.

Specifically, Chapter 1 introduces the overarching themes and claims of the book, situating them within the broader context of a more widely claimed recent "turn" to smart city, smartness discourses and variously described smart modes of urban analysis. The discussion here links "smartness" as the *emergent*, indeed trendy, meta-paradigm in global city-regionalism to the parallel notion of "transition," which refers not only to the world "beyond post-Fordism," following Alan Scott's (2011) recent work, but also to recent trends in and conceptualizations of, "post-authoritarian" societies. Chapter 2 next explores the literature on city-regions from an explicitly economic perspective, focusing thematically on city regions as originators of innovation and foci of enhanced competitiveness and global city-regions as putatively "Post-Westphalian" spaces pursuing sustainability through smartness and finally cities as both locales of economic investment and/or reflecting uneven visibility and "voice" in shaping national and international agendas. This last theme leads directly to a more explicit engagement with the political dimensions of city-regions in Chapter 3, which picks up and further develops in more detail, select themes broached toward the end of Chapter 2 on the emerging politics of global city-regionalism. In particular, Chapter 3 discusses new spaces of "clubbing together" (Scott, 2001), a general term which captures an array of new activities and self-organizing mechanisms of territorial governance at various scales of policy and programme activity (Moisio & Paasi, 2013). Increasingly, these include international city-networks, such as C40, as well as new tools for lobbying national governments. We contend in this chapter that such spaces are often "softly" institutionalized or "thinly" constituted – terms we detail here as well – in order to avoid threatening both traditional local entities as well as higher scale political authorities (Jonas & Pincetl, 2006). As a result, they are relatively easy to change and correspond with the opportunistic, time-dependent and goal-oriented nature of such arrangements.

The second part of this book likewise comprises three main chapters but with the addition of a short summary. As stated earlier, Chapter 4 establishes the overall analytical framework for the subsequent detailed empirical discussion. This framework help us to explore the main empirical questions raised by the case studies, namely: What are the policy-making processes and who are the key actors? What are the mechanisms of negotiation and involvement as well as of exclusion? How do specific political modalities, including established structures and ways of doing things, democratic traditions and electoral expectations about state involvement, impact governance? What are the main concerns and strategic goals of the key actors – and what are their key areas of activity and concern? What kind of decision-making and institutional cultures are present and – in particular – how do the broader transitional dynamics discussed above affect – perhaps condition – these cultures of decision-making and institutional behavior?

Chapters 5 and 6 present a series of comparative case studies in diverse world regions, which together consider different "external" and "internal" milieux as expressions of "dual transitions" affecting city-regional governance. For instance, one question concerns the balance between internal and external factors and its impact on city regional governance moving toward adopting principles of "smartness." The discussions focus especially on the themes of transition *beyond* inherited regimes of territorial governance, raising key questions around path dependency arguments, as a result of changing societal discourses, values, agendas and evaluations both within and outside specific city-regions at specific times. Chapter 5 focuses on the recent experiences of four globalizing city-regions in the long-standing economic "core" of North America and Western Europe, where state structures and governance practices have been long established; changes are closely associated with political discourse as rationale for changes, either initiated centrally or locally; and where federalization or centralization matter. The examples in North America and Western Europe reflect such differences. Vancouver and Seattle illustrate North American individualistic, (neo)-liberal ideology, yet also different degrees of "localism" as part of state structures and state involvement with local matters north and south of the border. Meanwhile, Lyon and Turin, while exemplifying Western European tensions between "welfare" and "workfare" (Jessop, 1993), also differ in their national contexts of a more centralized France and federalized Italy, respectively.

Chapter 6 next looks at "transition regimes" as external milieux for shaping smartness in city regional governance. As described above, they are characterized by dynamic changes, as they undergo extensive regimes changes producing uncertainties, yet also new opportunities to identify new ways of doing things. These transitioning contexts vary in their complexity and extent, including in post-communist Central Europe all three main spheres: economy, society and state, while in South Africa, regime change embraces crucial changes in society and the nature and operation of the state, although far less change in the workings of the economy (Marais, 1998). These transformative changes, we argue, have had major implications for the ways in which city-regions can function (Parnell, 2007; Pillay, 2004). In Central Europe, the main urban regions, especially the capital city regions, have been at the forefront of the post-communist transition process toward a democratic market economy Western-style. This has unearthed and also reinforced, underlying inequalities in opportunities, yet also engrained perceptions of the role of the state, territorially-based governance and policy agendas. Approximating "Western Europe" has been the explicit motivation of developments, driven further by the conditioning requirements for EU accession. Such European "adjustment pressures" obviously have not played a key role in South Africa, where, instead, global and national dynamics of societal change have been paramount (OECD, 2008).

Finally, Chapter 7 outlines the overall conclusions of this book, as they link the specific insights gained from the comparative analysis of case studies to the broader theoretical arguments and constructs outlined and developed in the first part of the discussion, especially as it relates to the overall notion of a societally embedded and more broadly discursively driven dual transition toward principles of "smartness" in city-regional governance structures and practices. Here again, we draw attention to how the "smartness" movement should really be interpreted as a politically open and institutionally dynamic effort to address both ideological and practical conundrums in policy-making. The chapter reemphasizes how, in each of the cases, "smartness" is energizing new territorial coalitions and development aspirations, building new city-centric networks at various scales of operation and, finally, creating new governance platforms – albeit in geographically variegated ways around the world – with varying degrees of "fit" into, or challenge to, existing state structures and societal values and aspirations. We provide a summary of how the many components of smartness are reconciled and operationalized in various cultural and historical settings and diverse institutional environments and how this in turn affects discourses at the city-regional level. We ultimately offer broad suggestions for both policy and further research on the conceptualization of governance at the city-regional level in an international context (Lackowska & Zimmermann, 2011).

References

Adler, G., & Webster, E. (1995). Challenging transition theory: The labor movement, radical reform, and transition to democracy in South Africa. *Politics & Society, 23*(1), 75–106.

Albino, V., Berardi, U., & Dangelico, R. M. (2015). Smart cities: Definitions, dimensions, performance, and initiatives. *Journal of Urban Technology, 22*(1), 3–21. doi:10.1080/106 30732.2014.942092

Allwinkle, S., & Cruickshank, P. (2011). Creating smart-er cities: An overview. *Journal of Urban Technology, 18*(2), 1–16. doi:10.1080/10630732.2011.601103

Anderson, J. (Ed.) (2002). *Transnational democracy.* London: Routledge.

Angelidou, M. (2015). Smart cities: A conjuncture of four forces. *Cities, 47*(0), 95–106. Retrieved from http://dx.doi.org/10.1016/j.cities.2015.05.004, accessed 10 Nov. 2017.

Arku, G. (2009). Rapidly growing African cities need to adopt smart growth policies to solve urban development concerns. *Urban Forum, 20*(3), 253–270. Retrieved from http://dx.doi.org/10.1007/s12132-009-9047-z, accessed 10 Nov. 2017.

Barber, B. (2013). *If mayors ruled the world: Dysfunctional nations, rising cities.* New Haven, CT: Yale University Press.

Batty, M. (2016). How disruptive is the smart cities movement? *Environment and Planning B: Planning and Design, 43*(3), 441–443.

Batty, M., Axhausen, K. W., Giannotti, F., Pozdnoukhov, A., Bazzani, A., Wachowicz, M., … Portugali, Y. (2012). Smart cities of the future. *The European Physical Journal Special Topics, 214*(1), 481–518. doi:10.1140/epjst/e2012-01703-3

Brown, M. A., & Southworth, F. (2008). Mitigating climate change through green buildings and smart growth. *Environment and Planning A, 40*(3), 653–675. doi:10.1068/a38419

Burchell, R., Listokin, D., & Galley, C. (2000). Smart growth: More than a ghost of urban policy past, less than a bold new horizon. *Housing Policy Debate, 11*(4), 821–879.

Caragliu, A., Del Bo, C., & Nijkamp, P. (2011). Smart cities in Europe. *Journal of Urban Technology, 18*(2), 65–82. doi:10.1080/10630732.2011.601117

Chapin, T. S. (2012). Introduction: From growth controls, to comprehensive planning, to smart growth: Planning's emerging fourth wave. *Journal of the American Planning Association, 78*(1), 5–15. doi:10.1080/01944363.2011.645273

City Protocol. (2014). *Community, collabortion, consensus, committment.* Retrieved from http://www.cityprotocol.org/principles.html, accessed 21 Oct. 2016.

Daniels, T. (2001). Smart growth: A new American approach to regional planning. *Planning Practice and Research, 16*(3–4), 271–279.

Deakin, M. (2013). *Smart cities governing, modelling and analysing the transition.* Hoboken, NJ: Taylor & Francis.

Dierwechter, Y. (2013). Smart city-regionalism across Seattle: Progressing transit nodes in labor space? *Geoforum, 49*(0), 139–149.

Dierwechter, Y. (2014). The spaces that smart growth makes: Sustainability, segregation, and residential change across Greater Seattle. *Urban Geography, 35*(5), 691–714. doi:10.1080/02723638.2014.916905

Dierwechter, Y. (2017). *Urban Sustainability through smart growth: Intercurrence, planning, and geographies of regional development across Greater Seattle.* Cham: Springer.

Downs, A. (2001). What does smart growth really mean? *Planning (APA), 67*(4), 20.

Downs, A. (2005). Smart growth: Why we discuss it more than we do it. *Journal of the American Planning Association, 71*, 367–378.

Evans, P. (Ed.) (2002). *Livable cities? Urban struggles for livelihood and sustainability.* Berkeley: University of California Press.

Giddens, A. (1984). *The constitution of society.* Cambridge: Polity Press.

Glasmeier, A., & Christopherson, S. (2015). Thinking about smart cities. *Cambridge Journal of Regions, Economy and Society, 8*(1), 3–12. doi:10.1093/cjres/rsu034

Goetz, E. (2005). *The big tent of growth management: Smart growth as social movement.* Paper presented at the *Policies for managing urban growth and landscape change: A key to conservation in the 21st Century*, St. Paul, MN.

Güssefeldt, J., 1980. Konsumentenverhalten und die Verteilung zentraler Orte. *Geographische Zeitschrift, 68*(H. 1), 33–53.

Harding, A. (2007). Taking city regions seriously? Response to debate on "city-regions: New geographies of governance, democracy and social reproduction". *International Journal of Urban and Regional Research, 31*(2), 443–458.

Harrison, J. (2007). From competitive regions to competitive city-regions: A new orthodoxy, but some old mistakes. *Journal of Economic Geography, 7*(3), 311–332. doi:10.1093/jeg/lbm005

Harrison, J. (2010). Networks of connectivity, territorial fragmentation, uneven development: The new politics of city-regionalism. *Political Geography, 29*(1), 17–27. doi:10.1016/j.polgeo.2009.12.002

Harrison, J., & Heley, J. (2014). Governing beyond the metropolis: Placing the rural in city-region development. *Urban Studies.* doi:10.1177/0042098014532853

Herrschel, T. (2005). *Global geographies of post-socialist transitions: Geographies, societies, policies.* London: Routledge.

Herrschel, T. (2013). Sustainability and competitiveness: Can smart growth square the circle? *Urban Studies, 50*(11), 2332–2348.

Herrschel, T. (2014). *Cities, state and globalization: City-regional governance in Europe and North America.* London: Routledge.

Herrschel, T., & Dierwechter, Y. (2015). Smart city-regional governance: A dual transition *Regions, 300*(4), 20–22.

Herrschel, T., & Newman, P. (2002). *Governance of Europe's city regions: Planning, policy and politics.* London Routledge.

Herrschel, T., & Newman, P. (2017). *Cities as international actors.* London: Palgrave.

Hess, P. M., & Sorensen, A. (2014). Compact, concurrent, and contiguous: Smart growth and 50 years of residential planning in the Toronto region. *Urban Geography, 36*(1), 127–151. doi:10.1080/02723638.2014.947859

Jessop, B. (1993). Towards a Schumpeterian workfare state? Preliminary remarks on post-Fordist political economy. *Studies in Political Economy, 40*(1), 7–39.

Jonas, A. E. G. (2012a). City-regionalism as a contingent "geopolitics of capitalism". *Geopolitics 18*(2), 284–298.

Jonas, A. E. G. (2012b). Region and place: Regionalism in question. *Progress in Human Geography, 36*(2), 263–272.

Jonas, A. E. G. (2013). Place and region III: Alternative regionalisms. *Progress in Human Geography,* published online 26 February.

Jonas, A. E. G., & Pincetl, S. (2006). Rescaling regions in the state: The new regionalism in California. *Political Geography, 25*(5), 482–505.

Kourtit, K., Nijkamp, P., & Arribas, D. (2012). Smart cities in perspective: A comparative European study by means of self-organizing maps. *Innovation-the European Journal of Social Science Research, 25*(2), 229–246.

Krueger, R., & Gibbs, D. (2008). "Third wave" sustainability? Smart growth and regional development in the USA. *Regional Studies, 42*(9), 1263–1274.

Kuzio, T. (2001). Transition in post-communist states: Triple or quadruple? *Politics, 21*(3), 168–177.

Lackowska, M., & Zimmermann, K. (2011). New forms of territorial governance in metropolitan regions? A Polish–German comparison. *European Urban and Regional Studies, 18*(2), 156–169. doi:10.1177/0969776410390746

Lafferty, W. M., ed. (2006). *Governance for sustainable development: The challenge of adapting form to function.* London: Edward Elgar.

Marais, H. (1998). *South Africa limits to change: The political economy of transition.* Cape Town: University of Cape Town Press.

Moisio, S., & Paasi, A. (2013). From geopolitical to geoeconomic? The changing political rationalities of state space. *Geopolitics, 18*(2), 267–283.

Morandi, C., Rolando, A., & Di Vita, S. (2015). *From smart city to smart region: Digital services for an Internet of Places.* Cham: Springer.

Munro, D. (2017). Is it okay for cities to track what's in your poop? Retrieved from http://www.macleans.ca/society/technology/is-it-ok-for-a-city-to-track-whats-in-your-poop/

OECD. (2008). *Territorial review: Cape Town metropolitan review.* Paris: OECD.

Parnell, S. (2007). Politics of transformation: Defining the city strategy in Johannesburg. In K. Segbers (Ed.), *The making of global city regions* (pp. 139–167). Baltimore, MD: Johns Hopkins Press.

Pillay, U. (2004). Are globally competitive "city regions" developing in South Africa?: Formulaic aspirations or new imaginations? *Urban Forum, 15*(4), 340–364. doi:10.1007/s12132-004-0013-5

Pozdena, R. (2002). Smart growth and its effects on housing markets: The new segregation. Retrieved from http://www.nationalcenter.org/NewSegregation.pdf

Schmitter, P. C., & O'Donnell, G. A. (2013). *Transitions from authoritarian rule: Tentative conclusions about uncertain democracies*. Baltimore, MD: Johns Hopkins University Press.

Scott, A. (2001). Globalization and the rise of city regions. *European Planning Studies, 9*(7), 813–826.

Scott, A. (2011). A world in emergence: Notes toward a resynthesis of urban-economic geography for the 21st century. *Urban Geography, 36*(2), 845–870.

Scott, A. (2012). *A world in emergence: Cities and regions in the 21st century*. Cheltenham, UK: Edward Elgar.

Shahrokni, H., & Brandt, N. (2013). Making sense of smart city sensors. In Ellul, Zlatanova, Rumor, & ALaurini (Eds.), *Urban and regional data management*. London: Taylor & Francis.

Simmonds, R. H. G. (2000). *Global city regions: Their emerging forms*. London: Spon Press.

Smith, A., Stirling, A., & Berkhout, F. (2005). The governance of sustainable socio-technical transitions. *Research Policy, 34*(10), 1491–1510. Retrieved from www.sciencedirect.com/science/article/pii/S0048733305001721, accessed 14 Dec. 14 2017.

Talen, E. (2012). Sustainability. In R. Weber & R. Crane (Eds.), *The Oxford handbook of urban planning* (pp. 120–140). Oxford: Oxford University Press.

Taylor, P. J. (2005). New political geographies: Global civil society and global governance through world city networks. *Political Geography, 24*(6), 703–730. Retrieved from http://www.sciencedirect.com/science/article/pii/S0962629805000259

The Economist. (2014). What's gone wrong with democracy? *The Economist*. Retrieved from http://www.economist.com/news/essays/21596796-democracy-was-most-successful-political-idea-20th-century-why-has-it-run-trouble-and-what-can-be-do, accessed 3 Aug. 2015.

Townsend, A. M. (2013). *Smart cities: Big data, civic hackers, and the quest for a new utopia* (First edition. ed.). New York: W.W. Norton & Company.

Ullman, E. (1941). A theory of location for cities. *American Journal of sociology, 46*(6), 853–864.

Wolfers, J., & Leigh, A. (2006). *Happiness and the human development index: Australia is not a paradox*. Cambridge, MA: National Bureau of Economic Research.

1 The smart turn

Tracing transitions to city-regional smartness

Introduction

The main themes and claims of the book outlined in the Introduction need to be situated within the context of the more widely touted "turn" to smartness discourses and modes of urban analysis (Dierwechter, 2017a; Haarstad, 2017). Within this context, this chapter begins the process of linking smartness as an emergent, perhaps trendy, if still heavily debated, meta-paradigm in global city-regionalism to the notion of transition. Our use of "transition" as a key analytical theme throughout this book refers not only to an emergent world "beyond post-Fordism," as Alan Scott (2011) argues, but also to recent and geopolitically diverse trends in and conceptualization of, "post-authoritarian" societies. Specifically, we explore "post-communist" Eastern Europe and "post-apartheid" South Africa later in the book as empirical contrasts to the "post-Fordist" experiences of Western Europe and North America. The Western/North Atlantic experience is not taken here, however, as the theoretical "norm" from which other societies depart, but as just one of several historical experiences worthy of attention. This more expansive and comparative sensibility we submit, allows us to draw greater attention to variegated path-dependent legacies as well as to geo-historical, political and (attempted) institutional *breaks* with past political economies.

Global contrasts highlight how cities in different national settings are all searching (differently) for what Parnell and Robinson (2012) have called "beyond neoliberal" solutions to the array of complex and often interrelated, challenges posed by "real-time" global capitalism (Barry, 2012); the deepening crisis of representative democracy and state-political legitimacy (Barber, 2013); and, especially, concerns with the role of cities in planetary-wide (un) sustainability (Seitzinger et al, 2012) and the global ecological crisis (Levine & Yanarella, 2011).Whereas the rise of city-regions and city-regionalism, about which more in Chapters 2 and 3, has been important everywhere since the early 1990s (Jonas, 2012), the global "smart turn" – indeed, the popularity of "smartness" in various forms and approaches – also suggests societal, political and economic reforms deemed increasingly *necessary* by key actors at various scales of authority to facilitate democratic and sustainable forms of urbanized socio-economic development. In consequence, this chapter argues, various kinds of city-regions, with otherwise divergent internal and external conditions, are nonetheless effectively embracing "smartness" discourses and, perhaps, new modes of governing space, as a way to reconcile often contradictory aspirations and territorial forces between inherited structures and practices in the face of projected agendas and aspirations.

Yet how has this popular term *evolved* over the past few decades? Our main aim here is to develop a conceptual map that allows us to begin to answer this key question.

In brief, we show that, while the intellectual history of contemporary policy debates around "smartness" dates mainly to the mid-1990s, the bloodlines of what we are calling smart city-regionalism arguably stretch back to the worldwide crisis of economic growth experienced in the 1970s and 1980s. Indeed, the core crisis of growth – economic-industrial and spatial-urban and with increasing reference to global ecological concerns – provides our initial point of departure. We then go on to explore the expansive literatures on smart growth, principally in the US/Canadian context and smart cities, particularly regarding Europe and other major world regions. We note that "smartness" has emerged in the present decade to integrate older and more recent concerns with growth, innovation, sustainability, regionalism, participation, etc. We conclude by restating our central claim that the unfolding search for smart city-regions might be usefully theorized through the lens of a "dual transition" that highlights both *internal* and *external* shifts in the path-dependent and geographically variegated governance of global(izing) city-regions. Our discussions in Chapters 2 and 3 then explore the political and economic dimensions of city-regions and city-regionalism, respectively. Part 1 of the book ends by turning to a detailed elaboration of our theoretical framework in Chapter 4, drawing together themes and claims of these first three substantive chapters.

The global growth crisis and the "sustainable development" challenge of the 1980s

The first half of the 20th century was shaped by two cataclysmic world wars and a long and damaging economic depression, while the quarter century that followed the return of peace in August 1945, was marked by economic growth and institutional recovery (Goldhammer & Piketty, 2014). This involved not simply the post-war experience of economic dynamism and consumption in Western Europe, North America and Japan, but expansion and, ultimately, political transformation in regions now remapped geopolitically by the Cold War as "third world" countries. Moreover, the Soviet Union and Soviet-led block in Eastern Europe also experienced economic progress, albeit one based on a cruder concentration of resources. For various reasons, however, this period of growth across the entire world economy slowed considerably in the

1970s and into the 1980s (Figure 1.1). Exceptions included the "Asian Tigers". Yet much of the 1980s saw major economic restructuring across the Western World, a period that many geographers have explored (via regulation theory) as the crisis of Fordism. The deceleration of economic growth partly explains the dénouement of the Cold War, the end of apartheid and certainly the structural shift to a new international division of labour that underpinned the global economy of the 1990s.

While overall growth slowed, powerful concerns finally emerged that questioned – more seriously than ever before – the overall environmental and political limits of industrialized society, whether capitalist, socialist, or mixed (Kassiola, 1990; Beck, 1992).

Though peripheral until the 1970s, these concerns had, of course, built up steadily over time. Aldo Leopold's influential *Sand County Almanac*, for instance, argued in 1949 for a new "land ethic" that challenged dominant land-use narratives and property norms. Within urban studies, Jane Jacobs' devastating critique of modernist planning, *The Death and Life of Great American Cities*, published in 1961, elevated popular appreciation of architectural diversity, mixed-use development and pedestrian-oriented public spaces that anticipated key themes now common in sustainable urban development literatures (Trudeau, 2013). A year later, Rachel Carson's *Silent Spring* drew attention to the environmental effects of pesticides. In 1968, Garrett Harden's

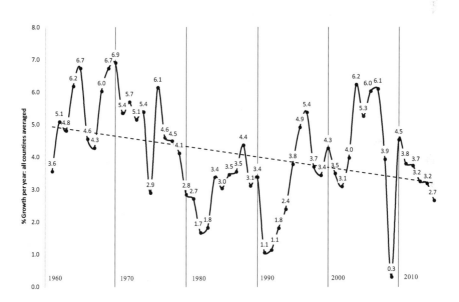

Figure 1.1 Average economic growth rate for all countries, 1961–2015.

Note: Calculated by authors: http://data.worldbank.org/indicator/NY.GDP.PCAP.CD?end=1975& start=1961

seminal article, "Tragedy of the Commons," punctured a major hole in the presumed public benefits of private self-interest – a linchpin postulate of unfettered capitalism since Adam Smith's writings in the late 18th century. Renewing themes in the neo-Malthusian school, Paul Erlich, also in 1968, warned of an approaching "population bomb." Barry Commoner's 1971 book, *The Closing Circle*, asserted that capitalist technology – not rising population – was doing the most to degrade global ecosystems. As Caradonna (2014) shows, national-level environmental legislation, such as the two Clean Air Acts of 1956 and 1965 in the United Kingdom (UK) and USA, respectively, also gathered considerable momentum. In 1972, Richard Nixon, who approved the use of Agent Orange in the jungles of Vietnam, paradoxically created the Environmental Protection Agency and signed the National Environmental Policy Act back at home.

The famous "Club of Rome" think-tank issued a dramatic global-scale report the same year that explored whether the linear expansion of new "technologies" – so central to smart city writings today – could ever mitigate the exponential demands of demographic growth and resource depletion. Without a considerable change in the basis of economic life, they modeled the likelihood of a major ecological breach by the mid-to-late 21st century; this thesis since has been developed and critiqued in the intervening decades (Clark, York, & Foster, 2010). Finally, again in 1972, at a United Nations conference in Stockholm, the term "sustainable development" first appeared under the leadership of the Canadian, Maurice Strong, although most observers today associate its subsequent popularity and rapid policy influence to the work of the Brundtland Commission in the mid-1980s (Adams, 2009; Rogers, Jalal, & Boyd, 2005).

Dismissed by some observers as an "oxymoron" (Redclift, 2005) and even a collective "mirage" (Foster, 2008), mainstream sustainable development discourses nonetheless accelerated a pre-existing "environmentalization" of public policy at various scales of governmental authority (Kershner, 2011). A new "greened up" internationalism in the global geopolitics of trade, aid, finance and development policy, for example, competed increasingly with what some authors now see as a more successful search for sustainability at the urban and regional scales of governance, particularly around climate action, as the 1990s gave way to the 2000s (Amen, Toly, McCarney & Segbers, 2012; Bulkeley & Betsill, 2005; Herrschel & Newman, 2017; Toly, 2008). In much of the world, the relationship between the global and urban scales of sustainability policy initially revolved around Local Agenda 21 projects conceived originally at the Rio Earth Summit in 1992 (Kern, Koll, & Schophaus, 2007; Llamas-Sanchez, Munoz-Fernandez, & Maraver-Tarifa, 2011; O'Riordan & Voisey, 1998; Owen & Videras, 2008). In the United States, however, the problem of how to ensure economic growth, but also contribute to global sustainability (and social equity), soon generated a new meta-concept in planning and public policy circles: smart growth, which promised to bridge conceptual and policy 'gaps' between growth, market interests and a concern about complex longer-term effects that stretch beyond business accounting or political time horizons.

North American smart growth as city-regional sustainability in the 1990s

The critique of sustainable development – or simply "sustainability," as it was increasingly called in the late 1990s – as "oxymoronic" and/or a "mirage" stemmed from global political efforts in the 1980s to merge the apparently syncretic goals of economic development, social equity and ecological resiliency. Yet herein also lay its socio-political strengths. Calling for better "balance" of these overall goals merged easily with comprehensive planning discourses at the state and local levels within the United States that had for decades similarly promised to balance competing pressures on local economies and societies. As the environmentalization of public policy mounted from the 1970s and as anti-growth coalitions in fast-changing suburbs gained greater political traction over the post-war pro-growth project, a new strategy was needed to manage metropolitan development. Smart growth emerged in the 1990s, as Dierwechter (2008) argues, to reconcile the unevenly experienced pressures of pro- and anti-growth politics within regions that suffered, like the wider world itself, from both too much growth in the form of low-density sprawl and fiscally-irresponsible overconsumption, yet, at the same time, too little growth in the form of economic opportunity within many abandoned (inner city and older suburban) communities and neighbourhoods. Growth *stricto sensu* was not really the main problem in smart growth theory. In fact, it was now recast into an opportunity (Chapin, 2012) and that was an important part of reconciling the seeming contradiction of growth, equity and sustainability: likely restrictions were not presented as losses, having to make do with less, but as a positive gain, as "more," even if in a broader sense than mere financial income terms. The real issue was the actual geography and design of development. As Pollard (2000, p. 253) put it, "growth is not inherently harmful. It is certain patterns of haphazard development that cause adverse impacts."

Communities could be "smart"; in other words, if they figured out how to channel fresh rounds of growth in ways that ameliorated, rather than created, problems – if they could change the patterns of "haphazard development," wherein the fragmentation, ill-placed subdivisions and strip developments, so characteristic of American space, could be reengineered over time into human-scaled urban fabric that required less energy to maintain and that generated more equitable opportunities for a wider set of workers (International City/County Management Association & Smart Growth Network, 2006). This involved, in short, the *locational* shift from greenfield to infill development; the *redesign* of homogenous, segregated, car-dependent zones into heterogeneous, mixed-use, multi-functional places; enhanced *connectivity* through multi-nodal transit options; and procedural efficiencies through, inter alia, *collaborative* decision-making and better *coordinated* regional and multi-scalar planning policies and capital improvements (Knaap & Zhao, 2009).

The physical-material and architectonic goals of smart growth – around location, design and connectivity, respectively – nonetheless, together highlighted the special importance of the last issue; that is, the procedural role of coordinated planning across a wider scalar platform, most prominently the global city-region as a key territorial space (Dierwechter, 2017a). Put more simply, smart growth resurrected and updated the older concern with regional planning in metropolitan areas (Daniels, 2001). In fact, the two major objectives of smart growth – urban revitalization and reduction of sprawl – implied and arguably even demanded, a long-term strategy that coordinated otherwise "local" applications of tools like comprehensive plans, urban growth boundaries, transit-oriented development, compact building codes, affordable housing incentives, priority funding areas, critical areas ordinances, transfers of development rights and so on (Fox, 2010). In this important sense, as J.W. Scott (2007) argues, smart growth essentially now offered a "pragmatic recoding" of the parallel calls in the New Regionalism literature. That literature – covered extensively in Chapters 2 and 3 – similarly called for robust forms of "city-regional governance" capable of responding more effectively to the new challenges of economic globalization and global sustainability (Basolo, 2003; Brenner, 2001; Deas & Ward, 2000; Frisken & Norris, 2001; Harrison, 2012; Jonas, 2013; Jonas & Ward, 2001; Mitchell-Weaver, Miller, & Deal, 2000; Rogerson, 2009).

By the early 2000s, the smart growth "movement" (Goetz, 2005), emanating out of land-use reforms in Maryland under Parris Glendening and the enthusiasm of the US Environmental Protection Agency during the Clinton/ Gore administration, had pulled together and made popular a number of interrelated policy streams – e.g. metropolitan planning, global sustainability and, no less, the relationships between technocracy and democracy – all as a way to resolve a series of governance "quandaries" (Braun & Scott, 2007). Some of its strongest policy and research advocates highlighted its most enthralling early promise as a planning programme. Tom Daniels (2001, p. 277), for instance, suggested that smart growth was not only a "new American approach to regional planning," but that it was a novel mechanism to implement what we today see as Brundtland-inspired sustainability; that is, "the best of both worlds: economic growth without the ugliness, congestion, environmental degradation and wasteful public subsidies or sprawling development." So while smart growth aimed to "impose a consciously chosen pattern of development upon the urban terrain" (Fainstein, 2010, p. 58), it nonetheless avoided a one-size-fits-all logic (a new "garden city" model, for instance, or a Radiant City modernism from Le Corbusier). Rather, smart growth suggested *reform* through a democratically inclusive, socially participatory, manner of collective mutual learning that (somehow) still generated economically efficient and technically rational decisions about specific urban changes with respect to the most vested parties in particular places. Rejecting such a planning logic would seem, its advocates reasoned, "dumb." In effect, put simply, it seemed to promise a win-win outcome for all.

Smart growth's "regionalist" framework for improved territorial management, like sustainability itself, thus fits comfortably within progressive-reformist rather than more radical interpretations of appropriate political action (Dierwechter, 2017a). This is evident, for instance, in how the American Planning Association (APA) framed and marketed the future of local development choices (APA, 2012). The APA emphasized, in particular, how smart growth promotes "choice" and "opportunity" by delivering efficient and sustainable land development. Central to their analysis, moreover, was and remains a strong concern with expanding people's right to choose "where and how they live, work and play" (ibid.). This is why it seems entirely reasonable to theorize smart growth as a "neoliberal" adaptation of Keynesian–Fordist planning culture (Krueger & Gibbs, 2008). But it is also possible to interpret smart growth as the "inter-currence" of multiple political orders, including past concerns with social segregation, current interests in securing private accumulation and, not least, nascent concerns with resiliency and sustainability (Dierwechter, 2017a). Here we emphasise the how players deploy "smartness" to reconcile competing or even conflicting interests and agendas. From this alternative perspective, smart growth is infused with strong market values and cultural discourses of individual self-realization, but not *only* so; at times and in certain places, it offers a significant challenge to "business-as-usual" development activity, particularly regarding the project of urban sustainability and the problem of social cohesion (ibid.). Indeed, it signals a willingness to look at the status quo of discourses and modi operandi in a fresh way to identify perhaps more imaginative and thus effective ways of responding to the complexities of multiple challenges across institutions, societies and geographic scales – global to local.

From roughly 1995 to 2005, it appears that smart growth planning practices diffused quite rapidly (if unevenly) across the United States and Canada and indeed, also started to influence urban development and design debates in China, sub-Saharan Africa, Scotland, Australia, Europe and many other societies (e.g. Arku, 2009; Chapin, 2012; Fox, 2010; Herrschel, 2013; Knaap & Zhao, 2009; MacLeod, 2013; Renne, 2008; Song, 2012). This expansion – or "policy mobility" (MacLeod, 2013) – has been accompanied by scholarly and practitioner work on its actually-implemented efficacy, shortcomings, contradictions, accomplishments and long-term prospects (Addison & Coomes, 2013; Dierwechter, 2014; Ingram, et al., 2009; Krueger, 2010; Litman, 2009, 2011; Margerum et al., 2013; Ruddiman, 2013; Wey, 2015). But just as smart growth practitioners tried to contain sprawl, paradoxically the discourse of "smartness" itself broke loose, sprawling out from the formal planning literature, where it was subsequently taken up – and redefined – by the data revolution of the new millennium.

By the late 2000s, of course, a different concern had clearly emerged: the "smart city."

Global smart cities and the data revolution in the 2000s

Just as the industrial revolution, the data revolution associated today with major and far-reaching advances in Internet and ICT is less a single "moment" – a jolt – than a steady accretion of – variably rapid – changes in both society and economy. The emergence of social media and "app" design, for example, could be traced reasonably to the use of the WorldWideWeb in the 1990s, or just as reasonably to the origins of the Internet in the 1960s (or even to the original work of Alan Turing and others in the 1940s, etc.). Following Newton, seeing farther down the road, means standing on the proverbial shoulders of giants. Still, the relatively recent and dramatic impacts of ICT-related research and policy concerns on the "smart city" concept are reasonably clear. According to the Web of Science citation index, scholarly work on the topic of "smart cities" has utterly exploded – from hardly anything in 1997 to over 2,600 citations by 2016. It certainly seems to have become academically "trendy."

Unlike work on spatial planning for smart growth, research on smart cities (such as sustainability) has involved a much wider number of disciplinary fields and areas of expertise, vastly complicating the discursive consolidation of an agreed definition of what smart cities actually might involve (though see, for example, Albino, Berardi, & Dangelico, 2015; Mosannenzadeh & Vettorato, 2014). This is shown in Figure 1.2 below, which lists the top ten most important disciplines in the production of research on smart cities (as a "topic") between 1998 and 2016. As might be expected, the interrelated scholarly fields of urban studies, geography and planning – traditionally focused on cities and

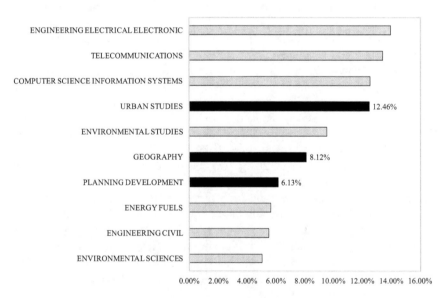

Figure 1.2 Top ten disciplines in the production of research on "smart cities," 1998–2016.
Source: Web of Science: wcs.webofknowledge.com.

urban analysis – are significant contributors to knowledge about smart cities, but they are nonetheless outpaced (fairly substantially) by more "technical" fields only incidentally or at best tangentially related to urban theory and general discourses of urbanism and urban development, notably: electronic and electrical engineering, telecommunications and computer science information systems. Other important disciplines in the production of original work on smart cities – energy fuels, civil engineering and environmental sciences – are also less oriented, at least historically, to urban-based policy and theory-building (while political science and sociology, somewhat unexpectedly, have figured far less).

Much work on smart cities, particularly where the focus is on the technology *per se*, thus falls beyond the detailed remit of this book. This work is significant, but we do not engage with questions of sensors or advanced sensing (Hancke, Silva, & Hancke, 2013), for instance, nor with algorithmic programs or even the "Internet of Things" as a socio-technical artefact (Zanella et al., 2014). Rather, our focus is on how social scientists, especially geographers, planners and urban studies researchers as the primary disciplines looking at the spatial manifestation of this "smartness," have explored the smart city as a parallel (or sister) concept to work on smart growth and city-regional development. That is still about a quarter of all published work so far, per the Web of Science; so, specifically, we are interested in what we call *smart transitions in global city-regionalism*. By this we mean, once again, an internal and external (or what has been theorized here as a dual) transition toward situated and variegated "smartness" discourses. This involves explicitly politico-economic and geographical problems, viz.: critiques of the "corporate" and "actually-existing" smart city (Hollands, 2015; Shelton, Zook, & Wiig, 2015); concerns with "empty rhetoric" (Wiig, 2015) and "techno-utopian policy mobilities"; and the putative forces that constitute actually-existing smart cities (Angelidou, 2015; Caragliu, Del Bo, & Nijkamp, 2011), especially the political and economic dimensions (Rossi, 2016).

Having said this, we recognize – and even emphasize – the profound significance of new technological capacities to generate exceptionally large amounts of data in real-time in various ways (e.g. handheld devices, apps, sensors, etc.) about an unprecedented number of mutable and protean socio-natural phenomena (e.g. consumption behavior, pollution rates, available parking spaces, etc.) to the smart city concept in recent years, both theoretical and applied. But for purposes of clarity alone, it makes sense, in our opinion, to associate the "smart city" concept *more narrowly* with "digitized urbanism" (sensors, Internet of Things, smart grids, embedded devises, networked actuators, etc.) along with the relatively novel role of ICT-mediated social interactions within society *and between society and state actors* in urban arenas. Allwinkle and Cruickshank (2011, p. 8) chart the development of this quality: from simply loading "static" information on city websites in the 1990s to, in more recent years, managing high-level programmes capable of meeting "the networking, innovation and creativity requirements of successful partnerships."

This does not mean that this book seeks to reduce the smart city concept only to top-down, company-driven visions, as in Songo, Masdar City or PlanIT (Naphade, Banavar, Harrison, Paraszczak, & Morris, 2011). Instead, expanding the perspective from the harnessing, diffusion and/or embedding of technologies like ICT per se (e.g. smart homes, smart building, etc.), to wider questions of institutional agility, civic capital and overall governance capability, we prefer the more synoptic and synthetic concept of "smartness." Indeed, as suggested in the introduction to this book, the just-cited "critiques," "concerns," and "expansions "of the smart city engagements with technology and data availability perhaps require now to jettison the dichotomy of "smart growth" and "smart city" in favor of something broader and more accommodating. In their place, in other words, the focus might shift to exploring various discourses of "smartness," wherein planning, regionalism, technology, politics, governance and geo-historical changes are creatively reassembled and re-theorized. For this book, now, that means, once again, linking this more expansive concept to city-regions currently undergoing a dual transition – a central theme we develop later on.

In doing so, we assume, of course, that cities form and grow over time through economic and cultural relationships of all kinds, yet are mundanely reproduced through various socio-technical complexes like power girds, transportation routes, solid waste systems and water distribution networks. The steady accretion of "encrusted bureaucratic systems" across the still-urbanizing world has managed these complexes through projects and programs of replacement, repair and/or reform (Araya & Arif, 2015, p. 1). From the 1970s, once again, key economies, particularly in the core of the world's economy, began to move away from a once-transformative paradigm based on oil, automobiles and mass production, towards one based increasingly on information, associated by what Araya (2015) sees as the "initiating revolution" of the Intel microprocessor in Santa Clara, California, roughly akin to Henry Ford's Model T manufacturing system in the late 1910s.

Initiating revolutions typically diffuse more quickly in the economic domain than in the political sphere, causing disjunctures, tensions and systemic asymmetries. Indeed, similar to the US railroad tycoons of the 19th century, the advent of new information and communication technologies from the 1970s have been captured and mobilized by large and increasingly globalized corporations, who naturally tend to emphasize economic rationalities, rather than, say, the promises of public accountability or collaborative decision-making as worthy ends in themselves. These are tensions that we see play out in several of our case studies. The discursive proliferation of the "smart city" from the late 1990s and into the 2000s thus owes much to the economic interests of IBM, Cisco and other large firms, looking for new markets by promising mayors and local leaders new managerial efficiencies associated with transforming the many "encrusted bureaucratic systems" inherited from previous decades of industrial transformation. Hollands (2008) and others have critiqued this development as the "neoliberal corporatization" of smart city ideals. Accordingly, one recent response to this critique is directed more sharply at the shifting relationships between ICT and democracy, with Araya and Arif (2015) and others calling for more research on how we might theorize smart cities as "democratic ecologies" rather than technological fixes.

Here "democratic ecologies" refer to how communication and joint decision-making consciously *embedded in the design* of cities can ultimately help to expand "democratic agency" by merging open government with open data. Here, too, there is, at least for us, a rather strong and at times overly-romantic, aversion (and even ethical-normative distrust) of the "top-down" culture associated automatically with "encrusted bureaucratic systems" of older urban management routines. In their place, the argument runs, democratic ecologies promise what Tapsott et al. (2008), for instance, imagine as community, collaboration and self-organization, rather than hierarchy and control. This is an almost neoanarchist theory of urban governance (or dynamic decision-making) that draws on the ethics of the previously mentioned Jane Jacobs, for instance, but that also comports with the hacktivist-as-citizen reading of civil society's energies and capacity for constant creativity and direct participation. Interestingly, the "community" is often taken to be good, grounded and bereft of class, race and gender cleavages or biases that too often tend to enervate collaboration and self-organization without a parallel process of exclusion and even oppression. Yet higher-level structures and institutions – from state-level policies to constitutional-legal arrangements – have emerged precisely because such assumptions rarely play out on the ground. Accordingly, smartness, again in our view, does not just offer romantic utopias of digitized, grassroots participation; it offers a way to reconsider state–society relations in a globalized and rapidly changing, city-regional environment.

Smartness discourses in the 2010s: towards diverse smart city-regions?

In their recent review of the smart city concept Albino et al. (2015) note that:

> Cities worldwide have started to look for solutions which enable transportation linkages, mixed land uses and high-quality urban services with long-term positive effects on the economy. For instance, high-quality and more efficient public transport that responds to economic needs and connects labor with employment is considered a key element for city growth. Many of the new approaches related to urban services have been based on helping to create what some call "smart cities."
>
> (p. 4)

This passage suggests crucial connections with the previously established smart growth and sustainability themes discussed above, leading in turn to "confusion among urban policy makers," as advocates and critics have not usefully limited the smart city concept narrowly enough "to the application of technologies to cities" (p. 10). In their view, the term, instead – as all terms inevitably do – has tried to span different "domains" (cf. Lombardi et al., 2012; Neirotti et al., 2014). The first of these is the so-called "hard" domain of smart cities, constituted by "buildings, energy grids, natural resources, water management, waste management, mobility and logistics, *where ICT can play a decisive role in the functions of the systems*" (Albino et al., 2015, emphasis added). The second domain, in contrast, is "soft," and refers to "education, culture, policy innovations, social inclusion and government, *where the application of ICT are not usually decisive*" (ibid., emphasis added).

With this language in mind, Figure 1.3 below provides a different conceptual map of the evolution of "smartness" as a now more expansive signifier of previous literatures and research programs. We do not suggest this "map" is meaningful for all research questions around smart cities and the smart turn more generally. So while others may wish/need to deploy the concept of the smart city even as they widen their investigations away from the "hard" domain of technology (Neirotti et al., 2014), in this book, we choose, instead, to deploy the notion of "smartness" as a more synthetic category produced from both the "hard" and "soft" domains and, indeed, from ongoing policy discourses around smart growth, sustainability governance and economic development challenges. Specifically, we see the *smart city* movement as a meaningful technological extension of smart growth concerns to reimagine (and better manage) the post-war growth project in cities, given the important intellectual impact of sustainability problems, even as these concerns have also directly informed various efforts in the 1990s to promote "intelligent cities," "digital cities," and so on. Furthermore, we see governance as a key bridge between smart growth's original focus on a more sustainable form of urban development and parallel arguments for a new city-regionalism.

For the purpose here, if not for other projects, "smartness" usefully captures efforts to govern city-regions differently – a theme we take up extensively in subsequent chapters through our heuristic of the dual transition – but also

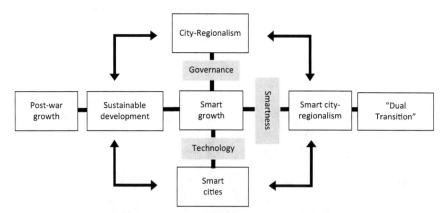

Figure 1.3 The conceptual evolution of smartness.

aptly summarizes many of the recent critiques, concerns, interventions of the smart city literature that, at least in its early stages, have focused more sharply on the technological dimensions of urban development. While part of our reasoning is a desire for simple clarity, we also worry, with Morandi et al. (2015), that too much of the smart cities literature is largely inattentive to problems of city-regionalism and regional development, which, again, has long been an important aspect of the smart growth contribution, given its concern with urban sprawl from the city into the wider region. Morandi et al. seek to shift the technological conversation away from, for instance, the "internet of things" (objects in space) to a more explicitly *territorial* and, for us, geo-political concern with the "internet of places" (communities sharing space) – all while still recognizing and taking very seriously the novel possibilities of "digital services." Those, as Neirotti et al. (2014, p. 26) put it, "obtain data from heterogeneous sources (e.g. sewers, parking spaces, security cameras, school thermostats, traffic lights, etc.)" in ways that progressively influence the conduct of spatial planning, urban design and regional governance. Morandi et al.'s work is an important inspiration for what we mean here by "smartness" as an integrative investigation that touches on (and thinks through) technology, governance, sustainability, regional planning, etc. in specific and diverse geographical and cultural settings.

As we argue *forward* through the concept of smartness, however, we also glance *backward* to useful literatures that anticipate some of its key features. In particular, work on urban smartness as we understand it here, captures notions of inter-institutional innovation and place-enhanced creativity developed in previous work within geography on so-called "learning regions" and related literatures in economic sociology, institutional economics and regional state theory (MacKinnon, Cumbers, & Chapman, 2002; MacLeod & Goodwin, 1999; Morgan, 1997). In his influential recent critique of self-proclaimed smart cities, for example, Robert Hollands (2008, p. 306) envisions truly smart cities as "territories with a high capacity for learning and innovation, which is built in to the creativity of their population, their institutions of knowledge production and their digital infrastructure for communication." While his attention to "digital infrastructure" that "undergirds" various urban systems reflects the hallmark of smart city research – about which more below – Hollands' concern that "real" smart cities should be able to provide compelling evidence of learning, innovation and creativity, is more familiar.

Kevin Morgan (1997), for example, not only suggested twenty years ago that innovation is "an interactive process" shaped by a "variety of social institutions other than the market," but also that innovation depends on "inter-organisational flows of information and knowledge" (pp. 490–3). *Regional* space-economies and their ancillary social institutions, moreover, provide in greater or lesser amounts what Michael Storper (1995) called the "supply architecture" for learning to occur and trust to sediment, which, in turn, emerges only though routines and repeated transactions. Others have broached the problem of "creativity" in ways that also anticipate themes common in the smart city literature. In his attempt to trace the uneven history and geography of particularly dynamic cities, Sir Peter Hall (1998) deployed the original and suggestive work of Gunnar Törnqvist (2004, p. 228), who has argued that creative processes, whether they deal with technological developments or other forms of creativity, such as product innovation, the visual arts, music and literature, "make special demands on their environments." Such environments include institutions (e.g. the Pasteur Institute in Paris in the 19th century) or, in fact, entire geographical arenas like cities at key moments: viz. ancient Athens; 15th century Florence; 16th century Amsterdam; 19th century Manchester; or late 20th century Silicon Valley.

Part of the generic promise of urbanized space, Törnqvist (2004) writes, is that cities offer several different types of advantages simultaneously, a point made famous too by, yet again, Jane Jacobs (1969) in her analysis of economic innovation. That said, the articulation and translation into policies and strategies require negotiation and prioritization – in itself a highly political process that responds to specific geographic and temporal situations. In addition, large urban environments – e.g. London, New York, Los Angeles, Paris, Vienna, etc. – are heterogeneous places refreshed by foreigners (and/or migrant outsiders) who often think differently from their urban hosts and thus act as a new, varying and, at times, perhaps unpredictable, dynamic. It is a point Richard Florida (2005) collapsed, rather too generically, into the "creative class." This means that cities, if sufficiently tolerant, can become "cultural smelting furnaces" (Törnqvist, 2004, p. 230). Such smelting can generate political heat, of course, but it can also create legitimate novelty and thus innovative potential and capacity, which then diffuses across space and time to change specific aspects of the extant world (Tellier, 2011).

As Amy Glasmeier and Susan Christopherson (2015, p. 3), *pace* Törnqvist, observe in their review of smart cities that urban environments are not simply "passive receptacles" for new technology. Instead, they add their own, specific, local political-economic and societal milieux as modifying agents. Moreover, various kinds of "smart" interventions, from mixed-use infill developments to "app" designs, actively seek to change the physical and virtual environments within which they appear and the utilization of these environments by functions and processes, suggesting and also producing a complex set of relationships between creativity, (technological, procedural and imaginative) smartness and place. It thus remains debatable whether smart technologies are, indeed, "deeply disruptive to the form and function of the city" (Batty, 2016, p. 441). Rather, the question of their utility may lie more in their ability to respond to specificities, to "learn" and to adjust to optimize their relevance and responsiveness.

In consequence, throughout this book, urban smartness is about more than hooking up local traffic lights with sensors that reduce unnecessary idling – the "hard" domain discussed above. Urban smartness is also and maybe, in particular, on the so-called "softer" side, a creative process that involves new capabilities in data storage, but not merely data storage. Having more data or information does not necessarily, by itself, produce insights and knowledge and, even less so, effective responses. Instead, it involves the analysis of data to help first gain and then instrumentalize insights and does so through leveraging existing "tools" (policies, local institutional set ups, personalities, etc.) to boost their utility in order to respond effectively to fast-changing circumstances and challenges, not at least in their prioritization and perceived importance and urgency. This rapid – and seemingly accelerating – pace of change all but rules out a matching pace of adapting "hard" instruments, including institutions and territories of governing. Using, instead, existing infrastructures in a novel, more creative and thus, eventually, "smart" way, so the argument here, provides much better scope for regulation to keep pace and remain relevant and "up to the job." This, in turn, may well shape the bargaining position of different policy fields and their advocates within and outside the government machinery, when it comes to negotiating resources, strategies and agendas vis-à-vis the challenges of environmental conditions, both internal and external to the region.

Smartness, in consequence, varies substantively over time and space. What counts as smart, may, after all, be imported exogenously, rather than nurtured endogenously from local capabilities and institutional cultures (Viitanen & Kingston, 2014). The latter may be much slower in coming about and bearing fruition than the former, perhaps too long for some policy-makers eying up the next election and seeking "effective' results" to suggest "success" in the face of emerging challenges. Thus, the popularity of one vision of urban smartness which imagines that policy progress is readily available, easy to implement and inevitably pragmatic. Large and powerful global-scale corporations like IBM, Cisco, Siemens, Oracle, Microsoft and Intel see opportunities in selling local governments what Hill (cited in Hollands, 2015, p. 68) calls a new "urban intelligence industrial complex." Central to this complex is pressure to standardize and normalize, to offer "tried and trusted" solutions, rather than tailor-made, locally-informed, instruments.

As a result, some have interpreted the "smart turn" as mainly a techno-utopian adaptation of established principles and rationales of a post-Keynesian, thoroughly neo-liberalized, opportunistically driven and overly techno-utopian adaptation of older forms of territorial and economic governance (Lafferty, 2004). Following this logic, new partnerships between cities and their governments, corporations, chambers, unions, citizen-consumers and NGOs mask deeper structural tensions in contemporary global capitalism. However, the degree to which this theorization really applies; the role public discussions acquire vis-à-vis political structures; and the adopted governmental and capitalist principles and practices – all this will, once again, vary, based on particular circumstances, histories and the political-economic-cultural conditions that facilitate an option: allow a locally-embedded creativity or adopt an imported attempt to side-step localized creativity. In between these two extreme ends, moreover, we might expect to find a variety of hybrid solutions that "download," yet also "customize," the ready-made packages to local circumstances, if only to make them *appear* to address local requirements and project strategic opportunities. Again, the "internal" dynamics of local city-regional policy-making and institutional contexts interact with an array of "external" processes and structural forces, including the power of global corporations to offer smart solutions. The many scholarly challenges in mapping what is, in our view, a variegated geographical and political story of a seemingly "universal" process (of adopting technology as producers of near perfect answers to urban problems) are, therefore, considerable, especially when directed at efforts to govern cities through new forms of city-regionalism that involve trans-local, multi-scalar policy coordination (Herrschel, 2005, 2014).

Smart transitions in city-regionalism: into the 2020s

The view offered in this book is that smart city-regions, which span questions of "hard" technology and "soft" governance, of new digital capacities and ongoing institutional adaptations, may well now represent new kinds of "transitions" in global urban space and territorial development, as various places around the world anticipate many common challenges into the 2020s. So, this is not subject to a singular global logic or simple linear convergence. We are not the first scholars to link versions of urban smartness – or smart cities – to the organizing theme of transition. Mark Deakin (2013), for example, has previously edited a helpful volume on the governance of smart cities as a form of transition. Nor are we the first to locate versions of urban smartness within an explicitly "city-regional" framework, although, as discussed above, with very few exceptions (Morandi et al., 2015), most of this work still reflects spatial planning discourses and particularly the narrower impacts of smart growth practices in North America (Allred & Chakraborty, 2015; Hess & Sorensen, 2015; McCauley & Murphy, 2013). The regionalization of smart city research has barely started (Dierwechter, 2017b).

Yet our analytical emphasis throughout this book on any given transition as both an internal and external dynamic does highlight, we argue, a variegated geographical story that is insufficiently developed in the extant comparative literatures on smart cities and urban smartness. As geographers, we are sensitive to long-standing tensions in the discipline between what Immanuel Kant originally charted as "nomothetic" (generalized and common) and "ideographic" (unique and contingent) traditions of empirical research epistemologies. In the present case, both the "smart turn" and the search for new forms of city-regional governance (city-regionalism) are, if not universal, then an increasingly generalized phenomenon, especially when the focus is on the adoption of hard digitized infrastructures. Everyone, everywhere, it seems, is "getting smart." Yet *differences* inherited from economic, historical and political experiences – the soft side of the problem – are important, too and in many ways more interesting and relevant.

The cases that we explore later in this book – Vancouver, Seattle, Turin, Berlin, Prague, Lyon, Cape Town and Johannesburg – reflect *not only* smart transitions in what Alan Scott (2011) and others see as a new urban world emerging "beyond post-Fordism" but also, in the instructive cases of Eastern Europe and South Africa, beyond different forms of "authoritarianism," whether post-socialist or post-apartheid. In doing so, we seek to develop the argument advanced by Parnell and Robinson (2012) that, as we investigate the politics and possibilities of cities in a more comparative global light, we need to "look beyond" the sometimes-totalized reductionism of neoliberalism. As they put it:

> [W]e want to reflect on the variety of processes other than neoliberalization that are shaping cities and argue that these need to be taken more seriously in their own right – i.e., that the range of urban processes shaping a diversity of urban contexts needs to be thought of as more than just contributing to the hybridization of urban neoliberalism.
>
> (p. 594)

This book acknowledges and takes up at different times in later empirical chapters, the "nomothetic" importance, for example, of real-time global capitalism in shaping the politics and possibilities of local regulatory choices and public investment. We acknowledge, too, the actually-existing powers of large corporations to sell the "urban-intelligence-industrial complex" to local leaders under profound pressure to deliver novel and trendy (if not too costly) solutions (Hill, cited in Hollands, 2015, p. 58) fairly rapidly. Furthermore, we note how various cities are responding pragmatically to the growing (increasingly shared) crises of representative (and often shallow) democracy and also ecological unsustainability. There are, the book shows, common stories here. Neoliberal forces are exceptionally powerful. Yet we circle back always to the variety of urban processes that Parnell and Robinson (2012) usefully foreground as central to how contemporary forms of urbanization are now playing out all around the world.

Conclusions

Various kinds of city-regions, with otherwise divergent internal and external conditions, are effectively embracing "smartness" discourses and novel modes of governing to try to reconcile often contradictory aspirations and territorial forces between inherited structures and practices in the face of projected agendas and aspirations. In this chapter, we have drawn an "intellectual map" of smartness as a concept that reflects the intellectual and pragmatic impacts of a range of challenges associated originally with the crisis of the post-war growth model, especially as experienced by the industrial west since the 1970s. The parallel concerns with both jump-starting growth through new rounds of competitiveness experiments, as well as the fast-mounting anxiety that such growth was ecologically and socially unsustainable in the 1980s, led eventually to novel meso-concepts in the 1990s such as "smart growth," in North America and then during the 2000s, "smart cities" seem nearly everywhere.

As we head into the 2020s, we conclude, more attention must be paid to a smart city-regionalism which can address not only questions of "hard" technology but also and perhaps particularly so, of "soft" governance. And this includes questions of how new digital capacities and ongoing institutional adaptations likely represent, as we have put it in this book, a new kind of "transition" in global urban space and territorial development. Accordingly, the book now turns to the rise of city-regionalism in more detail, first addressing its economic dimensions in Chapter 2 and then delving into more explicitly political themes in Chapter 3. Given the interdependence between these processes and topics, some thematic overlap between the two respective discussions is inevitable and, indeed, intended in places. Doing so in succession is meant to help appropriately territorialize the smartness literature, while also setting up the comparative case studies in Part II with their focus on the role of placeness in the transition process.

References

Adams, W. M. (2009). *Green development: Environment and sustainability in a developing world* (3rd edn.). London: Routledge.

Addison, C. S. Z., & Coomes, B. (2013). Smart growth and housing affordability: A review of regulatory mechanisms and planning practices. *Journal of Planning Literature* (OnlineFirst), 1–43. doi:10.1177/0885412212471563

Albino, V., Berardi, U., & Dangelico, R. M. (2015). Smart Cities: Definitions, dimensions, performance and initiatives. *Journal of Urban Technology*, *22*(1), 3–21. doi:10.1080/10630732.2014.942092

Allred, D., & Chakraborty, A. (2015). Do local development outcomes follow voluntary regional plans? Evidence from Sacramento region's blueprint plan. *Journal of the American Planning Association*, *81*(2), 104–120. doi:10.1080/01944363.2015.1067574

Allwinkle, S., & Cruickshank, P. (2011). Creating smart-er cities: An overview. *Journal of Urban Technology*, *18*(2), 1–16. doi:10.1080/10630732.2011.601103

Amen, M., Toly, N., McCarney, P., & Segbers, K. (Eds.) (2012). *Cities and global governance: New sites for international relations*. Farnham, UK: Ashgate.

Angelidou, M. (2015). Smart cities: A conjuncture of four forces. *Cities*, *47*(0), 95–106. doi:http://dx.doi.org/10.1016/j.cities.2015.05.004

APA. (2012). *APA Policy Guide on Smart Growth*. Retrieved from https://www.planning. org/policy/guides/adopted/smartgrowth.htm, accessed 10 April 2015.

Araya, D. (2015). Smart cities and the network society: Towards common-driven governance. In D. Araya (Ed.), *Smart cities as democratic ecologies* (pp. 11–22). New York: Palgrave.

Araya, D., & Arif, H. (2015). Introduction. In D. Araya (Ed.), *Smart cities as democratic ecologies* (pp. 1–10). New York: Palgrave.

Arku, G. (2009). Rapidly growing African cities need to adopt smart growth policies to solve urban development concerns. *Urban Forum*, *20*(3), 253–270. Retrieved from http://dx.doi.org/10.1007/s12132-009-9047-z, accessed 10 Nov. 2017.

Barber, B. (2013). *If mayors ruled the world: Dysfunctional nations, rising cities*. New Haven, CT: Yale University Press.

Barry, J. (2012). Climate change, the cancer stage of capitalism and the return of limits to growth. In M. Mark Pelling, D. Manuel-Navarrete, & M. Redclift (Eds.), *Climate change and the crisis of capitalism: A chance to reclaim self* (pp. 129–142). London: Routledge.

Basolo, V. (2003). US regionalism and rationality. *Urban Studies*, *40*(3), 447–462.

Batty, M. (2016). How disruptive is the smart cities movement? *Environment and Planning B: Planning and Design, 43*(3), 441–443.

Beck, U. (1992). From industrial society to the risk society: Questions of survival, social structure and ecological enlightenment. *Theory, Culture & Society, 9*(1), 97–123.

Braun, G. & Scott, J. (2007). Smart growth as new metropolitan governance: Observations of US experience. In H. Geyer (Ed.), *International handbook of urban policy: Contentious global issues, Volume 1.* Cheltenham, UK: Edward Elgar.

Brenner, N. (2001). Decoding the newest "metropolitan regionalism" in the USA: A critical overview. *European Planning Studies, 9*(7), 813–826.

Bulkeley, H., & Betsill, M. M. (2005). Rethinking sustainable cities: Multilevel governance and the "urban" politics of climate change. *Environmental Politics, 14*(1), 42–63. doi:10.1080/0964401042000310178

Caradonna, J. L. (2014). *Sustainability: A history.* New York: Oxford University Press.

Caragliu, A., Del Bo, C., & Nijkamp, P. (2011). Smart cities in Europe. *Journal of Urban Technology, 18*(2), 65–82. doi:10.1080/10630732.2011.601117

Chapin, T. S. (2012). Introduction: From growth controls, to comprehensive planning, to smart growth: Planning's emerging fourth wave. *Journal of the American Planning Association, 78*(1), 5–15. doi:10.1080/01944363.2011.645273

Clark, B., York, R., & Foster, J. B. (2010). *The ecological rift: Capitalism's war on the Earth.* New York: Monthly Review Press.

Daniels, T. (2001). Smart growth: A new American approach to regional planning. *Planning Practice and Research, 16*(3–4), 271–279.

Deakin, M. (2013). *Smart cities: Governing, modelling and analysing the transition.* New York: Routledge.

Deas, I., & Ward, K. (2000). From the "new localism" to the "new regionalism"? The implications of regional development agencies for city–regional relations. *Political Geography, 19*, 272–292.

Dierwechter, Y. (2008). *Urban growth management and its discontents: Promises, practices and geopolitics in US city-regions.* New York: Palgrave.

Dierwechter, Y. (2014). The spaces that smart growth makes: Sustainability, segregation and residential change across Greater Seattle. *Urban Geography, 35*(5), 691–714. doi:10.1080/02723638.2014.916905

Dierwechter, Y. (2017a). *Urban sustainability through smart growth: Greater Seattle, intercurrence and the new geography of regional development.* New York: Springer.

Dierwechter, Y. (2017b). What's smart growth got to do with smart cities? Searching for the "smart city region" in Greater Seattle. *Territorio, 83*, 48–54.

Fainstein, S. (2010). *The just city.* Ithaca, NY: Cornell University Press.

Florida, R. L. (2005). *Cities and the creative class.* New York: Routledge.

Foster, J. (2008). *The sustainability mirage.* London: Earthscan.

Fox, D. (2010). Halting sprawl: Smart growth in Vancouver and Seattle. *Boston College International and Comparative Law Review, 33*(1), 43–59.

Frisken, F., & Norris, D. F. (2001). Regionalism reconsidered. *Journal of Urban Affairs, 23*(5), 467–478. doi:10.1111/0735-2166.00101

Glasmeier, A., & Christopherson, S. (2015). Thinking about smart cities. *Cambridge Journal of Regions, Economy and Society, 8*(1), 3–12. doi:10.1093/cjres/rsu034

Goetz, E. (2005). *The big tent of growth management: Smart growth as social movement.* Paper presented at the *Policies for managing urban growth and landscape change: a key to conservation in the 21st Century,* St. Paul, MN.

Goldhammer, A., & Piketty, T. (2014). *Capital in the twenty-first century.* Cambridge, MA: Harvard University Press.

Haarstad, H. (2017). Constructing the sustainable city: Examining the role of sustainability in the "smart city" discourse. *Journal of Environmental Policy & Planning, 19*(4), 423–437. doi:10.1080/1523908X.2016.1245610

Hall, P. (1998). *Cities in civilization* (1st American edn.). New York: Pantheon Books.

Hancke, G. P., Silva, B. D. E., & Hancke, G. P. (2013). The role of advanced sensing in smart cities. *Sensors, 13*(1), 393–425. doi:10.3390/s130100393

Harrison, J. (2012). Life after regions? The evolution of city-regionalism in England. *Regional Studies, 46*(9), 1243–1259. doi:10.1080/00343404.2010.521148

Herrschel, T. (2005). *Global geographies of post-socialist transitions: Geographies, societies, policies.* London: Routledge.

Herrschel, T. (2013). Sustainability and competitiveness: Can smart growth square the circle? *Urban Studies, 50*(11), 2332–2348.

Herrschel, T. (2014). *Cities, state and globalisation: City-regional governance in Europe and North America.* London: Routledge.

Herrschel, T., & Newman, P. (2017). *Cities as international actors.* London: Palgrave.

Hess, P. M., & Sorensen, A. (2015). Compact, concurrent and contiguous: Smart growth and 50 years of residential planning in the Toronto region. *Urban Geography, 36*(1), 127–151. doi:10.1080/02723638.2014.947859

Hollands, R. G. (2008). Will the real smart city please stand up? *City, 12*(3), 303–320. doi:10.1080/13604810802479126

Hollands, R. G. (2015). Critical interventions into the corporate smart city. *Cambridge Journal of Regions, Economy and Society, 8*(1), 61–77. doi:10.1093/cjres/rsu011

Ingram, G., Carbonell, A., Hong, Y., & Flint, A. (2009). *Smart growth policies: An evaluation of program outcomes.* Cambridge, MA: Lincoln Institute of Land Policy.

International City/County Management Association, & Smart Growth Network. (2006). *This is smart growth.* Washington, DC: Environmental Protection Agency.

Jonas, A. E. G. (2012). City-regionalism as a contingent "geopolitics of capitalism". *Geopolitics 18*(2), 284–298.

Jonas, A. E. G. (2013). City-regionalism as a contingent "geopolitics of capitalism". *Geopolitics, 18*(2), 284–298. doi:10.1080/14650045.2012.723290

Jonas, A. E. G., & Ward, K. (2001). *City-regionalisms: Some critical reflections on transatlantic urban policy convergence.* Economic Geography Working Group (Working paper 01/01).

Kassiola, J. J. (1990). *The death of industrial civilization: The limits to economic growth and the repoliticization of advanced industrial society.* Albany, NY: SUNY Press.

Kern, K., Koll, C., & Schophaus, M. (2007). The diffusion of local agenda 21 in Germany: Comparing the German federal states. *Environmental Politics, 16*(4), 604–624. doi:10.1080/09644010701419139

Kershner, J. (2011). Senator Henry M. Jackson introduces the National Environmental Policy Act (NEPA) into the U.S. Senate on February 18, 1969. *History Link, Essay 9908.*

Knaap, G., & Zhao, X. (2009). Smart growth and urbanization in China: Can an American tonic treat the growing pains of Asia. In Y. Song & C. Ding (Eds.), *Smart urban growth for China* (pp. 11–24). Cambridge, MA: Lincoln Institute.

Krueger, R. (2010). Smart growth and its discontents: An examination of American and European approaches to local and regional sustainable development *Doc. Anal. Geogr., 56*(3), 409–433.

Krueger, R., & Gibbs, D. (2008). "Third wave" sustainability? Smart growth and regional development in the USA. *Regional Studies, 42*(9), 1263–1274.

Lafferty, W. M. (Ed.) (2004). *Governance for sustainable development.* Cheltenham: Edward Elgar.

Levine, R. S., & Yanarella, E. J. (2011). *The city as fulcrum of global sustainability*. London: Anthem Press.

Litman, T. (2009). *Evaluating criticisms of smart growth*. Retrieved from http://www.vtpi.org/sgcritics.pdf, accessed 9 Jan. 2014.

Litman, T. (2011). Can smart growth policies conserve energy and reduce emissions? *Center for Real Estate Quarterly Journal, 5*(2), 21–30.

Llamas-Sanchez, R., Munoz-Fernandez, A., & Maraver-Tarifa, G. (2011). The local agenda 21 in Andalusia, Spain: A model for sustainable innovation. *African Journal of Business Management, 5*(32), 12653–12663. doi:10.5897/ajbm11.2381

Lombardi, P., Giordano, S., Farouh, H., & Yousef, W. (2012). Modelling the smart city performance. *Innovation-the European Journal of Social Science Research, 25*(2), 137–149. doi:10.1080/13511610.2012.660325

MacKinnon, D., Cumbers, A., & Chapman, K. (2002). Learning, innovation and regional development: A critical appraisal of recent debates. *Progress in Human Geography, 26*(3), 293–311. doi:10.1191/0309132502ph371ra

MacLeod, G. (2013). New urbanism/smart growth in the Scottish Highlands: Mobile policies and post-politics in local development planning. *Urban Studies*, Online before print 19 June 2013. doi:10.1177/0042098013491164

MacLeod, G., & Goodwin, M. (1999). Space, scale and state strategy: Rethinking urban and regional governance. *Progress in Human Geography, 23*(4), 503–527. doi:10.1191/03091329 9669861026

Margerum, R., Parker, R., Brody, S., & McEwen, G. (2013). Metropolitan smart-growth centers: An assessment of incentive policies in four regions. *Journal of Transport and Land Use, 6*(2), 21–32.

McCauley, S. M., & Murphy, J. T. (2013). Smart growth and the scalar politics of land management in the Greater Boston region, USA. *Environment and Planning A, 45*(12), 2852–2867. doi:10.1068/a45307

Mitchell-Weaver, C., Miller, D., & Deal, R. (2000). Multilevel governance and metropolitan regionalism in the USA. *Urban Studies, 37*(5–6), 851–876.

Morandi, C., Rolando, A., & Di Vita, S. (2015). *From smart city to smart region: Digital services for an Internet of Places*. Cham: Springer.

Morgan, K. (1997). The learning region: Institutions, innovation and regional renewal. *Regional Studies, 31*(5), 491–503. doi:10.1080/00343409750132289

Mosannenzadeh, F., & Vettorato, D. (2014). Defining smart city: A conceptual framework based on keyword analysis. *Tema. Journal of Land Use, Mobility and Environment.*

Naphade, M., Banavar, G., Harrison, C., Paraszczak, J., & Morris, R. (2011). Smarter cities and their innovation challenges. *Computer, 44*(6), 32–39.

Neirotti, P., De Marco, A., Cagliano, A. C., Mangano, G., & Scorrano, F. (2014). Current trends in smart city initiatives: Some stylised facts. *Cities, 38*, 25–36. doi:10.1016/j.cities. 2013.12.010

O'Riordan, T., & Voisey, H. (1998). *Agenda 21: The transition to sustainability*. London: Earthscan.

Owen, A. L., & Videras, J. (2008). Trust, cooperation and implementation of sustainability programs: The case of Local Agenda 21. *Ecological Economics, 68*(1–2), 259–272. doi:10.1016/j.ecolecon.2008.03.006

Parnell, S., & Robinson, J. (2012). (Re)theorizing cities from the global south: Looking beyond neo-liberalism. *Urban Geography, 33*(4), 593–617.

Pollard, O. (2000). Smart growth: The promise, politics and potential pitfalls of emerging growth management strategies. *Virginia Environmental Law Journal, 19*, 247–285.

Redclift, M. (2005). Sustainable development (1987–2005): An oxymoron comes of age. *Sustainable Development, 13*, 212–227.

Renne, J. (2008). Smart growth and transit-oriented development at the state level: Lessons from California, New Jersey and Western Australia. *Journal of Public Transportation, 11*(3), 77–108. doi:10.5038/2375-0901.11.3.5

Rogers, R., Jalal, K., & Boyd, J. (2005). *An introduction to sustainable development.* Cambridge, MA: Harvard University Press.

Rogerson, C. (2009). The turn to "new regionalism": South African reflections. *Urban Forum, 20*(2), 111–140. doi:10.1007/s12132-009-9057-x

Rossi, U. (2016). The variegated economics and the potential politics of the smart city. *Territory, Politics, Governance, 4*(3), 337–353.

Ruddiman, E. (2013). Is smart growth fair growth: Do urban growth boundaries keep out minorities? *The Journal of Public and Professional Sociology, 5*(1), 1–34.

Scott, A. (2011). A world in emergence: Notes toward a resynthesis of urban-economic geography for the 21st century. *Urban Geography, 36*(2), 845–870.

Scott, J. W. (2007). Smart growth as urban reform: A pragmatic "recoding" of the new regionalism. *Urban Studies, 44*(1), 15–35.

Seitzinger, S. P., Svedin, U., Crumley, C. L., Steffen, W., Abdullah, S. A., Alfsen, C., … Sugar, L. (2012). Planetary stewardship in an urbanizing world: Beyond city limits. *Ambio, 41*(8), 787–794.

Shelton, T., Zook, M., & Wiig, A. (2015). The "actually existing smart city". *Cambridge Journal of Regions Economy and Society, 8*(1), 13–25. doi:10.1093/cjres/rsu026

Song, Y. (2012). Suburban sprawl and smart growth. In R. Weber & R. Crane (Eds.), *Handbook on urban planning* (pp. 418–435). New York: Oxford University Press.

Storper, M. (1995). The resurgence of regional economies, ten years later: The region as a nexus of untraded interdependencies. *European Urban and Regional Studies, 2*(3), 191–221. doi:10.1177/096977649500200301

Tapscott, D., Williams, A. D. and Herman, D. (2008). *Government 2.0: Transforming government and governance for the twenty-first century.* Retrieved from http://wiki.dbast.com/images/a/aa/Transforming_govt.pdf, accessed 21 Nov. 2017.

Tellier, L. N. (2011). *Urban world history: An economic and geographical perspective.* Montreal: Presses de l'Université du Québec.

Toly, N. (2008). Transnational municipal networks in climate politics: From global governance to global politics. *Globalizations, 5*(3), 341–356.

Törnqvist, G. (2004). Creativity in time and space. *Geografiska Annaler: Series B, Human Geography, 86*(4), 227–243. doi:10.1111/j.0435-3684.2004.00165.x

Trudeau, D. (2013). New urbanism as sustainable development? *Geography Compass, 7*(6), 435–448.

Viitanen, J., & Kingston, R. (2014). Smart cities and green growth: Outsourcing democratic and environmental resilience to the global technology sector. *Environment and Planning A, 46*(4), 803–819. doi:10.1068/a46242

Wey, W.-M. (2015). Smart growth and transit-oriented development planning in site selection for a new metro transit station in Taipei, Taiwan. *Habitat International, 47*, 158–168. Retrieved from doi:http://dx.doi.org/10.1016/j.habitatint.2015.01.020, 10 Nov. 2017.

Wiig, A. (2015). The empty rhetoric of the smart city: From digital inclusion to economic promotion in Philadelphia. *Urban Geography*, 1–19. doi:10.1080/02723638.2015.1065686

Zanella, A., Bui, N., Castellani, A., Vangelista, L., & Zorzi, M. (2014). Internet of Things for smart cities. *Ieee Internet of Things Journal, 1*(1), 22–32. doi:10.1109/jiot.2014.2306328

2 Economic factors in shaping city regionalism and "smartness"

Introduction

The previous chapter suggested that the evolution of smartness over the past few decades steadily merged in the 1990s with the "rise of city-regions" and parallel conversations and debates about a so-called new city-regionalism (Dierwechter, 2008; Herrschel & Newman, 2002; Jonas & Ward, 2007; Purcell, 2007; Segbers, 2007). Even as extant scholarship on the governance, politics and indeed geopolitics of city-regionalism offer important refinements of the literature (Evers & de Vries, 2013; Harding, 2007; Herrschel & Newman, 2002; Hidle & Leknes, 2014; Vogel et al., 2010), as Jonas (2013) points out, a preponderance of work on global city-regions and the new city-regionalism has focused on economic dimensions. This chapter highlights research into some of the main economic factors shaping the emergence of city-regions and parallel processes of city-regionalism and "smartness." This initial focus is merited, but following Jonas, does not reduce the important political dimensions, which are always empirically intertwined with economic dynamics.

Economic globalization over the past several decades has arguably elevated the territorial role of city-regions as key spaces of accumulation (A. Scott, 2001a, 2001b). In this book, then, city-regions are large geographic nodes characterized by dense socio-technical assemblages of firms, workers, shared infrastructures and variously scaled bio-physical systems of water, air, soil, etc. These nodes now sustain the production and reproduction of life in most societies all around the world. New trends in the democratic governance and professional management of city-regions, we note, have major consequences for how we study the new geographies of smartness in a comparative international context. For globalized processes of highly uneven *economic* development within (and between) city-regions, as well as within (and across) specific national settlement systems, have created both socio-economic winners and losers, a key organizing theme we develop at length in this chapter.

The city-regional concept is not new. The conceptual origins of today's globalized city-region as related directly to ecological sustainability and territorially embedded economies likely date back a century or more – at least to the work of Patrick Geddes and others creatively rethinking how to actively engage the costs and benefits of urban industrialization. Through the past several decades, however, discussions of city-regions have reflected wider historical and geographical changes in the space-economy of specific societies and their interrelationships with one another. The recent politics of anti-globalist populism – notably the Brexit vote and "Trumpism" in the UK and the United States, respectively – along with diverse urban geographies of longer-running city-regional transformations in different countries and world regions, simply foreground new challenges for researchers and practitioners alike.

In this chapter, we consider literatures on the uneven world of city-regional economies in relation to globalization. Our central concern is to tease out some of the social, spatial and political implications of uneven economic development within city-regions and between them, using diverse examples from North America and Europe especially. We then turn to a more specific discussion of how the winners and losers, associated with globalized processes directly challenge the parallel search for new forms of "smart(er)" governance and territorial management strategies. The final section considers how these dynamics are helping in turn to reshape global space from a "mosaic-like" world of clear defined state-static territories to a much more fluid space of economic flows, albeit one that produces more (and less) attractive corridors and nodes. Our overarching purpose throughout this discussion – and, indeed, the discussion that follows in Chapter 3 – is to forge more explicit linkages between the economic and political dimensions of globalized city-regionalism and the parallel literature just reviewed in Chapter 1 on the conceptual evolution of smartness. This helps us to offer an overall theoretical synthesis in Chapter 4, highlighting our central argument around interpreting smartness in city-regions as a "dual transition" in order to create the main analytical bridge to the comparative case studies that form Part II of this book.

Globalization and the uneven world of city-regional economies

City-regions are closely linked to economic processes and especially to those of globalization. At the turn of millennium, Allen Scott (2001a, p. 820) argued that:

> Over the last few decades and throughout the world, numerous suitably positioned urban centres have been transformed into super clusters whose massive recent expansion stems from the circumstance that many of the leading sectors of capitalism today are organized as dense and intensely localized networks of producers with powerful endogenous growth mechanisms and with an increasingly global market reach.

Such "superclusters" are evident in California, for example, as shown in Figure 2.1 below. With a GDP of more than $2.6 trillion in 2017 (Bureau of Economic Analysis, 2017), the Californian economy was and remains, the sixth largest in the world, roughly the same size of France. But most jobs in California are heavily concentrated in either the Los Angeles-Riverside-San Bernadino Core-Based Statistical Areas (CBSAs), or the extended "Bay Area'

CBSAs that link together San Francisco-Oakland and San Jose-Santa Clara. (Rural counties make up only 1% of all jobs.) These employment patterns illustrate a de facto metropolitanization of the national space-economy overall, in the United States as elsewhere, driven by the growing connectivity and flows of information, goods and people. City-regions benefit from agglomeration advantages as nodes in communication lines as well as centres of decision-making. Saskia Sassen (1991) first addressed this process in her "Global Cities" concept. She specifically stressed (Sassen 1994) how globalization processes, especially the rapidly growing trans-border mobility of capital, labour and ICT-enabled information, "ha[ve] spurred the fragmentation, dispersal and reorganization of productive activities" (Walks, 2001, p. 407). At the same time, globalization processes have precipitated rapid de-industrialization and loss of economic momentum in many Western (old industrial) cities. A few "global cities' have benefitted enormously from strategic head office functions, the growing presence and role of innovation and creativity in economic activity and what Richard Florida captured as the "creative class."

More than a quarter of a century later, all this has spawned a populist anti-globalization movement among those "left behind" who feel their economic losses have not been compensated for by "globalization wins." Inequality has reached across scales, manifesting itself *between* city-regions and between them and the wider non-urban regions, as well as between individual localities *within* city-regions and even *within localities* between neighborhoods. Reconciling these differences and also the seemingly competing and/or contradicting agendas of competitiveness, cohesion and, related to that, sustainability, thus

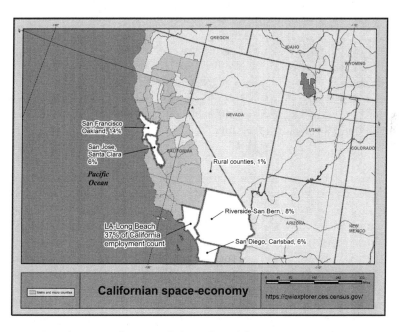

Figure 2.1 The uneven location of jobs in the Californian space-economy.

requires political imagination, courage and innovation, as well as decision-making capacity and institutional flexibility. "Smart" governance envisages a route to squaring this circle of competing demands across policy fields, types of actors and spatial-governmental scale.

In the United States, the intra-city–regional contrast manifests itself in the different fates of many inner-urban and early suburban neighbourhoods and the new suburbs and exurbs, with a growing gap between "winners" and "losers" (Voith, 1992; Walks, 2001). In Europe, depending on the quality of public transport/transit connectivity with the main centres of a conurbation/metropolitan area, "winners' include so-called "in-between cities" or *Zwischenstädte* (Sieverts, 2003), which fill the spaces between core cities and existing (older) suburban areas. They follow an exurban or "new urban" development design and rationale for work, living and services. Young and Keil (2010) consider whether this could be an expression of a post-Fordist rescaling and reorganising the economic landscape of and around, cities, with the regional scale gaining a particular role in the presentation of relational, rather than organizational, space: "Regions to some degree re-defined the space of political economies and shattered the methodological nationalism of scholars and practitioners alike" (ibid., p. 89). On the ground, this has produced urban sprawl, while also generating new concentrations as part of "new urbanist" developments with higher densities around infrastructure nodes. Often, this went in association with gentrifying urban trendiness as "glamour zones" by the "creative class" (ibid.).

The implications of unevenness at various scales have become an important part of the globalization story, as the political consequences of an effective differentiation of state territory and society into "winners" and "losers" are now much more evident. Indeed, as Scott (2001a, p. 821) also notes:

> the prospect of a mosaic of global city-regions, each of them characterized by an activist collectivity resolutely seeking to reinforce local competitive advantages, however, raises a further series of questions and problems. At the very least, *rising levels of concerted regional activism can be expected to lead to specific kinds of destabilization and politicization* of interregional relations, both within and across national boundaries.

> (emphasis added)

The economic context of city regions has thus undergone fundamental and continuous change as part of a shift toward global free trade arrangements that emphasize place-based competitiveness. The result has been a self-propeling, reinforcing process of cities growing into "their" regions, as people from more peripheral, rural parts seek to improve their chances by moving to urban/metropolitan areas. As many of these more mobile people are also more entrepreneurial, it is not far to Richard Florida's creative class as primary driver and beneficiary, of a growing metropolitanization of regions and states. The Brexit vote in the United Kingdom and the election of Donald Trump, reflect underlying tensions produced by this process, not just between a "metropolitan elite" and the non-metropolitan "rest," but also between successful and much less successful city-regions in their attempts to find their positions in a post-industrial, competitive, neo-liberal setting. City-regional development depends on particular conditions shaped by local economic structures and geographic location, but also on outwardly-oriented economic perspectives that in turn result from innovative, imaginative, "smart" policy-making.

The concern with city regions – or extended metropolitan areas – gained in attention and also urgency in the 1950s, when a rapid increase in personal mobility, especially in North America, accelerated an already growing dispersion of cities through suburbanization and the legendary pursuit of the American Dream. In Western Europe, this goal also gained traction, although at a slower pace, owing to a tighter regulative framework to protect landscapes and open space (and also an initially lower rates of car ownership). The eventual proliferation of the private automobile soon accelerated this process in a more ubiquitous way than was possible when public transport was the main driver of such a process, albeit in a much more spatially selective, linear way. The effects of "sprawl" attracted much attention not just because of its challenges to the rationale of development planning and control, but also to governance structures and principles, as administrative borders became transcended by functional relations and developments. In North America and the United States in particular, sprawl underscored the weakening of many urban cores to the advantage of the new suburban areas and exurban "cities." More affluent households and businesses migrated to larger, more car-accessible and lower cost locations. In Europe, meanwhile, such developments were resisted mainly for the environmental reason of landscape protection to prevent continuous suburbanization and cities became perceived as a regionalized phenomenon. Functional characteristics as expression of economic "relevance" and appeal to both people and economic activity and their physical manifestation in – largely unchecked and unstructured – expansion of built-up area, have become the primary criteria for describing city-regions as a phenomenon, be that in Europe, such concept as Boustedt's (1953) *Stadtregion* (literally, city region) in Germany, or, in the United States, Standard Metropolitan Statistical Areas (SMSAs) and, since 2003, Core Based Statistical Areas. As the name implies, establishing SMSAs was driven originally by a concern in the post-war United States with capturing the phenomenon of urbanization spreading – seemingly unchecked – into the regions through continuous suburbanization and finding appropriate governance answers on the basis of existing, locally-based, governing structures (Rosenwaike, 1970). In essence, though, the phenomenon of "metropolis" or, in today's term, city-region drew on positivist approaches to describing functional spatial relationships through statistical indicators, threshold values and calculations, such as travel-to-work linkages or telephone densities.

These models of city-regionalization seek to capture the fluid spatiality of economic opportunity-driven dynamics, as they challenge established formal governmental arrangements and push for a scaling to the regional level of governing mechanisms. The growing separation between city and suburb, in economic, societal and also in political terms and the formation of a more distinct suburban lifestyle and consciousness (Herrschel, 2014), added a complexity and challenge for a more collective regional approach in governance, as urban and suburban interests, superficially at least, diverged (see the Seattle case discussed in Chapter 5). This complexity goes beyond what statistical methods sought to capture about metropolitanism in the form of functional economic relations as far as the SMSA concept was concerned. Other models, such as the German *Stadtregion*, sought to include a more introspective view by taking internal physiognomic-functional patterns of city-regions into account. Also taken into account were preexisting structures outside a city-region, as they become subject to suburbanizing processes.

Subsequent conceptualizations continued a nodal perspective, including the "growth pole" idea of the 1960s and 1970s (Lasuen, 1969; Thomas, 1975). This has had a major influence on spatial planning (Parr, 1999), such as hub-and-spoke models (O'Kelly, 1998), as arguably advocated later by smart growth concepts with their focus on linear developments along public transport lines and, especially, around stations. This as been the case in Vancouver, for instance, and, to some extent at least, in Seattle. There, the interface between "city" and "region" is clearly structured and limited to "permitted" forms of engagement. Network theories (Bryson, Crosby, & Bryson, 2009; Murdoch, 1998) acknowledge more explicitly such a two-way, symbiotically functional relationship between core city/cities and the surrounding region, with mutual dependencies, as well as shared benefits, from pursuing common interests portrayed as win–win scenarios.

What these concepts share is a functionally, economically-led perspective of city-to-region relationships and thus the cross-scalar interdependencies between local and regional perspectives. The geographic reach of the nodal roles of cities within city-regions and of city-regions within national and international settings (contexts), provides the notional adhesive holding together a city-region as conglomerate of local entities (i.e. the main (core) city and surrounding more or less sub-urban municipalities). The main challenge of these opportunity-driven arrangements is linking them to the actual power of the relevant administrative-governmental structures and political systems. How can inherently static, fixed structures of power, responsibility and democratic legitimacy engage with fluid, functionally changing and (temporary) interest-defined relationships and engagements? This new economic reality creates new pressures for more imaginative, or smarter, policy solutions capable of quickly following changes in circumstances and requirements.

"Winners," "losers" and the challenges to "smart" governance?

In Europe, the 1996 European Union's Lisbon Agreement explicitly recognized city regions (referred to as metropolitan areas) as the drivers of both national and EU economic development (Wiechmann, 2009). This weakened adherence to spatial cohesion and territorial contiguity in public policy (Davoudi, 2007; Atkinson, 2001). As a compromise, "poly-centricity" is now being proposed in order to combine both competitiveness-driven localization and collaborative regionalism between local entities to advance their (individual) interests jointly (Davoudi, 2003). The financial crisis of 2008 and now Brexit and the election of Donald Trump, have focused more attention on the extent to which neo-liberally rationalized competitiveness has widened the gap between winners and losers of globalized economic competition to such a degree that it may turn into a systemic threat. Has the neo-liberal, globalist discourse actually now reached the end of the line? The unintended consequences of putting all eggs (of economic development and prosperity) into the metropolitan basket may thus be reconsidered. For city regions, differential opportunities are reflected in their internal structures, as well as relationships to each other and their wider hinterland. Here the notion of "metropolitanity" may be introduced, embracing physiognomic, functional-economic and political-administrative elements. Together, these qualities reflect, but also produce, in a reciprocal way, a sense of togetherness, of shared interests and, importantly, shared benefits, resulting from joint action at metropolitan/city-regional level. Yet, this will vary over time and in response to different degrees of social-economic cohesion at the local-regional scale and, at times, differences may seem to dominate perceptions, appearances and agendas.

By the same token, in response to this rising metopolitanity, those groups, actors, or places and spaces not feeling part of that metropolitanism and the associated ways of life and doing business as well as politics, may feel alienated, excluded and, as we can now see, become mobilized through growing populism, outright resentment and hostility toward the perceived elitism of the winners. Gaps and even "trenches," have become evident within, among and around interests. This affects the ways in which city-regions are perceived, see themselves and operate, in turn generating new challenges for policies to respond and bridge the gaps. Established and well-used formulae may no longer suffice, such as a continued repetition of the virtues of globalization and opportunities for all because of trickle-down economics. Instead, new narratives, innovative and, perhaps, experimental, may be required as underpinnings of "smart" governance responses that seek to keep up with the speed of change and thus the fluidity of challenges and expectations and their localization.

The decline of many of the older cities in the industrial heartland of the "Rust Belt" of the Northeastern and Midwestern United States, or, in Europe, in northern England, the German Ruhr, Northeastern France, or many parts of post-communist Eastern Europe, or, until quite recently, a continuous abandonment of the "old" urban cores for the new suburban expansions: whether called suburbanization, *Stadtflucht* or périurbanization, all have produced a sense that conventional cities as economic nodes may not necessarily be automatic "winners" *per se* of the growing metropolitanization of globalized (economic and life-style) space. Quite clearly, some cities are locationally and structurally better placed than others, leading to a growing divide between dynamically developing places with growth opportunities and those finding themselves increasingly on the margins and with reduced opportunities.

Thus, a few places begin to move ahead as their self-reinforcing concentrations of capital and structural capacities make them progressively
more efficient, in both static and dynamic terms. Success produces success
(up to some point of diminishing returns, at least) and "the advantages of
these places then become locked in, marginalizing competitor locations
and effectively crowding them out of the field.

(Scott and Storper, 2003, p. 584)

Yet, the notion of the *cohesive state*, underpinned by a Keynesian-style national –
and also European – economic policy aiming at comparable living conditions
across its territory, seems an outdated concept. Instead, alternative scenarios
lead to quite different, economic landscapes with varying degrees, characteristics and manifestations of city-regional clusters and their representation of
"new" and "old" urban and, especially, suburban qualities.

Some individual cities turn into "elite" places closely linked to the
"creative class," as suggested by Richard Florida, while a larger number of
cities – Detroit, Cincinnati, St Louis, or Middlesbrough, Duisburg or Douai,
respectively – have lost their old economic rationale and remain in search of
alternative post- or new industrial *raisons d'être* and identities. These struggling
cities illustrate the problem of "shrinking cities" (Bontje, 2005; Hollander,
2011) as an outcome of shifting economic interests – Castell's global economic
flows – and associated perceived greater or lesser opportunities in individual
localities. The tasks for and expectations from, city-regional governance are
thus likely to (need to) differ considerably between places as well as over time.

By contrast, winning cities have experienced major successes, either by
reinventing themselves, such as Boston, Chicago or Denver, or, in Europe,
Manchester, Leipzig, Lille or Gdańsk, by using existing locational strengths, or
appeal on the basis of image profiling as "liveable" and desirable urban spaces
as a lifestyle choice, such as Seattle, Portland, San Francisco and Los Angeles or
Malmö/Copenhagen, Freiburg, or Lyon – preferably in conjunction with the
adjective "eco," respectively. Indeed, by joining the arena on the back of new,
rapid growth, "sunshine economies," such as Dallas or Houston, the contrast
is thus not just between metropolitan areas and the rest, but also between economically successful cities and those urban areas that have lost out.

Figure 2.2 below highlights the uneven economic development across the
United States and thus a distinction between "winners" and "losers" among
large space economies in Europe, North America and the world as a result of
globalization-driven competitiveness. Two trends become especially clear. The
"spikes" that mark metropolitan areas/city regions indicate much of the respective continental territories as mere backcloth (Rodríguez-Pose & Crescenzi,
2008). In addition, the opposite nature of these spikes shows above average
increase of output and also above average decrease. While highlighting the
metropolitanization of state spaces, Figure 2.3 shows the diverse paths taken by
city regions in a globalized world, here, for the example of the United States.
The large, even dominant, contributions by metropolitan areas becomes very
evident. The "Rust Belt" shows a clustering of underperforming or shrinking

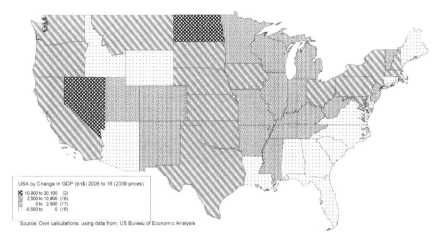

Figure 2.2 Uneven economic growth in the United States.

city-regional economies, while the Atlantic Seaboard, the "Sunshine States," and the Pacific Northwest see more rapid and sustained economic growth. The old industrial and peripheral non-metropolitan areas suggest different political-economic and societal requirements and circumstances for policy-making at the local and regional levels. There is, quite clearly, no "standard" national economic context for the development of city-regional governance. Rather, national context matters as a conditioning framework, not at least through the impact of national regulation and policies, which circumscribe scope and capacity for cities to act and seek to boost their chances on the global market place.

Figure 2.3 thus ultimately illustrates the resulting "fragmentation" of state territory through such individual actions, grouped into clear winners, losers and those "in-between." Transition here means a globalization-induced change from a more or less cohesive state space to that of a fragmented patchwork of winners and losers also among metropolitan areas. Yet, city-regions, so it seems, are the primary centres of sizeable growth. Evidence suggests that large and dense cities benefit from agglomeration advantages that increase productivity (Dijkstra, Garcilazo, & McCann, 2013; Melo, Graham, & Noland, 2009), so that a doubling of US city size appears to go together with an increase in GDP per capita by four to seven per cent (Dijkstra et al., 2013). As part of that, knowledge-related economic activities have a particularly important role to play (Porter, 1990). Agglomeration advantages produce self-selecting and reinforcing processes with growing differentials in economic opportunity and reward. "Cities are a necessary corollary of industrialization because they allow for complex ex agglomerations of specialized activities to emerge while economizing on infrastructure under conditions of national scarcity" (Scott & Storper, 2003, p. 583). Yet, just as positive selection based on locational strengths, cities may also get de-selected, if they lose or weaken their relative advantages. Self-selection may also involve "negative selection," that is, de-selection or exclusion. City size also seems to correlate

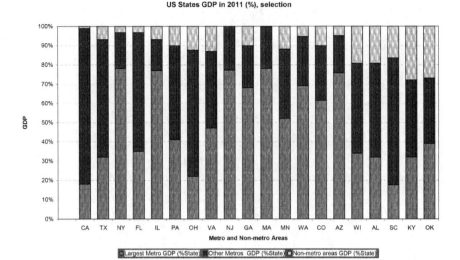

Figure 2.3 Contribution by metropolitan areas to the GDP of "their" US state in 2011 ($bn).

with sectoral diversity (Glaeser et al., 1992), supporting the basic assumptions of Christaller's Central Place Theory that conceptualized the link between size, functional diversity and geographic "reach" as an expression of economic appeal. Yet there seems to be a curve of diminished returns, as productivity gains through further agglomeration seem to slow down among large metropolitan areas (McCann & Acs, 2011), ultimately turning into disadvantages through excessive costs, be that living costs and thus appeal to a diverse labour pool, congestion, or labour costs. So it may not be surprising to find that "medium-sized" agglomerations of around one million inhabitants raise their appeal instead (OECD, 2006). There is thus evidence that the nodal effect of accessibility and connectivity matters more than mere size (McCann & Acs, 2011).

In Europe, too, as Figures 2.4, 2.5 and 2.6 all show, metropolitan areas are now the main centres of economic activity, generating a growing share of national populations and economic output. But just as in North America, not all metropolitan areas are winners. A number of urban regions and non–urban regions perform much less well economically. Nevertheless, metropolitan areas remain the key arenas for Europe's economic development (Figure 2.4). Moreover, at the global level, as Figure 2.5 indicates, large and especially medium-sized metropolitan areas will very likely provide most of the economic development capacity in developing countries. The Asian-Pacific region, for example, is a major contributor to a structural shift in favour of metro-politan areas (Jones &Douglass, 2008). This has accelerated the divide between urbanized regions and the rest within national territories. It remains to be seen, of course, to what extent the presumed trickle-down effects will material-ize and, importantly, whether people are willing to wait for such effects. As Douglass (2000, p. 2330) usefully observed several years ago now:

Uneven spatial development might not appear to be problematic in the short term. The efficiencies of giant urban agglomerations are widely touted to be superior to smaller cities and a spatial trickling-down of development impulses is still assumed by many governments to be inevitable despite countervailing tendencies at the moment. But some countries already show the consequences of long-term uneven development. In Japan and Korea, rural areas have been depleted of youth and basic urban functions such as bus and rail transport and schools are disappearing, leaving an extremely aged population to manage much of the agricultural economy.

In short, city-regions have now in a more exposed position as either successful or less successful nodes in their national space-economies, rather than remaining much less exposed, integral parts of these economy, as was the case in the past. This so highlighted "win" or "loss," of course, places major pressures on them to appear as "successful" and, in turn, affects their internal arrangements and structures with regard to policy outcomes.

Once again, this book emphasizes the "dual transition" of both external and internal changes as challenges to governance and policies. For this reason, it is equally important to take an intra-regional look in order to establish how far internal, intra-regional variations in economic performance and socio-economic status matter. This goes across scales and includes differentiating effects both between and within localities of a city-region. Furthermore, it may involve different parts of a city in different ways, such as urban centres with "elitization" through gentrification effects (Smith, 2002) or suburban versus core urban interests and political attitudes (Trumpist "anti-elitism"?) Older suburban cities may thus develop different strategic interests and priorities than newer, "exurban" ones, seeking to emphasize a version of "urbanity" that features in the currently so favoured smart growth agenda. Finding collaborative commonality in focus and emphasis of policies within such diverse city-regions may thus not be easy.

Already in 1964, before the term city-region became fashionable, Dickinson pointed to their two-fold role: as outward-reaching "zones of influence" – much in a Chrisllerian sense of market areas – , yet also as arenas of development that are shaped by the outside. This duality shapes both nature and scope of internal negotiations about common policy agendas as rationale of collective city-region-wide governance approaches which seek to bring together under one agenda roof differing, perhaps even competing, interests and expectations within and between localities. As such, city-regions are also "mental constructs," rather than, "as some planners and scholars seem to think, an area which can be presented on a platter to suit their general needs" (Dickinson, 1964-1972, p. 54). Instead, they are inherently fluid and possess multiple meanings at the same time as determined by a combination of external factors/processes and internal structures, values and imaginations. For businesses, city-regions offer distinct cluster (agglomeration) advantages or, as the case may be, disadvantages – and that may change over time –, which determine their attraction through likely (expected) opportunity gains. It is the sum of a

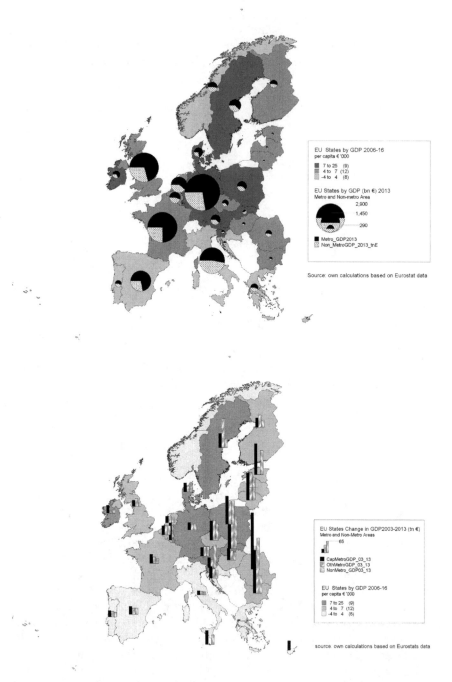

Figure 2.4 Growing importance of metropolitan and urban regions in the European Union.

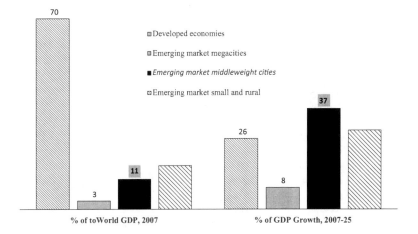

Figure 2.5 Mapping the power of cities.

Source: derived from data presented in http://www.mckinsey.com/global-themes/urbanization/
urban-world-the-shifting-global-business-landscape

city-region's internal locational factors, plus its external relations through physical and network connectivity, that jointly *through their interdependencies* define
its strength. The degree of their complementarity and cohesion decides how
far this leads to further (joint) economic capacity that may, ideally, benefit all,
or, instead, widens the gap between winners and losers.

Parr (2002) points to the fact that business–relevant agglomeration advantages
in a city region are a combination of different economies of scale, each relating
to individual policy fields, but requiring reconciliation through horizontal and
vertical deliberation and, where opportune, compromise and collaboration.
This, in turn, circumscribes (1) "economies of scope" as expression of the
potential and additional capacity gained from sharing interest and objectives
among economic activities between actors in pursuit of agreed shared interests
and (2) "economies of complexity." This denotes a reflection of organizational
arrangements across territorial, institutional and political-ideational boundaries
in the expectation of win–win outcomes from collective action.

Yet, such effective acceptance of likely "winner-takes-all" development
inherently contradicts a collective state-based perspective and political-
economic agenda as espoused by the post-war spatial Keynesianism, where
the promise of economic improvement for all served as the main legitimating
factor for capitalist economic policy. In Europe, the implicit social contract
between state and electorate about the to be expected economic improvement remained in place until the "discovery" of the neo-liberal discourse on
the back of globalization in the late 1970s. Regardless, the economic success
of space economies, at whatever multiple scales, remains a potent force in
shaping public policy by circumscribing scope and courage of policy-makers

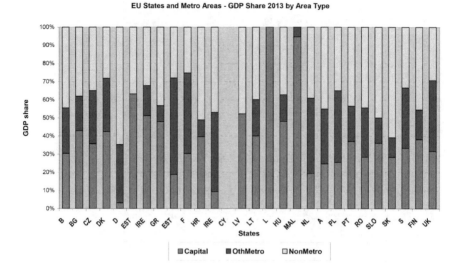

Figure 2.6 GDP per capita in metropolitan regions of the European Union.
Source: author's elaborations on data from Eurostat.

to look beyond tried and tested measures. As a result of the changes in universal discourse and derived policies, two different models of space economic development and related public policy emerged: (1) a conventional statist ("mercantilist") redistributive economic regionalism in the interest of maintaining a degree of spatial economic cohesiveness within national borders, in which regions are primarily containers for state delivered policies and (2) an abandonment of such on the back of doubts of public policy efficiency and a favouring of "going with the economic flow" as determined by market opportunism and accepting agglomeration advantages as self-propelling drivers of economic development in a globalized competitive setting. The outcome is metropolitan 'islands of prosperity' within a sea of largely by-passed, often invisible spaces that are not part of the "story." Veltz (2000) speaks of an "archipelago economy" that reaches from the global to the sub-national, with global processes creating locally selective inequalities.

In the United Kingdom, with its distinct primate city structure focused on London, a rapidly growing divide has developed between the wider London region and the 'rest' (Harding 2007) since the liberalization policies of the 1980s. These all but abandoned efforts to counteract such widening gap through (redistributive) regional policies. The Labour government of the 1990s and early 2000s sought to address the growing divisions, especially the North–South Divide, through devolution of the four national territories in 1997. These included attempts to regionalize England as the United Kingdom's largest national entity, and adoption of the 1960s regional economic planning entities that served as the basis of redistribution policies to shift economic growth from

London to the rest of the country (Pickvance, 1982). This clearly aimed at reducing London's outstanding economic pre-eminence within the United Kingdom. After the failure to establish English regions with more policy-making powers and capacities in the mid-2000s (Harding, 2007), city-regionalization appeared as an alternative to establish a number of economic growth centres outside London to counterbalance the economic tilt to the south. Quite clearly, this reduced "regionalism" to a rather selective "metropolitanity" of economic development opportunity, thus admitting that inequalities are there to stay. Regionalism in England has thus been established as de facto city-regionalism and has been done so quite visibly through newly to be installed elected metropolitan mayors as figureheads.

Since 2010, under Conservative Government leadership, there has been no interest in such a blanket regionalism with contiguous territories and fixed boundaries as "container" of all that lies within these boundaries and makes it subject to the same values and policy agendas. Instead, these entities are rather more fluid and weakly institutionalized ("virtual") city-regional spaces, based on self-selecting principles as expressed in the ides of Local Partnerships (Peck et al., 2013) instead. The concept of the Northern Way as a virtual region composed of a region-wide cluster – identified by the Government – of the larger cities of Northern England some 10 years ago, or the "follow-up mode" of the "Northern Powerhouse" (Lee, 2017), are attempts at state-sponsored city-regionalism as a form of a "grand plan" for rebalancing the national economy, based on cities, rather than the national territory as a whole. Yet, there was little involvement of local interests and structures in designing the policy, reflecting, rather, a centrally designed strategy based also on ideological priorities of "free enterprise" and market forces. So it may not be surprising that the somewhat grandly named Northern Powerhouse has so far been more a politically useful rhetoric than an actual developmental project on the ground to boost economic competitiveness among the provincial cities and regions outside London and the South East.

In essence, it is an idea borrowing from the polycentrism as favoured by the EU under its ESPON strategy as a seeming win-win policy that promises to be able to square the circle between individual city-centric competitiveness and wider, regionally collective cohesiveness as politically visible commitment to a cohesive (national) state space. Facing this conundrum between two competing and seemingly mutually exclusive discourses and concepts of spatial economic development between localized "market" and national "state," Harding (2007) questioned the salience of "conservative, backward-looking approaches to issues of spatial economic management in circumstances that are less suited to nation-specific 'spatial Keynesianism' than ever" (p. 456). Nearly 10 years on, facing the backlash of this inequality in the populist politics of Brexit and, in the United States, electing Donald Trump, such caution about seeking to reverse developments and policies of the last three decades have gained urgent relevance. Instead, what Harding proposed and what seems of greater importance now than perhaps realised before more widely, is "a much more fundamental rethink of what it means to be 'progressive' in an age characterized by perforated sovereignty and stretched urban hierarchies on one hand, but increased urban accessibility and more flexible work patterns on the other" (Harding, 2007, p. 456). It is the way of working on the back of rapidly changing information technology that is an important driver of globalization, permitting – and encouraging – inevitable competitive comparison of opportunity and thus ways of doing things differently, where opportune, but also creating opportunities to participate in economic opportunities in spaces deemed to be peripheral and too disconnected in a conventional sense of analogue communication. Simply rolling back the times, however, cannot offer credible answers to the need to square the circle between information-based comparative competitiveness, shifting opportunities through redefined connectivities and state-based sense of territorially and societally shared purpose, opportunity and commonality.

Economic structure thus provides a crucial variable for the development of city regions, both as an external determinant and an internal structural and political factor at the interface between local and regional interests. A more integrated, complementary and interconnected economy may be expected to facilitate a city-regional agenda not just at the political level, but also in public awareness as prerogative for continued political willingness to engage in collaborative inter-local and inter-regional action. It is the sense of likely shared economic benefit and inter-connectedness that can strengthen a city-regional agenda across socio-economic and political divisions and associated parochialism and introspection. Discourses of commonality clearly matter (Paasi, 1986), but there also need to be underlying genuine advantages – such as delivering improved living conditions and economic prospects – resulting from such a regional engagement for each actor individually, so as to justify – and legitimize – collective action as a win-win option for policy-makers, also against a public attitude toward such policies. Salet and Thornley (2007) thus include "economic structure" as a key determinant in the shaping of business-oriented intra- and trans-regional networks, respectively. They reflect the "internal" and "external" dimensions of city-regionalization as a framework for "domains of metropolitan action space" (ibid., p. 192). "City-region" as a term is thus very much shaped by functional and physiognomic characteristics associated with urbanization, whereby economic relationships and processes are of particular prevalence as "drivers" of the underlying logics. And capturing the complexity of interests, perspectives and preferred modi operandi requires innovative, at times experimental forms of governance, so as to allow policies to remain relevant and effective (see also Glaeser, 2011).

Outside city-regions: globalization, metropolitanization and economic state space

Since the rise of "globalization" as a distinct label and discourse a quarter of a century ago, when the emerging information technology (IT) revolution around the personal computer and the then infant Internet introduced a new era of seemingly unlimited communication and interaction at will, much of the focus has been on the economic, especially financial, aspect of globalization on the back of a Thatcherite, small-state, neo-liberal agenda. The presumption, propagated widely by Western political discourse, was that everyone would – ultimately – benefit from the expected economic growth. Yet, what is now becoming evident after more than 30 years is that (a) there is a growing gap between "winners" and "losers" – be that people, places, regions, or countries; and (b) people may no longer believe in the eventual arrival of the promised goods and demand their "fair" share now, or else challenge the system altogether. The presumptions and discursive hegemony of the Washington Consensus, which underpinned much of economic policy during that period, fundamentally altered the view and governance of state spaces across scales. The ease with which a digitally constructed virtual world can be constructed and brought to economic use through electronic information exchange, most visibly illustrated by the parallel universe of the Internet, led to an enthusiastic embrace of the concept of globalization as leading paradigm of a time dominated by a neo-liberal discourse as the "only show in town." This was especially so after the collapse of the communist world in 1989 (Herrschel, 2007; Fukuyama, 2006). Networks and lines of communication with preferred connectivity and relational interaction have replaced homogenous state territories which simply "contained" localities and regions.

As Brenner (2004a, p. 35) suggests, "[g]lobalization is a multifaceted concept that refers, at core, to the extension of spatial interdependencies on a worldwide scale," creating new, while reshaping and also abandoning, existing spaces and places. The notion of a global space has added a new scale to the otherwise strong focus on nation states as primary actors at the global level. The idea of a global space implies a degree of liberation from the confines of the national perspective and its boundedness. This offers opportunities for sub-national actors – regions and localities – to reach beyond conventional borders and boundaries, including national borders and engage directly with each other around the world. In effect, it is a scaling up to the global level of local and regional perspectives, ambitions and engagement. Yet, there will be considerable differences between these sub-national actors in their ability, capacity and capability to utilize this opportunity by defining own policies. Especially, the larger cities with a more internationally-oriented economy, may be expected to "reach globally" more enthusiastically – and competently and credibly – as individual actors, while others may lack such competence and confidence and seek to collaborate and thereby gain stature and opportunity, such as by being part of a city-regional conglomerate or other collaborative network (Herrschel and Newman, 2017). The main challenge in the latter case is finding and articulating a shared purpose and thus scope to secure a win-win outcome of collaborative city-region-based action.

The time–space compression claimed by David Harvey (1989) as underpinning the globalization processes of capital, surmounting and reducing ever more borders and boundaries in the process, including, eventually, the communist Iron Curtain (Herrschel, 2007, Deacon, 2000), has produced a new, shifting context for development policy-making. With neither scalar perspectives nor territorial certainties about responsibilities, scope and conventions no longer were fixed and settled, requiring, instead, continued adjustment. Likewise, reviews of policy agendas, creativity and experimentalism in finding strategies that promised policy success vis-à-vis local public expectations and voters' legitimation. And it is here that cities offer increasingly – and need to do so on a liberalized, competitive market arena – the most attractive economic spaces through their concentration of resources, including skills, innovative capacity, market access and connectivity. As a result, other areas with less "on offer" are increasingly marginalized as "in-between spaces." So, while "flows" certainly matter, places do as well, as flows seek – and need – nodes to connect. In so doing, they get defined by the nodes, while also shaping those nodes through increased (or decreased) connectivity and thus economic relevance (Macleod & Jones, 2007). Harvey (1982) describes this symbiotic relationship as a dialectic of fixity and fluidity of capitalism in its geographic manifestation: it is mobile in its search for the highest rent on investment at any one time, yet also requires specific locations/localizations for investments to meet resources and markets to be able to produce those returns in the first place. The emphasis between the two may vary, of course, differing between places and over time, as place specificities may be important for particular competitive evaluations, depending on the criteria used. Quality of life may well be part of these criteria.

This reflects a change in the main organizing principle of political economic geography, from a mosaic of clearly defined, static state territories – or "containers," with relationships between them defined by governments for specific reasons, to the notion of global flows of economic – capitalist – interest cutting across this mosaic. Castells (1991) argued that such "flows" produce new spatial differentiations and also fragmentations of state territories by determining linear corridors of preferential interaction and involvement and spaces of lesser interest in between those corridors.

The result is a spatially selective differentiation of more "attractive" (profitable) and less attractive (unprofitable) cities and regions – as seen from an investor's point of view. Those connected the most and the farthest by being important nodes of interaction are deemed the most lucrative and thus appealing; others are ignored and "left outside" the spaces of interest. For city-regions, this means that attracting and optimizing connectivity, both physically and informationally, needs to be top of the list of policy agendas. Thus, rather than facing a "flat world" (Friedman, 2006) as a result of flow-driven borderlessness, varying qualities in connectedness will produce a geography of places that matter and those that do less so, with city-regions favored by their inherent centrality for economic and administrative activity (Rodríguez-Pose & Crescenzi, 2008). Yet again, however, there are variations in that, based on internal factors (variables) of an economic, societal and political nature. And city-regional governance needs to respond to the external and internal dynamics and seek to fuse them into a strategic policy agenda that reconciles concurrent as well as divergent interests.

Scope, capacity and capability to do something about this will vary in reflection of political-institutional and statutory frameworks as a key (but not the only) descriptor of the combined effects of internal and external factors on developing and articulating new forms and practices of "smart" city-regional governance. As a consequence, while globalization has changed the notion, role, perception and utilization of space, "it has by no means undermined the significance of location, of *place*" (Martin, 1999, p. 16). This seemingly contradictory relationship has been captured in Swyngedouw's term "glocalization" (Swyngedouw, 1997, 2004). City-regions are thus both active players and passive locales of externally-shaped processes and "smart" governance that seeks to address and utilize local and regional perspectives and dynamics, needs to capture that in its modus operandi. There is thus a direct link, even feed-back loop, between internal city-regional qualities, external appeal, rise as economic node and thus shaper of wider space economies.

Globalization processes and forces are thus not just a "God-given," "out there" to impose its dynamic and rationale on all else, but, as Cox (1997) notes, is shaped by a framework of social, political and economic "conditions," as the sum of power relations, choices, past experiences and structural unevenness. Given the continuously changing nature of this framework, globalization may be viewed as a multi-scalar version of Polanyi's double transformation (Blyth, 2002) driven by the tension between embedding and dis-embedding processes, that is, cities integrating with "their" surrounding regions/states as part of collaborative arrangements, or following their own individual agendas without engagement with the "outside." While the former refers to the setting of the localized specific into the more general, wider context, the latter refers to the characteristics of the locally specific as its distinguishing (and separating) quality in relation to the broader regional/national/global context. It is thus about the dialectic between the "specific" and "general," something that needs to be addressed by governance arrangements. And, here, "smart" measures could seek to address this duality in order to make policies relevant and effective. Balancing the two seemingly contradicting processes of embedding (collectivity) and dis-embedding (individuality) will be shaped by particular political-economic cultures and histories and the values and priorities they produce. These reach from a more statist, protectionist tradition in Europe, to a more business-oriented, entrepreneurial, yet also more self-reliant tradition in the United States. What globalization has done is reduce the protective context of national political-economic space and its attempt at projecting (and achieving) a degree of cohesion, shared purpose and interest including all localities on its individual territory.

The notion of globalization is more than discourse and imagination. It is a technologically encouraged and permitted process of rescaling functional and strategic relations between actors and locations of (economic) opportunity and interest. As a consequence, state territoriality is being understood and utilized as a more fluid, fragmented and differential space of perceived opportunity and possible involvement. Under this new form of territoriality, in city regions as primary places of communication and competitiveness-driven opportunity, transcend scales and institutional structures and established ways of doing things. Brenner (2004b) draws two general conclusions from this metropolitanizing globalization, pointing to the dual process of change: (1) a continued belief in state-centric epistemologies – and this includes institutional, ideational (identity), democratic-legitimational and territorial dimensions and (2) the state as enabler, that is, an arena for "the profound transformations of state territorial and scalar organization that have played a crucial enabling role in the contemporary round of global restructuring" (p. 53). Some, like Brenner et al. (2003) or MacLeod (1999), have discussed this spatial shift "up" and "down" the hierarchy as "relativization of scale," something that Swyngedouw (1997, 2004) describes as "glocalization." This tries to capture the seeming contradiction between a general broadening of economic perspectives and engagement, on the one hand and a simultaneous localization of competitiveness-defined economic opportunities, on the other.

Effectively, therefore, a perceived topography of spaces of economic opportunity and dis-opportunity is projected onto the global surface through the very process of globalization and it is city-regions and large metropolises that stand out of this surface with their specific developmental capacities and economic paths. Yet, this "topography of opportunities" is also becoming more volatile, as competitive advantages and success may change quickly in response to technological innovations in communication and shifting global flows of preferential opportunities. Variability challenges established administrative structures and perceptions of "owned" and "controlled" territory. It's certainly not "flat" and static, subject merely to administrative fiat in its boundaries and control. Somehow, policy-makers need to find ways to attach themselves to these dynamics in order to remain relevant and able to define and implement relevant policies. The speed and extent of change in global economic relations and interactions is a major challenge for governing these developments and "smartness" as expression of new ways of doing things may be required to find novel, effective policy solutions to bring together trans-scalar interests, agendas and relations. There is more to regulation and government-to-capital interrelations than nation-state versus trans-national capitalism. The picture is becoming multi-layered and trans-scalar and thus more complex. On the one hand, at the sub-national level, new forms and principles of governance are emerging to respond to the differential effects of globalization, with city-regions gaining in relevance and visibility as primary arenas of this transformation. Elements of collaborative action may be needed that "stretch" established political and policy-making horizons and perspectives (and rationales) and thus give them some dynamic element of flexibility. The territoriality of the nation state matters. Yet, it includes a third dimension: the "thickness" of layered spaces of economic dynamics, governance and democratic legitimacy, something Brenner refers to as "plurilateral" forms of state power (2004a, p. 61). This needs to be translated into territorial regulation which communicates as part of a trans-scalar dialectic, while also acknowledging individuality.

The outcome of this twin process of localization and globalization is "assemblages of space," as Allen (1999) notes, where the arrangement of space in clusters or "assemblages" constructs institutional complexes out of the institutional underpinnings of the composite spaces. These are "integral to the ways in which particular forms of conduct are secured" (p. 202). In other words, the territoriality of power ideally follows the spatiality of strategic objectives and associated social actor relations. The challenge is finding a feasible mechanism to link the two, especially given their rather different inherent dynamics – static territoriality and fluid, rapidly changing spatiality. Power through collaborative association-building may extend laterally and vertically, seeking to link up actors with shared objectives and thus boost power. It is driven by political opportunity and the realization of potential win-win outcomes for all those engaging in collaborative action.

The global scale of city-regions is taken to the ultimate point in Doxiadis's 1960s vision of "Ecumenopolis" which embraces the whole globe as an urbanized space, guided by transport networks as manifestations of flows of connectivity. It is a rather amorphous, "flowing" arrangement whose internal structures differ by the varying degrees of connectivity and thus intensity of "urban life." Ecumenopolis, just like Gottmann's "Megalopolis," is an entirely relationally defined and functionally driven construct and reflects the spirit of the post-war technological era of the automobile and the mobility it brought, with a seemingly unlimited scope for connectivity right down to every person. Gottmann's "Megalopolis" revolves around notions of national and international flows of information, along which economic transactions occur between cities. Their inter-connectivity , as well as links with non-urban areas left "in between," is the "glue" that brings clusters of cities together as city regions. Megalopolis does not suggest a governance arrangement for such a mega city-region and, instead, revolves around "fluidity of urban life" (Gottmann & Harper, 1990, p. 238). Gottmann refers not only to the changing nature of the international organization of city regions and their interdependencies, but also the challenges posed to governance arrangements by these continuous dynamics, as established formal structures no longer "fit" once in place. Implicitly, he refers to a shift towards a self-organizing, bottom-up process of inter-municipal collaboration within a metropolitan area, led by perceived interests *within* the region, rather than pushed for by external interference, such as governmental decree.

Scope for regionally-scaled urbanism varies, depending on established practices and attitudes towards a regional perspective in principle and among voters and policy-makers alike. The problem of the regional scale is its position somewhere between the local and the national. Both the local and national levels have a clearer identity among the electorate. The local as representation of "community," and the state as representation and guardian of the "national," seem to possess a much stronger purpose and "following," and a (seemingly at least) clearer agenda and raison d'être. In addition, the sharp divisions between urban and rural and between core-urban and suburban, produce differing political affinities and ambitions. They contrast a more socially oriented with an inherently neo-liberal (look-after-yourself) mentality between core urban and suburban/rural constituencies. Such differences can build formidable obstacles to attempts at designing city-regional governance as collective action by localities and their actors. Such collectivity is driven by the recognition of win-win results for each actor involved and underlying structural differences and perceived inequalities in scope and opportunity are weakening the willingness for joint action. At the same time, growing interconnection between urban areas – absorbing suburban (and rural) areas in between "along the way," encourages the concept of the urbanized mega-region as super-sized city-region introduced in the mid-2000s (Carbonell & Yaro, 2005, Regional Plan Association 2006). Consequently,

> the institutional and spatial organization of a mega-region as a system of places can be conceptualized at two levels: as an interconnected network of places that serves as a component of a regional "growth machine" … and as a mosaic of autonomous political spaces created to exercise the sovereignty of "public choice", but with an exclusionary and differential outcome. Whereas the former construct has to do primarily with the nature of economic linkages and hierarchies within a mega-region, the latter is mainly about institutions and governance.
>
> (Banerjee, 2008, p. 90)

Conclusions

The emergence of smartness as a new governance strategy to reconcile tensions between competitiveness and sustainability – one of the principal claims developed in Chapter 1 – can be traced back to the worldwide "growth" crisis of the 1970s, the subsequent concern with ecological sustainability *through* global social development in the 1980s and the pragmatic role increasingly given to emerging urban areas – i.e. globalizing cities – in planning and managing these wider tensions in the 1990s.

While the use of "smart growth" in the United States arguably did the most to accelerate the *global* smart turn (Dierwechter, 2017), the data, digital and ICT revolutions of the 2000s soon quickly dominated "smart city" discourses (Townsend, 2013).

Yet the very notion of the "city" itself was also concomitantly changing, with scholars like Alan Scott, Ed Soja andy Jonas and many others now insisting on the new regionalization of urban functionalities into wider, more complex, more interconnected, territorial spaces – consolidating a new geographical concern with global city-regions and parallel processes of economic and political city-regionalism (Jonas, 2013).

In this chapter, we have highlighted mainly the economic dimensions of city-regionalism, arguing for the important territorial and socio-economic impacts of globalization. Perhaps the most important of these impacts has been the strong tendency for neo-liberal economic globalization to produce winners and losers, not only within city-regions but also across them – and indeed across entire, heretofore more "bounded," national space-economies. The recent electoral geographies that underpinned nationalist-populist-nativist support for Brexit and the victory of Donald Trump, as well as earlier developments in Poland like the anti-EU Law and Order Party, demonstrate the power of these changes. We have suggested that robust growth in the United States, for example, is actually "spiky," with clear winners like metropolitan San Francisco,

Seattle, Boston, Denver and Austin pulling up (and away) from a national space-economy that is, in many other areas, less productive, efficient, or able to generate high-tech economic opportunities. Such "in-between spaces" matter too. But the challenges are even more dramatic than simply shifting development geographies of national space-economies. Within the winning, "spiky" spaces – the so-called "winners" – growing inequality and social polarization and the attendant stagnation and even collapse of the "Fordist" middle class, is placing profound new pressures on collective action problems like transport, housing, social services and equitable environmental protection.

The smart transition in city-regionalism, then, is a dual transition shaped by an "external" transition that has been accelerated dramatically in recent decades by neo-liberal economic globalization as well as diverse national policy environments, but also an internal transition shaped by local efforts to deal with tensions between different kinds of older cities, different kinds of suburbs (some doing well, others losing their role). Although smartness is, in seems to us, an ambitious project to try to square the circle between competing values and problems, using ICT and other forms of institutional innovation and integration, the economic impacts of globalization of city-regionalism foreground some of the key issues that smartness is increasingly being forced to address.

References

Allen, J. (1999). Spatial assemblages of power. In D. Massey, J. Allen, & P. Sarre (Eds.), *Human geography today* (pp. 194–218). Polity Press.

Atkinson, R. (2001). The emerging "urban agenda" and the European spatial development perspective: Towards an EU urban policy? *European Planning Studies, 9*(3), 385–406.

Banerjee, T. (2008). Megaregions or megasprawls: Issues of density, urban design and quality growth. In C. Ross (Ed.), *Mega regions: Planning for global competitiveness* (pp. 83–106). Island Press.

Blyth, M. (2002). *Great transformations. Economic ideas and institutional change in the twentieth century.* Cambridge University Press.

Bontje, M. (2005). Facing the challenge of shrinking cities in East Germany: The case of Leipzig. *GeoJournal, 61*(1), 13–21.

Boustedt, O. (1953). Die stadtregion. Ein beitrag zur Abgrenzung städtischer agglomerationen. *Allgemeines Statistisches Archiv, 37*, 13–26.

Brenner, N., Jone, M., Jessop, B., & Macleod, G. (Eds.) (2003). *State/space: A reader.* Oxford: Blackwell.

Brenner, N. (2004a). *New state spaces.* Oxford: Oxford University Press.

Brenner, N. (2004b). Urban governance and the production of new state spaces in Western Europe, 1960–2000. *Review of International Political Economy, 11*(3), 447–88.

Bryson, J. M., Crosby, B. C., & Bryson, J. K. (2009). Understanding strategic planning and the formulation and implementation of strategic plans as a way of knowing: The contributions of actor-network theory. *International Public Management Journal, 12*(2), 172–207.

Bureau of Economic Analysis. (2017). *Gross domestic product by state: First quarter of 2017.* Washington, DC. Retrieved from www.bea.gov/newsreleases/regional/gdp_state/qgsp_newsrelease.htm, accessed 10 Nov. 2017.

Carbonell, A., & Yaro, R. (2005). American spatial development and the new megalopolis. *Land Lines, 17*(2), 1–4.

Castells, M. (1991). *The informational city: Information technology, economic restructuring, and the urban-regional process.* Oxford: Basil Blackwell.

Cox, K. (1997). Introduction: Globalization and its politics in question. In K. Cox (Ed.), *Spaces of globalization: Reasserting the power of the local* (pp. 1–19). Guilford Press.

Davoudi, S. (2003). European briefing. Polycentricity in European spatial planning: From an analytical tool to a normative agenda. *European Planning Studies, 11*(8), 979–999.

Davoudi, S. (2007). Territorial cohesion, the European social model and spatial policy research. In A. Faludi (Ed.), *Territorial cohesion and the European model of society* (pp. 81–104). Cambridge, MA: Lincoln Institute of Land Policy.

Deacon, B. (2000). Eastern European welfare states: The impact of the politics of globalization. *Journal of European social policy, 10*(2), 146–161.

Dickinson, R (1972) / [1964]. The regional relations of the city. In P. Schöller (Ed.), *Zentralitätsforschung* (pp. 54–68). Darmstadt: Wissenschaftliche Buchgesellschaft.

Dierwechter, Y. (2008). *Urban growth management and its discontents: Promises, practices and geopolitics in US city-regions.* New York: Palgrave.

Dierwechter, Y. (2017). *Urban sustainability through smart growth: Intercurrence, planning and geographies of regional development across Greater Seattle.* Cham: Springer.

Dijkstra, L., Garcilazo, E., & McCann, P. (2013). The economic performance of European cities and city regions: Myths and realities. *European Planning Studies, 21*(3), 334–354.

Douglass, M. (2000). Mega-urban regions and world city formation: Globalisation, the economic crisis and urban policy issues in Pacific Asia. *Urban Studies, 37*(12), 2315–2335.

Evers, D., & de Vries, J. (2013). Explaining governance in five mega-city regions: Rethinking the role of hierarchy and government. *European Planning Studies, 21*(4), 536–555. doi:10.1080/09654313.2012.722944

Friedman, T. L. (2006). *The world is flat: A brief history of the twenty-first century.* New York: Farrar, Straus and Giroux.

Fukuyama, F. (2006). *The end of history and the last man.* New York: Free Press.

Glaeser, E. (2011). *Triumph of the city: How our greatest invention makes us richer, smarter, greener, healthier and happier.* New York: Penguin.

Glaeser, E. L., Kallal, H., Scheinkman, J., & Schleifernd, A. (1992). Growth in cities. *Journal of Political Economy, 100*, 1126–1152.

Gottmann, J., & Harper, R. (1990). *Since megalopolis: The urban writings of Jean Gottmann.* Baltimore, MD: Johns Hopkins University Press.

Harding, A. (2007). Taking city regions seriously? Response to debate on city-regions: New geographies of governance, democracy and social reproduction. *International Journal of Urban and Regional Research, 31*(2), 443–458.

Harvey, D. (1982). *The limits to capital.* Oxford: Blackwell.

Harvey, D. (1989). From managerialism to entrepreneurialism: The transformation in urban governance in late capitalism. *Geografiska Annaler. Series B. Human Geography*, 3–17.

Herrschel, T. (2007). *Global geographies of post-socialist transition.* London: Routledge.

Herrschel, T. (2014). *Cities, state and globalisation.* London: Routledge.

Herrschel, T., & Newman, P. (2002). *Governance of Europe's city regions: Planning, policy and politics.* London: Routledge.

Herrschel, T., & Newman, P. (2017). *Cities as international actors.* London: Palgrave.

Hidle, K., & Leknes, E. (2014). Policy strategies for new regionalism: Different spatial logics for cultural and business policies in Norwegian city regions. *European Planning Studies, 22*(1), 126–142. doi:10.1080/09654313.2012.741565

Hollander, J. (2011). Can a city successfully shrink? Evidence from survey data on neighbourhood quality. *Urban Affairs Review, 47*(1), 129–141.

Jonas, A. E. G. (2013). City-regionalism as a contingent "geopolitics of capitalism". *Geopolitics, 18*(2), 284–298. doi:10.1080/14650045.2012.723290

Jonas, A. E. G., & Ward, K. (2007). Introduction to a debate on city-regions: New geographies of governance, democracy and social reproduction. *International Journal of Urban and Regional Research, 31*(1), 169–178.

Jones, G., & Douglass, M. (Eds.) (2008). *Mega-urban regions in Pacific Asia: Urban dynamics in a global era.* Singapore: NUS Press.

Lasuen, J. R. (1969). On growth poles. *Urban Studies, 6*(2), 137–161.

Lee, N. (2017). Powerhouse of cards? Understanding the "Northern Powerhouse". *Regional Studies, 51*(3), 478–489.

MacLeod, G. (1999). Place, politics and "scale dependence" exploring the structuration of Euro-regionalism. *European Urban and Regional Studies, 6*(3), 231–253.

Macleod, G., & Jones, M. (2007). Territorial, scalar, networked, connected: In what sense a "regional world"? *Regional Studies, 41*(9), 1177–1191.

Martin, R. (1999). *Money and the space economy.* New York: John Wiley.

McCann, P., & Z. J. Acs (2011). Globalization: Countries, cities and multinationals. *Regional Studies, 45*(1), 17–32.

Melo, P. C., Graham, D. J., & Noland, R. B. (2009). A meta-analysis of estimates of urban agglomeration economies. *Regional Science and Urban Economics, 39*(3), 332–342.

Murdoch, J. (1998). The spaces of actor-network theory. *Geoforum, 29*, 357–374.

OECD. (2006). *OECD territorial reviews: Newcastle in the North East, United Kingdom.* Paris: OECD.

O'Kelly, M. E. (1998). A geographer's analysis of hub-and-spoke networks. *Journal of Transport Geography, 6*(3), 171–186.

Paasi, A. (1986). The institutionalization of regions: A theoretical framework for understanding the emergence of regions and the constitution of regional identity. *Fennia, 164*(1), 105–146.

Parr, J. (1999). Growth-pole strategies in regional economic planning – A retrospective view part 1: origins and advocacy. *Urban Studies, 36*(7), 1195–1215.

Parr, J. (2002). Agglomeration economies: Ambiguities and confusions. *Environment and Planning A, 34*(4), 717–732.

Peck, F., Connolly, S., Durnin, J., & Jackson, K. (2013). Prospects for "place-based" industrial policy in England: The role of Local Enterprise Partnerships. *Local Economy, 28*(7–8), 828–841.

Pickvance, C. (1982). Physical planning and market forces in urban development. Critical Readings in Planning Theory. *Urban and Regional Planning Series, 27.*

Porter, M. E. (1990). *Competitive advantage of nations.* New York: Free Press.

Purcell, M. (2007). City-regions, neoliberal globalization and democracy: A research agenda. *International Journal of Urban and Regional Research, 31*(1), 197–206. doi:10.111 1/j.1468-2427.2007.00714

Regional Plan Association. (2006). *America 2050: A prospectus.* New York: RPA.

Rodríguez-Pose, A., & Crescenzi, R. (2008). Mountains in a flat world: Why proximity still matters for the location of economic activity. *Cambridge Journal of Regions, Economy and Society, 1*(3), 371–388. doi:10.1093/cjres/rsn011

Rosenwaike, I. (1970). A critical examination of the designation of Standard Metropolitan Statistical Areas. *Social Forces, 48*(3), 322–333.

Salet, W., & Thornley, A. (2007). Institutional influences on the integration of multilevel governance and spatial policy in European city-regions. *Journal of Planning Education and Research, 27*(2), 188–198.

Sassen, S. (1991). *The global city: New York, London, Tokyo*. Princeton, NJ: Princeton University Press.

Sassen, S. (1994). *Cities in a world economy*. Thousand Oaks, CA: Sage.

Scott, A. (2001a). Globalization and the rise of city regions. *European Planning Studies, 9*(7), 813–826.

Scott, A. (Ed.) (2001b). *Global city-regions: Trends, theory, policy*. Oxford: Oxford University Press.

Scott, A., & Storper, M. (2003). Regions, globalization, development. *Regional Studies, 37*, 579–593.

Segbers, K. (Ed.) (2007). *The making of global city-regions*. Baltimore, MD: Johns Hopkins University Press.

Sieverts, T. (2003). *Cities without cities An interpretation of the* Zwischenstadt. Hoboken, NJ: Taylor & Francis.

Smith, N. (2002). New globalism, new urbanism: Gentrification as global urban strategy. *Antipode, 34*(3), 427–450.

Swyngedouw, E. (1997). Neither global nor local: "Glocalization" and the politics of scale. In K. Cox (Ed.), *Spaces of globalization: Reasserting the power of the local* (pp. 140–142). New York: Guilford Press.

Swyngedouw, E. (2004). Globalisation or "glocalisation"? Networks, territories and rescaling. *Cambridge Review of International Affairs, 17*(1), 25–48.

Thomas, M. D. (1975). Growth pole theory, technological change and regional economic growth. *Papers in Regional Science, 34*(1), 3–25.

Townsend, A. M. (2013). *Smart cities: Big data, civic hackers and the quest for a new utopia* (First edn.). New York: W.W. Norton & Company.

Veltz, P. (2000). European cities in the world economy. In A. Bagnasco, & P. LeGalès (Eds), *Cities in contemporary Europe* (pp. 33–48). Cambridge: Cambridge University Press.

Vogel, R. K., Savitch, H. V., Xu, J., Yeh, A. G. O., Wu, W. P., Sancton, A., ... Zhang, F. Z. (2010). Governing global city regions in China and the West. *Progress in Planning, 73*, 1–75. doi:10.1016/j.progress.2009.12.001

Voith, R. (1992). City and suburban growth: Substitutes or compliments. *Business Review, Sept/Oct*, 21–33.

Walks, A. (2001). The social ecology of the post-Fordist/global city? Economic restructuring and socio-spatial polarisation in the Toronto urban region. *Urban Studies, 38*(4), 407–447.

Walks, A. (2004). Place of residence, party preferences and political attitudes in Canadian cities and suburbs. *Journal of Urban Affairs, 26*(3), 269–295.

Wiechmann, T. (2009). Raumpolitische diskurse um metropolregionen in Europa – Eine spurensuche. In J. Knieling (Ed.), *Metropolregionen. Innovation, wettbewerb, handlungsfähigkeit*. Forschungs-und Sitzungsberichte der ARL: Aufsätze, pp. 101–132. Darmstadt: Wissenschaftliche Buchgesellschaft, pp. 132–164.

Young, D., & Keil, R. (2010). Reconnecting the disconnected: The politics of infrastructure in the in-between city. *Cities, 27*, 87–95.

3 Political factors in shaping city regionalism and "smartness"

Introduction

This chapter develops select themes broached in Chapter 2 on the economic spatialities of the new global city-regionalism, but now with a stronger focus on the *political* dimensions of these changes. While cities are easily grouped as one entity, contrasting – and being contrasted – with non-urban areas, they also differ in standing and connectivity. Cities seek their own responses to match their scope, capacity, courage, ambitions and aspirations by building alliances both *inside* – that is, within city-regions as functional collaborative spaces – and *outside*, with other like-minded cities interested in like-minded problems, from climate action to immigration (Herrschel & Newman, 2017). In particular, the chapter discusses new spaces of "clubbing together" (A. Scott, 2001), a general term which captures, for us, an array of new activities around territorial governance at various scales of activity. Increasingly, these include national (Dierwechter & Wessells, 2013) and indeed international (Bouteligier, 2012) city-networks as well as new tools for lobbying national governments. We argue in this chapter that such spaces are often "softly" institutionalized (or "thinly" constituted) in order to avoid threatening both traditional local entities and higher-scale political authorities (Jonas & Pincetl, 2006). As a result, they are relatively easy to change and correspond with the opportunistic, time-dependent, and goal-oriented nature of such arrangements. They are, therefore, of central importance to what we see as "smart" transitions in city-regionalism.

Different examples from around the metropolitan world in various national contexts are addressed to illustrate the variety of these changes, although all are extensive and structural in nature as part of post-authoritarian and post-Fordist regime changes and re-constitutions of governing structures, practices and agendas. This includes growing evidence of a so-called new "geopolitics" of city-regionalism (Jonas, 2013; Moisio & Paasi, 2013). Here international city networks, like C40 Cities, City Protocol and the United Cities and Local Governments (UCLG), are seeking to by-pass, or at least to complement, the traditional central state apparatus, in order to pursue own interests and experiments (Barber, 2013). At the same time, the chapter strongly emphasizes the ongoing importance of established government regimes and legal-administrative structures (Orren & Skowronek, 1996), irrespective of regime changes under "transition." Accordingly, this chapter highlights the interactions of both relational and territorial forms of political space (Jonas, 2012c), which, together, shape the actual dynamics of city-regionalism, city networks and the role of more explicitly independent and locally opportunistic city politics. Claiming to pursue, and adopting discursive and practical, principles of "smartness" is part and expression of this shift. As new city-regional spaces and related, underlying agendas form, the state has to consider response strategies to maintain democratically the political cohesion of state spaces – including the "independent"-minded economically successful city regions (Parnell, 2007).

The discussion emphasizes that different dynamics of change – and subsequent discourses and responses – may be observed, such as between the more established, political-economic regimes of Western Europe and North America, versus what we interpret as the more dynamically changing conditions in "transition" regimes such as in Eastern Europe or South Africa (Pillay, 2004). In South Africa, post-colonial and Africa-specific elements come into play, as do, in Eastern Europe, the specific legacies of command economies and political totalitarianism. These add particular dimensions to shaping "smart" development, leading to a doubly dynamic (transitional) situation. The North Atlantic (Western) model serves as reference for "standard" (dominant) perspectives and interpretations (Lackowska & Zimmermann, 2011), as evident in international politics ("Washington Consensus") and heavily Anglo-Saxon-centric academic debates.

These differences in regime transition, this book suggests, matter for the particular structural provisions as "milieux" and practical modi operandi of city-regional governance vis-à-vis the proclamation of required transition towards, and adoption of, principles and practices of "smartness." The concept of "transition" (Adler & Webster, 1995; Ginsberg, 1996; Kuzio, 2001; O'Donnell & Schmitter, 2013) is developed as a key factor circumscribing the political-economic milieu under which city regionalism operates, identifies its agendas and faces challenges to modify established procedures.

Chapter 3 thus develops the theme that "transition" is a challenge to, but also driver of, smart city-regionalism – one searching to "square the circle" between a diverse range of policy agendas, policy practices and geographic relations and territorial scales, by using established structures and policy tools in novel and creative ways. "Smartness," we suggest, is both a *producer* of new discourses, agendas and ways of doing things, and a *product* of changing societal discourses, structures, experiences and value systems (as in state regimes). Changes here, such as under post-authoritarian transition, matter fundamentally in their effects on political agendas, public discourses and held values and aspirations, as well as ambitions and expectations. It is this that exercises pressure on governance modes and objectives to respond in order to deliver desired results – however complex, contradictory, changing, or elusive they may be – and thus obtain democratic legitimation. This sets the scene for finding the most efficacious ways of governing city-regions. Put more simply: "smartness" provides a redefining context for city-regionalism in the attempt to reconcile competing, even conflicting, but certainly dynamic, ambitions and agendas, primarily through using existing structures, mechanisms and tools in a creative, novel way.

The "city-region" as a political space

The steady if uneven and contingent consolidation of the nation-state over the past few hundred years, particularly in the Western world and, more recently, in Asia and Africa, has tended to efface the otherwise variegated political role of cities in world development. The logistical role of key cities in organizing vast world-empires, from Babylon to Rome to Xian-Chang'an to Constantinople/ Istanbul to London is well known; so too is the place of large capital cities like Paris or Toyko as national cultural-administrative centres.

But at different phases in world history, cities were loosely-networked city-states built around localized city-regional territorial spaces (Hall, 1998). This includes the riverine group of cities in ancient Sumeria – the world's first true urban system – and, more famously, the interacting and inter-continental city-states of ancient Greece, such as Athens, Syracuse, Alexandria, Byzantium etc. For hundreds of years, moreover, the "Hanse" cities in northern Europe – for example, Antwerps, Hamburg, Stockholm, Gdańsk, Lübeck etc. – constituted an "alternative modernity" of political-economic space (Lees, 2015). With the territorial rise of the United Kingdom, France, the United States, and many other nation-state systems though, cities were increasingly subsumed within, *and demoted by*, parcelized national regions. And while they remained places *for* politics they were no longer really seen *as* international political spaces. Even large and important cities like London and Boston were, as late as 1800, quite physically compact – dense and "walkable" – and thus nested well inside their eco-regional hinterlands. Together with the rise of the nation-state, cities appeared as sub-national, local, less important political spaces whose administrations focused on parochial issues.

That soon started to change. The mechanized industrialization of cities, originally in England, and then elsewhere, led to the "regionalization" of urban space (Soja, 2000). Cities broke decisively from their compact and contained moorings – generating new forces in society. More cities grew much larger. London and New York, for example, swallowed up their rural hinterlands over the course of the 19th century, causing a host of new coordination problems that, in turn, led to new calls for fundamental political reforms and institutional adaptations. Utopians like Ebenezer Howard propounded a "regional development" vision built around a planned necklace of "garden cities," while polymaths, such as Patrick Geddes, advocated "regional surveys" that placed cities organically within ecological and cultural evolution. Howard and Geddes – and later Lewis Mumford in the United States – are today seen not only as early advocates of regionalism, but also as key thinkers in sustainability, and Patrick Geddes, especially, an "inspirational pioneer" of the smart city movement (Townsend, 2013).

Clubbing together: from old to new regionalism(s)

As the 20th century opened, more pragmatic actors than Howard, Geddes and Mumford advanced a new kind of metropolitan reform that focused initially on the "consolidation" of smaller local governments and/or the creation of new authorities with special powers to manage region-wide issues, notably transportation, waste management, sewerage problems; that is, "the consolidation of existing government units or the creation of regional governments with significant powers to control land use and development" (Feiock, 2004, pp. 4–5). Present-day New York City, famously, was created in 1898 (and expanded through 1914) out of the consolidation of Manhattan, parts of the Bronx, Queens, Brooklyn and also Staten Island. In fact, a group of so-called "neoprogressives" continue to argue today that such political consolidation and/or regional institutional empowerment ("centralization") promotes economic development, reduces service inequalities and otherwise addresses a host of negative externalities and spillovers effects (Frisken & Norris, 2001). This overlaps strongly with smart growth arguments.

Examples of dramatic political consolidation of city-regional jurisdictions have been and remain today fairly uncommon, although prominent recent examples include the development of metropolitan municipalities or "unicities" in post-apartheid South Africa (OECD, 2008), about which more in Chapter 6. Strong(er) regional governments with political and regulatory powers over land use, housing and economic development policy, such as the *Rennes Metropôle* in France, are also uncommon worldwide. In the United States, for instance, only Metro in Portland, Oregon, and (to a lesser extent) the Metropolitan Council in Minneapolis-St. Paul, Minnesota, approach this neo-progressive model of regional governance and planning (Dierwechter, 2008, p. 145). Toronto, Canada, is also a well-known North American case of strong and influential metropolitan governance reform, dating back to the 1950s (Williams, 1999). Examples of city-county mergers, including Louisville, Kentucky, also merit attention in this regard (Savitch & Vogel, 2004).

For much of the latter 20th century, particularly within the United States, public choice scholars advanced the most influential theoretical case against the formal consolidation and/or centralization of city-regional institutions, or what is typically today called a "monocentric" project of "old regionalism" (Savitch & Adhikari, 2017). Figures such as Elinor Ostrom and Robert Bish, for instance, explored the putative advantages of locally "fragmented" governments, using Charles Teibout's (1956) claim that when local governments "compete" for citizen-consumers they approximate the beneficial rationality of the free marketplace. In other words, we should think about our local politics through the "polycentric" tools of (welfare) economics (Savitch & Adhikari, 2017). In response to these economistic critiques, updated arguments for a "new regionalism" reemerged in the 1990s – now focusing less on formal political reforms in the institutional structure of city-regions targeting efficiency gains in public administration, and, rather, more on the potential benefits of a variety of "collaborative" arrangements that foregrounded the logic of win-win propositions, especially regional economic growth and global competitiveness. The (North) America literature on this so-called new regionalist agenda is thus now considerable, particularly where it overlaps with planning (Clark & Christopherson, 2009; Frisken & Norris, 2001; Katz, 2000; Loh & Sami, 2013; Norris, 2001; Perlman & Jimenez, 2010; Provo, 2009; Rast, 2006). As Todd Swanstrom (2001) puts it in an early summary:

> The new regionalism [since the 1990s] can be viewed as an effort to shift the case for urban policy from the unstable terrain of values like equality and fairness to the solid rock of economic self-interest. The new regionalists argue that regional reforms can benefit inner cities and suburbs at the same time. Greenbelts, such as the one surrounding Portland, for example, will push development back toward distressed inner-city neighborhoods at the same time that they relieve the problems of congestion and loss of green space in the suburbs.
>
> (p. 481)

Even more specifically,

> The argument of much of the literature is that spatial inequalities should be opposed not just because they are unfair but also because they will harm regional economic competitiveness.
>
> (p. 482)

But even here there were (and are) differences. "Backdoor" regionalists such as Scott Bollens, for example, have long suggested new progressive reforms could (and do) occur in policy arenas like metropolitan-scale sustainability, transport and equitable housing, while "social movement" regionalists like Manuel Pastor, Chris Benner and others have emphasized the effects of society-driven rather than state-based reforms. More recently, as visualized in Figure 3.1 below, Savage and Adhirkari (2017) suggest a dialectical tension between the ongoing fragmentation of local autonomy and the policy integration of metropolitan action, generating what they see as a generalized state of "fragmented regionalism" formed from centrifugal and centripetal forces:

> We see here a desire for local autonomy pushing away from regionalism, whereas the necessity for collective action pulls toward it. The result is the embodiment of both tendencies in what we call *fragmented regionalism* – a condition of piecemeal, partial, and selective processes that induce some kind of a metropolitan-wide action while guaranteeing local prerogatives. [...] On one side, vigorous economic growth fills metropolitan regions

with more differentiation and more specialization. This invariably leads to a more independently minded middle class with a capacity to protect its assets (land values, revenue sources, school systems). On the other side, the maintenance of this prosperity brings about a need for better coordination, common policies, and shared public goods. Localities have sought to reconcile this paradox by bundling some services that fit within their territorial boundaries and unbundling other functions whose delivery necessitates a larger geographic scale. Unbundling requires that burdens be shifted to "third parties," like public authorities, whose territorial scope crosses multiple jurisdictions.

(pp. 348–9)

While these analyses relate mainly to the experiences of the United States, the wider literature on what Alan Scott (2001) and several others (Segbers, 2007; Simmonds, 2000; Vogel et al., 2010) have called "global city-regions" has similarly emphasized the growing theoretical and practical linkages between political city-regionalism, globalization and competitiveness. Much of this literature over the past fifteen years or so has explored a stronger competitiveness agenda shaped by the steady ascendance of "neoliberal globalization" after the denouement of the Cold War. In many places, this agenda has structurally necessitated what Neil Brenner (Brenner, 1997, 2001, 2004) has theorized as the political rescaling of state spatial structures in Europe and North America. Yet his hypothesized process of "rescaling" around key global city-regions as nationally-favoured spaces of accumulation has been geographically variegated, not only within countries, but also, and more importantly, across major world areas (Jonas & Pincetl, 2006; Jonas & Ward, 2001).

In South Africa, for example, the dramatic and relatively rapid post-apartheid creation of metropolitan municipalities between 1996 and 2000 arguably adopted many "old regionalist" arguments, particularly around efforts to redress profound service inequities inherited from the apartheid dispensation (Cameron, 2000). Over the course of only a few years, Cape Town, Durban,

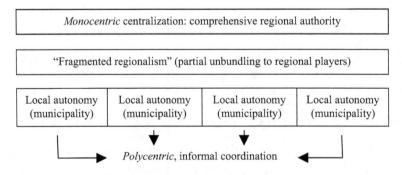

Figure 3.1 Various types of city-regionalism in the US context.

Source: Inspired by Savage and Adhirkari (2017).

Johannesburg and a few other larger conurbations eliminated, rationalized and amalgamated hundreds of apartheid-era local governments, while at the same time empowering the new city-regions *constitutionally* to deliver genuine trans- formation. Yet, early "neo-progressive" efforts in institutional reform arguably soon confronted wider pressures and contradictions associated with the neolib- eral global economy (Dupresson & Jaglin, 2014). Although both normatively and analytically skeptical of the "global city-region" concept in relationship to post-apartheid South Africa and other developing economies, Udesh Pillay (2004) nonetheless singles out Johannesburg-East Rand for special attention, linking it early on to the rising theme of smartness. "According to propo- nents," he notes, "Gauteng has made a strategic decision to move away from heavy traditional industry and low value-added products. The province is now committed to enhancing its reputation for being the country's 'Smart Centre'" (p. 359). As we shall see later, planners and public officials today frame smart- ness within Johannesburg both through sustainable urban development as well as ICT maturity nurtured through digitally-networked infrastructures.

What is particularly fascinating here is that the "footprint" of the newer, smarter city-region (or "centre") extends more widely (and often informally) than the "old" (formal) regionalisms of amalgamated metropolitan munici- palities put in place immediately after apartheid to redress traditional services inequalities between areas of different social status, and other profound socio- economic problems. This post-apartheid *hybridity*, within the context of South Africa's historically peculiar transition challenges, furthermore reflects earlier spatial development initiatives (SDIs) launched by the central state in the mid-1990s to forge new "corridors," "zones" and "centers" of industry and trade across the wider space-economy that are more capable of deepening the global sustainability project. This aimed in particular at poverty allevia- tion through targeted fast-tracked industrial support (e.g. agro-tourism). Here, South Africa has not looked only to Western experiences for insights, but to the experiences of adjacent African countries, as in the "Mozambique Development Corridor," as well as to China's record with Special Economic Zones (SEZs) as state-sponsored "islands" of neoliberal marketization in an otherwise state-led economy. Such policy efforts in South Africa nonethe- less broadly reflect too, in our judgement, Brenner's general theory of the "rescaling" of state spatial structures as well as what Martin Jones (1997) has elsewhere and earlier called the new "spatial selectivity of the state" (and see also McCauley and Murphy, 2013) More will be said in Chapter 6 about the specific "smart" turns in Johannesburg and Cape Town, respectively, but for the moment it should simply be noted that the transitions now underway have both "internal" and "external" features – scalar dualities – that require both theoretical and empirical attention.

Institutional and operational variety, and a complex "multi-scalarity" addi- tionally mark the emergent city-regionalisms of Germany and other European countries, particularly where these signal growing policy and programmatic interest in smartness discourses, modes of governance, and citizen and business engagement. The German case is interesting not simply because of the federal structure of the state, but also because of the historic transition to post-socialism within East(ern) Germany has merged with the broader post-Fordist transition elsewhere. In his work on German "metropolitan" or smart city-regional governance reforms, for example, Karsten Zimmerman (2016) identifies at least four distinct models of city-regional cooperation: norm-oriented, utilitarian, communicative and "dramaturgic," suggesting what are for him rather different combinations of actors, expectations, capabilities and projects – albeit all within a shared national and European Union policy environment. As in (North) America, formal experiments in consolidation, or centralization, are more exceptional, while efforts to build region-wide policy capacity revolve around often interlinked interests in sustainability, ICT and competitiveness proliferate. Much like Rennes in northwestern France, the Stuttgart area in southwest Germany enjoys a directly-elected regional assembly, while "softer" forms of city-regionalism, for instance the "European Region of Nuremberg," reflect efforts to overcome rural–urban tensions around otherwise shared territorial problems, such as carbon mitigation, transport and commuting networks, immigrant integration, innovation and economic competiveness (OECD, 2013).

For Lackowski and Zimmerman (2011), such variety, within Germany and also across former communist "transition" countries like Poland, nonetheless reflects a broader, global shift in the geo-political-economies of late capitalism. Drawing on both Brenner and Bob Jessop's work on the theorized transmutation of the "Keynesian social-welfare state" into the "postnational Schumpeterian workfare state," as well as the applied work on new regionalism by the Americans Sellers and Swanstrom, Lackowski and Zimmerman (2011) explore three key issues in eight case studies:

> (1) novelty in comparison with previous reform initiatives following the public choice approach (in the late 1970s and 1980s) and the metropolitan reform position (in the 1960s), (2) an explicit focus on economic development and competitiveness and (3) a governance arrangement that includes various forms of cooperation, that is, partnerships of public and private actors and/or networks.
>
> (p. 157)

This thematic and analytical triptych – historic novelty, competitiveness concerns and cooperative variety – provides one way to frame how processes of transition are working themselves out in diverse contexts, all the while paying close attention to the interscalar nature of these transitions. The Polish cases they discuss – Warsaw, Gdańsk, Katowice and Wrocław – generally suffer from the "almost non-existent" tradition of metropolitan cooperation, although the polycentric structure of Gdansk suggests limited progress. So, while clearly novel to the country, Polish city-regionalism was identified as remaining relatively weak, and varying from practical concerns with transport, for example, to narrower interests in accessing European Union (EU) funding.

In other words, they emerged as "single-purpose associations of neighbouring municipalities rather than multi-task associations encompassing whole city-regions" (p. 163). The German cases – Rhine-Neckar, Frankfurt, Hanover and Stuttgart – in contrast, are "multi-task associations," albeit not necessarily formal institutional entities that would otherwise threaten inherited territorial identities, especially those of the participating municipalities with their statutorily protected self-governing capacity. This work is especially relevant here, because it usefully underscores the diverse impacts of both "post-Fordist" *and* "post-authoritarian" transitions, and, as discussed later in the book, shows how these much wider ("external") transitions are influencing the "internal" smart turn within globalizing city-regions across Europe, as illustrated for the examples of Lyon, Turin, Berlin and Prague.

Offering their own (and much earlier) take on "fragmented regionalism," Counsell et al. (2007) charted obstacles in Yorkshire and the Humber in the United Kingdom to achieving a normative ideal of "strategic regionalism" after a period of devolution initiated in the late 1990s under the New Labour policies of Tony Blair's government. In particular, they highlighted multiple frictions and tensions that collectively stymied "joined-up thinking" and planning and policy integration in major policy and regulatory arenas like planning, economic development, housing and sustainable development. The *existence* of frictions and tensions across city-regional space-economies is, of course, hardly unique to Yorkshire and the Humber. Indeed, they characterize nearly all empirical efforts to coordinate development policies across scales, spaces and even "times," as various jurisdictions, organizations and agencies jostle different institutional priorities, funding streams and outlay periods, voter-blocks and multiple constituency expectations and demands. It is a condition that historical institutionalists working on political development in the United States and, more recently, Canada and the United Kingdom, have called "intercurrence" (Dierwechter, 2017c; Hodos, 2009; Orren & Skowronek, 1996; Wiedstrom, 2011). "Smartness," however, refers to the various ways in which variously engaged actors – both inside and outside relevant city-regions – forge new spaces and modalities of effective policy engagement to both manage and ultimately ameliorate these frictions and tensions. Again, such spaces will certainly vary from place to place as different assets, path-dependencies and external rules and norms shape both local possibilities and actualities. Counsell et al. (2007, p. 392) note, for example, "the emerging importance of the subregional scale as offering, potentially, a 'meeting ground' for different strategies for specific issues (housing, economic development, planning) in an unevenly developed policy landscape." In US regions, however, partial antidotes to "fragmentation" may well be found in the "smart" work of (too often) neglected "public authorities" operating *exactly at the regional scale* of service provision and/or planning (Savitch & Adhikari, 2017).

These themes further highlight the extent to which we should interpret the dual transition of smart city-regionalism – about which more in Chapter 4 – as a variegated, but generalized, response to the post-Cold War growth of

global competiveness pressures or, indeed, as a legitimately new way to navigate
the parallel pressures of sustainability as well – that is, "to square the circle"
between these two major concerns (Herrschel, 2013). More than that, much
of the above work foregrounds ongoing debates about the real meaning and
purpose of sustainability. Is sustainability a parallel environmental goal that must
be balanced with economic competiveness, or is it, in contrast, a new strategy to
ensure a new kind of accumulation (Jonas, 2015; Jonas & Ward, 2007; While,
Jonas & Gibbs, 2004)? If the latter, what grounds might there be to hope for a
more progressive politics of city-regionalism – smart or otherwise – that takes
environmental justice concerns seriously (Rast, 2006)? To what extent can a
so-called "community-based" regionalism contend with, for example, business-
driven regionalism (Swanstrom & Banks, 2007; Ward & Jonas, 2004). In his
analysis of transport policies in the search for a "smart city-region" in metropolitan Seattle, Dierwechter (2013) suggests that, to some extent,

> extant [policy] patterns comport with wider readings of capitalist restruc-
> turing – and therefore with themes common in geo-political discussions
> of neoliberal governance. [New transport] nodes are, in a word, subject
> to the politics of "entrepreneurial redevelopment"… edifying economic
> centers populated by social elites who, it seems reasonable to surmise,
> already enjoy multiple mobility choices.
>
> (p. 148)

At the same time, Dierwechter continues, drawing on the work of Jonas and
McCarthy (2009, p. 302):

> Smart city-regionalism in Seattle is also subject to an important new
> "rescaling of urban management institutions and the politics of redistri-
> bution" (op cit.). Transit nodes betray the impacts (and possibilities) of
> more progressive if inchoate coalitions of actors that stretch from, and
> interconnect, local and federal spaces; at times at least, such political spaces
> implicate community-based activists in new regional conversations about
> metropolitan sustainability. These are spaces of hope too.
>
> (Dierwechter, 2013, p. 148)

Such empirical claims about "Greater Seattle" (and see Dierwechter, 2017b)
are part of a larger body of literature, within North America, Europe and other
world regions, that interrogates the actual and potential politics of various
forms of city-regionalism, including places focused increasingly on "smartness"
(Harrison, 2012; Hidle & Leknes, 2014; Perlman & Jimenez, 2010; Rogerson,
2009; Swanstrom, 2006; Zimmerbauer & Paasi, 2013). Specifically, a robust
discussion asks whether or not – or to what extent, and how – the politics of
city-regions really can or do matter, especially in regard to ameliorating problems of growing income inequity and social justice (Clark & Christopherson,
2009; Greene, Treacy, & Cowling, 2007; Jonas, 2015; Lowe, 2014). Clark and

Christopherson (2009), for instance, envision a "progressive regionalism" based on the integration of "investment and equity," by which they mean policies focused on the "labor market as a whole" negotiated by "multiscalar coalitions" (p. 341). Others are less sure that progressive regionalism so defined provides an "actionable framework" for planning and policy going forward (Pezzoli, Hibbard, & Huntoon, 2006). More recently, Benner and Pastor (2012) have suggested that metropolitan regions within the United States, but elsewhere too, not only can achieve growth *with* equity but, in fact, they document cases of actual growth *through* equity, including less-studied, second-tier city-regions like Kansas City, Nashville, Jacksonville and Columbus.

Recognizing empirical variety and, certainly, the crucial role of multi-scalar coalitions, paradoxically complicates how city-regions *per se* are imagined, mapped, interrogated, and thus assessed. While it is usually possible to deploy common statistical categories to define bounded arenas, city-regions are functionally and unevenly perforated, more knotty assemblages, than stable nodes in local-national-global space (Thrift & Amin, 2002). Commuter sheds do not "match up" with ecological flows, for example, and cities' economic (and social) relationships now stretch across a multitude of protean landscapes in a multitude of different ways at any given time (Smith, 2003). This reality is further intensified by digitally-mediated sociologies of distance-interaction. This has led many observers to warn against reifying the city-region as just the newest valourized political space for policy efficacy and/or socio-economic transformation. John Harrison (2007), in particular, has critiqued Alan Scott's core claims that, first, "globalisation and city-region development are but two facets of a single integrated reality," and, second, they also now "function as territorial platforms for much of the post-Fordist economy that constitutes the dominant leading edge of contemporary capitalist development and as an important staging post for the operation of multinational corporations" (A. Scott, 2001, p. 4). For Harrison, city-regions – like regions before them – are still "objects of mystery." They are as much mental or epistemological fields, as they are material or ontological spaces "out there," to be methodologically identified, analyzed and constructed. At the same time, in so far as city-regions *are* "staging posts," their physical, social, economic and cultural constitutions are also forged by territorialized political forces, and, especially by the multi-tiered state. Yet for some critics, the actually-existing politics of city-regionalism are too often "lightly specified," or are simply "read off" neoliberal globalization without sufficient empirical support (Harding, 2007)

Scholars such as Andy Jonas (Jonas & Pincetl, 2006; Ward & Jonas, 2004) and Gordon MacLeod (MacLeod & Goodwin, 1999; MacLeod & Jones, 2001) anticipated Harrison's legitimate concern to "bring the state back in" (Erie & Mackenzie, 2009). Specifically, both highlighted the importance of political struggles around regionalism, even as the role of the state in society and economy has been central theme in neo-Weberian institutionalism and "state-building" research for many decades (Dilworth, 2009; King & Smith, 2005; Orren & Skowronek, 2004; Skowronek, 1982). Eugene McCann (2007) has explored the city-regional struggles of smart growth in Austin, Texas, while Pauline McGuirk (2007) has documented key state-scalar dynamics central to the rise of Sydney city-region. Mindful of this work, we thus build on Harrison's synoptic conclusion, shared by many others just cited, that:

> the capacity for self-determination in subregional territories continues to be constrained and blunted by the state's ability to direct and steer these new governance mechanisms towards what is perceived to be in the national interest – at the obvious expense of local and regional interests whose capacity to shape the city-region agenda is constrained by this process.
>
> (p. 329)

In particular, the concept offered here integrates these insights into the elaboration of the "dual transition" argument in relation to smart city-regionalism, and this is discussed further in the next chapter.

Moreover, the concern here is with recent developments in what Jonas (2012a) has elsewhere called the "geopolitics" of a now heavily globalized set of variegated, but also universal city-regional projects (and see Herrschel and Newman, 2017). For Jonas (2012b, pp. 822–4), in particular, the city-region is not only a "contingently produced geopolitical project." It is "a platform for examining struggles for social justice and urban environmental politics in late capitalism." In our view, geopolitical themes linked to various smartness concerns (Dierwechter, 2008), especially in the form of extra-urban global networks of advocacy, are indeed creating new kinds of tensions that remain under-explored in both urban studies and international relations (Herrschel & Newman, 2017), notwithstanding interesting recent interventions by scholars like Ben Barber (2013), Sophie Bouteligier (2012) and Mark Amen et al. (2012). This literature will be addressed next, before returning back to the main themes of this book.

A new networked geopolitics of globalized city-regions?

The opening discussion in this chapter about the city-region as a political space over the long history of urbanism and world development emphasized the more recent territorial consolidation of nation-states and the ancillary demotion of cities in world politics. The hypothesized "rise of city-regions" (A.J. Scott, 2001) as now globally favoured spaces of economic agglomeration since the denouement of the Cold War, however, has provoked urban researchers to reconsider the shifting geopolitics of "cities as international actors" (Herrschel & Newman, 2017). These concerns relate to explicitly ideological work deeply critical of the contemporary state. Some market liberals, for instance, want to "govern the world" via David Ricardo's original call for "a liberal internationalism" of truly free markets (Mazower, 2012), while radical critics like Michael Hardt and Antonio Negri (Negri & Hardt, 2000) argue that economic injustice could be abolished by undermining the territorial sovereignty of states and replacing it with what they call a networked, neo-anarchistic "multitude." The work reviewed here is more pragmatic, but nonetheless raises serious questions about the changing geography of politics in world affairs.

Some observers have blended normative with analytical claims, emphasizing the *desirability* of politically empowered urban actors no less than tracing actual empirical shifts in how international politics and policy mobilization occur (Amen et al., 2012). Ben Barber's (2013) recent research, for instance, emphasizes the growing crisis of liberal democracy and the urgent need to rediscover the "polis" where democracy was first born. Democracy, he argues, is in deep crisis, increasingly unable to meet global challenges like climate change, immigration, sex- and drugs-trafficking, etc. For Barber, city-led forms of global cooperation – groups spanning various scales, such as C40 and City Protocol (about which more below), constitute a legitimate institutional alternative to what he sees as the profound dysfunction of traditional nation-states, which are too small to manage globalization, but too big to secure meaningful democracy. Philosophically, Barber's project seeks to reject the "simplistic moral geometry of Thomas Jefferson and Benjamin Franklin," who romanticized the moral virtue of rural areas without at the same time evoking the "homilies of zealous urbanists who despise the country as a backwards wasteland" (p. 42). Modern cities, he argues, are best posed to meet the challenges of a global world because they are incubators of problem-solving. Mayors, he concludes, should rule the world:

> the more than 3.5 billion people (over half the world's population) who are urban dwellers and the many more in the exurban neighborhoods beyond could participate locally and cooperate globally at the same time – a miracle of civic "glocality" promising pragmatism instead of politics, innovation rather than ideology and solutions in place of sovereignty.
>
> (Ibid.)

Ultimately, Barber calls creatively for a "global parliament of mayors" more capable of binding together politically the variously entangled scales of our contemporary lives.

Other scholars have focused more on the empirical evidence, often in the form of new inter-city networks focused on global environmental governance and climate change (Bouteligier, 2012; Lee, 2012; Toly, 2008). Within this literature, authors have explored exactly how cities are (re)asserting themselves in world affairs, particularly, though not only, with respect to global climate action, often building theoretically (at least partly) on Saskia Sassens' seminal work on the "Global City" and Manuel Castells work on networked societies (Calder & Freytas, 2009). Bouteligier (2012) pays especially close attention to new action-networks like C40 and Metropolis, including how these groups interact with existing international organizations, as well as private corporations. What emerges from her work, the work of Barber and others, is that cities and their global city-networks are not only increasingly meaningful participants in international environmental governance, but, indeed, are probably now central to its success (Engelke, 2013). In particular, as Boutleligier shows, cities increasingly seek the capacity to construct novel governance arrangements in their attempt to foster and scale up local innovations. The broadest question here is whether or not the international political system in place since the Peace of Westphalia in 1648 – or at least 1815 – is undergoing a profound and potentially far reaching transformation (Calder & Freytas, 2009; Rosenzweig et al., 2010). An ancillary question is, therefore, how new actors who operate or think globally, including networked city-regions, are, increasingly, challenging the centrality of the nation-state (Amen et al., 2012; Nijman, 2009), or are at least pushing traditional institutions to rethink the *political role* of cities in world affairs (Calder & Freytas, 2009; Engelke, 2013). A final question is how recent "smartness" discourses now relate to questions about the new networked geo-politics of city-regions (Gascó, Trivellato, & Cavenago, 2016)?

A narrower focus may help illuminate this last question. A "smart" global network that has received recent attention is City Protocol, formed in Barcelona in 2012 as a joint-project in "smart cities" between the City of Barcelona and Cisco and subsequent participation of various knowledge institutions, cities and nonprofit organizations. According to its mission statement, the goal of City Protocol "is to define an interoperable city platform, which will allow cities to communicate and operate across silos and across communities, spawning an ecosystem of solution development and innovation," in other words "to define the Internet of Cities [that] will provide common solutions and solution platforms, crossing the silos within and between cities" (cityprotocal.org). This new Internet of Cities involves various subsystems *within* participant cities as well as improved systems of "learning and evolving" *across* the signature cities, corporations, academic entities and nonprofits, including, *inter alia*, Barcelona, Boston, Maputo, Milan, Tarragona and Torino as well as organizations like University of Chicago, the University of Sidney, the University of Virginia, Younsei University, ACEFAT, AENOR, Argonne National Lab, CIDEU, Citilab, Ecocity Builders and the European Network of Living Labs.

Table 3.1 below lists the empirical (or "taken-at-face-value") goals of City Protocol, now called the City Protocol Society. These goals reveal a great deal about how participants view "smartness" within the context of multi-scalar policy and programme relationships. For the language here is resolutely "win-win," collaborative, scientific, cool, participatory, yet at times shallow and weirdly corporate (e.g. "game-changer"). It reveals what might be called the allure of the "Ivory Tower of Practice." Desired discourses and narratives of self-intention stand in for an inchoate but emergent reality.

From a more critical perspective, as Gordon MacLeod (2013) has argued in his analysis of smart growth in Scotland, such goals are forged by "depoliticising consensus-inducing tendencies inherent in policy transfer and mobility" (p. 2199). This is not a criticism of the goals, which are largely unassailable (e.g. "Foster a culture for international cooperation"); it is a warning that

Table 3.1 "Take-for-granted" empirics of the City Protocol Society

---

- Enable better understanding and collaboration among the different constituencies (cities, industry, academia and society) that are involved in building better cities – worldwide
- Foster a culture for international cooperation that enables self-governance within the global community of cities, industry, academia, and society working and learning together
- Develop a system's approach (City Protocol) to rationalize, under a shared basis, city transformation and provide documentary evidence in the form of agreements, recommendations and standards
- Deliver a truly shared, trusted and universally useful Urban Anatomy to frame the processes of adopting, adapting and implementing real city transformations: If it is not transformational, it is not CPS
- Support the creation of Task-And-Finish-Teams (TAFTs) to create value-adding deliverables from game-changing urban transformation initiatives in different contexts worldwide
- Facilitate the responsible transformation of cities by accelerating city-to-city learning and by promoting an economy of urban innovation with resource-use efficiency, self-sufficiency, and social and economic progress in cities
- Support knowledge creation and capacity building on urban matters with the open activities and contributions of the City Protocol Task Force (CPTF)
- Establish partnerships with other organizations to adopt work already done and to maintain a network for education and knowledge sharing on urban matters.

Source: http://ibarcelona.bcn.cat/en/smart-cities/city-protocol

intensions are not the same thing as realities, that "protocols" are not the same thing as actually-existing urbanism, which requires an analysis deeply sensitive to the geopolitical economies of development and change in particular circumstances.

As discussed in Chapter 2, such work is now growing (e.g. Söderström, Paasche, & Klauser, 2014), and moreover is increasingly engaged with the specific politics of "smart" initiatives at various scales. March and Ribera-Fumaz's (2016) recent analysis of Barcelona's global leadership, for example, mobilizes urban political ecology to identify major contradictions in how smart buildings, networks and blocks both shape and are in turn shaped by wider relations of power. Their work furthermore illuminates how influential particular sets of ideas – theories of urbanism, sustainable cities and planning – can actually be in any given environment (Boelens, 2010; A. March, 2010).

In Barcelona, projects and programmes that seek "self-sufficiency" through various smart interventions haven been tied to Vincente Gaullart's attempt to theorize the city as an ontology of Internet topologies marred by pathologies created, in part, by modernist planning hierarchies and rationalities of management. While highly abstract when summarized like this, Gaullart's theories have informed the city's institutional merger of planning and infrastructure with the departments of housing, environment and ICT. They have also informed efforts to "upscale" pilot programmes from specific buildings, networks and blocks to the wider urban terrain (though not yet to the city-region). In one sense, March and Ribera-Fumaz (2016) argue, this is emblematic of the kind of results smartness discourses everywhere always promise. In another sense, however, Barcelona's search for self-sufficiency runs the same risks as smart growth plans in North America and Scotland. Progressive potential is easily sidelined by post-political rationalities. "There is an urgent need to repoliticize the Smart City debate," they accordingly conclude, "[o]therwise, the Smart City, can function to disguise entrepreneurial urban development and further privatization of urban services delivery under the veil of a new hype of ecological and technological branding" (p. 826). In so far as the innovation, creativity and experimental flare of Barcelona now has been put "in motion" through wider city-networks and global policy mobilities (González, 2011), the same concerns pulse through other cities and city-regions engaged politically in various kinds of smart turns.

Conclusions

While cities predate nation states by thousands of years, their rapid spatial expansion into *regional complexes* and their deepening functional importance to national economies paradoxically led to their political effacement in the 19th and 20th centuries. In recent decades, however, the global rise of large city-regions in particular has precipitated a new round of speculation that highlights how cities, often in the form of new transnational networks seeking improved sustainability, security, livability and competitiveness, amongst other goals, have "joined states" as international actors (Herrschel & Newman, 2017). While some authors now appear to all but equate the political rise of cities with the parallel demise of nation-states (Barber, 2013), it is still more appropriate to see the new politics of city-regionalism, including efforts to be smarter, as embedded within, and reflective of, extant territorial structures (Jonas & Moisio, 2016).

In that context, the city-region itself is a heavily contested space of relational governance, as "reframing" the city into a city-regional territory is much easier from an economic than a political perspective (Etherington & Jones, 2009). While key production complexes have thus stretched out across regional space-economies, extant systems of metropolitan governance – long fragmented – have struggled to adapt and reform in ways that might significantly improve the form, function, equity and efficacy of these space-economies through new modes of policy integration and political reform. With some notable exceptions here and there, such as in South Africa (Rogerson, 2009), efforts to consolidate institutional authority at the metropole-scale of regulation, investment, planning and overall economic and social governance – or what Savitch and Adhirkai call "monocentrism" – have largely failed to materialize, not only within the United States but most everywhere in the world. Instead, various forms of "fragmented regionalisms," in the US, Europe and other societies too, have emerged to try to balance local autonomy and democratic identity with the growing imperatives of metropolitan-wide patterns of economic accumulation, eco-metabolic change and social reproduction. As we noted in Chapter 1, though, much of the literature on "smartness" has focused squarely on individual cities, but not yet on entire city-regions, even as we are starting to see the steady emergence of this kind of work (Dierwechter, 2013, 2017a, 2017c, 2017d; Morandi et al., 2015; Zimmernann, 2016).

The next chapter thus develops a fresh theoretical framework for how to engage conceptually and analytically with what is understood here to be a diverse world of city-regional transitions shaped increasingly by the so-called "smart turn" turn in urban and regional policy-making and globalized political-economies.

References

Adler, G., & Webster, E. (1995). Challenging transition theory: The labor movement, radical reform, and transition to democracy in South Africa. *Politics & Society, 23*(1), 75–106.

Amen, M., Toly, N., McCarney, P., & Segbers, K. (Eds.) (2012). *Cities and global governance: New sites for international relations.* Farnham, UK: Ashgate.

Barber, B. (2013). *If mayors ruled the world: Dysfunctional nations, rising cities.* New Haven, CT: Yale University Press.

Benner, C., & Pastor, M. (2012). *Just growth: Inclusion and prosperity in America's metropolitan regions.* London: Routledge.

Boelens, L. (2010). Theorising practice and practising theory: Outlines for an actor-relational approach in planning. *Planning Theory, 9*(1), 28–62.

Bouteligier, S. (2012). *Global cities and networks for global environmental governance.* Hoboken, NJ: Taylor & Francis.

Brenner, N. (1997). State territorial restructuring and the production of spatial scale: Urban and regional planning in the Federal Republic of Germany, 1960–1990. *Political Geography, 16*(4), 273–306.

Brenner, N. (2001). Decoding the newest "metropolitan regionalism" in the USA: A critical overview. *European Planning Studies, 9*(7), 813–826.

Brenner, N. (2004). Urban governance and the production of new state spaces in Western Europe, 1960–2000. *Review of International Political Economy, 11*(3), 447–488. https://doi.org/10.1080/0969229042000282864

Calder, K., & Freytas, M. (2009). Global political cities as actors in twenty-first century international affairs. *SAIS Review of International Affairs, 29*(2), 79.

Cameron, R. (2000). Megacities in South Africa: A solution for the new millennium? *Public Administration and Development, 20*(2), 155–165.

Clark, J., & Christopherson, S. (2009). Integrating investment and equity: A critical regionalist agenda for a progressive regionalism. *Journal of Planning Education and Research, 28*(3), 341–354.

Counsell, D., Hart, T., Jonas, A. E. G., & Kettle, J. (2007). Fragmented regionalism? Delivering integrated regional strategies in Yorkshire and the Humber. *Regional Studies, 41*(3), 391–401. doi:10.1080/00343400601135864

Dierwechter, Y. (2008). *Urban growth management and its discontents: Promises, practices and geopolitics in US city-regions.* New York: Palgrave.

Dierwechter, Y. (2013). Smart city-regionalism across Seattle: Progressing transit nodes in labor space? *Geoforum, 49*(0), 139–149.

Dierwechter, Y. (2017a). The smart state as utopian space for urban politics. In A. E. G. Jonas, B. Miller, K. Ward, & D. Wilson (Eds.), *The Routledge handbook on spaces of urban politics*. London: Routledge.

Dierwechter, Y. (2017b). *Urban sustainability through smart growth: Greater Seattle, intercurrence, and the new geography of regional development*. New York: Springer.

Dierwechter, Y. (2017c). *Urban sustainability through smart growth: Intercurrence, planning, and geographies of regional development across Greater Seattle*. Cham, Switz.: Springer.

Dierwechter, Y. (2017d). What's smart growth got to do with smart cities? Searching for the "smart city region" in Greater Seattle. *Territorio, 83*, 48–54.

Dierwechter, Y., & Wessells, A. (2013). The uneven localisation of climate action in metropolitan Seattle. *Urban Studies, 50*(7), 1368–1385.

Dilworth, R. (Ed.) (2009). *The city in American political development*. New York: Routledge.

Dupresson, A., & Jaglin, S. (2014). Governing Cape Town: The exhaustion of a negotiated transition. In D. Lorrain (Ed.), *Governing megacities in emerging countries*. Burlington, VT: Ashgate.

Engelke, P. (2013). *Foreign policy for an urban world: Global governance and the rise of cities*. Washington, DC: Atlantic Council.

Erie, S., & Mackenzie, S. (2009). The LA school and politics noir: Bringing the local state back in. *Journal of Urban Affairs, 31*(5), 537–557.

Etherington, D., & Jones, M. (2009). City-regions: New geographies of uneven development and inequality. *Regional Studies, 43*(2), 247–265. doi:10.1080/00343400801968353

Feiock, R. (2004). *Metropolitan governance: Conflict, competition, and cooperation*. Washington, DC: Georgetown University Press.

Frisken, F., & Norris, D. F. (2001). Regionalism reconsidered. *Journal of Urban Affairs, 23*(5), 467–478. doi:10.1111/0735-2166.00101

Gascó, M., Trivellato, B., & Cavenago, D. (2016). How do southern European cities foster innovation? Lessons from the experience of the smart city approaches of Barcelona and Milan. In J. R. Gil-Garcia, T. A. Pardo, & T. Nam (Eds.), *Smarter as the new urban agenda: A comprehensive view of the 21st century city* (pp. 191–206). Cham, Switz.: Springer.

Ginsberg, D. (1996). The democratisation of South Africa: Transition theory tested. *Transformation, 29*, 74–102. Retrieved from http://pdfproc.lib.msu.edu/?file=/DMC/African%20Journals/pdfs/transformation/tran029/tran029006.pdf, accessed 29 Nov. 2017.

González, S. (2011). Bilbao and Barcelona "in motion": How urban regeneration "models" travel and mutate in the global flows of policy tourism. *Urban Studies, 48*(7), 1397–1418. doi:10.1177/0042098010374510

Greene, F. J., Tracey, P., & Cowling, M. (2007). Recasting the city into city-regions: Place promotion, competitiveness benchmarking and the quest for urban supremacy. *Growth and Change, 38*(1), 1–22.

Hall, P. (1998). *Cities in civilization* (1st American edn.). New York: Pantheon Books.

Harding, A. (2007). Taking city regions seriously? Response to debate on "city-regions": New geographies of governance, democracy and social reproduction. *International Journal of Urban and Regional Research, 31*(2), 443–458.

Harrison, J. (2007). From competitive regions to competitive city-regions: A new orthodoxy, but some old mistakes. *Journal of Economic Geography, 7*(3), 311–332. doi:10.1093/jeg/lbm005

Harrison, J. (2012). Life after regions? The evolution of city-regionalism in England. *Regional Studies, 46*(9), 1243–1259. doi:10.1080/00343404.2010.521148

Herrschel, T. (2013). Sustainability *and* competitiveness: Can smart growth square the circle? *Urban Studies, 50*(11), 2332–2348.

Herrschel, T., & Newman, P. (2017). *Cities as international actors*. London: Palgrave.

Hidle, K., & Leknes, E. (2014). Policy strategies for new regionalism: Different spatial logics for cultural and business policies in Norwegian city regions. *European Planning Studies, 22*(1), 126–142. doi:10.1080/09654313.2012.741565

Hodos, J. (2009). Against expectionalism: Intercurrence and intergovernmental relations in Britain and the United States. In R. Dileorth (Ed.), *The city in American political development* (pp. 44–63). New York: Routledge.

Jonas, A. E. G. (2012a). City-regionalism as a contingent "geopolitics of capitalism". *Geopolitics, 18*(2), 284–298.

Jonas, A. E. G. (2012b). City-regionalism: Questions of distribution and politics. *Progress in Human Geography, 36*(6), 822–829. doi:10.1177/0309132511432062

Jonas, A. E. G. (2012c). Region and place: Regionalism in question. *Progress in Human Geography, 36*(2), 263–272.

Jonas, A. E. G. (2013). City-Regionalism as a contingent "geopolitics of capitalism". *Geopolitics, 18*(2), 284–298. doi:10.1080/14650045.2012.723290

Jonas, A. E. G. (2015). Beyond the urban "sustainability fix": Looking for new spaces and discourses of sustainability in the city. In D. Wilson (Ed.), *The politics of the urban sustainability concept*. Champaign, IL: Common Ground.

Jonas, A. E. G., & McCarthy, L. (2009). Urban management and regeneration in the United States: State intervention or redevelopment at all costs? *Local Government Studies, 35*(3), 299–314.

Jonas, A. E. G., & Pincetl, S. (2006). Rescaling regions in the state: The new regionalism in California. *Political Geography, 25*(5), 482–505.

Jonas, A. E. G., & Ward, K. (2001). *City-regionalisms: Some critical reflections on transatlantic urban policy convergence*. Economic Geography Working Group (Working paper 01/01).

Jonas, A. E. G., & Moisio, S. (2016). City regionalism as geopolitical processes: A new framework for analysis. *Progress in Human Geography*. doi:10.1177/0309132516679897

Jonas, A. E. G., & Ward, K. (2007). Introduction to a debate on city-regions: New geographies of governance, democracy and social reproduction. *International Journal of Urban and Regional Research, 31*(1), 169–178. doi:10.1111/j.1468-2427.2007.00711.x

Jones, M. (1997). Spatial selectivity of the state: The regulationist enigma and local struggles over economic governance. *Environment & Planning A, 29*, 831–864.

Katz, B. (Ed.) (2000). *Reflections on regionalism*. Washington, DC: Brookings Institution Press.

King, D., & Smith, R. (2005). Racial orders in American political development. *American Political Science Review, 99*(1), 75–92.

Kuzio, T. (2001). Transition in post-communist states: Triple or quadruple? *Politics, 21*(3), 168–177. doi:10.1111/1467-9256.00148

Lackowska, M., & Zimmermann, K. (2011). New forms of territorial governance in metropolitan regions? A Polish–German comparison. *European Urban and Regional Studies, 18*(2), 156–169. doi:10.1177/0969776410390746

Lee, T. (2012). Global cities and transnational climate change networks. *Global Environmental Politics, 13*(1), 108–127. doi:10.1162/GLEP_a_00156

Lees, A. (2015). *The city: A world history*. Oxford: Oxford University Press.

Loh, C. G., & Sami, N. (2013). Death of a planning department: Challenges for regionalism in a weak mandate state. *Land Use Policy, 32*(0), 39–49. doi:doi.org/10.1016/j.landusepol.2012.09.015

Lowe, K. (2014). Bypassing equity? Transit investment and regional transportation planning. *Journal of Planning Education and Research, 34*(1), 30–44. doi:10.1177/0739456x13519474

MacLeod, G. (2013). New urbanism/smart growth in the Scottish Highlands: Mobile policies and post-politics in local development planning. *Urban Studies, 50*(11), 2196–2221.

MacLeod, G., & Goodwin, M. (1999). Reconstructing an urban and regional political economy: On the state, politics, scale, and explanation. *Political Geography, 18,* 697–730.

MacLeod, G., & Jones, M. (2001). Renewing the geography of regions. *Environment and Planning D: Society and Space, 19*(6), 669–695. doi:10.1068/d217t

March, A. (2010). Practising theory: When theory affects urban planning. *Planning Theory, 9*(2), 108–125.

March, H., & Ribera-Fumaz, R. (2016). Smart contradictions: The politics of making Barcelona a self-sufficient city. *European Urban and Regional Studies, 23*(4), 816–830. doi:10.1177/0969776414554488

Mazower, M. (2012). *Governing the world: The history of an idea, 1815 to the present.* New York: Penguin Press.

McCann, E. (2007). Inequality and politics in the creative city-region: Questions of livability and state strategy. *International Journal of Urban and Regional Research, 31*(1), 188–196.

McCauley, S. M., & Murphy, J. T. (2013). Smart growth and the scalar politics of land management in the Greater Boston region, USA. *Environment and Planning A, 45*(12), 2852–2867. doi:10.1068/a45307

McGuirk, P. (2007). The political construction of the city-region: Notes from Sydney. *International Journal of Urban and Regional Research, 31*(1), 179–187. doi:10.1111/j.1468-2427.2007.00712.x

Moisio, S., & Paasi, A. (2013). From geopolitical to geoeconomic? The changing political rationalities of state space. *Geopolitics, 18*(2), 267–283.

Morandi, C., Rolando, A., & Di Vita, S. (2015). *From smart city to smart region: Digital services for an Internet of Places.* Cham, Switz.: Springer.

Negri, A., & Hardt, M. (2000). *Empire.* Cambridge, MA.: Harvard University Press.

Nijman, J. (2009, October 29). The rising influence of urban actors. *The Broker.*

Norris, D. F. (2001). Prospects for regional governance under the new regionalism: Economic imperatives versus political impediments. *Journal of Urban Affairs, 23*(5), 557–571.

O'Donnell, G., & Schmitter, P. C. (2013). *Transitions from authoritarian rule: Tentative conclusions about uncertain democracies.* Baltimore, MD: JHU Press.

OECD. (2008). *Territorial review: Cape Town metropolitan review.* Paris: OECD.

OECD. (2013). *Rural–urban partnerships: An integrated approach to economic development.* Paris: OECD.

Orren, K., & Skowronek, S. (1996). Institutions and intercurrence: Theory building in the fullness of time. In I. Shapiro & H. Russell (Eds.), *Nomos XXXVII, Political Order* (pp. 111–146). New York: New York University Press,

Orren, K., & Skowronek, S. (2004). *The search for American political development.* Cambridge: Cambridge University Press.

Parnell, S. (2007). Politics of transformation: Defining the city strategy in Johannesburg. In K. Segbers (Ed.), *The making of global city regions.* Baltimore, MD: Johns Hopkins Press.

Perlman, B. J., & Jimenez, J. (2010). Creative regionalism: Governance for stressful times. *State and Local Government Review, 42*(2), 151–155. doi:10.1177/0160323x10380616

Pezzoli, K., Hibbard, M., & Huntoon, L. (2006). Introduction to symposium: Is progressive regionalism an actionable framework for critical planning theory and practice? *Journal of Planning Education and Research, 25*(4), 449–457.

Pillay, U. (2004). Are globally competitive "city regions" developing in South Africa? Formulaic aspirations or new imaginations? *Urban Forum, 15*(4), 340–364. doi:10.1007/s12132-004-0013-5

Provo, J. (2009). Risk-averse regionalism: The cautionary tale of Portland, Oregon, and affordable housing. *Journal of Planning Education and Research, 28*(3), 368–381. doi:10.1177/0739456x08319202

Rast, J. (2006). Environmental justice and the new regionalism. *Journal of Planning Education and Research, 25*(3), 249–263. doi:10.1177/0739456x05280543

Rogerson, C. (2009). The turn to "new regionalism": South African reflections. *Urban Forum, 20*(2), 111–140. doi:10.1007/s12132-009-9057-x

Rosenzweig, C., Solecki, W., Hammer, S. A., & Mehrotra, S. (2010). Cities lead the way in climate-change action. *Nature, 467*(7318), 909–911.

Savitch, H. V., & Adhikari, S. (2017). Fragmented regionalism. *Urban Affairs Review, 53*(2), 381–402. doi:10.1177/1078087416630626

Savitch, H. V., & Vogel, R. K. (2004). Suburbs without a city: Power and city-county consolidation. *Urban Affairs Review, 39*(6), 758–790. doi:10.1177/1078087404264512

Scott, A. (Ed.) (2001). *Global city-regions: Trends, theory, policy*. Oxford: Oxford University Press

Scott, A. J. (2001). Globalization and the rise of city-regions. *European Planning Studies, 9*(7), 813–826. doi:10.1080/09654310120079788

Segbers, K. (Ed.) (2007). *The making of global city-regions*. Baltimore, MD: Johns Hopkins University Press.

Simmonds, R. H. G. (2000). *Global city regions: Their emerging forms*. London: Spon Press.

Skowronek, S. (1982). *Building a new American state: The expansion of national administrative capacities, 1877–1920*. Cambridge : Cambridge University Press.

Smith, R. (2003). World city actor-networks. *Progress in Human Geography, 27*(1), 25–44.

Söderström, O., Paasche, T., & Klauser, F. (2014). Smart cities as corporate storytelling. *City, Analysis of Urban Trends, Culture, Theory, Policy, Action, 18*(3), 307–320.

Soja, E. (2000). *Postmetropolis*. London: Sage.

Swanstrom, T. (2001). What we argue about when we argue about regionalism. *Journal of Urban Affairs, 23*(5), 479–496.

Swanstrom, T. (2006). Regionalism, equality, and democracy. *Urban Affairs Review, 42*(2), 249–257.

Swanstrom, T., & Banks, B. (2007). *Going regional: Community-based regionalism, transportation, and local hiring agreements (Vol. Working paper 2007–17)*. Berkeley, CA: Institute of Urban and Regional Development.

Thrift, N., & Amin, A. (2002). *Cities: Reimagining the urban*. Cambridge: Polity.

Tiebout, C. M. (1956). A pure theory of local expenditures. *Journal of Political Economy, 64*(5), 416–424. doi:10.1086/257839

Toly, N. (2008). Transnational municipal networks in climate politics: From global governance to global politics. *Globalizations, 5*(3), 341–356.

Townsend, A. M. (2013). *Smart cities: Big data, civic hackers, and the quest for a new utopia* (First edn.). New York: W.W. Norton & Company.

Vogel, R. K., Savitch, H. V., Xu, J., Yeh, A. G. O., Wu, W. P., Sancton, A., … Zhang, F. Z. (2010). Governing global city regions in China and the West. *Progress in Planning, 73*, 1–75. doi:10.1016/j.progress.2009.12.001

Ward, K., & Jonas, A. E. G. (2004). Competitive city-regionalism as a politics of space: A critical reinterpretation of the new regionalism. *Environment and Planning A, 36*(12), 2119–2139. doi:10.1068/a36223

While, A., Jonas, A. E. G., & Gibbs, D. (2004). The environment and the entrepreneurial city: Searching for the urban "sustainability;fix" in Manchester and Leeds. *International Journal of Urban and Regional Research, 28*(3), 549–569.

Widestrom, A. (2011). *The political development of public policy: Institutions, intercurrence, and the Community Reinvestment Act.* Paper presented at the Western Political Science Association 2011 Annual Meeting. Available at SSRN: http://ssrn.com/abstract=1767096, accessed 13 Nov. 2017.

Williams, G. (1999). Institutional capacity and metropolitan governance: The Greater Toronto area. *Cities, 16*(3), 171–180.

Zimmernann, K. (2016). *Smart city-regional governance: The German perspective.* Paper presented at the *Smart city-regional governance for sustainability: experimental smartness Dresden,* Germany (6–October).

Zimmerbauer, K., & Paasi, A. (2013). When old and new regionalism collide: Deinstitutionalization of regions and resistance identity in municipality amalgamations. *Journal of Rural Studies, 30,* 31–40. doi:10.1016/j.jrurstud.2012.11.004

4 Going for "smartness"

Reframing city-regionalism

Introduction

This chapter provides an overall analytical framework for the empirical application of the conceptual fusion of transition and smartness in city-regional governance. The evaluation adopts two comparative perspectives based on our synoptic concept of a "dual transition," which we argue shapes the ways in which specific city-regions move towards adopting smart governance principles and practices. The dual transition consists of changes to the *external* context, that is, the situation of city-regions, as well as changes to their *internal* conditions. In addition, we propose that both transitions are circumscribed by place-specific interactions between structure and agency. We thus study these interactions at two scalar levels: *within* and *outside* city-regions. The key idea advanced throughout our discussion is that interactions between external and internal transitions produce time- and place-specific circumstances for the adoption and concrete manifestations of smart governance. In this sense, we emphasize the nature and relative "weight" of the two processes of change, that is, the negotiated *balance* between external and internal factors as they impact the city-regional adoption of smart governance. This includes the primary rationales, values and goals underpinning established "orders" in governance regimes for city-regions and how they help to address competing interests and expected policies (both electoral and special-interests).

One example is the current tension between globalization-based competitiveness and socio-spatial cohesion within (and especially in Europe, *between*) states. The role of the state thus differs between fostering competitiveness, actively facilitating economic development through state support, and seeking to maintain cohesiveness through redistributive interventions and economic and fiscal equalization measures. These rationales, and their respective importance, manifest themselves in public and political discourses and values which shape justifications, expectations and modi operandi of governance in city-regions. Indeed, place-based factors matter too, such as established values concerning the interest of the individual vis-à-vis that of the collective, historic experiences with municipal self-government versus a centralized state system or just the simple habits and inherited routines of governing. Importantly, we further posit that the ways these traditions, views and ways of doing things are brought together, and practically elaborated, in response to changing contexts – especially when they conflict with one another – *are empirical signs of "smartness" in governance*. Building upon the themes introduced in Chapter 1, smartness is therefore broadly understood in this and subsequent chapters to include deliberation and negotiation – or "creativity" and "learning" – in the ongoing search for more effective and responsive governance structures and policies, viewed against agreed objectives and expectations, and within what we furthermore call the "power field" between external and internal structural and dynamic factors.

Our initial framework of a "dual transition" in city-regional smartness is illustrated in Figure 4.1, which reflects analytical and normative considerations.

Analytically, we explore the *external transition* specifically through three main "orders," which embody more concrete regime principles and rationales of control and operation between the development-political "poles" of competitiveness and cohesiveness. These orders help to define the external position

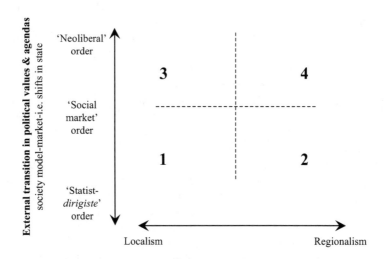

Internal transition in city-regionalism
Propensity for policy innovation and collaborative action
based on internal political-economic milieux

1 = ***statist/localist***, *non-collaborative, hierarchical, dependent, defensive*
2 = ***statist/regionalist***, *collaborative through state-incentives/intervention, also reaching across scales*
3 = ***neo-liberal competitive/localist*** *(metropolitan elitist), self-centred ('independent-minded'), feeling 'held back' by struggling neighbouring localities, or seeking support by 'clinging on' successful*
4 = ***neo-liberal-competitive/regionalist***, *opportunistic-collaborative at different scales, internationlist in networking, 'elitist' metropolitanist, confident*

Figure 4.1 Smart city-regionalism as "dual transition."

of city-regions as crucial nodes of economic activity and policy-making in relation to locally-defined priorities as well as developments and policies in wider national settings. For instance, are city-regions allowed to "leave behind" their respective national territories in pursuit of their own opportunities and policy agendas? Alternatively, are key city-regions required to follow external trends and national processes as part of a strictly hierarchical, top-down political-administrative project? (The remarkable insistence by hundreds of US cities to ignore in toto the Trump administration's high-profile withdrawal from the Paris Climate Agreement in 2017 is a recent example of the growing conflicts in American society between "internal" and "external" transitions and shifting political values.)

Different principles connect to different types of city-regional governance experiences, based on pre-dominant rationales, the relative roles of the state and capital in shaping space-economies and of course policy approaches. Accordingly, *equitable* (social market economy, neo-Keynesianism), *dirigiste* (socialism, ideology/idealism, statism) and *competitive* (market-centric, neo-liberal) principles give rise to:

1 a "neoliberal market" order, which is largely business-driven and set in a free-market, corporate understanding of individualism, globalization, and associated uneven opportunities between inevitable "winners" and "losers";
2 a "Social market" order, which is driven by greater socio-spatial equity, democratic accountability and social justice, such as reflected in conventional, territory-based equalisation policies in the EU's Structural Fund scheme; and
3 a "Statist-*dirigiste*" order, which is more driven by the state apparatus in a neo-mercantilist tradition, wherein city-regions are "pushed out" as the best (competitive) horses in the race for economic opportunities and appeal to (presumed) globally footloose capital. City-regions are thus expected to act both individually (to be successful) and on behalf of the state as a whole.

The "choice," or, as the case may be, requirements, among these orders is a product of the "dual transition" advocated here: that is, the time-dependent varying interactions between two main (changing) factor dimensions, and the negotiated aspirations around topical priorities and modi operandi of governing a city-region. The result may be different, place-specific, "paths" towards adopting smartness in city-regional governance, as shown in Figure 4.1.

The conditioning impact of external parameters on actors within city-regions, combined with place-specific internal factors, circumscribe the acceptability of policies among local electorates. This shapes the conditions within which policy-makers feel able, as well as compelled, to deliver policies more likely to lead to political reward at the next election. It is here, once again, that "smartness" may (need to) be developed to utilize existing possibilities, overcome inherent obstacles and pursue novel agendas in order to reconcile politically and more effectively seemingly conflicting, competing or, at times, contradicting expectations. Smartness thus involves continuous adaptability among policy-makers, as neither external nor internal factors are static. They are subject to the pressures and expectations emanating from globalization, technological innovation and individual, as well as institutional, learning among political and economic actors and the public. Established values, priorities or agendas may need to be revised. Structures matter, too, as they set the framework and scope for, and interest in, flexibility, individuality and experimentalism in policy-making. Flexibility contrasts with simply following orders "from above" – pursuing politically safe, largely technocratic solutions. The underlying dynamic also questions, and/or continuously requires to review, established and typically more familiar frameworks of power arrangements and sources of legitimacy, including the perceived scope for policy success.

This framing allows us to explore broader questions of territorial development and embedded path-dependencies, of the policy choices and governance principles of city-regions. These may sit between, on the one hand, a rather *laissez-faire* approach by their respective states, with varying degrees of devolved powers and thus scope for own action, and, on the other hand, a much more state-*dirigiste* approach, in which cities are effectively reduced to mere agents of national agendas and policies and, thus, little more than *locales* for the "acting out" of such externally-defined policies and developments. For instance, in the former scenario, city-regions are permitted to do their "own thing" – indeed, they may be required to do so to protect their own interests and prospects in the absence of a state-provided "safety net." Examples include an increasingly more widespread venturing onto the global stage (see also Herrschel and Newman, 2017) as self-managing actors to pursue opportunities unavailable within the confines of their states.

These differences in context are likely to have fundamental implications for the formation of city-regions, and, especially their governance and policy directions as shaped by localist versus regionalist sensibilities. In Figure 4.1 we capture this as the *propensity for policy innovation and collaborative action* based on *internal* political-economic milieu. A change in context, such as through shifting national policy interests, or structural contexts in the wake of globalization, are bound to impact also on the nature of city-regional governance. Specifically, this may affect the ways in which complex and usually conflictual issues and agendas are addressed. The external dimension's focus on structural and ideational concerns refers to how different national contexts help influence actors' minds, expectations and political interest in finding new policy agendas and approaches. Choices may consider national guidelines, funding arrangements for local initiatives and, in particular, expectations and responses by the local electorate and particular interest/lobby groups. This dimension of transition thus draws attention to key tensions both in terms of scale – between national and international interests – and topical perspectives (policy fields).

Our framework also helps us to explore the main empirical questions raised by the case studies about place- and time-specific preponderance for shaping and adopting "smart" city-regional governance. This includes the nature of, and main actors in, policy-making processes; the mechanisms of negotiation and involvement, or exclusion, of participants; the identified goals, the effects of place-specific as well as more general political modalities, democratic traditions and electoral expectations about policy outcomes and state involvement in achieving those. In other words, there is a place-specific and broader, more general, political milieu as product of institutional cultures and established ways of defining and implementing policies.

This interplay between structure and agency applies to both the territorial (relational versus place-based geography) and institutional (structuralist versus actor-centric) interpretations. The latter is closely linked to relational geography, such as expressed in notions of "soft spaces" or "virtual regions" (Walsh, 2012, 2014; Herrschel, 2011, 2012) as part of the concept of "new regionalism" (Söderbaum & Shaw, 2003; MacLeod, 2001; Keating, 1998) or "soft institutionalism," which contrast with conventional, more institutionalized regionalism. The "soft" varieties of territorial governance focus on agency as part of innovation in political strategies and policy applications, rather than being merely shaped and conditioned by given territorialities. Inevitably, there will be tensions between the two perspectives, so that smartness will need to be applied to the ways in which structures can be made more responsive by adding elements of agency. At the same time, agency needs to be "organized" within structures in order to provide a dose of continuity and predictability, as well as credibility and state-administrative capacity. Reconciling the two approaches is where we see "smartness," as actors seek to negotiate between contrasting traditions and thus generate novel forms in city-regional governance. It is the interaction between external and intra-city-regional parameters that circumscribe the propensity among actors and the general public to accept and engage with "smart" principles in political discourse and practical policy approach.

In the end, as seen in the "heart" of Figure 4.1, we argue that all these various dynamics generate *four different types* of city-regional "transitions." More will be said of these quadrants later in this chapter – and indeed in subsequent chapters. But for the moment, in brief, we note only that city-regions located in the first quadrant ("1") are defined by the "external" legacies of state-*dirigisme* and the "internal" absence of new forms of collaborative regionalism. For its part, the second quadrant ("2") reflects much greater evidence of city-regional collaboration, but nonetheless remains also shaped by the external state-market dynamics of state-*dirigisme*, albeit in rather different forms in different world regions. The remaining two quadrants show a greater impact of neoliberal values and agendas with the main difference between them the effect of place-specific factors. Accordingly, the third quadrant ("3") includes city-regions shaped by neoliberal competitive/localist dynamics, including greater struggles to initiate new forms of regional collaboration, while the fourth and final quadrant ("4") are city-regions that reflect variegated admixtures of both neoliberalism and regionalism.

Finally, the book openly acknowledges at the outset that our "dual transition" theory in city-regional smartness also includes a strong *normative* element in addition to the analytical dimensions just presented. Ideally, in our view, "smartness" implies that differently-situated city-regions all around the world should converge towards new and more effective forms of city-regional collaborations, and that, moreover, these new collaborative efforts in creative policy innovation *should strengthen* and reflect wider political-economies characterized by social-market values and more equitable forms of governance. Put another way, our dual transition framework is significantly informed by our ethical-philosophical sense of an ideal "smart city-region" that is collaborative, creative and dynamic, but also – and no less importantly – socially equitable and ecologically resilient, even as the bulk of this book is focused more on a detailed empirical exploration of "actually-existing" city-regional transitions in different social, historical and geographic contexts.

Transition as directional regime change

The term "transition" *per se* points to a transformational process towards an envisaged ultimate stage of development. For this to be achieved, the widespread notion had been the need for satisfying certain formal, structural preconditions to allow democratization to take a foothold. Illustrating the longevity of the structuralist perspective nearly half a century ago, Rustow (1970) pointed to the role of structural variables in shaping political-economic transitions (mainly in relation to liberal democratization), especially historic factors found in a locality. As a result, he argued, regime transitions may vary between "rapid" and "gradual" speeds of change, and also in their depth of change, reflecting the varying senses of urgency and desired extent of change in a place and at a particular time. Referring to developments in Central and Eastern Europe after the end of communism, for instance, Stark and Bruszt (1998) pointed to the influence of place-specific factors in the various countries, as they compete for prevalence, including past experiences, historic legacies, existing network relationships and own agendas. They include a communist-era culture of doing things (Seleny 1994), attached to a distinct statist tradition (Szarvas 1993), with expectations that things will get taken care of "by the state." It is these particularities, Haggard and Kaufman (1995) argued, that encourage subsequent political processes. "For example," Anderson and O'Dowd (1999, p. 11) elaborated, "variations in historical patterns of state formation between coercive and capital-intensive paths and in their reliance on external or international dynamics may well create cultural and social structural predispositions toward certain types of political regime." The underlying notion of path-dependency is thus less structurally determined – although that varies between places – than process-based, and thus ultimately haphazard, unpredictable and contingent; it does not necessarily follow a predictable linear route. These structural divisions included the resurfacing and clear manifestation of underlying differences in economic opportunities and competitiveness, as assessed by the newly and abruptly applied market criteria in the immediate post-socialist years.

Prior to the end of the communist regimes, "transition" referred primarily to developing countries and their expected progress towards a Western-style market democracy as envisaged ultimate evolution. Such a rather one-dimensional understanding of the outcome of societal development was strongly advocated during the 1980s, with the struggle between communism and liberal market democracies now seen as won by the latter. Indeed, Fukuyama (1992) famously claimed "an end to history." The so-called "transition paradigm" (Diamond et al., 2014) maintained that a country in transition was one embarking on a process of democratization. The transition paradigm takes as its starting point an authoritarian (military, single party or personality-based) regime (Huntington, 1991) which then shifts towards liberal democracy. Each type of authoritarian regime presents different prospects for the realization of democracy: perhaps surprisingly, military rulers are not considered to pose significant institutional obstacles to democratization (Rafti, 2007, p. 8). In other words, the concept of transition presumes an automatic process of "adjustment" to democracy as the "naturally" preferred choice, given an absence of suppressive or, in particular, obstructive ideational obstacles. Democracy as the outcome of a natural flow of regime development is thus an inherently normative assumption of the alternative to authoritarianism. The transition paradigm focuses on the choices made by the political actors, and much less those from business and civil society, including the negotiation of power transfers between old and new elites. One question here is the extent of "rupture" versus processes of institutional continuity and gradual change of norms and routines (p. 9).

As Nofosi (2005) points out, three main modes of transition may be distinguished, based on the different nature of processes of change and underlying dynamics: reform, compromise and overthrow. Under "reform," the existing political elite remains engaged and actively participates in shaping the transition process. Here, there is little opposition to their leading roles. The focus is on continuity, not at least in terms of holding power. In contrast, "compromise" is required in instances of power parity between the old regime and the propagators of a new agenda and political discourse. The allocation of power in such circumstances needs to be changed, with the old elite seeking to retain as much as possible. Lastly, "overthrow" is the most radical type of transition. It is a response to an old regime reluctant to accept change and loss of power and insisting on maintaining the status quo. Under conditions of rupture, the new regime has the support for the most far-reaching changes in access to power and control of policies, often based on high expectations of improvements to conditions for the general public.

Once in motion, the simplistically linear "transition paradigm" suggests a process divided into three steps/sequences: first, *opening* the process of change through discursive challenges, then, as second step, *breakthrough* denotes the process of transformation, where the new values, actors and agendas manage to replace the existing elite and discourse. Lastly, the *consolidation* phase encapsulates the general acceptance of the new regime, its discourse and agenda, as well as lead actors and holders of power. That achievement, so the "transition paradigm" holds, is first and foremost the result of personal agency of key actors (individuals or groups) and is not shaped and/or predetermined by structural factors. In other words, transitions can be ubiquitous and ad hoc. Their nature, however, varies as different circumstances affect speed, extent, objectives and outcomes. In practice, therefore, transitions are not always clear-cut, simply reaching from A to B. Rather, they may involve compromise and incorporation of local conditions, including established power structures and political conditions, which may lead to a fusion between old and new, with varying inputs by the two. Consequently, transitions can become stuck in a "grey zone," somewhere between the old and new regimes, and this to incomplete transitions, where democratization is used as criterion. Here it is very difficult for new arrangements to emerge as "good practices"– made too unclear by the circumstances and directions of agenda, interests and expectations. This includes variations across scales between particular local, regional and national experiences and ambitions, as well as across society. The currently observed acceptance of authoritarian elements of governing in parts of Eastern Europe, but also in the Western world, suggests that experiences with, expectations of, and thus support for, democracy can vary temporally, geographically and socially. This suggests that a one-way linear expectation of the transition desired is too simplistic, even naïve.

The focus of debates on regime transition has been on a neoliberally informed understanding of competitive political economy and the resulting spatial and institutional arrangements, in close conjunction with expected democratization of political processes. Increasingly, other economic development agendas have been acknowledged, too, including alternative values and a broader perspective than merely least cost production and maximum profitability. Examples include alleviating climate change, protecting and/or boosting environmental qualities or questioning lifestyle. Indeed, responsibility for climate change has become a critical issue as part of globalization and the need for cross-scalar governance.

Debates on regime transformation may be divided into two main theoretical strands: one focusing on structural determinants of action, and the other placing greater emphasis on people-based determinants of actor agency. Sinpeng (2007) refers to this as contrasting structuralist and voluntarist approaches Adeney and Wyatt (2004, p. 1) call this the "structure-agency dichotomy," insinuating that the two are, in effect, mutually exclusive. But that need not be the case. Almost 50 years ago, Rustow (1970), for instance, questioned the (then) prevailing notion in academic and public debate, rooted in structuralist views, that democratization needs a specific set of supportive factors as prerequisites to establish itself and keep a foothold in a society. These included such broad variables as economic prosperity, level of education and widespread adherence to liberal or democratic values. Instead, he turned the focus on agency, process and the bargaining between actors, moving away from a primary concern with structures and institutions, and thus broke new ground in the interpretation and analysis of transitions to democracy. Questions of leadership, networks and imagined opportunities become major elements in this agency perspective.

Despite the contrasting debates on different rationales and purposes, "structure" and "agency" are not, of course, mutually exclusive but, as our opening chapter suggests, co-constitutive (Giddens, 1984). Their respective impact and relevance, however, varies. *Structuralists* argue that regime changes are facilitated and shaped by specific structural contexts, such as economic patterns, power structures, political traditions, experiences and socio-political milieux, historic legacies of ways of doing things, values and so on. In contrast, *voluntarist* approaches place human behaviour at the centre of regime transformation. From this perspective, behaviour reflects actor interests and agendas as well as personalities. Career ambitions, personal convictions and ideological beliefs drive political engagement. This can have a major impact on initiating, directing and implementing regime change processes and outcomes. There is thus no structurally predetermined course of events and developments, but, instead, considerable scope for steering developments on the basis of actor will.

It is here that Cultural Theory introduces its focus on the role of particular societal traits, such as histories, social practices, memories and identities in shaping political-economic regimes. Culture, in this context, is understood as the combination of values and beliefs and social relations. Inevitably, this implies place-specificity as well. Cultural Theory thus includes what we consider an important aspect of agency – the relations between places and their "contents." Thompson et al. (1990) refer to these as the two dimensions of *sociality*: "groups" and "grids" capture the environment's impact on socio-economic decisions. There is thus reference to both territorially- and relationally-defined factors. "Groups" refer to bordered territorial order, and thus an essentially static system of economic activities, in which actors are organized in like-minded and like-interested groupings. In our cases, here, this corresponds with the population of a city or city-region, which, of course, expresses underlying values and agendas. "Grid" by contrast refers to the linkages and relations that reflect interdependencies and dependencies, as well as power relations, and these two may embrace territory and society as actor reference.

The intersection between those two dimensions, Thompson et al. (1990) argue, produces two sets of contrasting variables as descriptors of power relations and sources of value systems: (1) egalitarian vs hierarchical and (2) collectivism vs individualism. The emphasis varies in terms of the organization and location of power and the role of identified collective interests versus individual advantages. Both are, of course, interdependent, even if that is not always evident to local actors (and the electorate). Major external changes can be expected to influence the range of actors involved, the prioritization of values and agendas, and thus the relative positions, and publicly and politically perceived relevance, desirability and capability of actors and their interests. And this, in turn, circumscribes the nature and rationale of groupings and their interactions and likely agreements on joint actions and agendas. Such major context includes globalization and the retreat of the state vis-à-vis capital as part of a dominant belief in neoliberal principles since the late 1970s; democratization as the shift away from authoritarian rule in several waves (Huntingdon, 1993); and, more recently, a growing awareness of global ecological interdependencies and dangers. The collapse of communism in Eastern Europe, the demise of apartheid in South Africa, or post-colonial changes elsewhere, are each examples of such major political-economic shifts in the external environment of city-regions at the national level.

Actor relations with their underlying priorities and searching for opportunities are thus considered at least as important as structure in shaping regimes. Interests and calculations may well go beyond mere economic interests and follow personal or group-specific aspirations. Existing value systems, political and public narratives and discourses about desirable developments and developmental priorities matter for the acceptability of, support for and likely political capital from, decisions made by actors. This provides greater or lesser support/pressure for policy choices. Structure also comes into play as place- and time-specific conditions, albeit not as pre-determinants. Actor agency may seek to counteract them, rather than follow the easiest path. Actors may or may not encounter and consider them, as they map out, and seek to pursue, their goals, including changes to an existing political-economic regime (Mahoney & Snyder, 1999).

Looking at actually-occurring regime transitions from communism to liberal market democracy in Eastern Europe, the crucial role of which way becomes evident in which changes take place. Anderson and O'Dowd (1999), for instance, point to the importance of the process of transition; especially, how power is transferred as a key factor in shaping the likely path (and success) of democratization. This can be orderly, through negotiations between old and new political actors, allowing the old elite to shape the new regime and thus ensuring a degree of continuity of governance; or it can be abruptly, through revolutionary processes. When revolutionary, there is a decisive, clear break with the past and a new beginning, with completely different actors and governmental arrangements, rationales and practices. This, they argue, contributes to the emergence of individual country-specific circumstances, and underlying dynamics, rather than the mere "rolling out" of a standardized, one-size-fits-all approach.

Observations of actually-occurring regime changes have thus highlighted that there is not just one path of, for instance, post-authoritarian development, nor just one standard type of liberal democracy as the universal outcome for all. "Transition" has therefore also been challenged as much too normative, with "transformation" a favoured alternative. The question of normativity matters here, as there is some indication that some political agendas and discourses become non-negotiable, as they are deemed to be "without alternative" in a post-political sense (Swyngedouw, 2014). Alleviating climate change and ecological sustainability have become such post-political, universal agendas.

In contrast, place specificity suggests the outcome is not clear-cut, as existing circumstances and policy-making cultures generate "hybrid" regimes that fuse aspects of old and new values and practices in governing. Among political-economic regime transitions, fusions between elements of authoritarianism and democracy often may be the result (Case, 1996a; Collier & Levitsky, 1997; Carothers, 2002; Ottaway, 2003). Effectively, this is a way of having it both ways: staying with the familiar old, while also seeking to try out something new.

But such hybrids may be unstable. Competing interests push in different directions as they attempt to gain influence. Structural challenges and different forms and personalities of political agency also seek to shape policies and governance in the image of their values and agendas. Indeed, it is their "in between" nature that gives them an inherent dynamic as part of an experimental process of shaping regimes. This, of course, has fundamental implications for the ways in which sub-national governance can emerge, articulate itself and function, as it depends on the established degree of devolution, the scope and capacity to govern, and adherence to multi-level governance between (localist) individualism and (regional) collectivism. "Hence," as Rafti (2007, p. 9) notes, "political transition ultimately entails *regime change*, which in turn entails a procedural, ideological and/or behavioral change."

Dual transition of structure and agency

As discussed earlier, the main concept used here to underpin the different examples of city-regional governance is that of "dual transition" as a product of two intersecting processes at different spatial and societal scales: one external and one internal to the locus of governing city-regions, now developed further in Table 4.1.

The notion of "external" and "internal" itself applies to two scalar relationships: the international vis-à-vis the national arena and the national vis-à-vis

Table 4.1 Dual transition and the adoption of smartness: concurrent changes of internal and external structural factors and discourses

Level of inter-action	"External" factors (general dynamics and values)	"Internal" factors (domestic, territory/place-specific)
T1 National Transition: changing discourses and challenges	Globalization, international politics by international organizations, international discourses, international regulation	National political-institutional structures, political traditions, societal values, public discourses
T2 City-Regional (sub-national) Transition: changing discourses and policy-making practices (e.g. collaborative action)	National political-institutional structures, political traditions, societal values, public discourses	City-regional governing structures, econ conditions, public discourse city-to-region (suburbs), policy-making capacity, leadership

the city-regional. Both, of course, are interconnected via the (national) state as interlocutor between the two scales of relationships which are shaped by political-economic circumstances and dynamics, established practices and policy-making structures. The latter include centralized, hierarchical decision-making, on the one hand, and more devolved, self-organizing arrangements within city-regions, on the other. This dichotomy is underpinned by held values and expectations in public discourse, such as the role of competitive individualism versus "responsible" collectivism. We see the political implications of this tension in the current rise in populism on the back of criticizing globalization for its production and/or reinforcement of inequalities. These *wider external variables*, at both the national and international scale, may include moments of major regime change in societal-economic and political-institutional terms, which alter the points of reference, scope and capacity for actors to effect policies and claim legitimacy for the criteria used in the principles of practiced governance at city-regional level. This can be focused on the choice between fragmented localism or collaborative regionalization.

There are thus two arenas of held values and perceived priorities and urgencies, which may also undergo greater or lesser degrees of change, or "transition": Transition 1 (T1) at the national (state) level, and Transition 2 (T2) at the city-regional scale. Both T1 and T2 are shaped by a combination of "external" and "internal" factors which sit at the international-to-national interface (T1) and national-to-city-regional interdependency (T2). Both may go concurrently and thus produce greater dynamics of change, including possible ruptures, by encouraging, or even discursively or circumstantially requiring, bolder or radically different governance approaches locally. Alternatively, changes of T1 and T2 may point in the opposite direction and thus create tensions between, or even counteract, each other in their goals and effects on governance choices. The result may then be that "internal," that is, city-regional, scope to modify governance agendas, mechanisms and principles changes very little, AND even stagnate. It thus shows few, if any, signs of developing and adopting novel and imaginative, perhaps "smart," responses to identified challenges in governing city regions. The extent of this scope for city-regions to innovate policies and governance may be expected to vary with the degree of concurrency – or discurrency – of external and internal transition dynamics.

Smart governance involves the innovative, task- and place-specific utilization of existing, conventional state structures and territorialities and the associated powers and responsibilities. In particular, it involves the opportunity to marry flexibility (but also inherent uncertainty of innovativeness in its likely effects) with needed reliability and efficacy offered by territorial and institutional state structures. Connecting and fusing the inherent experimentalism of *agency*, as expressed in new network relations, with the predictability of static *structure*, and doing so in response to place-based applications, is the essence of smart city-regionalism, *a process aided, but not determined, by new digitized technologies*. The actual outcome thus depends on the respective influence of

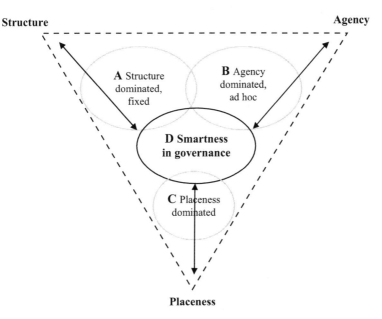

Structure   **Agency**

A = governance scenarios still dominated by structures
B = governance scenarios dominated by actor relations and
    ad hoc networks
C = governance scenarios still dominated by specific local
    factors
D = position in equilibrium between all three factors of
    influence

Figure 4.2 Smart city-regional governance in a power field between structure, agency and placeness.

three factors – structure, agency and placeness – and thus includes variations in the use of clearly defined powers and responsibilities in relation to more *ad hoc* actor relations and networks of power and influence (Figure 4.2)

The outcome may thus be a particular, more or less harmonious, combination of place-specific "tie-ins" between, on the one hand, relationally-defined, opportunistic and imagined spaces of policy-making ambition, and, on the other, established static, state-administrative territorialities and institutionalizations of power and public authority. Examples include emancipating and re-energizing cities and their economic and political-ecological regions, as they build city-centric networks around particular policy goals and thus seek to merge local and regionally scaled interests and opportunities. The inherent selectivity of the relational, network-based way of policy-making and governance has obvious implications for democratic participation and representation of the (state-) territorial heritage. And so a tie-in with established structures of democratic control, legitimacy and participation may well be a precondition for necessary political support by the local electorate for such regional engagement through inter-local collaboration and required compromise.

Dual Transition – Dimension 1: The "big picture" of transition among external parameters: national and international changes in values, agendas and regimes

As discussed above, Dimension 1 of transition involves the effect of *external* structures and processes at the wider international and national level. Such structures may drive, or hinder, the dynamics of regime and agenda change in city-regions. They include the predominant globalization discourse and neoliberal policies, emphasizing borderlessness, openness and competitiveness between places and spaces, with a clear focus on individuality in obtaining success. This push for individuality, through the competitiveness agenda, becomes evident in the growing role of place-specific profiles, such as place marketing, a feature of globalized competitiveness that Swyngedouw (1997b, 2004) calls "glocalization." In addition, over the past 30 years or so, the hegemonic forces of neoliberal globalization, reaching the point of a post-political status "without alternative," have ruled, until recent populist contestations. The end of communism reinforced neoliberal globalization by provoking the notion of a systemic and moral Western political-economic superiority. And that reinforced the impression of a compulsory, all but inevitable, "one-size-fits-all" globalism. Yet, upon closer inspection, there have been different Western approaches to internationality. The EU as political-economic framework offers a different "version" of "Westernism" than North America and, especially, the United States, with much stronger statist traditions that valourize redistributive interventions in economic processes in the interest of maintaining societal and geographic cohesiveness. However, increasingly, this has been undermined by the apostles of free market capitalism and the putative gains it promises for everyone, even if only within rather unspecified time horizons.

Importantly, as recent political developments in Europe and beyond have shown, there is no simple one-directional shift in values and ways of doing things from "there" to "here," as suggested by the binary logic of the word transition. In particular, the process of establishing and deepening liberal democracy, as in Poland for instance, has been notably difficult. Authoritarian aspects of governance may, in fact, be preferred, seemingly offering more certainty, less struggle and less responsibility for people to worry about, especially if the individual rewards of democratic principles and practices are not immediately clear nor manifested in economic improvements. At the city-regional level, that means collaborative action among municipalities may blossom only where individual (i.e. local, institutional, actor-specific) rewards can be identified and clearly attributed to the current regime. If not, collaboration may be in vain and, instead, give way to either self-centred individualism or a more centralized, top-down, *dirigiste* approach by the state, as it seeks to organize city-regional matters by decree in the interest of its own priorities and strategic ambitions.

Past experiences with, and attitudes towards, particular regime practices may further influence the susceptibility to engage in city-regional governance or, rather, merely administer policies determined elsewhere.

As a result, *transitions follow diverse routes* in response to external and/or internal structural heterogeneity of a city-region. It is the particular combination of internal and external changes that produce specific city-regional circumstances which, together with a pre-existing local policy-making milieu, for example, the adoption of an inward-looking localist (individual) versus outward-looking regionalist (collective) perspective, produce place-specific policy solutions and governance structures and practices. For instance, while there may be a general transition to adopting "smartness" as a new phase in governance, including a particular set of narratives, priorities and ways of doing things, their local/regional manifestations and applications may vary considerably between adopting such narratives wholesale as "without alternative," as associated with the so-called rise of city-regionalism (e.g. Jonas, 2013), or just seeking to resist such change, opting instead to continue as before.

The inherent dynamics of both dimensions, in their interdependence, mean that the whole system of dual transition is in constant flux. This makes it difficult to capture its characteristics, directions and destinations. As globalization and technological changes continuously redefine societal-economic parameters, values and political agendas, they, in turn, set the scene for the adoption of flexible responses through innovative policies which draw on past experiences. Additionally, responses may seek to reconcile structure and agency across spatial and institutional divisions. Importantly, as suggested in previous chapters, such broad changes include *a general shift from post-Fordist, neoliberal paradigms,* to "beyond post-Fordism" (Scott, 2011). Alternatively, they refer to climate change which demands changes to the ways we conduct our economies and daily lives and frame relevant policies across all scales. What they share, is an underlying change in values and discourse which, in turn, circumscribe the nature and range of arguments that policy-makers may employ to justify and support their choices. Here, economic structures may matter, such as a sense of participation versus exclusion; success versus vulnerability through weak performance; or domination by few large, international corporations, versus a more balanced, regionally-based, small business structure more embedded and interested in the locality of a region. Particularly, when policy decisions are more contentious and/or contested, references to external pressures of wider changes and decisions made elsewhere, can serve as an excuse for mistakes and, hence, reduce the heat from local/regional policy-makers. The simplistic arguments brought forward by populist politicians during the Brexit campaign in 2016, or the presidential campaign by Donald Trump, have illustrated this.

The importance of external effects has become starkly evident in transforming societies and economies, as in post-communist Eastern Europe and post-apartheid South Africa. Regime changes here have cut up existing, and established new, patterns in economic opportunities, granting some parts, especially the main urban regions, new and greater opportunities than perhaps available to other, more peripheral (or old industrial), parts of the territory and/or society. Negotiations about the urgency of sustainability vis-à-vis competitiveness (Herrschel, 2013) have been fundamentally affected by these far-reaching socio-political and quite broad transitions and the rifts they have produced elsewhere. In the United States, and in different parts of Europe, such as between East and West, or North and South, such discussions have become leading debates over the past 30 or so years, albeit with differing degrees of emphasis and enthusiasm. This reflects variations in dominant societal values and discourses about neo-liberalism versus the social market economy.

The outcome of the dual transition process, here the governance concept of *smart city-regionalism*, is thus understood as opening up, and pressing for, important new ideas about democratic legitimacy and political inclusion in the consideration of interests and concerns. This may involve reaching across social, economic, sectoral and geographic divisions and differences. Yet in order to do so more effectively, context matters as supporter or inhibitor of such developments. Public discourse, for instance, may encourage or discourage policy-makers to stick out their necks when it comes to innovative policies. This may include private views by citizens, institutional assessments, or corporate or political interests and their expressions. Likewise, state policies and statutory/structural provisions may either enhance or inhibit moves towards new, more innovative and enterprising policy approaches. This may be either owing to insufficient power, or political reward systems which are tilted against such attempts (Hauswirth, Herrschel, & Newman, 2004). In addition, direct central interventions can impose new approaches from "above," as in France with the creation of metropolitan regions (Hoffmann-Martinot & Sellers, 2013).

Kuzio (2001) also recognizes the complexity of transitions, as they consist of several concurrent processes with varying degrees of congruence, each with particular dynamics. He thus develops the concept of "quadruple transition," which refers to the political, economic, societal and state/nation (identity)-based factors in shaping transition processes, be they open-ended or more focused on a particular outcome as part of a wider trend. Structure matters, yet so do dynamic factors, such as actor-specific and wider societal experiences, concerns and values, as well as political relationships and internal dynamics of parties, society, public administration.

Relationships between context and processes of change in socio-technical regimes affect the ways in which actors, institutions and networks behave in response to policy challenges, whether within or outside a particular locale, such as a city-region. In particular, they react to differences in the degree of coordination effecting such change, and identify four different contexts for regime change: (1) "purposive transitions" (change effected by outside actors), (2) "endogenous renewal" (change initiated by regime members themselves), (3) "re-orientation of trajectories" (ad hoc modifications to established modi operandi in response to changing relationships and dynamics within a regime) and (4) "emergent transformations" as the unintended consequence of changes initiated by outside regimes and arrangements.

External factors are recognized as potentially important, albeit not predominant, drivers of regime change with two dominant factors identified. The first factor distinguishes primarily between intended and unintended ("imposed") regime changes, which, in turn may be planned and initiated by the regime (its agents) itself, or, alternatively, by a set of actors *within* the regime using established relations and networks. The second factor concerns the availability of required fiscal and executive resources to effect and direct regime transition. These may be readily available either within the existing regime, or outside the regime with limitations to access. The *locus* of the resources determines the ease of their access and availability and thus likely vulnerability to external factors/interests.

Dual Transition – Dimension 2: "Internal transition". City-regionalism and factors of smartness in city-regional governance

Internal arrangements of city-regions vary, be that on grounds of the number of localities involved or the size of any negotiation "team" and variety of voices involved. Then, there is the internal hierarchy between places, being either organized around a dominant city or metropolis (monocentric), or several competing cities, such as in polycentric arrangements (Herrschel & Newman, 2002; Krätke, 2001). In either case, local traditions, competitive thinking and notions of local pride, all play a role in the willingness to collaborate. As shown in Table 4.1, several variables have been used to establish the societal-political and economic milieu in a city region, including the preferred agenda, methods of political implementation, the type of policies and range of actors involved and the detailed operational empirics. Viewed together, they allow the establishment of not just spatial variations, but also those based on values and paradigms. These are identified and evaluated with regards to their manifestation of the three main overarching political-economic models that impact on the scope to adopt and shape smart governance in city regions: equitability, state *dirigisme* or competitiveness. They are reflected in the ways in which the main indicators used express themselves: nature of politics, types of actors or goals pursued.

Keeping a fine balance between local particularities and collective opportunity is usually translated back into particular local advantages and benefits from such collective action. "Smartness" here is taken as a rationale and modus operandi effecting, and responding to, such *internal city-regional* structures as well as interests, as they form around the local-regional nexus, seeking to strike a balance that suits individual local interests in such a city-regional collectivity. This may push for exploring new forms and targets of engagements and thus a transition in governance in purpose and/or modus operandi to a different way of doing things. This involves adopting a more regional, rather than narrowly local, perspective when assessing policy-making needs and likely outcomes. Concern is with reconciling seeming contradictions between established growth agendas and a rising concern with a broader range of qualitative parameters, for instance, such as societal and territorial cohesion in "quality of life." Once again, since emerging as a planning concept in North America during the mid-1990s to tackle urban sprawl (Dierwechter, 2008), as discussed earlier in Chapter 1, the smartness concept has steadily morphed to capture more reflective and innovative way of doing things, well beyond planning, land-use and transportation approaches (Caragliu, Del Bo, & Nijkamp, 2011).

Having concentrated initially on the morphology of urban space and its functioning as a way of creating a new urbanity, "smart" cities now typically incorporate wider concerns with economic competitiveness, ecological sustainability, energy budgets, improved administrative efficacy, data integration and coordination, technology, citizen empowerment, and, ultimately, a more agile, "intelligent," efficient, and problem-oriented culture of territorial (e)governance. Yet, what they all share is a focus on improving efficiency in achieving set objectives, thinking in new ways and trying to depart from/set paths of past development to reach new goals, which all requires looking for more information to obtain task-specific answers. Smartness thus has become a by-word for a more holistic, yet also more complex, multi-layered and critically reflective policy-making perspective that recognizes, and seeks to address, the multiplicity and, at times conflictual, nature of the political task to reconcile multiple goals and turn them into "do-able" policies through "intelligent decision-making and efficient political dynamics within and between cities and city regions" (Shahrokni & Brandt, 2013, p. 117). Yet, the context varies considerably, being more encouraging, or less, drawing on pressures to act (or be seen to act) on behalf of different incentives or disincentives. These are subject to changes, such as through new discourses, political agendas and economic shifts.

Building on Chapters 2 and 3, the following sections now look at the second main transition, that is, *within* city regions. These sections sketch out external scenarios as a framework for regime transition processes and their impact on the ways in which city-regional governance manifests itself.

Transition as political-economic and societal regime change: from state *dirigisme* to liberalized market democracy in Eastern Europe

The phenomenon of regime collapse and subsequent transition to a different mode of organizing state power, society and socio-economic relations and structures has attracted considerable attention in the context of former communist Europe (Altvater, 1993; Gowan, 1995), especially because of its unprecedented scale which meant a de facto end to the Cold War. It also created a sense of superiority among Western countries that liberal market democracy was the now "only show in town" – not by force, but simply as a matter of choice. Yet, while "structure" remained an important consideration in explaining the cause of regime change, such as economic (under)performance, absence of markets and thus consumption as incentives to innovate, and a de facto fossilization of the status quo, arguments also revolved around the nature of change, as an important factor in shaping the outcome. It mattered, so the argument held, whether the process would be ad hoc and complete (Sachs, 1993; Sachs & Lipton, 1990), very much in the mold of "shock therapy" (Popov, 2007), or more gradual like "transformational recession" (Kornai, 1993, 1994) or "rebuilding the boat in the open sea" (Elster, Offe, & Preuss, 1997).

As evident from this, much of the focus was on the economic dimension of change, that is, the shift from state *dirigisme* to a dominance of market forces. In other words, it was a shift from "big state" to "small state." In particular, the redistributive role of the state, locating economic activity on the basis of utilizing productive capacity also outside the – from a competitiveness perspective – less attractive areas. Overruling market rationale for the sake of political expedience meant lost productivity, innovativeness and thus wealth creation. On the other hand, it produced a social-economic system with smaller differences and "gaps" between the urban centres and the more rural (and small town) periphery. The far-reaching abandonment of that striving for cohesion in favour of more competitiveness under the impression of globalization is now producing political tensions that challenge existing narratives and presumed certainties about democratic representation and the advantages of Western liberal democracy. Structures thus clearly matter, as also evidenced by the Arab Spring of 2011/12, where the limits of agency like the "Facebook revolution" vis-à-vis established patterns of societal and economic arrangement became evident in the face of varying distributions of power.

Referring to extant changes in former communist Eastern and Central Europe since 1989, Bunce (2010) points to the variations in democratic transitions there and also other parts of the world and the much less clear outcome in terms of democratization and liberalization than many had presumed, until quite recently. This, she argues, ought to also be seen in light of the expectations around the Arab Spring which, again, were frequently – and immediately – understood in the West as a sign of the inevitability of democratization (Huntington, 1991; Carothers, 2002). And prior to that, enabling a "natural" development towards democratization once a dictatorship had been removed, served to justify intervention in the second half of the 2000s in relation to Iraq. She differentiates between external (international) and internal (domestic) factors that may be held responsible for the differences in adopting democracy – both in terms of quality and timing it took to emerge, and thus nature and dynamic of transitional processes and pressures of change resulting from those. Transition is thus viewed as a time- and place-specific combination of domestic, that is, local (intra-city-regional) factors/determinants, including histories, historic experiences and political cultures (comprising experience with city region building, established institutional structures and qualities), as well as people's engagement and attitudes towards city-regional cooperation, and external factors. Such include proximity to Western states and the EU as ideational and political reference point for intended "adjustment." Attempts at qualifying to join the EU serve as "conditioning factor." The outcome is a variety of transitions, and applied to democratization, they stretch from authoritarianism, at one end of the scale, to liberal democracy, at the other, with a range of hybrid arrangements in between.

So, once again, transition is not a clearly prescribed, linear shift from one regime to another, but may lead to a wide range of mediated regimes combining elements of competing scenarios into individual, place and time-specific "versions" of a – here democratic – regime. And this will then have implications for the emergence of governance arrangements during that process of change. For instance, the existing degree of centralization will shape the scope for local governments to act on their own behalf, including building co-operative regions, and will also shape the likelihood of sufficient political resolve to pursue more autonomous city-regional politics, and thus an acceptance of regions as actors (Herrschel & Tallberg, 2011). As a result, policy solutions are likely to vary considerably, and with them any notions and practicalities of "smartness" as a value system or political goal. Referring to the regime changes after the end of communism, Bunce (2010, p. 38), however, rejects any notions of structuralist ideas of path-dependency and, instead, argues that, "The problem here, however, is that the variations in post-communist political trajectories are *not* predicted by the age of the state." Instead, the time a regime has had to establish itself, and a combination of factors inside and outside a regime's territory, need to be considered. There cannot be a "one-size-fits-all," one-directional inevitability with no alternative, as was implied by discussions in the United States about the Iraq from 2002 to 2009, resulting from the end of the bipolar world in 1991. This means that the outcome of transition is far from certain when it comes to democratization. Current support for populism and propagation of less liberalism in Europe and North America, illustrates that. Indeed, as we can currently observe in Poland, Hungary, Russia or Turkey – and perhaps even the United States – democratization may also be reversed or, at least, severely corroded. Nofosi (2005) speaks even of a "reverse wave" of democratization as a form of backlash.

In any case, context changes and is likely to produce its own momentum for city-regional governance in its focus, manifestation and operation, resulting in different ideas that may be competing on the basis of local and national dynamics in regulation. These variations question the dominance of a singular transition paradigm, such as liberal (Western) democracy or, at the city-regional level, sustainability or, indeed, smartness. Smartness under such circumstances may now involve taking into consideration not just different paths of transition, but also outcomes with a degree of unpredictability. This limits, of course, the scope to "sell" a political agenda, or copy policy-making and policies across places, as so conveniently suggested by notions of good practice and policy transfer on the back of shifting discourses and agendas. And, with democracy having largely been considered a "natural" process of political development, so evidently popularized by Fukuyama's "end of history" thesis, the collapse of the communist regimes across Eastern Europe raised many new questions about the likely nature, forms, processes, variations and mechanisms of transitions, and whether there was an inherent tendency to catch up with the West

(Kolodko 2001). Important have been both a sense of missing out and being left behind from global, especially economic, developments and associated envisaged higher standards of living. Important, too was a growing frustration with the great inefficiencies of a highly bureaucratic state-centric regime dispensing a one directional, top-down flow of governing orders, which stifled, indeed inhibited, individual entrepreneurialism and initiative, and, instead, turned collectivism and adherence to official political doctrine into the primary *raison d'état.*

By the end of communism, a distrust of state regulation and bureaucracy was deeply entrenched, affecting the ways in which new structures could emerge, find acceptance and thus manage to gain efficacy. Following the long-time "anti-model" of Western market economy, for many the United States seemed the way to go, made attractive as the place where previously unfulfilled wishes and aspirations would seem achievable. Indeed, the anti-model of market forces and low levels of state regulation embodied the antidote to the communist regime, with its total control of personal lives. The more the market ruled the greater the distance from communism.

Central European countries chose different paths of adopting Western liberal market-democratic principles, sometimes meandering between more or less state control of the economy and, as evident recently, varying degrees of authoritarian input in governing. Thus, for instance, in Poland and the Baltic States, but also former East Germany, neoliberal ideology was widely adopted, favouring market-driven development over state regulation in local and regional development. Yet, as recent developments suggest, the sharp difference between "winners" and "losers" in society from economic change, especially between the urban centres and the more rural peripheries, has created a political backlash in the form of support for rightist, even authoritarian, and certainly reactionary, populism. Such divisions were not entirely new as such, because the communist system also knew differences in the allocation of investment and consumer product allocation by the state authorities; most of the resources went to the capital city as "shop window" of the respective nation state's political-economic development.

In East Berlin, for instance, in the late 1970s, the East German regime wanted streets to look more "Western" by populating them with a greater number of Western cars, so that they ordered 10,000 VW Golf cars as part of a trade deal between East and West Germany. These cars were only available to East Berlin residents, many linked to the state administration. Such preferential treatment of the capital city, followed by the next tier of regional cities, created resentment among the rest of the population outside these centres, where consumer goods and public investment were much more difficult to obtain – if at all. This resentment has lingered, making collaborations between cities and surrounding hinterlands more difficult, as both the cases, Berlin and Prague, in Chapter 6 aptly illustrate. New municipal rights in the wake of democratization produced a new sense of empowerment at the local level and thus attempts at taking a stand against the (still) dominant cities by the more rural municipalities.

This also became evident in the re-organization of the former communist states, where the regional level was at first largely resented as the main relay point for distributing national resources and political agendas to the respective subordinate municipalities. In Eastern Germany, for instance, the boundaries of the new formal planning regions were in several instances cut in such a way as to obscure their association with their socialist-era predecessors (Herrschel, 2000). Likewise, in several central European states, there were attempts to avoid giving regions place-names that refered to the respective regional capitals and, instead, choose more "egalitarian" names based on geographic landscapes instead, even if little known outside those regions. Role and rationale of the geography of planning regions was thus guided by post-socialist ideological concerns (Elander, 1997), such as municipal equality in administrative powers and responsibilities, rather than the pragmatic necessities of economic development policy and management. So, desirable collaborative action from an administrative rationality point of view was resisted for reasons of emphasizing local governing autonomy. This autonomy was considered a crucial sign of democratization by most concerned, including the international organizations supporting Washington Consensus policies of marketization, liberalization and democratization. After the end of communism, it thus was the local level that gained most attention, as it also promised to be best suited to foster democratic principles and practices (Andrusz, Harloe, & Szelényi, 2011; Herrschel, 2007). Municipalities were strengthened as a sign of moving away from centralist, top-down managerialism to more devolved and decentralized grass-roots decision-making at the local level – understood now as "democracy in practice."

The effects of such localist agendas varied, however, between different states, based on their varying histories in organizing the state, for example, Poland, the Baltic states, the Czech Republic or Slovakia. Nevertheless, the former communist states all have in common a centralized state system that limits the scope for local policy-making and, indeed, has a historic antipathy to regions as more autonomous policy-making entities. Also, only the main cities, especially the capital cities, possessed sufficient political and economic clout, as well as institutional capacity and expertise, to engage in more strategic local policy-making, including at the city-regional level. Interestingly, both Prague and Berlin established strategic development offices in the 1990s. The Berlin-Brandenburg Joint Planning Office (Hauswirth et al., 2003) and the City Development Authority Prague with a Strategic Planning Department (Turba, 2005), respectively, were positioned outside the main administrative hierarchy, enjoying a degree of independence and access to the city leadership. As shown in Chapter 6, both were also seen as efforts to look "beyond" planning-technical perspectives that tend to end at the city limits. Yet, with little enthusiasm for the regional scale of governance after new-found municipal empowerment, governance at that level, therefore, needs to work primarily through informal, collaborative arrangements, using state-defined structures.

Market forces, and the drive for competitive advantage and opportunity, favoured the main urban areas, especially the capital cities with their access to governmental power and decision-making, while largely ignoring the more peripheral, rural parts. This affected, in particular, sparsely populated and structurally weak border regions with little economic appeal. Those areas experienced disinvestment as state-backed enterprises and economic structures were abandoned as no longer competitive on market principles. The only visible investment the more peripheral areas experienced was in the form of warehouse complexes along major transport arteries cutting through the peripheries. Inevitably, growing divisions between successful cities and functionally and structurally dependent surrounding municipalities have grown. Legacies from the previous regime's hierarchical system favouring the main cities in the form of resentment by the smaller municipalities, and newly gained local powers, have created a mix that tends to work for localism and against collaborations.

Among those benefiting less from the transformation process, low participation in elections, voting for radical or single issue parties as an alternative to the "mainstream" governing parties, or voting for former communists, are expressions of discontent and disillusionment (Taras, 2015). But they also reflect an emerging newly defined, often nostalgic (Velikonja, 2009), but also increasingly assertive, "Eastern" identity vis-à-vis the perceived threat of "all-out Westernization" and loss of local characteristics and ways of doing things, including local histories and particularities. It is a concern also voiced now vis-à-vis globalization and "open borders" by newly rising nationalist-populist parties. This trend is quite evident from recent elections in Eastern Germany (regional elections), Hungary or Poland (Bútora et al., 2007), where either former communists or newly-nationalist conservative parties have gained considerable support, especially from outside the main metropolitan areas and among the older generation with memories of the communist years. Such tendencies seem to move towards a more authoritarian, centralized form of governance, such as is currently observed in Hungary and Poland, thus reducing scope for independent local policy-making, including in city regions.

The legacies of the communist period have had an important impact on the subsequent economic and regulatory development of the Central and Eastern European countries. While showing basic similarities in the main features of the planned economic geography created under state socialism, country-specific particularities remained in the form of the implication of communist era practices in governing and administration. The initial simplistic and somewhat naive understanding held in the West was increasingly challenged in the second half of the 1990s, when the fundamental problem of developing a new economic structure became more apparent to now more seasoned policy-makers. This included the realization that market forces *alone* would not bring about effective governance and successful economic development was a precondition for a "feel-good factor" under the new market democratic arrangements. Consequently, as evidenced by more recent developments, alternative self-help solutions emerged in those regions where policy-makers grasped the wider situation and adopted a broader perspective more rapidly than elsewhere. As part of that process, the meaning of "region" has slowly begun to extend beyond the étatiste *planning region*, and obtained a more competitive, marketing-oriented and business-focused dimension, accepting and utilizing the role of networks and relations, rather than structure and hierarchy alone. This may include international engagement and greater visibility beyond state borders (Herrschel & Newman, 2017).

Focusing on networks and shared interests and agendas among actors encouraged the building of new virtual (conceptual) regions of collaborative engagement, based on common policy objectives between localities and actors, rather than fixed, structured arrangements of interconnection. For instance, the need to project an attractive place image and offer business-friendly "responsive" policies has encouraged collaborative governance at the regional level, so as to boost visibility and appeal among external investors. This includes the agreement to develop the region as projection space and platform for new initiatives, rather than viewing it simply as a spatial subdivision of the territorial state and its administration. The case studies illustrate this approach, for example in the promotion of Berlin's Capital City Region, which includes parts of two federal states. The focus is on emphasizing functional spaces based on actual communication and exchange of shared interests, rather than the simple implementation of pre-defined fixed policy objectives handed down the administrative hierarchy and guarded by bureaucracies competing for influence and control.

As a result, varying combinations of the two traditions – planning centred and policy based – have emerged, adding to the complexity and multi-layeredness of territorial governance in "transition countries." The cases provide interesting examples of the interaction between "internal" (local societal) and "external" (national institutional and global economic) factors and their impact on the nature and process of city-regionalization when seeking to address complex agendas, such as economic development and increased sustainability. The external parameters affecting this form of regionalization exercise two types of impact: (1) attracting interest by projecting a clear place image for external consumption by different interest groups, and (2) establishing operational relations and paradigms of potential gains, which are shared among actors and drive coordinated policy-making. In Eastern Europe, the socialist legacy is one important common historic experience, shaping identity, establishing practices and providing societal reference points. The other main factor is the sudden exposure to the forces of globalization in 1990, which quickly unearthed inequalities that had been obscured by state politics and investment decisions across state territory, following political, rather than market, rationales.

Keynesian cohesiveness and neoliberal competitiveness in Western Europe and North America?

Western Europe's transition is marked by two main trends in public and political discourse: economic globalization and the rise of concern with sustainability and climate change. The former is characterized by an ideological as well as practical shift from Keynesian-style regional equalization policy aimed at levelling out inequalities in opportunity and quality of life across state territories and societies, to a much more selective, individualist competitiveness agenda driven by neoliberal rationale. Suggesting a trickledown effect in expected positive development effects from such deregulatory approach was to counteract criticism about likely growth in inequality (Allen et al., 2012). While the intended goal had been to set up a North American-style competitive, entrepreneurial, urban (metropolitan) localism (Hall & Hubbard, 1998), the result has been a de facto abandonment of a traditional direct support to "lagging regions" by individual states and the EU, so as to limit an emerging gap between "winners" and "losers" from an opportunity- and rent-seeking market economy. Role, view and status of cities and city-regions have thus experienced a fundamental re-interpretation and re-presentation: from being mere parts of a region and state territory, to standing out as places and actors in their own right, performing now as nodes (or central places) of relations and connections linking opportunity spaces/places across administrative boundaries and also national borders.

Naturally, these changes have affected the ways in which cities and city-regions seek, but also have been required, to define and implement own policies. The main challenges have been a growing withdrawal of blanket support for regions – and cities as part of those – that was originally put in place to counteract inequalities in economic development – in favour of targeting cities and city-regions, especially those with success, as "beacons" of national competitiveness and success. In Eastern Europe (or Central Europe), the shifts have been even greater. In Western Europe, the growing role of the sustainability debate is often projected as in direct conflict with the modernist "growth" agenda which has predominated in postwar politics up until the present day. This has required learning to do things differently to tailor policies more specifically to individual cities' and city-regions' characteristics to achieve greater policy efficacy – albeit within the changing demands and circumstances set by national and international regulations and political pressures. Finding their particular solutions to the conundrum of competing and conflicting agendas and expectations across policy fields and scales requires "smartness" as understood here in its innovative, experimental and entrepreneurial meaning.

Europe's city-regions are part of a multi-level governance arrangement which stretches from the local to the international. Outside Europe, the international layer of governance, as provided by the institutions of the EU, is largely absent, with merely a few international organizations, especially the United Nations (UN) and World Trade Organization (WTO) and the International Monetary Fund (IMF), framing policies that influence city-regional governance. Thirty years ago, the 1987 Brundtland Report drew attention to the importance of cities in challenging and, eventually helping to address, sustainable development as a global task. A few years later, the 1992 UN Conference on Sustainable Development in Rio de Janeiro explicitly placed *local* government in a leading role to seek and develop partnerships with local stakeholders and communities in working towards local sustainable development. This included efforts to strengthen participatory, democratic processes in governance vis-à-vis conventional political elitist managerialism with emphasis on devolved decision-making to reflect the trans-scalar nature of the challenges and thus the required answers.

One of the policies that came out of this has been Local Agenda 21 which, in the United Kingdom for instance, has translated into a framework for developing "sustainable communities" (Bulkeley & Betsill, 2005, p. 42). In Germany, sustainable urban development featured in a federal competition for good practice in planning and developing the "City of the Future" (BBR, 2004), and also developing "Urban Strategies to Tackle Climate Change." As a result, climate change has become a dominant agenda in, and explicit task of, local governance. Conditions attached to international loans to national governments also circumscribe favoured provisions for city-regional governance. In North America, structural changes have been fewer as compared with Europe, and especially Central Europe. Agenda changes have thus been more important at the policy-making level, working through established structures, rather than creating new ones. Political and policy changes are thus mostly a matter of change in emphasis, public discourse and leading personalities. Nevertheless, the radical change in political discourse emanating from a White House under Donald Trump in relation to the Paris Climate Summit Agreement has triggered strong metropolitan responses of defiance and, instead, continuing to adhere to the Summit-agreed agenda (Boffey, 2017; Comstock, 2017).

Successive European treaties have increased the penetration of European programmes into Europe's cities and regions. Programmes impacting directly on cities and regions include those concerned with transport policy (for example, completing the Trans-European Networks); environment policy (for example, the standardization of approaches to assessing environmental impacts since the Environmental Assessment Directive of 1985); and regional policy supported by a range of funds to support weaker regions. Since the end of the 1990s, an important issue has been the increasing attention to policies that specifically focus on urban, as opposed to wider regional, issues. For Europe's cities and regions, there are important issues of both policy-making and policy change and institutional adaptation to European policy. This dual focus of change has facilitated rescaling of policy-making and institutional innovation, including a shift to the city-regional level, whether formally institutionalized or a more "virtual" form based on collaborative arrangements (see Chapter 3).

The development of European institutions has from the start been a political process and the development of regional policy no less implicated in the machinations of political relationships between member states, while aiming at the sub-national regional scale as primary platform for implementing its structural policies. The primary driver of EU policies has been greater harmonization of living standards and opportunities as a means to enhance greater integration and a sense of "Europeanness." This common objective encouraged a continuous

"Europeanization" of once nationally defined, if EU supported, regional policies. The result has been greater EU control and definition of policy objectives
and eligible projects right down to the local level. Systematic regional intervention started essentially as a supra-national exercise, with little regard to a
state's federal or unitary organization and thus the specific role and position
of regions and municipalities to obtain control of support funding and pursue
their own policies.

The inclusion of poorer countries, starting in 1986, challenged the existing distribution of regional funds on the basis of a much widened inequality.
Member states agreed in the Maastricht Treaty to substantial changes to
European treaties to create a single European market and thus heightened pressure for greater competitiveness through more open borders. At the heart of
this concept was the acknowledgement of the political relevance of dispari-
ties between rich and poor regions and a shared objective that these divisions
should not widen because of closer economic integration and, so, increased
competitive pressures. Quite the contrary, improving prospects in the disadvantaged areas should muster support for the EU and its policies. And regional
policy was an important instrument in pursing these seemingly contradictory
aims. In addition to this new environmental focus, the economic project of the
single market went beyond the conventional territorial approach and acknowledged the growing importance of relationally defined spaces of economic
activity and opportunity: European transport planning and the idea of TENs
(Trans-European Networks), highlighted the relevance of linking together
cities, regions and states through strategic transport investment across Europe.

For cities and regions, location on new strategic road and rail links or, the
absence of such, could have as profound an economic impact as the flow of
regional development funds, although the former has a more locally selective
effect. Not gaining access to the new network would seem to cement peripherality and reduced relevance, setting those localities on a self-reinforcing spiral of
stagnation or decline. Quite evidently, such policies were still in the Keynesian
tradition of public investment (and thus the state) directing markets, including
through "enablement" and "incentivizing" by creating competitive advantages.
And this intention gained efficacy and visibility through a series of initiatives
concerned with spatial planning as a more direct form of centrally-directed
policy-making. Focusing at first, in the early 1990s, on "trend scenarios" of
trans-national super-regional development, such as the Atlantic Arc, as part of
an emerging EU-wide development planning to at first counteract inequalities,
(Herrschel & Newman, 2002), the formalized European Spatial Development
Perspective (ESDP) was to bring in a more implementation-oriented approach.
The term "Perspective," however, signals a rather "soft" approach; it was
chosen to avoid the fear of top-down policy implementation suggested by
the word "Plan," something that could undermine regional self-government,
especially in federal states, as well as notions of national sovereignty. The ESDP
argued for stronger integration of European regions into the global economy
to improve the competitiveness of the European economy and thus quality

of life. At the same time, the ESDP acknowledged inter-regional differences in competitiveness and opportunities, when it identified regions as "global economy integration zones" (Atkinson, 2001).

This reflects the contradiction between favouring cohesion through a broader spatial approach, and competitiveness, focused on *selected* locales, and especially, metropolitan areas. While the ESDP has marked a significant development in European urban and regional policy, funding support to effect policy developments is limited and strictly spatially targeted, with cities and city-regions increasingly at the top of the list of support. In the studies for the Europe 2000 and Europe 2000+ projects, urban Europe came to the fore (see CEC, 1994, 1992). And here, city-regional approaches, based on collaborative arrangements between neighbouring and functionally connected municipalities, gained greater visibility. The shift towards such a more competitively focused approach reflected the growing appeal of neoliberalism vis-à-vis established, post-war Keynesianism (post-war consensus), and was made explicit in the launch of the urban-centric URBAN programme in 1994 with 85 individual programmes focused on infrastructure and measures to tackle high unemployment (Herrschel & Newman, 2002).

As discussed above, national policy-making and governing traditions and political frameworks matter for the extent and speed of changes to governing regimes, such as the respective established roles of the state vis-à-vis capital interests, or, in other words, reliance on statism rather than neoliberalism. Northern and northwestern European cities have developed more experience of dealing with Brussels in the decades of emerging EU regional policies. This has increasingly included collective bargaining and lobbying through networks, such as Eurocities, reaching across national territories and governing systems. Meanwhile, southern European cities have held traditionally a much greater reliance on the national level to filter information, channel funding and allow local interests to become involved. Dependence on often inefficient national administrations, therefore, contrast with the more locally based entrepreneurial attitudes developed in the north, frequently driven by a retreat of the state under the impact of neoliberal ideology. Indeed, leading European cities organized in the Eurocities network, a lobbying organization of self-defined dynamic cities, shared technical knowledge and expertise, and sought to get the European Commission to grant them specific competence in urban as well as regional governance.

The ideal city imagined in Brussels was very much a northern city and one which had shrugged off its industrial past, looking instead to innovativeness, hi-tech and direct engagement on the international and global market (Herrschel & Newman, 2017). Southern cities, more used to relying on the certainties of state agency, may well lack the technical administrative capacities of many northern cities. And so there is varying preparedness for engaging in partnerships with other actors and scales of governance, which go beyond usual experiences. Paradoxically, the leading (city-) regions are regarded as "models" for the less successful and less developed ones to follow as part of "good practice," but that may not necessarily be the most appropriate or, indeed, realistic, path to take. Most of the big cities have by now direct representations in Brussels to lobby for funding (Herrschel & Newman, 2017) and thus seek daily to enhance their international status by undertaking large projects (Swyngedow et al., 2002).

The shift in Western European policies from the regional to urban (and city-regional) scale reflects ever closer linkages between cities and European institutions and a new set of ideas about the dynamic properties of city regions in the European economy. The "Europe of the Regions," which had seemed to represent the future of European economy and institutions at the end of the 1980s and into the 1990s, has been ousted by an image of city-regions as the *real* economic motors and new focus for European policy intervention. Political attention and policy focus has thus shifted away from an egalitarian and integrationist concern with support for lagging areas to avoid their being left behind and the undermining of the envisaged equal quality of life across the EU's territory and so the sense of benefiting from the European Project. Yet, capacity to follow this new approach, and be successful in an economically focused way, varies, and so the likelihood of a "filtering down" of gains made in the successful urban nodes to the "rest." Inequalities are likely to grow, with the most pro-active and innovative and politically apt cities and city-regions able to boost their opportunities and move ahead. This gives a completely new meaning to the Thatcherite mantra of "freeing enterprise."

The North American context for the shaping of city regional governance differs from that in Europe in terms of the role of historic complexity and "depth," the perceived and accepted role of the state, equally, and the role of the business community and the weight of its voice and political relevance in matters of economically relevant policy-making. A multi-level federal arrangement is found in both the United States and Canada, although there are differences in the degree to which – in relation to direct local matters – central government (provinces, states) are permitted to become active locally and intervene in local affairs. Also, the role of ethnicity and its geographic manifestations in the cities as driver of local unevenness differs between the United States and Canada. Canada allows for more direct intervention by the provinces in local matters, as municipalities are creatures of provincial parliaments, allowing city-regions to be created and abolished as seen fit at the time. The Toronto city region of Greater Toronto is one such example (Slack, 2000; Savitch & Vogel, 2009). This is less evident in the United States, where municipalities in most states enjoy so-called home rule, protecting their territorial status through secured fiscal provisions and protection from state intervention (Vanlandingham, 1968). Changes, such as building city-regions, are more likely through bottom-up, collective agreement among local governments.

In the United States, despite a lackluster pursuit of city-regional governance, such discussions go back to the beginning of the last century, when local government reformers were attracted by managerial practices in the business world and the concern with raising efficiency and effectiveness of the administration and provision of services. This normative perspective contrasted with the public choice-based view of competitive localism as a means to improve service delivery efficiency, as advocated by Ostrom et al. (1961), for instance. There, as first suggested in Chapter 2, a more top-down approach was suggested, with a clear emphasis on "governing" which also involved a dedicated metropolitan government, and thus a link between metropolitan governance with regionalism. For instance, Mathewson's (1978) Regionalist Papers, sought to make a collective case for metropolitan regional government. In this collection of a broad range of contributions, Mathewson used the term "metropolitan region" as synonymous with "city-region." Indeed, such metropolitan regions are defined by functional relationships rather than administrative boundaries of responsibilities. The "glue" holding such a metropolitan region together he considered to be a sense of "regional community" as a product of the lived interdependence of urban and suburban interests. Such a regional community, he suggested, draws on shared values, aspirations and a *"regional ethic."* In other words, metropolitan regionalism is understood as comprising a sense of togetherness and interdependency (p. 8). These units should be run on the basis of self-government, a *regional version of "home rule"* (p. 15).

The focus was thus on adding *another* layer of government at the regional level and shift some local responsibilities to that level, while also subordinating local, especially planning, responsibilities to the region-wide strategic objectives formulated by that new governmental level. Yet, such a move, in most places, faced considerable resistance, as it involved re-structuring the territoriality of existing governments through either merging existing units or inserting an additional tier of metropolitan-wide (regional) government, directly challenging the notion of municipal self-government (home rule). On those grounds, in the United States local public involvement and support is required whenever municipalities are to be merged or otherwise modified in their territoriality and capacity. This makes attempts at re-organization – whether through horizontal merger, or additional vertical layers at the regional level – inherently more difficult and political than in Canada, for instance. Removing a locality from existence through merger affects its very existence as an entity and thus goes to the foundations of the notion of localism as an expression of the historic right of self-governing autonomy. Informal, network-based and self-organizing principles of "scaling up" local government to the city-regional level have thus become the more "acceptable face" of metropolitan regionalization, as it is perceived as less interventionist, less permanent and not imposed but instead locally "owned." The view is of a pragmatic, workable and, ultimately, effective compromise between the need for acting "bigger," yet remaining locally rooted and controlled (Savitch & Adhikari, 2017).

And it is under such conditions that a regional agenda is, on the one hand, needed to retain an overall cohesion of developments to avoid counterproductive localist non-cooperation, such as a competitive race to the bottom in taxation in the pursuit of securing politically useful "successes" in securing the location of new businesses. There are variations in the application and "severity" of home rule principles. Thus, in the Pacific Northwest, for instance, compared with other parts of the United States, for example the South East, there is a stronger sense of shared responsibility for maintaining the natural resources as a key ingredient of a generally much valued quality of outdoor life, which, in turn, provides a crucial factor in promoting economic development, especially at the high end innovation-centred sector. Yet, different perspectives and priorities exist among cities and city regions as to the utility of Nature as an economic resource versus its value as key contributor to quality of life and "amenity" (Dierwechter, 2008; Seltzer, 2004). What North American cities share, however, is a distinct sense of local enterprise and entrepreneurialism, with local business playing an important role in local politics and policy-making, again as discussed initially in Chapter 2. Unlike in Europe, the state has historically been an extensive safety net provider for municipalities, generating a distinct need and preparedness to adopt entrepreneurial policies to boost a locality's standing. Yet, as in Western Europe, there is no hard and fast rule, and local leadership may make a big difference. The much-reported success of Barcelona in preparing for the Olympics and developing a new sense of urbanity and urban action (Garcia-Ramon & Albet, 2000), illustrates that entrepreneurialism, "smartness" and southern-ness may well go together.

Transitions in South Africa: managerial city-regionalism under disintegrating neo-mercantilist conditions?

Finally, we note that the post-apartheid transition in the geopolitical economy of South Africa provides a complement to the other world-regional cases in North America and Eastern Europe. In particular, the nature of the South African state cannot be reduced to the hypothesized "post-colonial" problems of many other African states, particularly in terms of bureaucratic-administrative incapacity to govern, although these problems cannot be ignored either. Moreover, while South Africa still strives to replicate liberal democratic values that arguably bind it to (originally) "Western" norms and principles of state–society relations, notably regarding constitutional-legal rights, South Africa also shares (with many Asian societies) a parallel set of organizational expectations that characterize neo-mercantilist debates about the so-called Developmental State. South Africa is, therefore, concomitantly of/in Africa, peculiarly Western-liberal and also "developmentalist," yet at the same time none of these exactly, at least not in toto. Steven Robins (2005) provides a particularly compelling summary:

> While the South African state is, by African standards, a massive and well-resourced apparatus, its capacity to govern and meet the social, economic, health and housing needs of citizens is severely compromised and limited. [...] The South African state, it would seem, is caught between its contradictory and ambivalent desire to extend its reach and delivery development ... and the neoliberal imperatives of the downsizing,

rightsizing and outsourcing state. [...] It is not a classic neoliberal state and neither is it a textbook modernist social democracy or socialist state. Instead its policies appear to be the product of perpetual improvisation and pragmatic maneuvers.

(pp. 10–11)

There is a sense, in other words, of something we call here neo-mercantilist improvization, particularly in regard to the recent elevation of key city-regions like Cape Town and Johannesburg as crucial scalar platforms for economic development and social transformation in a now demonstrably unsustainable world order. Here we mean not only that national authorities are indeed trying, albeit pragmatically and often inconsistently and unevenly, to affect the "competitive advantages" of city-regional territories, as Roberto Campagni (2002) might put it, but to help improve the socio-cultural functionality and ecological sustainability of these same spaces too. Again, smartness has emerged as a key governing discourse through which such a critical territorial project might move forwards, at least in theory.

Context and caveats, however, are important. Concerns with "dysfunctional" and "corrupt" central state practices – that is, with the otherwise common post-colonial pathologies of African state (dis)formation, political (dis)order and institutional decay (Fukuyama, 2013) – have been growing much louder since the ousting of Thabo Mbeki by Jacob Zuma (Russell, 2009). One of contemporary South Africa's most strident critics, R. W. Johnson (2015), ultimately questions how long the country as presently configured territorially can "survive." He draws attention especially to high-level corruption among the ANC (African National Congress) elite, to the ascendance of a rent-seeking kleptocracy, as well as fiscal mismanagement, patron–client tribalism and (relatively) insufficient state capacity and technical expertise given extant challenges and aspirations. Forty years ago, Johnson (1977) asked the same question of apartheid South Africa in the late 1970s. Apartheid collapsed; South Africa did not. While open civil war (and territorial disintegration) could well have occurred throughout the 1980s and early 1990s, particularly in/from Kwazulu-Natal, less alarmist readings since 1994 tend to emphasize South Africa's otherwise common "middle-income" problems, notably the extreme contrasts in wealth produced by the still strong path-dependencies of a once primary sector resource-extractive economy (Butler, 2005). Like other such economies around the world (e.g. Brazil), the South African economy grew robustly in the 1950s and 1960s, averaging between 4 and 6 per cent per annum. But as first discussed in Chapter 2, the post-OPEC crisis of the mid-1970s sharply impacted economic growth dynamics in South Africa. The subsequent fiscal crisis of the now heavily "militarized" apartheid state, the anti-apartheid movement and, ultimately, the global divestment campaign further depressed growth rates throughout the 1980s – to around only 1.5 per cent per annum through the end of the apartheid system. More fundamentally, and from a more radical perspective, apartheid collapsed under a number of contradictory pressures engendered mainly by an accumulation strategy that depended on cheap, expendable African labour and capital-intensive industrialization (Marais, 1998, p. 37).

Post-apartheid South Africa's main problem, then, has been "jobless growth" (Banerjee et al., 2008). While the economy finally picked up again in the early 2000s, large-scale structural unemployment has remained stubbornly at between 25 and 40 per cent, depending on the exact definition of unemployment used. Thus, the obvious importance of the country's key city-regions to the overall national project, even the "survival" of South Africa as presently conceived, if Johnson's critique is accurate. As we shall show in Chapter 6, for example, the province of Johannesburg-Gauteng alone generates about one-third of South African GDP, and 40 per cent of value added (New York, by contrast, produces 8 per cent of US GDP). The profound irony of the project is that the strategic elevation of city-regions by central authorities may paradoxically accelerate new "post-Westphalian" forms of what Sheering and Wood (2005) call "nodal governance" and "denizenship." Deploying the classical theme of "security" services associated with the state, they argue that:

> We have, for or the past several decades, been living in an age where the empirical regularities that we took for granted have changed radically. Today, as studies of the governance of security are making clear, the relationship between nodes of governance is considerably varied [...] People now live within a world full of crisscrossing memberships that operate across and through multiple and layered governmental domains.
>
> (pp. 100–101)

Still another paradox is that while the hypothesized "rise of city-regions" (Scott, 2001) may eventually undermine the traditional Westphalian model of the territorially and culturally hegemonic liberal nation-state, the expansion in, for example, the nodal governance of security within city-regions like Johannesburg is leading to a "defensive urbanism" characterized by "spatial partitioning" and a "fortification aesthetic" (Murray, 2011). "Johannesburg is a city," Murray specifically notes, "... scattered over vast distances, surrounded by protective barriers, buffered by vacant dead space, and connected by high-speed freeways" (p. 213). Smart efforts to overcome such "partitioning" through improved urban spatial policy integration, as Behrens and Wilkinson (2003) have shown specifically for housing and urban passenger transport, are profoundly challenging, and certainly not amenable to simplistic policy transfers from elsewhere. South Africa is interesting and worth studying in comparative perspective, in consequence, because its main city-regions are managed and shaped within a neo-mercantilist framework dealing simultaneously with deep race and class cleavages, path-dependent economic inefficiencies and insufficient, but also quite ambitious, state capacity. In addition, mounting concerns with kleptocratic pathologies (Rotberg, 2004) cannot be waved away either.

Reflecting again upon our opening themes here, we thus theorize South African city-regionalism mainly through a "managerial" rather than neoliberal or equity lens per se – notwithstanding the importance of both these latter discourses. This book attempts to show later on that the "external" transition in South Africa to neo-mercantalist improvization – that is, neither "neoliberal" nor "social democratic" – has shaped, in turn, an "internal" transition within city-regions like Cape Town and Johannesburg. The overarching search for "smartness" implies a place-based institutional and political capacity to reconcile competing demands and interests; this, in turn, entails ongoing debate, productive deliberation, social learning and careful negotiation in the search for appropriate structures and policies for regional development. Smartness promises to overcome socio-spatial fragmentation, civic disengagement and the concomitant goals of competitiveness, sustainability and cohesion. This, too, is theoretically producing new spaces of regulation and nascent modes of governance and institutional experimentation, however inchoate, improvized and likely reversible. In city-regions like Cape Town, what we see in this book as examples of smartness – such as the Knowledge Transfer Program – concretely reject the "best practices" argument that "singular, inflexible, non-context specific, universally applicable and accepted practice can lead to policy change" in favour of what Patel et al. (2015, p. 201) have called a more creative search for "fine practices," which explicitly foreground "adopting modes of work that are contextually grounded, as well as sectorally and organisationally specific."

Mapping smart *transitions* in city-regionalism: the empirical cases going forward

As we move forward in the coming chapters with our detailed empirical invitations of smartness and transition, it is perhaps helpful here to summarize the overall narrative we shall present by synthesizing visually the above conceptual tools, themes and core claims. This is done in Figure 4.3 below, which applies the same basic heuristic framework deployed in Figure 4.1, but now adds the various *"smart transitions"* in city-regionalism that we aim to tease out in Chapters 5 and 6 – and indeed that make up the overall title and subject of this book.

Specifically, the four quadrants illustrate the relative "positions" of our eight city-regions as they show different engagements with, and acceptance of, various elements of "smartness" in their approaches to their multi-scalar governance. Nonetheless, it needs to be emphasized at the outset that – as a heuristic device only – such positions, or "mappings", are simply symbolic; they are deployed in the coming chapters to assist our interpretations of smartness in the empirical context of the contested and inchoate production of economic and political city-regionalism around the world. In this sense, Figure 4.3 is not derived directly from, for instance, rigid quantitative assessments, "ranking"

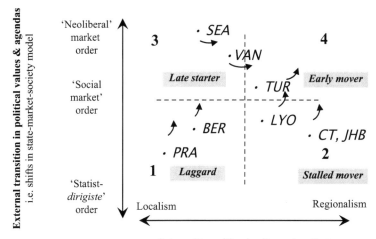

External transition in political values & agendas
i.e. shifts in state-market-society model

'Neoliberal' market order

'Social market' order

'Statist-*dirigiste*' order

Internal transition in city-regionalism
Propensity for policy innovation and collaborative action
based on internal political-economic milieux

1 = ***statist/localist****, non-collaborative, hierarchical, dependent, defensive*

2 = ***statist/regionalist****, collaborative through state-incentives/intervention, also reaching across scales*

3 = ***neo-liberal competitive/localist*** *(metropolitan elitist), self-centred ('independent-minded'), feeling 'held back' by struggling neighbouring localities, or seeking support by 'clinging on' successful*

4 = ***neo-liberal-competitive/regionalist****, opportunistic-collaborative at different scales, internationlist in networking, 'elitist' metropolitanist, confident*

Figure 4.3 Transitions toward "smartness" in existing city-regionalism.

exercising or index-statistical benchmarking – all of which are increasingly popular techniques in both smart city and global city discourses (e.g. IESE Business School, 2016).

We have provocatively suggested a normative "zone" for "ideal smartness" as *both more effectively "regionalist" and strongly "social-democratic" in nature* – as discussed earlier in this chapter and in later chapters too. That said, our actually-existing evaluations of smartness are based on reviews of political and policy debates over the last few decades in those localities and regions. In addition to interviews with key stakeholders, we have analyzed meta-themes, formal statements and specific project initiatives. Furthermore, the analysis engaged critically with policy documents and Web-based discourses. The objective, here, is to provide a sense of the attitudes to regional engagement and policy-making as they shape moves towards adopting smart principles. Important to our discussion, then, are the general directions of transitions, including starting points and likely destinations, albeit all within the power fields defined by external and internal circumstances. And again, as also earlier discussed in this chapter, these dynamics are shaped by place-specific combinations of internal and external factors that "push" or "pull" policy-makers in key directions. There is no common starting point, nor a uniform outcome, just the synoptic claim that these variables exert pressures and eventually lead to policy responses in scale and agenda over time. Within this context, we see four broad categories within the wider context of our theory of a dual transition in the external and internal dynamics of city-regions. In the first quadrant, illustrated in this book by the cases of Prague and Berlin, we see *"laggards."* Here the propensity for policy innovation and city-regionalist collaborative action – that is, for "smartness" – is less evident, even though "post-socialist" shifts in state-market society model are obviously important. We suggest specifically that Prague has struggled far more than Berlin to shake off the various legacies of the previous statist order, even as both city-regions, we also claim, are relatively *non-collaborative, hierarchical, dependent and defensive.* In quadrant 2, we contend that transitions to city-regionalism are more advanced in both Cape Town and Johannesburg, but are today also *"stalled"*, in part because their (socio-spatial and institutional) shift away from the manifold of legacies of apartheid are not sufficiently supported by a smart "external" transition as the central state apparatus increasingly shows signs of patrimonial rent-seeking and abject corruption. Reflecting stronger traditions of social-market political economies, both the cities of Turin and (especially) Lyon are structurally closer to the normative smart zone we discussed earlier. Both show evidence, for example, of policy innovation and collaborative action – of local agency – across local borders and scales of governance. Yet smart city-regionalism in Lyon reflects French traditions of state-incentives/intervention, whereas Turin has been an *"early mover."* We also see the Canadian city-region of Vancouver, British Columbia as an "early mover," with relatively advanced discourses and practices of regional collaborations but also, like nearby Seattle, Washington, in the United States, shaped more significantly by North American-style neo-liberalism. Unlike Vancouver, however, we show that Seattle's efforts are more recent, thus a *"late starter,"* even as its high-technology economy produces smart city innovations.

Conclusions

The notion of "smartness" has become somewhat of a catch-all label in public policy, even though the actual added value of "smart" as adjective is not always clear at all when it comes to city-regional governance. The primary reason is the growing complexity of city-regionalism and its governance as conventional ways of governing – through fixed institutional structures, lines of representation and accountability, and sources of power, just as much as a reliance on the caring state – no longer seem to be able to produce effective answers to the challenges and changes triggered by globalization.

Both discourse and practice are going through a dual transition as intersection of, firstly, wider political-economic regime change, and, secondly, place-specific changes to values and modi operandi of defining and making "smart" policies. Differences in the wider context, marked as Transition 1, set the framework for the development of an in-principle acceptance of city-regionalism as a desirable governance level in public and political discussions. They set the external "stage" for the formation of an internal place-specific milieu, for accepting the utility of such arrangements and thus the general direction of, and emphasis in, city-regional development per se. Changes in the internal approach in city-regions to their own governance, labelled here as Transition 2, shape the local political milieu and thus local readiness to adopt principles and practices of "smartness," as described above, in policy-making. Changes in technology, and a sheer awareness of challenges and opportunities, may produce greater or lesser impact on the course of this second transition within city-regions.

The following two chapters investigate the interdependence of the two transitions – extra- and intra-city-regional – of the proposed dual transition in city-regional governance and their determination of the role of "smartness" as discourse and agenda. In particular, the role of a paradigmatic *leitbild*, a leading vision and concept, as found in different national governing traditions, will be explored.

References

Adeney, K., & Wyatt, A. (2004). Democracy in South Asia: Getting beyond the structure-agency dichotomy. *Political Studies, 52*(1), 1–18.

Allen, J., Cochrane, A., Henry, N., Massey, D., & Sarre, P. (2012). *Rethinking the region: Spaces of neoliberalism*. London: Routledge.

Altvater, E. (1993). *The future of the market: An essay on the regulation of money and Nature after the collapse of "actually existing socialism"*. London: Verso.

Anderson, J., & O'Dowd, L. (1999). Borders, border regions and territoriality: Contradictory meanings, changing significance. *Regional Studies, 33*(7), 593–604.

Andrusz, G., Harloe, M., & Szelényi, I. (Eds.) (2011). *Cities after socialism: Urban and regional change and conflict in post-socialist societies*. Chichester, UK: John Wiley & Sons.

Atkinson, R. (2001). The emerging "urban agenda" and the European spatial development perspective: Towards and EU urban policy? *European Planning Studies, 9*(3), 385–406.

Banerjee, A., Galiani, S., Levinsohn, J., McLaren, Z., & Woolard, I. (2008). Why has unemployment risen in the new South Africa? *Economics of Transition, 16*(4), 715–740.

BBR (Ed.) (2004). *Städte der Zukunft, Kompass für den Weg zur Stadt der Zukunft. Sonderveröffentlichung*. Bonn: BBR.

Behrens, R., & Wilkinson, P. (2003). Housing and urban passenger transport policy and planning in South Africa cities: A problematic relationship? In P. Harrison, M. Huchzermeyer, & M. Mayekiso (Eds.), *Confronting fragmentation: Housing and urban development in a democratising society* (pp. 154–174). Cape Town: UCT Press.

Boffey, D. (2017). Mayors of 7,400 cities vow to meet Obama's climate commitments. *The Guardian*, 28 June 2017.

Bulkeley, H., & Betsill, M. (2005). Rethinking sustainable cities: Multilevel governance and the "urban" politics of climate change. *Environmental Politics, 14*(1), 42–63.

Bunce, V. (2010). The regional transition. In V. Bunce, M. McFaul, & K. Stoner-Weiss (Eds.), *Democracy and authoritarianism in the post-communist world* (pp. 30–59). Cambridge: Cambridge University Press.

Butler, A. (2005). *Contemporary South Africa*. New York: Palgrave.

Bútora, M., Gyárfášová, O., Mesežnikov, G., & Skladony, T.W. (2007). *Democracy and populism in Central Europe: The Visegrad elections and their aftermath*. Bratislava: Institute for Public Affairs.

Camagni, R. (2002). On the concept of territorial competitiveness: Sound or misleading? *Urban Studies*, *39*(13), 2395.

Caragliu, A., Del Bo, C., & Nijkamp, P. (2011). Smart cities in Europe. *Journal of Urban Technology*, *18*(2), 65–82.

Carothers, T. (2002). The end of the transition paradigm. *Journal of Democracy*, *13*(1), 5–21.

Case, W. (1996a). Can the "halfway house" stand? Semidemocracy and elite theory in three Southeast Asian countries. *Comparative Politics*, *28*(4), 437–464.

Case, W. (1996b). *Elites and regimes in Malaysia: Revisiting a consociational democracy* (No. 38). Clayton, VIC: Monash University Press.

Collier, D., & Levitsky, S. (1997). Democracy with adjectives: Conceptual innovation in comparative research. *World politics*, *49*(3), 430–451.

Commission of the European Communities (CEC). (1992). *Europe 2000: The development of the Community's territory*. Luxembourg: Office for Official Publications of the European Communities.

Commission of the European Communities (CEC). (1994). *Europe 2000+: Cooperation for European territorial development, Volume 93*. Luxembourg: Office for Official Publications of the European Communities.

Comstock, A. (2017). US cities and states want to implement the Paris Climate Accord goals: It's not that simple. *The Washington Post*, 13 June 2017.

Diamond, L., Fukuyama, F., Horowitz, D. L., & Plattner, M. F. (2014). Reconsidering the transition paradigm. *Journal of Democracy*, *25*(1), 86–100.

Dierwechter, Y. (2008). *Urban growth management and its discontents: Promises, practices and geopolitics in US city-regions*. New York: Palgrave.

Edvardsen, U. (1997). A cultural approach to understanding modes of transition to democracy. *Journal of Theoretical Politics*, *9*(1), 211–234.

Elander, I. (1997). Between centralism and localism: On the development of local self-government in postsocialist Europe. *Environment and Planning C: Government and Policy*, *15*, 143–159.

Elster, J., Offe, C., & Preuss, U. (1997). *Institutional design in postcommunist societies: Rebuilding the ship at sea*. Cambridge: Cambridge University Press.

Fukuyama, F. (1992). *The end of history and the last man*. New York: Free Press.

Fukuyama, F. (2013). *Political order and political decay*. New York: Farrar, Strauss and Giroux.

Garcia-Ramon, M. D., & Albet, A. (2000). Pre-Olympic and post-Olympic Barcelona: A "model" for urban regeneration today? *Environment and Planning A*, *32*(8), 1331–1334.

Giddens, A. (1984). *The constitution of society*. Cambridge: Polity Press.

Gowan, P. (1995). Neoliberal theory and practice for Eastern Europe. *New Left Review*, *213*, 3–60.

Haggard, S., & Kaufman, R. (1995). *The political economy of democratic transitions*. Princeton, NJ: Princeton University Press.

Hall, T., & Hubbard, P. (1998). *The entrepreneurial city: Geographies of politics, regime, and representation*. Chichester, UK: John Wiley & Sons.

Hauswirth, I., Herrschel, T., & Newman, P. (2003). Incentives and disincentives to city-regional cooperation in the Berlin-Brandenburg conurbation. *European Urban and Regional Studies*, *10*(2), 119–134.

Herrschel, T. (2000). Regions and regionalization in the five new *Länder* of eastern Germany. *European Urban and Regional Studies, 7*(1), 63–68.

Herrschel, T. (2005). "Competing regionalisation" through territory and cluster networks: Experiences from post-socialist eastern Germany. *GeoJournal, 62*(1), 59–70.

Herrschel, T. (2007). Regions between imposed structure and internally developed response: Experiences with twin track regionalisation in post-socialist Eastern Germany. *Geoforum, 38*(3), 469–484.

Herrschel, T. (2011). Regional development, peripheralisation and marginalisation and the role of governance. In T. Herrschel and P. Tallberg (Eds.), *The role of regions: Territory, scale, governance* (pp. 85-102). Christianstad: Region Skåne.

Herrschel, T. (2012). Regionalisation and marginalisation: Bridging old and new divisions in regional governance. In M. Danson, & P. de Souza (Eds.), *Peripherality, marginality and border issues in Northern Europe*. Routledge *Regions and Cities* series (pp. 30–48). London: Routledge.

Herrschel, T. (2013). Sustainability *and* competitiveness: Can smart growth square the circle? *Urban Studies, 50*(11), 2332–2348.

Herrschel, T., & Newman, P. (2002). *Governance of Europe's city regions*. London: Routledge.

Herrschel, T., & Newman, P. (2017). *Cities as international actors: Urban and regional governance beyond the nation state*. London: Palgrave.

Herrschel, T., & Tallberg, P. (Eds.) (2011). *The role of regions – networks – scale – territory*. Kristianstad: Region Skåne.

Hoffmann-Martinot, V., & Sellers, J. M. (2013). The emerging metropolitan political ecology of France. In J. Sellers, D. Kübler, R. A. Walks, & M. Walter-Rogg (Eds.), *The political ecology of the metropolis: Metropolitan sources of electoral behaviour in eleven countries* (pp. 161–198). Colchester, UK: ECPR Press.

Huntington, S. (1993). *The third wave: Democratization in the late twentieth century*. Oklahoma: Oklahoma University Press.

IESE Business School. (2016). *Ranking the world's smartest cities*. Retrieved from https://www.forbes.com/sites/iese/2016/07/06/the-worlds-smartest-cities/#5ad9aa3a4ab9, accessed 13 Nov. 2017.

Johnson, R. W. (1977). *How long will South Africa survive?* New York: Oxford University Press.

Johnson, R. W. (2015). *How long will South Africa survive?* London: Hurst & Co.

Jonas, A. E. G. (2013). City-regionalism as a contingent "geopolitics of capitalism". *Geopolitics, 18*(2), 284–298.

Keating, M. (1998). *The new regionalism in Western Europe: Territorial restructuring and political change*. Cheltenham, UK: Edward Elgar.

Kolodko, G. (2001). Globalization and Catching-up: From Recession to Growth in Transition Economies. *Communist and Post-Communist Studies, 34*, 279–322.

Kornai, J. (1993). *The socialist system: The political economy of communism*. Oxford: Clarendon Press.

Kornai, J. (1994). Transformational recession: The main causes. *Journal of Comparative Economics, 19*, 39–63.

Krätke, S. (2001). Strengthening the polycentric urban system in Europe: Conclusions from the ESDP. *European Planning Studies, 9*(1), 105–116.

Kuzio, T. (2001). Transition in post-communist states: Triple or quadruple. *Politics, 21*(3), 168–173.

Lock (1994).

MacLeod, G. (2001). New regionalism reconsidered: Globalization and the remaking of political economic space. *International Journal of Urban and Regional Research, 25*(4), 804–829.

Mahoney, J., & Snyder, R. (1999). Rethinking agency and structure in the study of regime change. *Studies in Comparative International Development, 34*(2), 3–31.

Marais, H. (1998). *South Africa limits to change: The political economy of transition.* Cape Town: University of Cape Town Press.

Mathewson, K. (ed.) (1978). *The regionalist papers, 2nd edn.* Detroit: Metropolitan Fund.

Murray, M. (2011). *City of extremes: The spatial politics of Johannesburg.* Durham, NC: Duke University Press.

Nofosi, I. (2005). A new conceptual framework for political transition: A case-study on Rwanda. In *L'Afrique Des Grands Lacs. Annuaire 2004–2005* (pp. 71–94). Paris: Editions L'Harmattan.

Ostrom, V., Tiebout, C. M., & Warren, R. (1961). The organization of government in metropolitan areas: A theoretical inquiry. *American Political Science Review, 55*(4), 831–842.

Ottaway, M. (2003). *Democracy challenged: The rise of semi-authoritarianism.* Washington, DC: Carnegie Endowment for International Peace.

Patel, Z., Greyling, S., Parnell, S., & Pirie, G. (2015). Co-producing urban knowledge: Experimenting with alternatives to "best practice" for Cape Town, South Africa. *International Development Planning Review, 37*(2), 187–203.

Popov, W. (2007). Shock therapy versus gradualism reconsidered: Lessons from transition economies after 15 years of reforms. *Comparative Economic Studies, 49*(1), (March), 1–31.

Rafti, M. (2007). *A perilous path to democracy: Political transition and authoritarian consolidation in Rwanda.* IOB Discussion Paper 2008-03, Nov. 2007. Institute of Development Policy and Management, University of Antwerp. Available from www.uantwerpen.be/images/uantwerpen/container2143/files/Publications/DP/2008/03-Rafti.pdf, accessed 30 Nov. 2017.

Robins, S. (2005). Introduction. In S. Robins (Ed.), *Limits to liberation after apartheid: Citizenship, governance and culture* (pp. 1–21). Athens: Ohio University Press.

Rotberg, R. (2004). Strengthening African leadership. *Foreign Affairs, 83*(4), (July/August), 14–18.

Russell, A. (2009). *Bring me my machine gun: The battle for the soul of South Africa from Mandela to Zuma.* New York: Public Affairs.

Rustow, D. (1970). Transitions in democracy: Toward a dynamic model. *Comparative Politics, vol. 2.* Here re-printed in L. Anderson (Ed.) (1999). *Transitions to democracy* (pp. 14–41). New York: Columbia University Press.

Sachs, J. (1993). *Poland's jump to the market economy.* Cambridge. MIT Press.

Sachs, J., & Lipton, D. (1990). Poland's economic reform. *Foreign Affairs, 69*(3), 47–66.

Savitch, H., & Adhikari, S. (2017). Fragmented regionalism. *Urban Affairs Review, 53*(2), 381–402. doi:10.1177/1078087416630626

Savitch, H., & Vogel, R. K. (2009). Regionalism and urban politics. *Theories of Urban Politics, 2,* 106–124.

Scott, A. (2001). Globalization and the rise of city regions. *European Planning Studies, 9*(7), 813–826.

Scott, A. (2011). Emerging cities of the third wave. *City, 15*(3–4), 289–321.

Seleny, A. (1994). Constructing the discourse of transformation: Hungary, 1979–82. *East European Politics and Societies, 8*(3), 439–466.

Seltzer, E. (2004). It's not an experiment: Regional planning at Metro, 1990 to the present. In C. Ozawa (Ed.), *The Portland edge: Challenges and successes in growing communities* (pp. 35–60). Washington, DC: Island Press.

Shahrokni, H., & Brandt, N. (2013). *Making sense of smart city sensors.* Paper presented *Urban and Regional Data Management, UDMS Annual 2013.* Proceedings of the Urban Data Management Society Symposium 2013, pp. 117–127, London.

Sheering, C., & Wood, J. (2005). Nodal governance, denizenship and communal space. In S. Robins (Ed.), *Limits to liberation after apartheid: itizenship, governance and culture* (pp. 97–112). Athens, OH: Ohio University Press.

Sinpeng, A. (2007). Democracy from above: Regime transition in the Kingdom of Bhutan. *Journal of Bhutan Studies*, *17*, 21–47. Retrieved from https://core.ac.uk/download/pdf/1323039.pdf, accessed 30 Nov. 2017.

Slack, E. (2000). A preliminary assessment of the new city of Toronto. *Canadian Journal of Regional Science*, *23*(1), 13–30.

Söderbaum, F., & Shaw, T. (2003). *Conclusion: What futures for new regionalism?* Basingstoke: Palgrave Macmillan.

Stark, D., & Bruszt, L. (1998). *Postsocialist pathways: Transforming politics and property in East Central Europe.* Cambridge: Cambridge University Press.

Swyngedouw, E. (1997a). *Excluding the other: The production of scale and scaled politics.* London: Arnold.

Swyngedouw, E. (1997b). Neither global nor local: "Glocalization" and the politics of scale. In K. Cox (Ed.), *Spaces of globalization: Reasserting the power of the local* (pp. 137–166). New York: Guilford Press.

Swyngedouw, E. (2014). *The post-political and its discontents: Spaces of depoliticization, spectres of radical politics.* Edinburgh, UK: Edinburgh University Press.

Swyngedouw, E., Moulaert, F., & Rodriguez, A. (2002). Neoliberal urbanization in Europe: Large-scale urban development projects and the new urban policy. *Antipode*, *34*(3), 542–577.

Szarvas, L. (1993). Transition periods in Hungary: The chances for democracy? *Journal of Theoretical Politics*, *5*(2), 267–276.

Taras, R. C. (2015). *The Road to disillusion: From critical Marxism to post-communism in Eastern Europe.* London: Routledge.

Thompson, M., Ellis, R., & Wildavsky, A. (1990). *Cultural theory.* Boulder, CO: Westview Press.

Turba, M. (2005). The city of Prague: New challenges. *Presentation at METREX – XIX Meeting of the Network, Nürnberg,* June 2005. Available from http://www.eurometrex.org/Docs/Meetings/nurnberg_2005/Presentations/Milan_Turba_Prague.pdf, accessed 13 Nov. 2017.

Vanlandingham, K. E. (1968). Municipal home rule in the United States. *Wm. & Mary Legal Review*, *10*, 269–290.

Velikonja, M. (2009). Lost in transition: Nostalgia for socialism in post-socialist countries. *East European Politics and Societies*, *23*(4), 535–551.

Walsh, C. (2012). Spatial planning and territorial governance: Managing urban development in a rapid growth context. *Urban Research & Practice*, *5*(1), 44–61.

Walsh, C. (2014). Rethinking the spatiality of spatial planning: Methodological territorialism and metageographies. *European Planning Studies*, *22*(2), 306–322.

5 Beyond post-Fordist regimes?

Smart city-regionalism in North America and Western Europe

Introduction

This chapter now focuses on the recent empirical experiences of four city-regions in the long-standing economic "core" of North America and Western Europe, respectively, where state structures and governance practices have been long established but also differ in key respects, notably the degree of federalism and regulatory cultures of state–market relationships. Seattle, Washington and Vancouver, British Columbia serve as leading examples of the North America-specific context for city-regional governance, following a more individualistic, (neo)liberalized ideology than arguably seen in Western Europe. At the same time, they differ in the degrees of "localism" as part of their respective state structures and, especially, state involvement with local matters north and south of the border, as well as the role of business interests in shaping local political agendas. Seattle and Vancouver are, to borrow Norbert MacDonald's (1987) felicitous term, "distant neighbors" – that is, they show distinct similarities, but also equally distinct differences. Meanwhile, Lyon and Turin both exemplify the Western European tradition of urban development and governance, especially the tensions between "welfare" and "workfare" as ideological backdrop, while also differing in their national contexts: that is, a centralized France and a federalized Italy.

Following the book's overall theoretical argument, our empirical discussion throughout this chapter – as well as next in Chapter 6 – highlights the synoptic concept of a "dual transition" to smartness in conceptionalizing and operationalizing city-regional governance. In this chapter, now, we focus especially (though not exclusively) on the external dimension of our concept of dual transition. This centres on a broader societal and ideological search for an "after" (or beyond) post-Fordist regulatory and investment regime at the city-regional level, because it is this fundamental political-economic and societal shift that provides a stark form of transition at the supra-local level, just as the previous era change from Fordism to post-Fordism more than 30 years ago. Most of the debate saw a shift in capitalist societal and economic organization from standardization of production (including social reproduction) and bureaucratized government to more flexible, responsive forms of organization and ways of doing things. It is this broad trend that underpins all four case studies examined here as a common challenge, but also an opportunity. By the same token, the four case studies illustrate variations in their internal circumstances for shaping city-regional governance as the second dimension of our "dual transition" concept (see Chapter 4).

Thus, while these four cases illustrate particular city-regional economic, political and cultural contexts, they show in common the second dimension of the "bigger trends" as external shared parameters. This comparative perspective of difference against a background of important commonality argues strongly for their comparative treatment, so as to highlight variegated but homologous experiences in a new city-regionalism. This adopts elements of virtuality, as it reaches for characteristics conceptualized under the umbrella term of "new regionalism." Attention is given to city-regions situated in a Western, post-industrial/post-Fordist political-economic and societal milieu, setting the scene for a growing requirement to develop innovative efforts at city-regionalism to achieve effective policies and outcomes. This, so the argument here runs, requires "smart" practices of governance. The Western examples further illustrate continuing political arguments about scalar governance and the position of city-regions as policy-making and economic entities in their own right, albeit within well established state and societal structures. Bringing together individual agency and collective structures is central to the notion of "smartness."

North American smart(er) city-regionalism: balancing central and local impetus in the Vancouver and Seattle city-regions

The United States and Canada exhibit their own distinctive national "urban systems," even as scholars such as Maurice Yeats (1990) have long emphasized a common set of morphological and socio-economic features of a "North American city," that provides useful contrasts with Asian, European, Latin American, African and, to some extent, Australian cities. How much is similar and how much is different, of course, is a matter of interpretation and research inquiry, and whether comparisons are made *within* North America or *across* major world regions (Walker, 2016).

Superficial commonalities of the "North American" city-region are easy enough to spot: for example, Central Business Districts, edge cities, renewed urban core gentrification, low-density/auto-based suburbanization, declining "inner ring" suburbs, etc. (Burnett, 2014; Filion & Kramer, 2012; Rothblatt, 1994). Like the United States, moreover, Canada has also seen the rise of what Richard Florida (2017) now calls (more darkly) "superstar cities." Canadian cities, however, are less racially and economically segregated and invariably safer – while the regulatory and investment roles of Canadian provinces and federal agencies differ (albeit not radically) from US institutional patterns (Addie, 2013). Nevertheless, as Hackworth (2016) aptly points out, despite "racialization" on both sides of the border, Canada has "no Detroit."

It is similarly compelling to provincialize the spatialities and pathologies of US city-regions for their "remarkable historical-geographical contingency" (Wyly, 2004, p. 738). Here, though, we want to focus our explicitly comparative interests in smartness more narrowly on the "distant neighbours" of Seattle and Vancouver in their city-regional setting (Figure 5.1). This involves making specific empirical references to our overall theory of a dual transition in two different federated structures, with varying emphasis on local autonomy in governance, and degree of local self-government. Both have been shaped by neoliberal globalization and wider concerns with equity and collective interests, such as in the balance between a focus on competitiveness and sustainability, and through *evolving* smartness discourses (Herrschel, 2013). Nevertheless, distance despite proximity remains evident in their varying policies and priorities, not least reflected in the fact it has taken some 20 years for the Washington State Governor and Premier of British Columbia to have shared a stage, on this occasion to announce a new Innovation Corridor to be developed as part of the virtual region of Cascadia between Seattle and Vancouver (Business Council of British Columbia, 2016).

The specific urban comparison here is, we suggest, particularly apt considering the later analysis of Turin and Lyon, where comparable local structures and ambitions intersect with different state structures, political cultures and

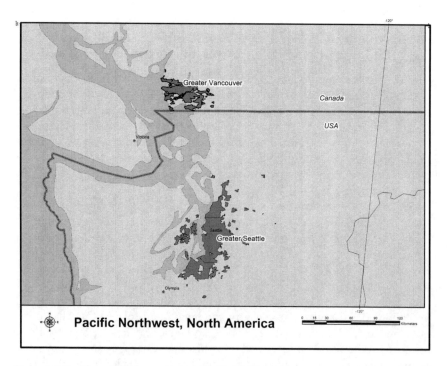

Figure 5.1 Seattle and Vancouver in the Pacific Northwest.

policies. In this instance, now, although similarly embedded within different national polities and state-territorial histories, Seattle and Vancouver share a wider ecological region and, to some extent, natural resource and Pacific Rim orientation in lifestyle, valuing the "great outdoors" and awareness of ecological and climate change challenges. Both city-regions are today touted globally and repeatedly for their putatively innovative and influential urban sustainability policies, high quality of life and, albeit more recently, "superstar" status as two of the most dynamic, desirable (as a place to live and work) and, indeed, "smart" economic engines within a shared North American urban system that arguably has been further integrated since the mid-1990s by the North American Free Trade Agreement (NAFTA) (Studer-Noguez et al., 2007).

Moreover, while Canadian planners and urban managers, including those in Vancouver, quickly adopted and adapted smart *growth* regional planning discourses and practices first seen in the United States (Fox, 2010; Herrschel, 2014), advocates of stronger forms of city-regionalism and green management within the Greater Seattle area have long looked to Canadian cities, including Vancouver and Toronto, for policy lessons and institutional insights (Dierwechter, 2017, ch. 5). Both places are starting to build over time smart(er) city-regional economies and societies, expanding inherited planning, economic and environmental policy and institutional structures in ways that, we argue here, seek to move beyond post-Fordist modes of regulation and regimes of accumulation and look to more interventionist was of directing development in the interest of greater than mere economy-centric concerns about competitiveness. Tensions, though, pervade this process, as multi-scaled states reposition these two city-regions in ways that amplify their strength and weakness as well inherited path-dependencies of institutional and material development.

Seattle as "late starter": smart(ish) city-region between regional competitiveness and urban (un)sustainability

Understanding the dual transition first across the Seattle city-region highlights, once again, the intersection between internal transition to (and evolution of) "smartness" *within* the region as well as a broader "external" transition in political agendas and perspectives in both the state of Washington and the United States (Figure 5.2).

Following the work of Alan Scott (Scott, 2001, 2012), Andy Jonas (Jonas, 2012a, 2012b, 2015; Jonas & Ward, 2001; Jonas & Ward, 2007) and others, including our own past research on the area (Carlson & Dierwechter, 2007; Dierwechter, 2008, 2010, 2013a, 2013b, 2014, 2018; Herrschel, 2014; Herrschel & Dierwechter, 2015; Herrschel & Newman, 2017; Modarres & Dierwechter, 2015) the "building" of smart city-regionalism within the Greater Seattle area has both economic and political dimensions, with their territorial, institutional and representational questions of particular importance. The Greater Seattle metropolitan area – or the Seattle city-region, as

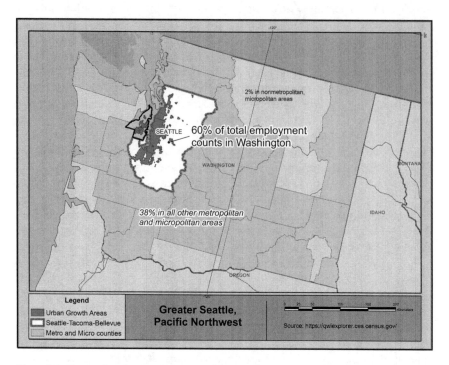

Figure 5.2 Greater Seattle city-region, Washington, USA.

we describe it here – is today a four-county conurbation of formerly more distinct and territorially conscious, metropolitan spaces, notably Seattle-King County and Tacoma-Pierce County, respectively, as well as smaller "nodes" of growth based around the urbanized municipalities of Bremerton and Everett (Figure 5.2). Moreover, various state-level and federal agencies have unevenly supported specific development patterns in ways that reflect supra-local concerns and territorial strategies with how to manage economic performance and, ideally, counteract ecological degradation (Katz, 2000; Rabe, 2011).

For much of the mid-20th century, of course, Seattle meant Boeing, which almost single-handedly inscribed a "hub-and-spoke" industrial structure across the regional space-economy – leading to frequent periods of boom and bust (Gray, Golob, & Markusen, 1996). Boeing's technical innovations incubated a highly-skilled workforce and business-service complex that, in hindsight, ultimately helped to set off a "more diversified developmental process" (Markusen, 1996, p. 302). As Mayer (2013) explains in her study of spin-off firms, Microsoft's post-1970s regional presence in the evolutionary wake of the hub-and-spoke economy helped facilitate an "entrepreneurial ecology" conducive to localizing more start-ups: "Spinoffs inherit knowledge and skills from their parents and therefore they benefit from knowledge spillovers," she theorized, "diversify[ing] into new markets and therefore creat[ing] new layers to the regional economy in not identical but closely related industries" (p. 1731). The "Microsoft economy" diversified, it now seems clear, into a high-tech, IT-based eco-*system* of globalized firms anchored in the Seattle-King County area, leading to, and further attracting, well-educated workers to an eco-*region* that has become a synonym for a high quality of life and strong commitments to urban sustainability and progressive politics.

Boeing's economic success, though, was ensured *externally* by what Kirkendall (1994) originally and memorably called America's "Metropolitan-Military Industrial Complex," which (geo-)politically favoured West Coast city-regions like Seattle and Los Angeles, who were after World War II beneficiaries of a "military remapping" of the county's overall industrial base – away from the "rustbelt" in the Midwest towards this new "gunbelt" (Markusen et al., 1991). The region, in other words, was favoured by the "spatial selectivity" of a geopolitically-militarized federal state self-charged with policing the planet's Cold War security problems (Jones, 1997). The steady militarization of the federal state also favoured Tacoma-Pierce County and Bremerton, though in the form of armed service facilities which were relatively stable but less economically generative. Tacoma, in particular, settled into a slow-growing, "blue collar-based" trajectory around its port, never quite able to diversify as quickly or successfully as Seattle and King County and, by the 1980s, performing a new role as a cheap "reproduction" frontier for the more expensive "production" complex emerging around Seattle, especially with respect to providing a regular supply of low-density suburban ("sprawling") housing to keep labour costs down. By the early 1990s, the contradictions of the city-region – which represented *two-thirds* of Washington State's value added – led to major state-level reforms in land-use planning, regional coordination and transportation policy (Dierwechter, 2017).

But with 38 municipalities there are also variations in King County. Given that number, it is unsurprising that there are informal groupings around shared agendas, such as in southern King County to boost a public transport hub (Renton City Council, Mayor's Office, interview, 5 Nov 2003), while in the northern part the focus has been more on widening and improving existing roads. "King County is a weird animal," one informant observed. It views itself as advocate of the non-urban parts of the region, although its council is elected by all (cities, suburbs and un-incorporated "grey areas"). Many of the smaller parts are unattractive to cities (for incorporation), as they suffer from years of underfunding in infrastructure, social deprivation and crime (interview Renton City Council. Mayor's office, 5 Nov 2003).

Reconciling these different agendas, and their political underpinnings, both within the two counties between the different municipalities and their socio-economically based political interests, those of Seattle and its immediate suburbs, and Tacoma, creates a complex and variable dynamic of alliances and collaborative interests. It also creates competition and localist protectionism that requires political skill and imagination to produce a regional agenda satisfying all parties and, still, producing tangible outcomes to justify such as approach to a critical public. And it is the term and associated (varying) meanings of "smart" that may take on the role as "unifying" umbrella agenda that allows actors to project commonality irrespective of underlying differences in priorities, perspectives and interests. Having multiple meanings associated with it, "smart" may thus, indeed, be able to contribute to reconcile competing interests, because it provides a virtual table and agenda around which the different actors can rally, maintaining their individuality, while learning about those of the other participants and thus open the door to identifying possible common interests as the basis of, in this instance, a regional agenda.

As this point gradually gained traction in the 1990s, as the "external" reforms took institutional root, the *first iteration* of "smartness" first appeared across the Seattle city-region (Dierwechter, 2008). Smartness first meant, in our view, better urban growth management, improved coordination across long-fragmented local planning regimes, and, perhaps most importantly, the institutional elevation of two key regional bodies eventually known as (1) the Puget Sound Regional Council (PSRC), the city-region's federally-designated Metropolitan Planning Organization, and (2) Sound Transit, the regional agency now trying to provide a viable public transportation alternative to heavily congested and dangerous highways and other major arterials, a congestion that was causing considerable economic cost and led to Boeing threatening to pull out of the region, if improvements to connectivity within the region were not achieved (Herrschel, 2013). It was such high-profile corporate pressure onto policy-makers, not least through raising awareness of the economic risk of doing nothing to address a region-wide problem with transportation and connectivity (delays through traffic jams) among the public (threat to jobs), that helped push a "smarter," region-wide approach to key elements of development planning to alleviate economically costly dysfunctions and, "along the way," also address issues of sustainability.

Following smart growth *planning* theory, the region from the 1990s now committed itself to much stronger – if still inadequate – regimes of sprawl containment through regionally-negotiated "urban growth boundaries" as well as new policy efforts to occasion "transit-oriented development" that tightly flanked long-term investments in light – and commuter-rail services (Dierwechter, 2013a). This pro-regional development was facilitated further in 1990/91 by a significant external push: the Growth Management Act, which required that most cities and counties adopt an area-wide comprehensive development plan that addressed sprawl, road congestion and the limited provision of public transport outside the central city area. In response, the region followed many of the key principles of smart growth, while adopting elements found in Vancouver's own regional plan, notably provisions for higher density (urban) centres and "urban villages" (Fox, 2010) connected by public transport corridors. Over time, also in the public's eye, the environment became more than a simple economic resource, but, rather, an economic asset in its own right (see also Herrschel, 2013). Having raised public awareness as support base of regionally-targeted policies, the PSRC's 2040 Vision strategy elevated "people, property, planet" (PSCR, 2009), in an attempt to publicly reconcile (individual) economic interests, expressed in property ownership and its value, and global sustainability with its repercussions (Freilich et al., 2010).

As such city-region-wide planning regimes are still fairly rare in the US and to lesser extent Canadian context (Dierwechter, 2014), it is worth emphasizing the legal and policy changes alone, even as the many contradictions and outright social injustices of new regional development patterns should also give considerable pause to inordinately generous assessments of local innovation and policy efficacy (Abel, White, & Clauson, 2015; Balk, 2014; Benko, 2011; Gardheere & Grant, 2014; Gregory, 2015; Minard, 2014). Seattle is getting richer, for example, but its Black households are getting poorer (Balk, 2014) – and there is predicable resistance to both densification and desegregation in multiple communities (Benko, 2011; Driscoll, 2015). Such inequalities between winners and losers of unfettered competitiveness under conditions of minimal state regulation have become increasingly evident – and widespread, especially since the 2008 financial crisis and subsequent budget constraints. These have found their outpouring in rapidly growing support for populist anti-globalization narratives, on the one hand, and more pro-active policy-making, on the other. Climate change and a more widespread realization that some coordinated response is required, also helped shift public opinion to a more "open ear" for collaborative policy-making in the region beyond conventional localist agendas.

All the same, the region's internal efforts at these early forms of smartness invariably attracted external federal support in many other ways too, especially as the Obama administration sought to re-energize new forms of institutionally-integrated regionalism and urban sustainability after a period of policy neglect during the administration of George W. Bush from 2001 to 2009 (Environmental Protection Agency, 2009b; Ziegler, 2010). In particular, three key federal agencies with long-standing but usually "siloed" metropolitan development policies – Housing and Urban Development, the Department of Transportation and the Environmental Protection Agency – forged an "unprecedented agreement … to work together to ensure that housing and transportation goals are met while simultaneously protecting the environment, promoting equitable development, and helping to address the challenges of climate change" (Environmental Protection Agency, 2009a). Seattle-area planners, particularly with the PSRC, worked to access federal funds around "sustainable communities" as part of their regional planning visions and programmes, "drawing down" the federal government in ways many other metropolitan regions did not (Bakkente, 2012, interview).

These federal changes were of a piece, moreover, with a widening of the smartness discourse at various scales of policy-making, or, what we see as the *second iteration* of smartness in and directed at the city-region. Efforts to make federal policies "smarter" not only meant supporting ICT-oriented projects that promised improved administration and management – although such initiatives certainly grew more important (White House, 2015). It also meant renewed efforts to integrate institutional action across multiple scales and programme areas, and to coordinate their developmental and ecological impacts in promising city-regions with strong regional planning regimes and policy matrices. What we referred to in Chapter 2 as "hard" smartness, though, has emerged unevenly across the region. Unsurprisingly, "smart city" projects emerged rapidly within the city of Seattle, drawing on existing strengths in progressive sustainability programmes (Portney, 2003), a "green" corporate sector, as well as strong research facilities at the University of Washington – the classic "triple helix" model so frequently associated with smart city innovations, especially during the first decade of this millennium (Leydesdorff & Deakin, 2011). One example is the recent development of city-wide temperature sensors analyzed by university-based engineers to gauge trends in energy resource usage. Another example is "Seattle 2030 District," a collaboration between property owners, the city and utility providers, that seeks to improve building management through enhanced energy efficiency. Interestingly, while such initiatives involve the built-environment, Alawadhi and Scholl (2013, p. 1698) in their review of smart city projects within Seattle a few years ago found – at that time at least – more emphasis on "Smart City government." In their judgement, this meant "proactive action and service to and interaction internally as well as with citizens, businesses, and other government entities" via a technologically-mediated "openness" and "transparency" in data generation and information sharing (ibid.). More recently, the city of Seattle has dominated (so far) in the regional production of spaces strongly associated with the smart, creative, green, sharing, innovative, indeed "after" post-Fordist economy, such as new "coworking" facilities (Mariotti, Pacchi, & Di Vita, 2017) (Figure 5.3).[1]

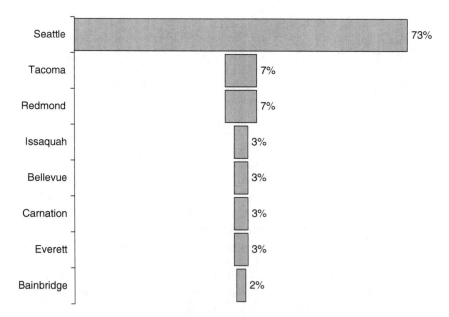

Figure 5.3 "Coworking" facilities across the Seattle city-region, *c.* 2017.

Source: derived from crowd-sourced data found at the following site: http://wiki.coworking.org/w/page/16583695/CoworkingSeattle [*c.* July 2017].

Finally, the behemoth Amazon, anchored in the heart of Seattle, is now using Living Lab techniques to re-think the future of retailing by using sensors that eliminate cashiers (Wingfield, 2017), although here, micro-economic efficiency gains and thus profitability are a major driving force of such innovation.

This *second* iteration, this so-called "hard turn" in the longer-running development of internal and external smartness away from smart growth *per se* to more broadly conceptualized, smart city projects, such as ICT-related services, co-working spaces, smart governance, energy monitoring, e-retailing, etc., raises obvious questions here about extant processes of smart city-regionalism as a dual transition across Seattle. In Chapter 4 we theorized that, when compared with other forms of smart city-regionalism around the world, Seattle and Vancouver – but especially Seattle – exhibit strong imprints of North American-style neoliberalism *even as* processes of (incomplete) regionalism are also discernable. Fordist Boeing bequeathed a high-tech economy that subsequently helped create a post-Fordist, Microsoft-driven IT ecosystem, although the company itself is undergoing changes to remain part of that new societal-economic dynamic. But it is now global companies like Amazon that really represent the cutting edge of "hard" smartness, in Seattle as elsewhere. Amazon perfectly embodies, for us, the US corporate culture of neoliberalized smartness – of radical product innovation; of constant risk-taking; of cut-throat competitiveness; of long hours and excessive labor demands – that one employee described to *The New York Times* as "purposeful Darwinism" (Kantor & Streitfeld, 2015).

Paradoxically, this survival-of-the-fittest culture in "smart economy" firms like Amazon enervates, rather than edifies, a public culture that has long emphasized the need for regional cooperation, inter-jurisdictional policy collaboration and mutual co-benefits. Since planning and transport reforms, as well as renewed federal support in the 1990s, the regional scale has slowly (and very delicately) entered the political process around strategic economic policy and urban development priorities (interviews at Tacoma EDU 6 Oct 2002 and Seattle Corporate Planning Dept, 5 Oct 2002). To be sure, the region's somewhat anodyne name, Puget Sound, reflects an abiding concern to appease "localist" concerns (Fox, 2010). As elsewhere in the world, municipalities across the region are still seen as "little kingdoms" by public and elected officials in smaller cities and surrounding suburbs (interview, 5 Nov 2003; Howard, pers. comm. YD, 2014). The business community, as expressed by the Trade Development Alliance of Greater Seattle, prefers "Greater Seattle" as a more effective name when marketing the region internationally (interview Greater Seattle Trade Alliance, 19 Feb. 2014). But the low-key compromise to regionalization is reflected in PSRC's web address extension ".org." The organization is nominally outside the governmental hierarchy without excessive powers that might cut deeply into local control and thus be "suspicious" in terms of potential interference with local matters.

In their novel analysis of digital services and urban nodes between Milan and Turin, Morandi et al. (2015) reflect on Seattle as a possible case of a nascent novel "smart city-regionalism" (Dierwechter, 2013a). Yet such regionalization has, until quite recently, focused more on the first iteration of smart growth governance than on second-generation smart city initiatives that are also *region-alized*. Still, there is evidence of some change. The eCityGov Alliance, for example, represents a special case of "smart-city collaboration" between neigh-bouring municipalities (within King County) who are focused on providing smart services to citizens and businesses that no single municipality could have provided alone (Scholl & AlAwadhi, 2016). This is an important institutional development, albeit one associated as much with the (externally imposed) necessities of fiscal austerity, as the fountains of political creativity – and still not "scaled up" to the entire city-region. So, what we know about the spaces and places of smart *city* initiatives in around Greater Seattle – as elsewhere in the world– still feels fragmented, project-bounded, central city-centric, and, by and large, inconsistently inattentive to the wider political and institutional frameworks associated with smart growth regional planning policy, including the major initiatives just described (e.g. White House, 2015).

Irrespective of its formal institutional (non-)powers, the PSRC nonetheless offers a publicly visible political arena for local actors to engage with local and trans-local developments and required policy agendas – an "arena" shaped by participants, rather than a higher authority. In addition, this particular arrange-ment signals a clear willingness – to both internal and external actors – to engage region-wide, across boundaries and divisions, and to tackle supra-local development and transportation challenges that produce more effective answers and that seek to maintain the region's sustainability and competitiveness. This capacity has functioned as a catalyst of a regional policy-making dimension, sitting at the centre of our notion of smartness in contemporary city-regional governance. The emphasis has been on *a process of negotiation and deliberation* between competing, even contradicting, interests and agendas, in order to find a "bigger" solution that offers a win-win outcome to all concerned. Its stated mission since the 1990s has been "to ensure a thriving central Puget Sound now and into the future through planning for regional transportation, growth management and economic development" (psrc.org, accessed 5 April 2012).

From a regional perspective smartness thus means, first, smart *growth*: that is, (sustainable) economic development, sprawl containment, efficient public trans-port, "green" architecture, etc. This understanding is still rooted in an essentially modernist, growth-oriented world of technology-driven development. Yet there is also, albeit less explicitly, an ongoing attempt to use "smartness" as a more politically oriented modus operandi with the aim *to reconcile, and thus more effectively govern* an increasingly complex mesh of *competing and conflicting interests* across spatial, ideational, topical and institutional, as well as societal divides. The importance of being able to do so has become evident in the growing support for populist promises of easy solutions and support for those who feel hard one by and ignored by the prevailing system of output-focused competitiveness. The many boundaries and divisions crisscrossing the region – social, mental and administrative – represent major obstacles to regional collaboration between different localities and their communities, however defined. This especially involves fears of losing financial control (e.g. over the use of tax money), which is important for local politicians, who want to get re-elected on a local ticket, with local popular support. The 2040 Vision strategy thus claims to focus on "people, property, planet" and guide the Growth Management, Environmental, Economic and Transportation Strategy for the Central Puget Sound Region; quite clearly an attempt to reconcile openly (discursively) varying economic interests, political agendas, and societal aspirations and expectations (Puget Sound Regional Council, 2009).

The tensions that now increasingly pervade the political-economy of 21st-century regional development in leading urban areas, notably that between "Darwinian competition" and these new forms of regional collaborations, nonetheless illustrate structural challenges in building a new kind of smart city-regionalism "beyond" post-Fordist regimes of regulation and accumulation. Overcoming structure and adopting variable, flexible and virtual forms of governance arrangements no longer is sufficient in its own right. Instead, the very essence of policies, their agendas and mechanisms of identifying goals, framing objectives and going about implementing them needs to evolve into a "smart" way of governing. This includes moving beyond spatial planning concerns with growth as a seemingly non-negotiable hegemonic paradigm, allowing land-use and circulation to be guided by novel concerns in conjunction with the rollout of digital economies and a digitized state apparatus which enhances the scope for democratic participation and thus legitimacy of political decisions beyond core, "superstar" cities and a few select suburbs as successful, "trendy" places of innovation and constant political-economic evolution, leaving large parts of the remaining territorial state behind.

Vancouver as "early mover": smarter city-region – virtual space for sustainable competitiveness

Much like its Pacific Northwest urban "neighbor," Vancouver, British Colombia, is described by some as a "superstar city" (Florida, 2017), especially with respect to its record on urban sustainability (Rossiter, Cameron, & Harcourt, 2007), but also, if less glowingly, in regard to its increasingly bifurcated "new urban crisis" status wherein gaps between the haves and have-nots are growing (Florida, 2017; C. E. Jones & Ley, 2016; Walker, 2016) (Figure 5.4).

As indicated earlier, comparisons with Seattle in the United States are helpful as both city-regions share a common ecological setting and emerged historically on the Pacific Coast over roughly the same period of time. They are also shaped today by common global economic pressures, as well as underlying liberal, environmentally-conscious values as shared characteristic in the Pacific Northwest. By the same token, these two cities are separated in crucial ways by a national border – demarcating distinct political and cultural traditions and ways of doing things – that has, accordingly, institutionalized

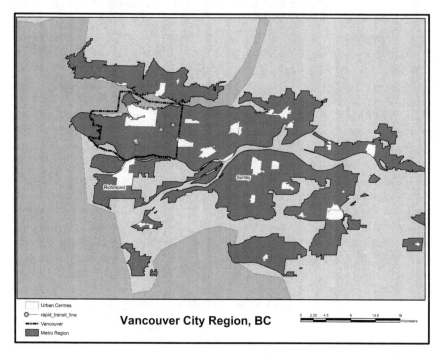

Figure 5.4 Greater Vancouver, British Columbia.

different regulatory and investment regimes which portray comparative "distance" too. When compared with Seattle, this book argues, Vancouver has made greater progress on smartly "regionalizing" its territorial governance strategies, although, in other arenas related to new smart *city* developments, Vancouver has lagged Seattle, at least by its own admission.

One example of a (perhaps temporary) lag with Seattle is a 2013 self-analysis by the City of Vancouver (2013) of its own "digital capabilities," defined here as "a broad range of technology that enables new methods of engagement and service delivery supported by a robust and accessible digital infrastructure and open government ecosystem" (p. 3). The city's self-analysis, reproduced in simplified form in Figure 5.5, also suggests a focus on the technology aspect of new competitiveness and, of course, point towards this aspect of "smartness" as expression of technology-induced changes to governing and organizing economic activity. According to the city's review, digital capabilities in cities and regions emerge unevenly in distinct stages across four main assets: *viz*, "online," "mobile," "social" and "infrastructure and data." Progress *per se* can be interpreted as development over time from "absent" capacities through "connected" capacities that research "maturity", after an initial period of "exploring" followed by a more active phase that "enables" a digital environment. So, interestingly, "progress" is connected to "digital" as a matter of fact.

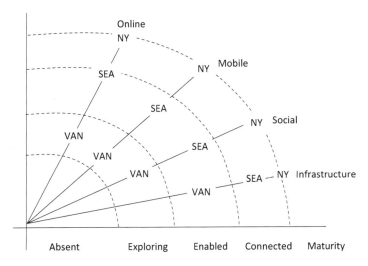

Figure 5.5 "Digital capacities" along four fronts: Vancouver vs. Seattle.
Source: redrawn and simplified from City of Vancouver. (2013).

Adopting this criterion, Seattle and Vancouver both putatively lag beyond "global leaders" in digital capabilities such as New York. Yet, as of 2013, Seattle had made more progress overall than Vancouver, even as Vancouver was the first Canadian city to launch a Digital Strategy Plan that aimed to catch-up to its competitors within a few years (Alizadeh & Sipe, 2016).

In their work on smartness in Vancouver, Alizadeh and Sipe (2016) note that investing in digital services basically represents a new and increasingly crucial kind of strategic planning. Such planning has been long associated with outlays in large-scale public infrastructures that necessarily underpin, stimulate and ultimately shape private sector growth and overall urban development patterns and social interactions. Like traditional "bulk" infrastructures, over – and under-ground – digital services, particularly telecommunications, influence participatory planning, public safety, disaster management, local and regional economic development, employment growth, sustainable development, transport management, governance, development assessment, and, of course, the efficient performance of other kinds of traditional infrastructure, for example, energy, water, waste and road systems (p. 2). Indeed, as discussed in Chapter 2, much of the "hard" literature on the meaning and impacts of "smart cities" is just an extended examination of these themes. But it also shows that digitally-focused smartness is not entirely "new" and "different," because it relies on, and projects, physicality of networks and their presence.

The last of the traditional outlays just mentioned – road systems – provides a significant contrast between the developmental histories of Seattle and Vancouver, and, particularly, in the ways in which "external" dynamics differed on either side of the national border (MacDonald, 1987). While both metropolitan areas experienced significant suburbanization in the fast-growing decades following World War II, federal and provincial authorities in Canada were less committed to urban freeways in cities than their American counterparts. Both Vancouver and Seattle experienced highways revolts in the late 1960s, but the development of the Vancouver city-region was not shaped as decisively as Seattle by the geographies, financing and territorial politics of automobility. The creation of an elevated highway that separated Seattle from its waterfront illustrates this difference in the automobile's prominence: there has been no such physical dominance in Vancouver. The more limited national programme of highway spending, which was relatively costlier in Canada owing to lower population densities, "tended to discourage outward movement," and generated greater density in Vancouver compared with Seattle (ibid., p. 192). Such density arguably reinforced an antecedent pro-city culture more reminiscent of European cities; but as MacDonald notes, the greater vitality and appeal of Vancouver occasioned by greater density and more limited suburbanization also reflected the *absence* of Black-White racial tensions, urban violence, and ghetto poverty – a general characteristic of Canadian cities – and with it, federal-scale interventions in urban (re)development that arguably exaggerated these tensions and conditions (ibid.). Regardless, Vancouver's "urban" advantages over Seattle meant a much earlier and more significant commitment to public transit systems, including light rail. Again, external factors in what is today routinely considered "smart" urbanism mattered too. The 21-kilometre transit system linking Vancouver with the suburban city of New Westminster, for instance, was largely financed by provincial authorities at a time when Seattle, in contrast, had just barely financed regional bus services – and was still years away from shifting to light and commuter rail investments (Crowley, 2000; HistoryLink Staff, 2002). By the same token, political changes at provincial level may change from tailwind to headwind as far as regional perspectives and related public investment are concerned. This may go right down to deciding on the running of the regional transit company, TransLink (interview BC Govt, 21 June 2016).

Transportation matters for the Vancouver city region, because its polycentric nature requires efficient communication across the city-region to allow its multiple and complex functional interdependencies to work. While the city of Vancouver is the most recognized and, from its image and functionality, the dominant urban node, but there are also several large suburban cities, notably Surrey, which at 500,000 residents actually rivals the size if not global reputation of Vancouver's population of 650,000. The result is a competitive neighbourliness which affects the whole city region and provides a common ground for all municipalities in the region, including the vehemently competing suburban cities of Surrey and Richmond (interview Surrey EDU, 26 Oct 2004). And here, the mayors, as leading policy-makers, are of vital importance. If they cannot "get on," regional cooperation between municipalities will be difficult to achieve (Surrey Chamber of Commerce, 26 Oct 2004).

Density, but also a general concern about quality of life and an appreciation of the beautiful natural landscape as a key component in this quality, has been a key driver of accepting a regional perspective, despite inter-local competition, and so it is not surprising that the main regional body, the Greater Vancouver Regional District (GVRD), now called Metro Vancouver – in, albeit reluctant, recognition of the city's strong international recognition factor – has environmental and green space management as its primary responsibility. At the same time, there is latent concern within local government, and among the public, about how this regionalization "is done" – imposed top-down by central government (the Province) or bottom up through local co-operation. There is little appetite for the former variant (interview Vancouver Board of Trade, 3 Nov 2003). City-regionalism in Vancouver has thus emerged essentially on the back of development planning control to manage land-use, and here the loss of open space in recognition of the value to the community of maintaining open space. This view goes back to the city's first development plan of 1929, designed upon request by the provincial government of British Columbia to protect land resources from urban expansion (Donald, 2005). While technocratic concerns, such as transport planning, are the main drivers of regional cooperation, such regional perspective competes with a strong sense of municipal independence and local policy-making autonomy.

GVRD is a collective body controlled by the participating municipalities. Regional and local interests have been closely intertwined, with local agendas the primary perspective. As such, GVRD is a service provider for local areas (GVRD, interview, 3 Nov 2003). As governing board members,

> they are good localists, that is they place local interest first. They view their primary role to be on the board to ensure that the region and regional decisions do not affect local interests negatively. Their participation is driven by an essentially negative, defensive, approach to the region. Regional decisions are only acceptable, if they support local matters.
>
> (GVRD interview, 3 Nov 2003)

This situation has changed little since. Regionalization "sells" politically, also to the public, if there are tangible benefits for local interests.

In Vancouver, and not just in the city itself, public debate expressed, and reinforced, a preparedness to accept the principles of development control in a bid to enhance urban living and quality of life as early as the beginning of the 1970s. The then liberal political middle-class movement, TEAM (The Electors' Action Movement) gained control of the Vancouver city council in contested elections against the backdrop of a perceived assault on "urban living," and social equity and inclusion by rapid urban expansion on the "edges," supported by extensive road building, as a result of, so it was then seen, the self-serving interests of a narrow local political elite of "inaccessible politicians" (Ley et al., 1992, p. 281). The result was a mood receptive to the discourse of "sustainability," largely expressed through the concept and political agenda of "smart growth," and this has been an important driver in fostering a sense of "shared purpose" without the underlying competitiveness latent in economic development policies. Being "sustainable" reflects concerns with the overall environmental quality of a city-region, wherein key policy-makers also perceive physical landscapes and natural amenities as major economic assets.

This requires more strategic, longer-term perspectives as guidance to local policy decisions, than economic development often does, including cooperation with neighbouring municipalities to address the "bigger picture" of sustainability. The regional agenda benefits from such public awareness and, indeed, is essential for political collaboration across municipal boundaries to be viewed by local policy-makers as a political gain. Public support for such engagement can make a difference (Vancouver Board of Trade interview, 3 Nov 2003), and getting businesses "on board" can make a significant difference. It has not been easy, however, to get the region's businesses interested in engaging with economic development policy: most are small- to medium-sized, doing relatively well and thus remain in their "own worlds." There are none of the big international behemoths found in Seattle that act as a global sounding board for the city and drive an outward-looking agenda and policy. In the United States there are also more local and regional banks than in Canada, which can help articulate a regional business perspective and agenda (GVRD interview, 3 Nov 2003), something also found in other countries with a strong tradition of municipal and urban independence, such as Germany or Italy. In more centralized states, such as Canada or France, for instance, a few national banks with regional and local branches tend to be more widespread.

The main "voice" for economic development is the small organization, Vancouver Economic Committee (VEC), an advocacy group that seeks to operate "thinly" institutionalized in a business-like fashion. It is well connected to the business community and equally well to the city council (the city mayor is the VEC chairman). Its primary mission is to promote Vancouver as a place to invest and act as a platform to communicate business interests and concerns to the administration, and do this as a lobbying organization more so than the more "club-like" chambers of commerce with their local, rather than regional, memberships. And this includes drawing on the city's credentials as livable and "green" and thus, by extension, "smartness" in its governance. VEC thus sees itself as a key player among the "context people" focusing on strategy, rather than detailed implementation of policy (interview with VEC, 23 Oct 2006). Its recent Economic Development Strategy document (available from: vancouver.ca/ctyclerk/cclerk/20120131/documents/rr1.pdf) shows sustainability clearly presented as an integral economic quality, inherent in the city as a "smart," economically successful location. "Smartness" is thus an integral part of Vancouver's policy-making and becomes synonymous with its name, as the Mayor's strategy shows.

The then mayor's decision to use "greenness" as an obvious boosterist policy tool to promote the city's competitiveness is an extension of this expertise through the Greenest City 2020 Action Plan launched in 2009 (available from http://vancouver.ca/greenestcity/, accessed 5 April 2012), just ahead of the 2010 Winter Olympics as the then touted "most sustainable" Games. It is an attempt to further strengthen the perception of Vancouver as innovative and creative in successfully bringing together often conflictual policy fields and pursue an economically successful sustainability agenda. This includes propagating a shared vision as accepted, negotiated guidance for shaping local and individual agendas (Healey 2003) within an agreed overall framework of development principles. Interestingly, it is the private sector that has taken a lead role, by focusing on particular problems as "rallying point" for concerted action, so that the advantages of doing so can also be recognized by the public. And this, in turn, provides an important support base for policy-makers to dare and stick their heads above a localist parapet. So, it is important for its functioning and efficacy for the GVRD to operate within societal values. For this, "you need flags to rally around" (GVRD interview, 3 Nov 2003), that is, there needs to be defining issues that help to focus the mind, provide a clearly recognizable justification for policy choices, and help develop a regional identity, that is, a relationship to the relevant space/territory as sense of ownership.

> In the past, it was the governments providing that role as a conduit for territorial identity, but following the neoliberal shift towards business as local and regional actors, it is them who should have taken on that role, but they didn't.
>
> (GVRD interview, 3 Nov 2003)

And it is here that the corporate structure in Seattle, with its universally recognized global actors, is in a much stronger position to provide that identity-making local reference.

The sustainability agenda took on this role, not at least because of its consistently high discursive standing in the public sphere, going back to the Sustainable Region Initiative started in 2002. This was early in the publicity of the Smart Growth campaign among policy-makers, and followed shortly afterwards, that is in 2008, by a more explicitly "growth oriented" "Sustainability Framework" for a Regional Growth Strategy (Metro Vancouver, 2008). It was approved by all municipalities in the city region as "shareholders" in Metro Vancouver.

Comparing approaches to "smart governance" in a North American setting

Seattle and Vancouver are both recognized exemplars of smart *growth* (Fox, 2010), but for this and other reasons, Vancouver, in our judgement, illustrates a stronger and probably more instructive North American version of *smartness* as part and parcel of a wider territorial project in "smart city-regionalization" with a distinct involvement of the public as both initiator and also supporter of adopting regional perspectives in the city-region's governance (Dierwechter, 2013; Herrschel, 2013). Similar to the Seattle city-region,

Greater Vancouver's political and policy commitments to sustainability and competitiveness are often (theoretically) balanced through broad "livability" discourses that mobilize smart growth planning and management principles in the enveloping context of neoliberal globalization, for example containment, transit and housing choice, greater design flexibility, and so on (Greater Vancouver Regional District, 2002). But this livability discourse also means a policy discourse and rationale that is very accessible to the public at large, allowing regional policies to gain support and recognition – not at least at the ballot box at the next local elections.

Unlike Seattle, Vancouver has managed to more effectively link spatial and policy-sectoral perspectives to a strategic-conceptual "bigger picture" by, in effect, facilitating multi-actor communication, collaboration and political negotiations (Herrschel, 2013, p. 2334). More simply, it has fused together more effectively than has Seattle the planning concept of smart growth with the governance concept of new regionalism, offering a novel set of "virtual" governance spaces around improved inter-sectoral policy coordination and inter-local coordination that merit global attention and scholarly reflection (Herrschel, 2014). So, whereas Seattle may well have enjoyed greater "digital competencies" in the mid-2010s, Vancouver's *governance* advantages – its past, current and future efforts to build one of North America's most advanced examples of "smart city-regionalism" – could easily change this state of affairs, if it has not done so already. Being "smart" is less a matter of technological wizardry than governance capabilities. Vancouver has moved and matured the second "iteration" of smartness in North America in ways that strongly suggest it will be able to more effectively "square the circle" of sustainability and competitiveness, even as it also suffers from the impacts of pathologies of neoliberal globalization and growing societal inequalities. And being able to gain public support, including from the business community, has been an important element in the ability to link concept to practical policy-making on the ground at the city-regional level. If nothing else, such engagement of the public also aids important legitimacy for collaborative regional policies when governing the (largely virtual) Vancouver city region.

Smart city-regionalism in Western Europe: reconciling state parameters, economic perspectives and municipal standing in Turin and Lyon

The two Western European cases now discussed here, Turin and Lyon, are not just competing regions separated by the Alps and the Franco-Italian border, albeit now connected by a high-speed rail line; they also share the experience of seeking to expand their metropolitan reach and profile. This includes strategies to move towards a globalized form of international post-Fordism, and, as part of that, adopt "smart" strategies as expression of political, economic and social innovation. In fact, innovation is the leading discourse to overcome post-industrial decline, insufficient standing in the internationalized world, the perceived need to map out a path for the re-invention of the city as international, entrepreneurial, innovative and experimental. While these strategies began to take shape some 15 years ago (Herrschel & Newman 2002) – all key ingredients of strategic "smartness" – they have become recently subsumed under the "smart" label. In both Turin and Lyon, internationality has been a major narrative to reach beyond the confines of traditional functionality within a national urban hierarchy. In both instances, the state, through policies and administrative measures, has been an important actor in shaping the new agenda of metropolitanization of the national and regional economies. The focus on international and innovative policies serves to mark the breaking out of the confines of the old Fordist-era city image, functionality and space qualities.

This city-focused regionalism has been highlighted by Lefèvre as a general "renaissance of metropolitan governments" in the new regionalism of the 1990s (Lefèvre, 1998). In effect, therefore, regions in Italy may be seen as little more than aggregations of individual localities which act as the centres of *actual* decision-making and provide the grounding in civil society. Regions are effectively the result of regional clustering of a "multitude of local societies which have their networks, strategies and cohesion at the municipal and the provincial levels" rather than a genuine, separate regional scale of government (Bagnasco & Oberti, 1998, p. 162). As a result, there is no genuinely regional interest or dynamism to translate into region-based policies and networking within the state system. Other, more firmly established representations, such as the counties (provinces) can step into the fray, if a regional task requires. The absence of regionally-scaled institutions and forms of governance reflects the multiplicity of local communities and established identities, as expressed in the many small, yet independent municipalities.

This makes the development of appropriately scaled, responsive, credible and thus "efficient" territorial regions more difficult (after Putnam, 1993, referred to in Bagnasco and Oberti, 1998, p. 150). Regardless of this, the state continues to apply some *dirigiste* pressure to address this fragmentation of voices and interests and circumstances at the local level, so as to reach a more coordinated and cohesive approach to policy-making and thus credibility. As a result, there are regulated state-regional conferences convened by the state government in Rome, and there are also local-regional conferences hosted by the regions to discuss collaborative work between the regional administration and the relatively powerful municipalities, drawing on the historically well entrenched – especially urban-centric – localism in Italy. "The strategic plan is the instrument which cities adopt nowadays to identify and put into practice whatever is necessary for growth in the new world context" (Associazione Torino Internazionale, 2000).

Turin's reach for a regional dimension has largely been a locally driven, urban initiative, albeit with some encouragement by the national government's not particularly successful attempts at supporting a degree of metropolitanization of the regional level of governing at the expense of the provinces which are, in effect, hinterland entities around larger cities. Not surprisingly, this was resisted by the provincial governments, not least because of a fear of job losses (interview, Torino Internazionale, 29 Jan 2004). In France, national policies have gone in a similar direction, albeit more explicitly *dirigiste*, by seeking to build metropolitan regions as national economic champions under the auspices of the larger cities. Yet, given France's centralized system, the state put more explicit pressure on the main city-regions to enhance their profile internationally through administrative re-organization that imbued the metropolises with greater governmental powers. As a result of the different external determinants (Transition 1), Figure 4.4 in the previous chapter shows Turin as an *"early mover,"* while Lyon is characterized as a *"stalled mover."*

Smart City Torino: "early mover" reclaiming the "regional" as part of political innovation

Turin, in northern Italy, exemplifies a city which, facing an economic crisis after the collapse of its dominant industrial base in car production, needed to reinvent itself and rediscover its historic role as a leading historic urban centre for a large region, and Italy, this involved looking beyond city limits (again) and rediscovering and nurturing its historic role as a major regional capital, which meant viewing the surrounding region as its natural "sphere of interest" and engagement (Figure 5.6).

Preparations for the 2006 Winter Olympics required – and, as a result, promoted – collaborative engagement between municipalities and regional

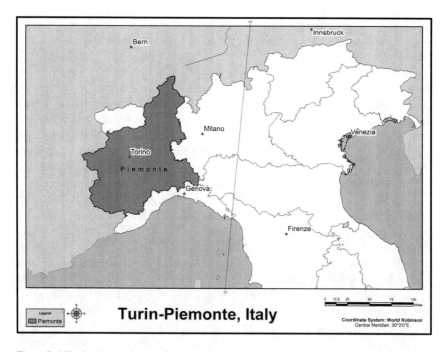

Figure 5.6 Turin city-region, Italy.

authorities within the city region (Caruso & Saccomani, 2017; Bondonio & Campaniello, 2006). A few years later, these experiences and strategies merged into the new narrative of Smart City Torino as overarching strategy and development agenda. Strong local leadership in Turin, and attempts at de-politicizing this process, led to a fundamental repositioning of the city within a regional and, especially, international context. In the early 1990s, Turin discovered that, after the loss of its century-long status as the "home" to the car maker Fiat, a new economic base had to be found or, more accurately, rediscovered. A strong city mayor, with a business, rather than conventional administrative (party-political) background, promoted "Torino Internazionale" as a new initiative to open up the city to international business and competition (interview, Torino Internazionale, 29 Jan 2004), while also giving the city a clear purpose and focus in its urban renewal and development strategies. All urban projects were located within that plan to ensure they added up to the overall agenda of raising the city's national and international profile, and the whole is more than the sum of its composite parts.

As an arm's-length company, Torino Internazionale was set up as part of a new urban governance to promote and direct the new initiative, and, importantly, act as ambassador of the new internationality. The projects and the name Torino Internazionale became a new image-maker and shaped the local political milieu in response to the evident pressures from a loss of competitiveness in its manufacturing base (globalization), a new national agenda of regionalism in governance regional agenda and a strong urban culture and civility, led to a comprehensive policy framework to connect the city outwardly – to the region, and beyond as a way of stepping out of the confines of the "industrial city" of the 20th century. A vision of post-industrial international (global) connectivity and trans-local reach, with the city as a vibrant, innovative hub, replaced conventional political battles about administrative procedures and party-political competencies. In effect, the city understood itself as reaching out into the region in the sense of a Greater Turin.

Torino Internazionale has thus been the city's new (and novel) way of responding to globalization and its shifting, and to open up to the world advocating a regional approach, although it is essentially a local initiative by the dominant city of Turin to reconnect with its pre-industrial urban characteristics and capacities and project those into the post-industrial future. This project and publicly-promoted city-wide narrative of the first decade of the 2000s had thus key features of "smartness" in that it was innovative and creative in its approach to policy-making and mapping out a vision as vehicle for confidence building among the Turin citizenry and political establishment. The focus was not so much on ways of how to govern the metropolitan area, even though the city was formally extended into the region when the Italian parliament introduced the city-region (*città metropolitana*) as a conceptual construct to the debate. Yet, this strategic objective was never really properly implemented, and the political narrative was somewhat overtaken by state-sponsored, locality-focused regionalization initiatives. These focused on relational, locality-based network regions, where the municipalities signed a contract of cooperation with the formal, territorial region for a range of specified policy fields.

This arrangement was therefore not so much an *ex ante* redistribution and formalization of powers as part of a scalar re-arrangement of the state, but, rather, a problem-specific and time-limited informal agreement about specific tasks for a clearly specified group of participating municipalities with shared policy objectives. The primary goal was to put the main metropolitan regions in the driving seat for moving ahead regional and national economic development. This was a reaction by the federal government in Rome to the slow progress of self-organizing regionalization among municipalities since the initiation of this policy in 1990, seeking to propel the process forwards by encouraging the core cities to identify and suggest "metropolitan areas" and a definition of the tasks required to give this new level of regional governance credibility and effectiveness.

Torino was the first city to develop a metropolitan area strategy, that is, one that went beyond city limits (interview, Torino Internazionale, 29 Jan 2004). Only if the two are combined – territory and powers – would the new government level make sense and justify its addition to the existing structure. The envisaged new tasks were focused on economic development – thus reflecting the driving role of competitiveness – and included transportation and urban planning as key policy areas for implementing any metropolitan-area-based policy (interview, *Regione Piemonte*, 29 Jan 2004). And these are the "typical" policy fields that opened up to the smartness agenda. This notion of doing things differently was also behind the focus on self-organizing, informal collaboration and cooperation, rather than new institutionalization. The challenge then, of course, is linking the emerging networks to the existing institutional structures, a challenge that was explored by a committee under Bagnasco's chairmanship with a focus on more horizontal linkages (interview, Torino Internazionale, 29 Jan 2004), rather than hierarchical arrangements as part of a re-structured, re-scaled state. Views on this differ among municipalities, with the main cities favouring strong metropolitan mayors as drivers of city-regionalization and their governance, while the smaller municipalities fear loss of voice in comparison to their current position in the provincial as administrative "doughnut" around the major cities (interview, Torino Internazionale, 29 Jan 2004)

Without providing clear guidance to implementing such regional competencies and responsibilities "on the ground," cities thus had to develop their own forms and mechanisms of operationalizing a city-regional perspective and agenda. It was not clear how this was meant to manifest itself in practice in terms of governmental territoriality and capacity. This urban focus of the regional scale, however "fuzzy," reflects the realization that it is successful urban economies that will drive the regional and national economies, and that it is "government" that needs to be extended and enhanced. This matters, as there is already governmental presence at the regional level in the shape of the official NUTS 1 regions (such as Regione Piemonte) and the counties as groupings of municipalities. The problem is the delimitation of such regions, as different tasks use different territorial boundaries to best match collaborative interests and policy necessities, but also available powers and fiscal capacities (interview, Regione Piemonte, 29 Jan 2004). The challenge now is how to reconcile this different territories and policy spaces to avoid conflicts and inefficiencies through counter-effects. The "moving target" of policy objectives as determinants of the new metropolitan area has been one of the main sticking points, and so placing the main cities and their strategies, such as Torino Internazionale, in the driving seat of such collaborative, self-organizing regionalization efforts seems a good idea (Regione Piemonte, 29 Jan 2004).

The issue of multiple geographies as an expression of variable, multi-layered interests between adjoining municipalities in a city region, also over time, has been a key driver behind the shaping of Torino Internazionale as a non-governmental, thinly institutionalized organization – with a small office suit, few, but dedicated and innovative staff, and a website – the hallmarks of virtual regionalism (Herrschel, 2010). By its very nature, it resembles an open membership organization for municipalities in the wider Turin metropolitan area to join without the threat of perhaps permanently surrendering powers of local self-government. In effect, it is a form of layered regionalization á la carte, where individual municipalities may participate for a clearly defined range of policy fields (or agendas), and do so with a select group of like-interested municipalities. Much of this approach draws on political and policy innovation, as there are no ready-made answers "off the shelf," by the very nature of this form of regionalism; no fixed, prescribed lines of communication and authority. Responses need to be defined and implemented in an ad hoc manner and thus cannot be one-size-fits-all solutions. It is here that smart solutions are required. Such include variations in policies with varying degrees of "novelty" and thus inherent elements of experimentalism, a possibility permitted by the virtual and thus less binding and committing nature of many collaborative engagements (see for example, the comparative study by Bobbio and Rosso, 2003). The possibility to retreat from such a form of collaboration also eases the way for "giving it a go" as a way of experimenting with new policy-making approaches, as there is little danger of lasting disadvantages if such attempts fail to deliver.

Yet, notions of power and credibility matter for such regional constructs to give them implementational scope and efficacy, and thus also political credibility. And it is here that established, formal, institutionalized organizations become important with their defined powers and territorially circumscribed responsibilities and legitimacy. They tie in the ideational and programmatic "virtual" with the "actually existing" reality of political agendas, projects and power. In so doing, they also maintain the "virtual" as indirect, "loose coupling" (Orton et al., 1990) between the local and regional perspective in political ambition, interest and capacity, which allows local, individual interests to engage and also disengage with those of the regional level – be that defined as collective of local interests, or institutionalized regional entity of the state-governmental structure. Perhaps unsurprisingly, the formalized, state-defined region of Piemonte confirms this dual approach, but also a concern about being left out of informal power relations, when claiming that, "Torino Internazionale is a good idea, but the region needs to participate" in any such enterprise, and thus be part of the regionalization game (interview, Regione Piemonte, 29 Jan 2004). At the same time, there was a claimed need for allowing variable geographies of collaboration within any regional construct to accommodate different sub-areas of shared agendas and interests – and thus a sense of shared purpose and reward. In effect, therefore, there has been a realization that regions ought to serve as vehicles to help local areas develop, and, importantly, be locally seen and perceived to be able to provide this support and opportunity.

Yet external incentives through higher tier government may vary in response to shifting political agendas and governmental majorities. When the current regions were set up in 1970, the associated regional government was meant to acquire some powers, but devolve others to localities. But the national government cut funding for these regional powers, so they are mainly on paper without implementational "teeth." This inequality is a particular problem for Piemonte region with its differences between urban cores and remote rural mountainous areas. Interests and perspectives vary widely, and Turin-based urbanity means more to some than others. With Turin itself still undergoing a process of reinvention and repositioning (Vanolo, 2008), agendas and perspectives on the relationship between city and region are in flux, with regional interests changing in their perceived importance. In the run-up to the 2006 Winter Olympics, regional engagement clearly led to specific local advantages as chosen locations of events, also providing a sense of connectivity and participation in a joint large project. Yet, with the city's functional and reputational dominance in the region, especially from an external perspective, there is a danger of reducing the region too much to a narrow, metropolitan understanding of city-region for marketing reasons (interview, Regione Piemonte, 29 Jan 04) and forget the rest as it "disappears" under the umbrella of the notion of a greater Turin.

This regional orientation represents a major shift for Turin from an insular, inward-looking view during its "industrial phase," when it functioned primarily as the location for Fiat's globally operating business and thus served as a mere host to a international network of the corporation. It was Fiat that brought international recognition, perhaps something that Boeing used to do for Seattle before it became internationally known as a destination and actor in its own right. Turin as a city was not the economic centre of the region, from which it was perceived to have withdrawn, functionally disconnected. City and metropolitan area (Provincia di Torino) were separate entities (interview, Regione Piemonte, 29 Jan 2004). Turin had effectively been reduced to a location in Fiat's production network, rather than a metropolitan centre and source of development in its own right. Instead, the region was looking to Milan as the "trendy," international city for metropolitan impulse and international reach. As a result, the sense of "region-ness" (see also Hettne &

Söderbaum, 2000) is developed much less than, for instance, in neighbouring Emilia Romagna with its industrial districts and "Third Italy" arrangements (Boschma, 2005; Bianchini), and a sense that the region is the sum of its cities with their individual economic specialisms which are nevertheless an integral part of the internationally operating regional economy.

It is here that the vision of Torino Internazionale emerged to re-/establish the city as a recognized metropolitan place, a regional centre and internationally connected and visible locality, with its own, specific characteristics and potential for further development. Actors involved included a broad range of interests across scales and sectors. The first step involved the governmental and institutional actors, such as Piemont regional and provincial governments, various branches of the Chambers of Commerce (Foreign Department, Brussels office), trade associations, the University, the Polytechnic, religious and consular organizations (Torino Internazionale, report and interview 29 Jan 2004). In the second stage, the local communities and resources were the focus, such as study centres, training centres, cultural and social institutions, and organizations with ongoing international relations.

Preparations for the Winter Olympics in 2006 provided extra impetus to deliver projects and make things happen "on the ground," rather than engage solely in designing grand strategy in virtual space. As a result, Torino Internazionale has come to be accepted not just as think-tank with "fancy ideas" but also as a relevant policy-maker. It has become part of the political establishment, they proved their credentials. One outcome of this has been the growing emphasis on "do-able" projects, proposed by the concept, so as to deliver results and convince policy-makers and the public alike of the feasibility and "realness" of the proposed re-invention of the city. This greater emphasis on doing things was also possible, because of the principle of cooperating, an initially new concept among relevant actors within the city, and between it and the region with its many small municipalities in the Turn hinterland (interview, Torino Internazionale, 29 Jan 2004). Driven by a technocrat, rather than political mayor, two strategic avenues were taken to make projects "happen": consultations (3 years) to connect the project with the public and establish a general acceptance of its purpose and ways of implementation (legitimation), and (2) openness, "listening" and seeking a broad coalition of actors and interests to minimize conflict, delay and obstruction (Associazione Torino Internazionale, 2000).

The new Metropolitan Conference served the purpose of a talking shop and negotiating table, and followed in its nature a central government's requirement for such a platform as part of the regionalization agenda. The Conference represents the visible political-institutional expression of a network-based, collaborative and consultative approach connecting horizontally municipalities and other relevant actors in the city-region (Associazione Torino Internazionale, 2000). In essence, it is a platform for discussion and negotiation between local representatives, with participating local governments, through their delegates sent to the Conference. And this provides indirect democratic legitimacy. The key task remains to convince the other urban municipalities of the benefits of closer cooperation with Torino, for example, through infrastructure measures that improve their economic prospects. In this respect, the strategic plan is a mere guidance for further development, as it takes governmental capacity to implement projects "on the ground."

Torino Internazionale operates at two levels: the grand strategy meta-level, involving strategic perspectives and involving public debate and participation beyond the government, and a detailed, project-based approach, where ideas are put into practice (Pinson, 2002). The link between "meta" and "project" is crucial for the sum of the projects adding up to a bigger strategic and "real" whole. There is thus a distinct separation between a non-state, non-governmental organization as collaborative platform for negotiations of interests, and an institutionalized governmental arrangement to implement agreed project. Tensions between the established public sector actors and policy-makers, and the organizational "new kids on the bloc" about control and influence are inevitable. The experimental novelty of this approach is in the attempt to scale-up Turin's imagined placeness as a city of historic importance, with a distinct societal and political-economic "milieu" (ibid.), to that of a strategic city-region with international standing and improved competitiveness.

This milieu is now being developed further as a distinct quality of the city that is expected to run under the now fashionable label of "smart." The city's strategic agenda is now subsumed under the Torino Smart City label, something not altogether novel as such. There are quite a few self-proclaimed "smart A-city" about. In this instance, however, both the city and surrounding region of Piemonte lay claim to that adjective, suggesting a link between city and region in strategic terms.

The Torino Smart City project interprets "smartness" as referring to a city "in which the quality of life improves with the ability to promote a clean and sustainable mobility, reducing the [*sic*] energy consumption, producing high technology, offering culture, be accessible" (www.torinosmartcity.it/English-version/, accessed 29 Mar 2017). This understanding involves, not surprisingly, conventional staples of "smartness," such as infrastructure and sustainability, but also goes beyond these by including culture as a field of innovativeness, and quality of life. Consequently, the strategy lists five core themes as guidance for policies and projects: energy, inclusion, integration, life & health, mobility (ibid.). Organizationally, Smart City Turin follows the structure of Torino Internazionale by being a foundation and thus sitting outside the city's bureaucratic hierarchy, yet also tied in with it for access to policy-makers. Yet, this arm's length position allows it to step out of the bureaucratic hierarchy and find new ways of engaging with the public in an effort to reach out and obtain a broader public support for the city's policies. Torino Internazionale did this through a trendy exhibition gallery in the main shopping street, and repeated adverts in the city explaining the intention/idea behind each relevant project/policy. Overall, therefore, Turin's development strategy:

aims at triggering urban innovation, and open innovative approach. It lever-ages on lean instruments to support fluid processes of innovation, sharing of the [*sic*] innovation risks, no closed [=open] governance system to develop the local ecosystem [through] collaborative knowledge and action, creating a multi-actor local ecosystem as well as a new open culture.

(Piero Fassino, mayor of Turin:
transition from Industry to Innovation,
www.cittametropolitana.torino.it, accessed, 18 Mar 17)

The strategy is thus clearly rooted in notions of innovation and re-/invention, drawing on the city's historic qualities and functions, including its urban life and civicness. As part of this, the strategy seeks to combine three main paths: develop a stakeholder network to reach out to, and draw on know-ledge of, the citizenry and civil society actors beyond civic hall, emphasize collaboration to boost political and policy learning, and use a set of targeted, "innovative initiatives co-develop by the city," such as PPPs to "co-develop innovative solutions for smart communities," use of public procurement to "deliver smart innovation" and engage in social innovation through the Torino Social Innovation (TSI) initiative. This includes three main "thematic priorities" around "people," the local community as a whole (civic society) and networks of communication. The latter are based around linking together social networks using interactive maps of neighbourhoods and the policy tools from the EU project WeGovNow (Fassino, 2017). As shown in Figure 5.7, the main policy fields comprising Turin's approach to "smartness" involve the variable overlapping of "participation" (democratic reach), "initiative" (inno-vation, engagement), "innovation for citizens' direct participation" (open, equitable governance), "innovation inside policy areas" and "markers and start-ups" (lighthouse projects). Innovativeness and flexibility and, associ-ated with that, learning, are thus key ingredients in Turin's understanding of smartness and its impact on, and facilitation through, the city's governance, including administrative innovation as a caption for "innovative," perhaps also creative, funding of local projects.

Torino Smart City emerged in 2011 out of integrated territorial programme *Sustainable Energy as Local Competitiveness Factor: A Plan for Turin in 2007*, the year after the 2006 Winter Olympics had brought the city and region together and generated a sense of pride and determination to achieve, to utilize the momentum and achieved international image, also building on the experience with Torino Internazionale. Similarly, Torino Smart City Foundation is about implementing governance, rather than state-based government, by bringing in key local stakeholders, such as the city's university and polytechnic, chamber of commerce and the municipalities of the metropolitan area, that is, the city-region. The approval of the Turin Action Plan for Energy (TAPE) in 2010 laid one cornerstone of the meaning of "smart" in Turin: sustainability and quality of life. This plan was developed further into the more comprehensive Torino Smart City Platform as organizing backbone for the emerged focus on

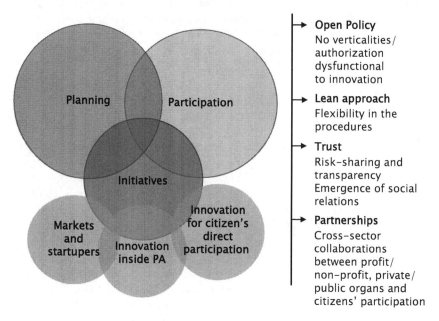

Figure 5.7 Turin's multi-dimensional approach to smartness.

Source: Mayor's web blog www.cittametropolitana.torino.it

"urban innovation policy" and policy-making innovation to achieve inclusive and sustainable growth. This Platform is more than a fixed foundation and starting point for the development of policies of spatial development, but, rather, serves as an evolving reference framework for policies and projects to foster inclusion, innovation, especially by drawing in young people and entrepreneurs (Torino Be Young as a social innovation project), competitiveness and related investment and innovation in financial and management structures (ways of doing things (Stefano Pisu, Project Manager, Torino Wireless). These are complex and, at times, competing, agendas, requiring a squaring of political circles (Herrschel, 2013). The smart city project in Turin involves an e-government service portal Torino Facile, access to city data AperTO [also = "open"] and encourages citizen participation through planned City of Turin web 2.0 services.

So, overall, in terms of governance, "smartness" comes in through emphasis on innovation in ways of doing politics and governing, with a focus on increased participation to broaden legitimacy of action, and collaboration with other actors across the city region, including municipalities. Policy innovation began with the Torino Internazionale project in the early 2000s, and this theme continues to be an important part of the city's efforts at transcending scales in its strategy to boost the city's visibility and recognition as major metropolitan player. The city's website shows a specific "international affairs" section and lists under this heading annual accounts of international missions by city delegates, going back to 2003, when such action was pursued more vigorously. In 2016, there were 15 such visits (www.comune.torino.it/relint/inglese/missioni/, accessed 29 March 17).

At the regional level, formal region Piemonte also seeks to gain a "smart" image, focusing on its tradition of technological innovation. But despite the mobilization of popular debate outside government, Torino Internazionale, is, in essence, an elitist project (Pinson, 2002) put in place, and shaped, by a group of technocrats around the then mayor, inspired by the success achieved with such "grand visions" and strategic approaches in Barcelona and Lyon. It is the personality of the mayor and his immediate collaborators, who act as the connector between "inside" and "outside" of government, that brings diverse interests and perspectives together in an agreed framework of shared interest. Yet, public institutions have remained central to the development and implementation of broader governance structures and discourses, acting as linchpins between institutionalized, territorially-bounded and locally-tied government, and relationally-expanded governance, that reaches across spaces, territories, institutions and the division between inside and outside of government. And it is in this ability to connect interests, actors and varying spaces of engagement and projected opportunity that smartness is required in the form of innovative, imaginative and thus learning forms of policy-making and governance, responding to intra- and extra-metropolitan dynamics or pressures and expectations.

Lyon: "stalled mover" – state-driven metropolitanization and the shift to "smart" labelling

Lyon is an interesting case of a metropolitan area that has grown from a rather vague metropolitan-ness hovering somewhere above the existing territorial structure of municipalities, region and *départements*, to a high-profile, image-making spatial narrative seeking to transcend boundaries between types of actors (public private), different scale administrations – within or without government. At 1.3 million, the conurbation is the second French metropolitan area after Paris, albeit with a sizeable gap (Figure 5.8).

The main goal of the city's leaders is to reach beyond the metropolitan region to the international, even global economic scale as part of its drive for greater competitiveness and visibility on the global economic arena. For this, in 2009, the logo of OnlyLyon was created – deliberately in English, to highlight internationality, rather than Frenchness (www.onlylyon.com/en/). Only Lyon has been set up as a roof organization – all virtual – of economic development and place marketing efforts, run by the city region's economic development arm – ADERLY (Lyon Area Economic Development Agency) – and also serves as portal for all leading economy and internationally related topics and organizations. It embraces local and regional governmental and non-governmental actors relevant to economic competitiveness and locational

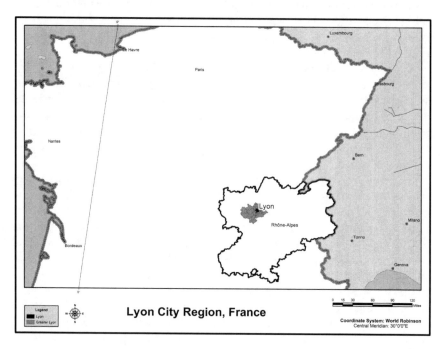

Figure 5.8 Lyon city-region, France.

appeal as a place to outside (foreign) investment. And this includes projecting a broad alliance and thus credibility to the public. Bodies involved include: Greater Lyon, Rhône County, University of Lyon, as well as key regional business representations as a reflection of the main target groups of this initiative: the Lyon Chamber of Commerce and Industry, ADERLY, Lyon Saint-Exupéry Airport, Lyon-Rhône Employers Association (MEDEF) and the Confederation of Small and Medium-sized Businesses (CGPME) (source: www.onlylyon.org, accessed 7 April 2013). There are thus clear elements of a triple helix arrangement.

This new arrangement goes well beyond the original venture into regionalizing the city's economic strategy in 2000, in response to the then French government's push to establish key city-regions as lighthouses (*poles*) for national economic competitiveness and success (Wendelin, 2014). It is part of a continuing process of spatially "upscaling" Lyon's strategic approach of profiling and internationalizing, embracing the regional to the international level as target. Much of this multi-agency approach depends on key persons in the emergent network, where the Lyon mayor holds a central position. The head of Grand Lyon and the COE of Lyon Chamber of Commerce jointly launched in 2013 the new branding campaign of "addicted to Lyon," focusing very much on personal qualities and impressions generated by the city and its population as a unique strength of international appeal. It follows the growing shift towards quality of life as a central dimension in competitive economic policy, of the kind that appeals to the so-called "creative class" as described by Richard Florida (2002).

Such a regionalization approach seeks to cut through compartmentalized administrative responsibilities as found in the rather complex setting of French local government with its multi-tiered, nested arrangement of governmental territories. This suggests "big government" (Morris, 1994) with overlapping and competing responsibilities and competencies and thus limited efficacy in foster- ing economic competitiveness. They reach from the sub-local *arondissements*, via communes and collaborative municipal associations – *communeautés urbaines* –, to the *départements* as regional subdivisions of the state. Then, there are the "official" regions as – from an EU perspective – more virtual, strategic, bodies with limited, yet specific powers, such as providers of regional public trans- port. Institutionally, they are not in a strict line with the centralized scalar state hierarchy, but, rather, are something of an additional "adjunct" scale and thus create some overlaps in geographic delimitation of powers and responsibilities. The hierarchically arranged, nested configuration of locally effective adminis- trative responsibilities adds to the local policy-making "milieu," also referred to as "local chord" (Randles & Dicken, 2004, 2017). Given this institutional "thickness," any new spatial unit, such as place marketing or arrangements for economic development and the space it applies to, is kept outside the state hierarchy to not add to this complexity. Thus, ADERLY, the Lyon economic development agency, has been set up as such an organization: an essentially virtual (or "soft"), institutionally thin umbrella organization. Its role is to act as interlocutor between business, especially inward investors, and the metropoli- tan bureaucracy by helping to cut through the layers of bureaucratization and bringing together otherwise separate, yet economically relevant, actors. These include the local universities and business organizations as important players with international links – and important bonus for the attempts of internationalizing the city region. Again, the triple helix model of cross-sectoral collaboration and innovation seems to have served as inspiration. At the same time, this arrange- ment marks a shift from state-directed government towards *city-regionally shaped governance* with a stronger self-organizing, bottom-up dynamic. Inevitably, as frequently found in city-regions, the challenge has been to negotiate, and bal- ance between, the two primary scales of policy-making – localist and collective, regional perspectives. This includes the search for ways how best to articulate and translate this scalar tension into effective policies.

The struggles between central state and city for setting the city-regional development agenda goes back to the 1960s, when, as expression of state centralism, a metropolitanization initiative (OREAM) by Paris established broad metropolitan planning organizations as spatial containers to capture socio-economic trends underpinning the development and prospects of met- ropolitan areas. In particular, this involved a "remit to promote the orderly economic development of the country at a time of rapid economic expansion" and "address the growing imbalance between Paris and the Île-de-France and the rest of the country by building up the major provincial cities" (Booth et al., 2001, p. 481). For Lyon, the proposed region included other major cities that thus lost part of their visibility and scope to boost their positions: St Etienne to the west and Grenoble in the east (Booth et al., 2001). This was the first explicit focus in national development policies on metropolitan areas as a specific phenomenon – of growing economic importance – making them stand out from the regions they used to be considered an integral part of. Yet, it was the centrally imposed *dirigiste* nature of the strategy that was viewed by the main metropolises as an attempt by Paris to extend its primary role and reach right through the state hierarchy to shape policy-making at the local level and thus also interfere with the, in France so important, local decision-making capacity (democratic legitimacy). Such de facto enhanced central orchestration of city-regional matters was thus met with considerable reservation (Randles & Dicken, 2004) and resulted in the abandonment of the plan in 1970 (Booth et al., 2001).

Although inherently ambitious in its geographic scope (Jouve, 2001), the main interest of the state was not, however, to micro-manage metropolitan development per se, but rather place them into a national economic policy framework to utilize secondary effects of metropolitan successes for the whole of the national economy in the interest of cohesiveness. This included counterbalancing the heavy concentration of activity in the Paris region. The critique of state meddling in local, especially metropolitan, affairs meant that the idea of centrally-directed metropolitan planning regions gave way to the smaller, more urban-focused metropolitan inter-communal cooperation – the aforementioned *communeautés urbaines*. Although, in principle, still drawn up by Paris, they provided more scope for local voice by being smaller entities, but managed to address two main concerns of central government: firstly, increased inefficiency through reduced localist thinking and policy-making, and, secondly, the potential for some of the large and powerful central communes, like the city of Lyon, to go their own ways. Pushing for a more regional scale of strategic thinking and acting sought to statutorily require four of the largest urban areas to form *communautés urbaines* which would provide a large range of services on behalf of the communes they represented. Though in principle the communes remained the base unit, the 11 services (including the preparation of land-use plans) transferred to the *communautés urbaines* represented a real threat to communal independence, and there was thus initial resistance to this external imposition. Yet, soon, the larger cities realized these *communautés* could also serve as sounding boards for their own ambitions and boost both their visibility and influence (Booth et al., 2001).

Developments in metropolitan governance in Lyon over the past 40 or so years have quite clearly shown multiple changes in the scale at which policy-making has been undertaken between, on the one hand, an interest in defining Lyon's metropolitan area as widely as possible to capture most of the functional connections, and, on the other, a focus on the actual built-up area of the city of Lyon proper as urban space. Bringing together difference, or following existing connectivity and cohesiveness are thus the alternative poles describing the options, so that it has been challenging to create a policy document for the metropolitan region with sufficient detail and thus negotiated interests, to serve as basis for policy decisions. It is here, that questions of local as against regional interests, perspectives and expectations need to be addressed and negotiated into a joint agenda so as to allow effective policy-making to emerge. And it is here that political leadership gains in importance as the third main topic of metropolitanization in the Lyon area: political influence and lobbying capacity, with individual mayors. Especially those serving a longer period of time, producing consistency in policy-making that also generates trust, predictability and reliability in political agendas, will find it easier to achieve negotiated outcomes that manage to square the circle between competing, or even contradicting, interests, by being able to agree a win–win outcome for all participants. Under such conditions, finding negotiated outcomes that manage to square the circle between competing, or even contradicting, interests is more likely to be achieved by suggesting a win–win outcome for all participants.

In line with other, similarly organized and rationalized collaborative arrangements at the city-regional scale, the *communautés* are indirectly legitimated in their policy-making though delegated councillors appointed to its board from the member municipalities (see for example, Vancouver, Seattle). In the case of Lyon, Greater Lyon (Grand Lyon) acts as the crystallization point, and centre of governance, of a grouping comprising the city and 54 surrounding municipalities. Given its size and functional and political connections and relevance, the city of Lyon possesses inherently considerable weight in this association of municipalities, which causes unease among the smaller members about being potentially drowned out and "pushed along," while not being given sufficient voice in any metropolitan-wide decisions (Randles & Dicken, 2004). Nevertheless, this imbalance does not seem to have created an anti-Lyon "ganging-up" among the 54 municipalities outside Lyon, based on a realization that value added can be achieved for each of them vis-à-vis both Paris and growing pressure for international competitiveness. A realization of ultimate mutual benefit arising from the collaborative undertaking seems to more than outweigh anxieties about metropolitan dominance.

The origins of the communal association of Grand Lyon go back to concerns about efficiency gains in delivering municipal services by pooling their provisions, One example is rubbish collection, a function that first brought the association to public awareness (interview, Grand Lyon, 28 Jan 2003). Only later, in the 1990s, economic development became more of a leading local policy objective; and so Grand Lyon was given the new remit of devising economic development strategies for the city region on behalf of the municipalities, also supported by a central government push for a stronger focus on (internationally-oriented) competitiveness-enhancing policy measures. Inevitably, that meant a leading role for the city of Lyon whose then mayor sought to open up the city to the outside world as a way of boosting the city's standing, especially vis-à-vis Paris. A high profile project of this internationalization strategy is the upmarket office development on the river Rhône near the city centre, the Cité Internationale, with international architecture in a river front location. Image and narrative around this project stands in direct opposition to the city's established inward-looking self centredness (interview, Grand Lyon, 28 Jan 2003), and included branding Lyon a European city. The European focus was underpinned by the city's leading role in setting up the Eurocities network, together with Glasgow (Herrschel & Newman, 2017). This strengthened, ambitious profile of the city boosts its already dominant position within the municipal association Grand Lyon, raising suspicions and concerns among the smaller municipalities subsumed under the Grand Lyon banner and concerned about losing their scope for self-government. Yet, to alleviate these concerns and potential obstacles for effective city-regional governance, Lyon invests considerable effort to consult the smaller municipalities, and other players, to gain broader support for its policies and strategies (Randles & Dicken, 2004). It is this platform function of Grand Lyon, offering a round table for negotiating regional priorities and policy agendas into a regional strategy and investment pattern, which legitimizes such policies and gives all members a sense of being equally part of the policy-defining process.

Collaborating closely with the Lyon Chamber of Commerce, its economic development arm, ADERLY supports and markets Lyon as an international city, promoting in particular the Cité International office development on the River Rhône. This collaborative network of players within and outside government very well illustrates the nature of governance by being institutionally thin, located outside established hierarchical territorial structures, and thus not adding to a regional scale already crowded with actors, but, instead, drawing on, and orchestrating, their existing arrangements as their individual contributions to ADERLY's implementational capacity. Meanwhile, the primary role of the construct of Grand Lyon is to provide a city-regional platform for bringing together the different types of stakeholding policy-makers, each embedded in their particular forms of organizations and organizational cultures, as well as spatial/territorial contexts, which, collectively, add up to Grand Lyon's policy-making efficacy. Sitting outside the immediate governmental hierarchy, the city-region's economic policies work primarily through the regional business community, and as such it seeks to build new forms of collaboration, while operating from little more than an office, some staff and a website. Its main assets and routes of operation are the connections into the business community, in close collaboration with the chamber of commerce, which it then seeks to connect to international corporate and political interests and networks.

As a result, the spatial model of the Lyon city-region shows a combination of differently scaled governmental territories and governance spaces, with most showing a more or less concentric pattern around the city (Figure 5.9): City of Lyon in the centre, then Grand Lyon, followed by the functionally defined, virtual urbanized space *"aire urbaine"* with some 300 municipalities, and, then, the equally virtual *"région urbaine."* This embraces other cities, such

as St Etienne, as the next neighbouring large city. In scale terms, regionalization is, in effect, going back to the 1960s description of state-led OREAM,
although then, it was meant to be a spatial container for centrally-defined
development policies, while the *région urbaine* is based on the opposite, bottom-
up approach of regionalization. It is based on existing functional connections
and inter-dependencies and thus defined indigenously from within the region
through regional actors and their collaborative engagement. Established in the
late 1980s through collaboration between Grand Lyon and the four *départements* underpinning the city region (Rhône, Isère, Ain, Loire), the *aire urbaine*
seeks to follow established functional relations and linkages in the city region
across administrative boundaries as a collaborative effort by the participating
municipal and governmental entities. In effect, therefore, metropolitanization
as a functionally defined, virtual space of cross-boundary collaboration was
raised to the level of the regional representation of the central state.

This brought into the game influential regional players with considerable
formal powers and fiscal capacity – the *départements*. It is these that ADERLY,
as virtual roof organization, can draw on and link up with to shape policies,
especially in the areas of public transportation (accessibility), sustainable development, metropolitan functions and improved cooperation between businesses,
planners and regional marketing people. This joined-up work has been considered crucial for fostering – but also projecting to the "inside" and the world

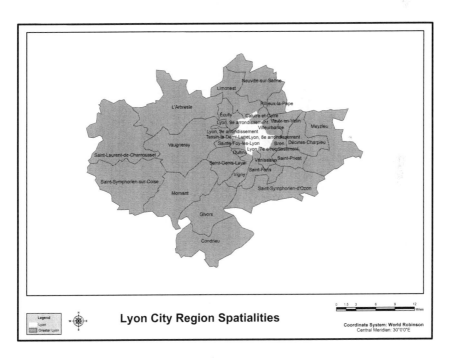

Figure 5.9 Lyon region territoriality/spatiality.

"outside" the city-region – successful development and good economic prospects. Nevertheless, ADERLY has had no specific powers of its own, but needs to bring together, and work through, the formal structures and institutions at local and regional level (*départements*, Grand Lyon) as recognized, not least also to boost their indirect legitimacy (interview, ADERLY, 28 Jan 2003).

Jointly, now, these actors have adopted "smartness" as a leading narrative, in line with many other cities seeking to appear "in trend." This involves a broad range of activities and projects between a greater focus on technology and one on innovation and creativity, including in politics. And such may also mean international engagement with technology companies elsewhere. Thus, for instance, Grand Lyon announced in 2013 "A New Partnership between NEDO and Greater Lyon to Undertake a Smart Community Demonstration Project in the Lyon Confluence from 2011 to 2015" (Le projet Lyon Smart Community à Lyon Confluence (www.grandlyon.com/projets/lyon-smart-community-confluence.html, accessed 26 Mar 2017) (Figure 5.10).

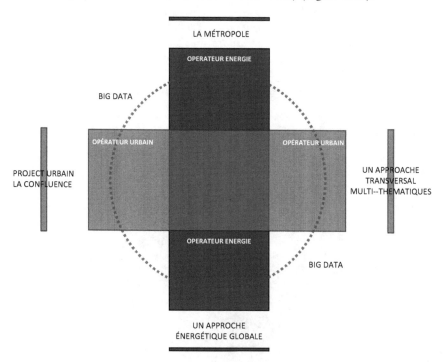

Figure 5.10 Lyon Confluence as smart project at the interface between global and urban processes in "smart energy" and "smart community."

Note: Lyon Confluence and the metropolis of Greater Lyon (Métropole Grand Lyon) as a three-dimensional intersection of variables: multi-party, multi-scalar and horizontal cross-sectional (sectoral), embracing, *inter alia*, basic provisions (water, energy), transportation (mobility) and democratic participation (engagement).

Source: Consortium: Pilote: Métropole Grand Lyon, Bouygues, SPL Lyon Confluence, GE/Alstom.

Looking at the role of "smartness" in Lyon as a way of innovatively responding to changing competitive opportunities, three main issues come to the fore: (1) the Lyon Confluence project as new "eco quarter" (Eco Quartier) and a public–private partnership, certified by WWF (and that matters for credibility) as a new river front residential and office development, (2) the new technology-based inter-connection with the population ("smart community") and (3) international engagement, such as through the link to Japan through NEDO (New Energy and Industrial Technology Development Organization), a Japanese public agency which promotes research and development and the dissemination of energy, environmental and industrial technologies. It was the innovative, experimental nature of this new development that proved particularly attractive, not at least for image reasons. And metropolitan smartness revolves around the concept of "smartness" also involves such now conventional policies as enhancing urban mobility (transportation), a policy field that finds itself widely circumscribed by national guidelines defining basic organizational principles which seek to reconcile mobility requirements of the population with sustainability (environmental) concerns, all written into a national urban mobility master-plan (UMMP). Set out in 1982 as a first and foremost transport planning document, it morphed increasingly into a more sustainability-embracing policy agenda (energy use) and became mandatory in conurbations of a population in excess of 100,000. The Lyon UMMP reaches across all *55 communes* of Greater Lyon (Communautès). In terms of governance, the Plan works through a dedicated consultative committee to coordinate and monitor the actions agreed between the decision-making partners across all scales of government: state, region, *département*, and the city region of Greater Lyon, plus economic partners and, as a sign of democratic "outreach," four user representatives. This model clearly represents a conventional "soft" arrangement of collaborative governance with minimum institutionalization and thus infringement of local powers and responsibilities. And so Lyon advertises itself as "Grand Lyon: la métropole intelligente qui fait rugir l'innovation" (www.grandlyon.com/elus/karinedogninsauze.html, accessed 23 Mar 2017) in relation to fostering new technologies as a "source of progress." Such fostering involves managing and strategically supporting economic change, as well as transforming spaces of production to accommodate new organisational forms and modi operandi, including adopting ecological methods of production and transportation. And this is to be facilitated by customized ITC and the use of "big data." As part of that, Grand Lyon announced in 2013 its Smart Data web presence in the shape of interactive maps including such things as location of city bikes or drinking water fountains.

Much of this is about redesigning the city to optimize its usability as part of a smart city concept under the title of "Lyon Smart City – La métropole intelligente de demain," which highlights the fact that Lyon was chosen in 2013 as the first smart city in France (M2OCity), with economic dynamics and sustainable development as primary criteria (descriptors). These were combined with image-changing large urban development projects, such as Confluence Lyon (https://www.aderly.fr/pourquoi-lyon/grands-projets/lyon-confluence/, accessed 26 Mar 17), which seeks to encourage and utilize imagination of, and building spaces for, new forms of urban living and working (www.aderly. fr/filieres-dexcellence/smart-city/smart-city/, accessed 26 Mar 2017). Such encouragement seeks to work through innovative solutions to economic challenges and opportunities to "create new businesses" and facilitate "energy transition" (tied in with new "solutions to transportation") www.business. greaterlyon.com/international-relations-48.html, accessed 26 Mar 2017).

Part of the policy innovation implied in conjunction with the Lyon Confluence project (devolved out of the Cité International project of the early 2000s) is the explicit internationalization strategy that the city has been pursuing for more than a decade now. This includes "boosting its visibility and its influence on the European and international scene by mobilising all the vital forces in the territory, and via partner cities, institutions and strategic international networks." www.business.greaterlyon.com/international-relations-48.html, accessed 26 Mar 2017). "Smartness" in Lyon rests on four pillars in its application to the concept of "smart city": (1) addressing environmental and energy challenges, (2) facilitate horizontal collaboration between policy fields and different types of actors, (3) reach out to, and involve more, citizens through user participation to shaping product/service delivery, and (4) facilitate the integration of new technologies to allow new ways of usage and addressing problems (www.aderly.fr/filieres-dexcellence/smart-city/smart-city/, accessed 23 Mar 2017).

The implicit innovativeness is also expressed in the label of Lyon as "intelligent metropolis" (*Métropole intelligente*), which also, inevitably, includes a sense of learning, and is given a time horizon of two to three decades to achieve the four objectives listed earlier: a global outlook, people focus, working collaboratively and multi-scalarly, with political imagination and strategic operation. The conceptual "intelligent metropolis" embraces four main dimensions: new forms of mobility (*ville agile*), digital services with easy access (*ville facile*), innovation in energy use (*ville durable*) and support for innovativeness (*ville de expérimentation*) (www.economie.grandlyon.com/smart-city-lyon-metropole-intelligente, accessed 26 Mar 2017). Intelligence and smartness are closely intertwined in Lyon's conceptualization of its Confluence neighbourhood in particular, but also the city in general. And here "smart community" serves as a key descriptor. As shown in Figure 5.11, this involves as multiple transition over five years from 2011 to 2016. This involves five parallel processes of managed change – or transition: the overall project as a whole, and, then, four parallel developments of specific themed projects related to eco-city characteristics: energy efficiency of buildings, electric mobility, eco-redevelopment of the city of Parrache and installation of a Community Energy Management System (Joss, 2011). And along each of the illustrated five transition paths, there are specific projects with allocated time slots to "make them materialize" over the five-year period.

Summing up developments in Lyon, it becomes evident that the Chamber of Commerce has been a key driver behind these informal,

Year	2011	2012	2013	2014	2015	2016	June
General overall planning of the project	Project selection		sign contracts with private sector	annual progr report	annual progr report	annual progr report	final report
Measures of energy efficiency improvement (*project goal 1*)	Project selection		project start (1st phase)		completion of measures		
Expand use of electric vehicles in public transport, incl sharing (*project goal 2*)	Project selection			inauguration of service / solar power system 'on'	end of demonstration period		
Retrofit home energy monitoring system, *Cité Parrache* (*project goal 3*)	Project selection			start fitting energy efficiency system	end of demonstration period		
Install community 'smart' energy management system (*project goal 4*)	Project presentation		opening 'big data' centre	local project presentation		end of demonstration period	

Figure 5.11 Eco-transition for Smart Community project in Lyon.

Based on Lyon Smart Community, at confluence of energy and the environment, media kit, available under: www.economie.grandlyon.com/fileadmin/user_upload/fichiers/site_eco/20121121_gl_lyon_smart_community_dp_en.pdf

thinly institutionalized and spatially virtual policy arenas which provide the backdrop to the re-imaging and re-organising of the city as a "smart city." ADERLY is a prime example of the new form of informal institutionalization as a way to overcome administrative divisions and the challenges that call for "speaking with one voice" for the whole city region vis-à-vis the outside (globalized) world. Straddling four *départements*, and sitting at the "edges" of three French regions, Grand Lyon, and its key advocator, ADERLY, illustrates the complex cross-border situation of the Lyon city-region. Here, different cultural and geographic regions meet, each with their own regional identities. The city provides an important common focus and interest that manages to reach across inter-institutional and inter-regional boundaries and govern the functional spatiality of the Lyon city region as though a conventional territorial reality. The competitive economic success of the city-region is recognized as advantageous by all relevant actors, with its "soft," virtual nature an important factor in its broad acceptance. There is no perceived threat to established actor autonomy and relevance, as the city-region phenomenon appears to just hover above the complex underlying administrative structures, rather than being imposed on them and cutting through established relations.

ADERLY, and now OnlyLyon, fit the bill of a "soft" platform and network for communication, negotiation and coordination, by offering, rather than imposing, an open platform – or "round table" – for different actors, with their various "owned" forms of territorialization and institutionalization kept largely out of play and thus unchallenged. This avoids adding more – potentially competitive – institutionalization and associated conflictual claims for power and control. Instead, the metropolitan (functional) area is the background and rallying point for the, in effect, virtual metropolitanization through ADERLY's voice, not administrative structures. In fact it is only through the institutional thinness and organizational lightness, that ADERLY can gain support and acceptance and thus become effective. Being under the stewardship of both the municipalities and the Lyon Chamber of Commerce, ADERLY's primary mission is to act on behalf of both local businesses and local governments, and doing so in an advocacy role without formal powers. The main tool at its disposal is its network, connecting policy-makers across institutional, territorial and strategic boundaries, and between business and local government. It is thus a clear illustration of regionalization through "soft power," relying on connections and networks – both as an existing as well as expanding resource – through which it generates increasing attractiveness and gains influence. As is the case with such thinly institutionalized, spatially virtual and network-based organizations and policy processes, there are questions about transparency and legitimacy, and it is here that the close connection to, and involvement of, the formal governmental institutions at local and regional level matter.

Smart governance and metropolitanized internationalization under post-Fordism in Turin and Lyon

Both cities, Turin and Lyon, illustrate the role of internal and external factors in their particular combination and inter-action in a city-region, and the specific interpretations and manifestations of "smartness" they produce. In both instances, external factors, such as state policies and the position of local and regional government in the state hierarchy matter, as do national policies to boost metropolitan-ness as a way to boost national economic competitiveness.

In Turin, smartness has much to do with re-establishing the city as metropolitan centre and actor nationally and, especially internationally and step out of the shadow of its industrial age under the dominance of the Fiat car maker. Political leadership, especially the fresh approach of a "non-traditional" mayor from outside the political machinery, provided new perspectives and ways of doing things, and, in conjunction with national policies of giving regional governance a more explicit metropolitan focus, and the designation of Turin as host of the Winter Olympics 2006, jointly provided the impetus needed to develop – and strategically pursue – a comprehensive agenda under the banner of "Torino Internazionale." Smartness, here, focused less established buzz words related to ICT and/or environmental issues per se, rather the advantages of more integrated and collaborative governing across the city-region horizontally, between municipalities, as between different types and actors. Smartness during that phase of the first decade of the 2000s thus clearly revolved around municipal leadership and re-/building a post-industrial city as part of a city-regional set-up, underpinned by promised – and expected – region-wide advantages from doing so. This sense of "getting up and go," that was expressed in the whole project, very much was shaped by the then mayor of the city – after changes here, the strategy lost its novelty flair and became more "traditionally" bureaucratic in its focus (institutional and administrative procedures). Smart City Torino as new metropolitan agenda sets out to update that agency, together with a new direction in focus towards innovativeness in societal, political-economic and urban development. This includes a more participatory form of governance to boost democratic legitimacy and discussion in urban policy-making. In other words, Smart City Turin has a lot to do with new, innovative and experimental ways of governing, using technology as a tool to develop more responsive and inclusive governance at the city-regional level.

In Lyon, metropolitanization and a shift to "smartness" as a public discourse follow national policy guidance and changes in the administrative structure to favour metropolitan leadership at the regional scale. This external impetus met an internal dynamic of internationalizing the city – not at least also, as second city in France, in competition with Paris, and turned the focus on sustainability and "smartness" into a clear label for the city's politics and profiling. The project Cité Internationale of the early 2000s, a large mixed-use development in a river front location morphed into Confluence Lyon as "smart city" example, combining international ambition, technology and business–government collaboration into an image-making project of an "eco city." Similar to Turin, this new emphasis on "smartness" surely also following a current trend, seems a natural evolution of earlier, innovative local projects into a new "version," in response to external incentives and attractions. This has led to particular local manifestations of this intersection between external and internal changes, leading to "transition" even at project level, such as Lyon's Confluence project.

Conclusions

The four cities in this chapter, Vancouver, Seattle, Turin and Lyon, clearly illustrate the respective effects of internal and external conditions for the adoption of innovative, novel policies that seek to marry competitiveness with a growing focus on people, be that as part of civil society and its multiple interests in economic wellbeing and quality of life, or residents aspiring to urban living. Such aspirations may sit at different scales, expressed in international, national or local discourse and agendas. In the four cities, local dynamics in developing novel policies were clearly affected by external factors, such as state structure and thus local powers, or policy incentives and projects that push local decisions in a particular direction. This may include re-organizing the territorial state, making available infrastructure money or setting out strategic plans that push for the recognition of "smart" criteria. This, then, has resulted in the different positions of the four cities in Figure 5.11 above in the power field of the two transitions – internal and external – and thus the earlier and more pro-active adoption of "smart" elements in governance, or, a much slower and more hesitant adoption of such policies.

Note

1 According to one Seattle-based volunteer group, for example, "coworking spaces are key aspects to a sustainable urban environment because they provide a platform for community among independent workers. When those communities form, all sorts of good things happen. New business opportunities are discovered, resources you didn't know existed are suddenly sitting at the next desk, personal relationships are formed and the rest of the local community grows stronger." See: http://collaborativespaces.org/.

References

Abel, T., White, J., & Clauson, S. (2015). Risky business: Sustainability and industrial land use across Seattle's gentrifying riskscape. *Sustainability, 7*(11), 15718–15753.

Addie, J-P. D. (2013). Metropolitics in motion: The dynamics of transportation and state reterritorialization in the Chicago and Toronto city-regions. *Urban Geography, 34*(2), 188–217. doi:10.1080/02723638.2013.778651

Alawadhi, S., & Scholl, H. J. (2013). *Aspirations and realizations: The smart city of Seattle.* Paper presented at the 46th Hawaii International Conference on System Sciences, Honolulu, Hawaii.

Alizadeh, T., & Sipe, N. (2016). Vancouver's digital strategy: Disruption, new direction, or business as usual? *International Journal of E-Planning Research, 5*(4), 1–15. doi:10.4018/IJEPR.2016100101

Assoziazione Torino Internationale (2000). *The Strategic Plan of Torino Internazionale 2000–2010.* Unpublished document. Available from http://images.torino-internazionale.org/f/Editoria/SP/SP.pdf, accessed 1 December 2017.

Bagnasco, A., & Oberti, M. (1998). Italy: "Le trompe-l'oeil" of regions. In P. Le Galès, & C. Lequesne (Eds.), *Regions in Europe* (pp. 150–165). London: Routledge.

Baker, M. (1998). Planning for the English regions: A review of the Secretary of State's regional planning guidance. *Planning Practice & Research, 13*(2), 153–169.

Bakkente, B. (2012, 23 April). Interview.

Balk, G. (2014, November 12). As Seattle gets richer, the city's black households get poorer. *Seattle Times.* Retrieved from http://blogs.seattletimes.com/fyi-guy/2014/11/12/as-seattle-gets-richer-the-citys-black-households-get-poorer/, accessed 22 July 2016.

Benko, E. (2011). *Overcoming resistance to density and desegregation in Seattle: Developing a model for high-density integrative transit oriented development.* Unpublished Master's Thesis, University of Washington, Seattle.

Bianchini, F. (1991). The Third Italy: Model or myth? *Ekistics, 58*(350/351), 336–345.

Bobbio, L., & Rosso, E. (2003). Torino tra Lione e Milano: politiche e istituzioni di livello metropolitano. Paper presented to the conference *Alta capacità Lione – Torino – Milano: Cooperazione o competizione fra aree metropolitane europee?*, Turin, 21 Feb 2003. Retrieved from www.comune.torino.it/atlantemetropolitano/pdf/Bobbio-Rosso.pdf, accessed 7 Jan 2018.

Bondonio, P., & Campaniello, N. (2006). Torino 2006: What kind of Olympic Winter Games were they? A preliminary account from an organizational and economic perspective. *Olympika: The International Journal of Olympic Studies, XV*, 1–33. Available from http://library.la84.org/SportsLibrary/Olympika/Olympika_2006/olympika1501c.pdf

Booth, P., Poxon, J., & Stephenson, R. (2001). The implementation of strategic land use policy: Lessons from the Lyon conurbation. *Regional Studies, 35*(5), 479–485.

Boschma, R. (2005). Social capital and regional development: An empirical analysis of the Third Italy. In R. A. Boschma, R. Kloosterman, & J. G. Lambooy (Eds.), *Learning from clusters: A critical assessment from an economic-geographical perspective* (pp. 139–168). Dordrecht, Netherlands: Springer.

Burnett, K. (2014). Commodifying poverty: Gentrification and consumption in Vancouver's downtown eastside. *Urban Geography, 35*(2), 157–176. doi:10.1080/02723638.2013.867669

Business Council of British Columbia. (2016). *News release*, 20 September 2016, available from http://bcbc.siraza.net/news-releases/2016/cascadiarelease, accessed 4 Aug 2017.

Carlson, T., & Dierwechter, Y. (2007). Effects of urban growth boundaries on residential development in Pierce County, Washington. *Professional Geographer, 59*(2), 209–220.

Caruso, N., & Saccomani, S. (2017). 4 Turin metropolitan region. In *Post-metropolitan territories: Looking for a new urbanity* (pp. 53–74). London: Routledge.

City of Vancouver. (2013). *Digital strategy*. Retrieved from http://vancouver.ca/files/cov/City_of_Vancouver_Digital_Strategy.pdf, accessed 15 Oct. 2016.

Dierwechter, Y. (2008). *Urban growth management and its discontents: Promises, practices and geopolitics in US city-regions*. New York: Palgrave.

Dierwechter, Y. (2010). Metropolitan geographies of US climate action: Cities, suburbs and the local divide in global responsibilities. *Journal of Environmental Policy and Planning* 12(1), 59–82.

Dierwechter, Y. (2013a). Smart city-regionalism across Seattle: Progressing transit nodes in labor space? *Geoforum, 49*(0), 139–149.

Dierwechter, Y. (2013b). Smart growth and state territoriality. *Urban Studies, 50*(11), 2275–2292.

Dierwechter, Y. (2014). The spaces that smart growth makes: Sustainability, segregation, and residential change across Greater Seattle. *Urban Geography, 35*(5), 691–714. doi:10.1080/02723638.2014.916905

Dierwechter, Y. (2017). *Urban sustainability through smart growth: Intercurrence, planning, and geographies of regional development across Greater Seattle*. Cham, Switz.: Springer.

Dierwechter, Y. (2018). The smart state as utopian space for urban politics. In A. E. G. Jonas, B. Miller, K. Ward, & D. Wilson (Eds.), *The Routledge handbook on spaces of urban politics*. London: Routledge.

Donald, B. (2005). The politics of local economic development in Canada's city-regions: New dependencies, new deals and a new politics of scale. *Space and polity, 9*(3), 261–282.

Driscoll, M. (2015). Friction is to be expected, but development in Proctor shouldn't catch anyone by surprise. *Tacoma News Tribune*. Retrieved from www.thenewstribune.com/2015/05/20/3801181_matt-driscoll-friction-is-to-be.html?rh=1, accessed 21 May 2015.

Environmental Protection Agency. (2009a). EPA dministrator Lisa Jackson, DOT Secretary Ray LaHood and HUD Secretary Shaun Donovan announce interagency partnership for Sustainable Communities. *Partnership sets forth 6 "livability principles" to coordinate policy*. Retrieved from http://yosemite.epa.gov/opa/admpress.nsf/0/F500561FBB8D5A08852575D700501350, accessed 21 Nov. 2017.

Environmental Protection Agency. (2009b). *HUD, DOT and EPA Partnership: Sustainable Communities*. Washington, DC: EPA. Retrieved from www.epa.gov/smartgrowth/pdf/dot-hud-epa-partnership-agreement.pdf, accessed 21 Nov. 2017.

Fassino, P. (2017). *Mayor of Turin: Transition from industry to innovation*. Retrieved from www.torinosmartcity.it/English-version/, accessed 29 Mar. 2017.

Filion, P., & Kramer, A. (2012). Transformative metropolitan development models in large Canadian urban areas: The predominance of nodes. *Urban Studies, 49*(10), 2237–2264.

Florida, R. L. (2002). *The rise of the creative class: And how it's transforming work, leisure, community and everyday life*. New York: Basic Books.

Florida, R. L. (2017). *The new urban crisis*. New York: Basic Books.

Fox, D. (2010). Halting sprawl: Smart growth in Vancouver and Seattle. *Boston College International and Comparative Law Review, 33*(1), 43–59.

Freilich, R. H., & Popowitz, N. M. (2010). The umbrella of sustainability: Smart growth, new urbanism, renewable energy and green development in the 21st century. *The Urban Lawyer, 42*(1), 11–39.

Gardheere, U., & Grant, J. (2014). Seattle housing authority rent proposal would hurt working poor. *Seattle Times*, 29 Sept.

Gray, M., Golob, E., & Markusen, A. (1996). Big firms, long arms, wide shoulders: The "hub-and-spoke" industrial district in the Seattle region. *Regional Studies, 30*(7), 651–666. doi:10.1080/00343409612331349948

Greater Vancouver Regional District. (2002). *Annual Report: Livable region strategic plan.* Vancouver.

Gregory, J. (2015). Seattle's Left Coast formula. *Dissent, 62*(1), 64–70.

Hackworth, J. (2016). Why there is no Detroit in Canada. *Urban Geography, 37*(2), 272–295. doi:10.1080/02723638.2015.1101249

Healey, P. (2003). Collaborative planning in perspective. *Planning Theory, 2*(2), 101–123.

Herrschel, T. (2010). Cities, suburbs and metropolitan areas: Governing the regionalised city. In M. Clapson, & R. Hutchison (Eds.), *Suburbanisation in global society.* Series: Research in Urban Sociology, Volume 10, pp. 107–130. Houndsmill, UK: Palgrave-Macmillan.

Herrschel, T. (2013). Competitiveness and sustainability: Can "smart city regionalism" square the circle? *Urban Studies, 50*(11), 2332–2348.

Herrschel, T. (2014). *Cities, state and globalisation: City-regional governance in Europe and North America.* London: Routledge.

Herrschel, T., & Newman, P. (2002). *Governance of Europe's city regions: Planning, policy and politics.* London: Routledge.

Herrschel, T., & Dierwechter, Y. (2015). Smart city-regional governance: A dual transition *Regions, 300*(4), 20–22.

Herrschel, T., & Newman, P. (2017). *Cities as international actors.* London: Palgrave.

Hettne, B., & Söderbaum, F. (2000). Theorising the rise of regionnes. *New Political Economy, 5*(3), 457–473.

HistoryLink Staff. (2002). Voters reject rail transit plan and three other Forward Thrust bond proposals on May 19, 1970. *History Link, Essay 3961.* Retrieved from www.historylink.org/File/3961, accessed 12 April 2015.

Jonas, A. E. G. (2012a). City-regionalism: Questions of distribution and politics. *Progress in Human Geography, 36*(6), 822–829. doi:10.1177/0309132511432062

Jonas, A. E. G. (2012b). Region and place: Regionalism in question. *Progress in Human Geography, 36*(2), 263–272.

Jonas, A. E. G. (2015). Beyond the urban "sustainability fix": Looking for new spaces and discourses of sustainability in the city. In D. Wilson (Ed.), *The politics of the urban sustainability concept.* Champaign, IL: Common Ground.

Jonas, A. E. G., & Ward, K. (2002). A world of regionalisms? Towards a US–UK urban and regional policy framework comparison. *Journal of Urban Affairs, 24*(4), 377–401.

Jonas, A. E. G., & Ward, K. (2007). Introduction to a debate on city-regions: New geographies of governance, democracy and social reproduction. *International Journal of Urban and Regional Research, 31*(1), 169–178. doi:10.1111/j.1468-2427.2007.00711.x

Jones, C. E., & Ley, D. (2016). Transit-oriented development and gentrification along Metro Vancouver's low-income SkyTrain corridor. *Canadian Geographer / Le Géographe canadien, 60*(1), 9–22. doi:10.1111/cag.12256

Jones, M. (1997). Spatial selectivity of the state: The regulationist enigma and local struggles over economic governance. *Environment & Planning A, 29,* 831–864.

Joss, S. (2011). Eco-cities: The mainstreaming of urban sustainability – key characteristics and driving factors. *International Journal of Sustainable Development and Planning, 6*(3), 268–285.

Jouve, B. (2001). Sectors and territories in territorial planning in Lyons. *Planning Theory & Practice, 2*(2), 222–230.

Kantor, J., & Streitfeldd, D. (2015). Inside Amazon: Wrestling big ideas in a bruising workplace. *New York Times,* 16 August, p. A1.

Katz, B. (2000). The federal role in reducing sprawl. *The Annals of the American Academy of Political and Social Science, 572*(Nov.), 66–77.

Kirkendall, R. (1994). The Boeing Company and the military-metropolitan-industrial complex, 1945–1953. *The Pacific Northwest Quarterly,85*(4), 137–149.

Lefèvre, C. (1998). Metropolitan government and governance in western countries: A critical review. *International journal of urban and regional research, 22*(1), 9–25.

Ley, D., Hiebert, D., & Pratt, G. (1992). Time to grow up? From urban village to world city, 1966–91. In G. Wynn, & T. Oke (Eds.), *Vancouver and Its Region* (pp. 234–267). Vancouver: UBC Press.

Leydesdorff, L., & Deakin, M. (2011). The triple-helix model of smart cities: A neo-evolutionary perspective. *Journal of Urban Technology, 18*(2), 53–63.

MacDonald, N. (1987). *Distant neighbors: A comparative history of Seattle and Vancouver.* Seattle: University of Washington Press.

Mariotti, I., Pacchi, C., & Di Vita, S. (2017). Co-working spaces in Milan: Location patterns and urban effects. *Journal of Urban Technology, 24*(3), 47–66. doi:10.1080/1063073 2.2017.1311556

Markusen, A. (1996). Sticky places in slippery space: A typology of industrial districts. *Economic Geography, 72*(3), 293–313.

Markusen, A., Hall, P., Campbell, S., & Deitrick, S. (1991). *The rise of the gunbelt: The military remapping of industrial America.* New York: Oxford University Press.

Mayer, H. (2013). Entrepreneurship in a hub-and-spoke industrial district: Firm survey evidence from Seattle's technology industry. *Regional Studies, 47*(10), 1715–1733. doi:1 0.1080/00343404.2013.806792

Metro Vancouver (2008). *Metro Vancouver sustainability framework articulates vision, charts course for the region.* Media release 18 June 2008. Available from www.metrovancouver. org/media-room/media-releases/MediaReleases/2008-06-18-MetroVancouverSustain abilityFramework.pdf, accessed 1 Dec. 2017.

Minard, A. (2014). Developers sue to make Seattle more developer-friendly. *The Stranger.* Retrieved from www.thestranger.com/seattle/developers-sue-to-make-seattle-more-developer-friendly/Content?oid=18781207, accessed 29 Jan. 2014.

Modarres, A., & Dierwechter, Y. (2015). Infrastructure and the shaping of American urban geography. *Cities, 47*(Supplement C), 81–94. doi:https://doi.org/10.1016/j.cities.2015.04.003

Morandi, C., Rolando, A., & Di Vita, S. (2015). *From smart city to smart region: Digital services for an Internet of Places.* Cham, Switz.: Springer.

Morris, P. (1994). *French politics today.* Manchester: Manchester University Press.

Orton, D., & Weick, K. (1990). Loosely coupled systems: A reconceptualization. *The Academy of Management Review, 15*(2), 203–223.

Pinson, G. (2002). Political government and governance: Strategic planning and the reshaping of political capacity in Turin. *International Journal of Urban and Regional Research, 26*(3), 477–493.

Portney, K. E. (2003). *Taking sustainability seriously: Economic development, the environment, and quality of life in American cities.* Boston: MIT Press.

Puget Sound Regional Council (PSCR) (2009). *VISION 2040.* Seattle: Puget Sound Regional Council. Available from http://psrc.org/growth/vision2040/pub/vision2040-document/, accessed 5 April 2012.

Rabe, B. (2011). Contested federalism and US climate policy. *Publius, 41*(3), 494–521.

Randles, S., & Dicken, P. (2004). "Scale" and the instituted construction of the urban: Contrasting the cases of Manchester and Lyon. *Environment and Planning A, 36*(11), 2011–2032.

Rossiter, S., Cameron, K., & Harcourt, M. (2007). *City making in paradise: Nine decisions that saved Vancouver.* Vancouver: Douglas & McIntyre.

Rothblatt, D. N. (1994). North American metropolitan planning: Canadian and US perspectives. *Journal, American Planning Association, 60*(4), 501–520.

Scholl, H. J., & AlAwadhi, S. (2016). Smart governance as key to multi-jurisdictional smart city initiatives: The case of the eCityGov Alliance. *Social Science Information, 55*(2), 255–277. doi:10.1177/0539018416629230

Scott, A. (2001). Globalization and the rise of city-regions. *European Planning Studies, 9*(7), 813–826.

Scott, A. (2012). *A world in emergence: Cities and regions in the 21st century.* Cheltenham, UK: Edward Elgar.

Studer-Noguez, I., Wise, C., Studer, I., Studer-Noguez, I., Wise, C., & Studer, I. (2007). *Requiem or revival? The promise of North American integration.* Washington, DC: Brookings Institution Press.

Vanolo, A. (2008). The image of the creative city: Some reflections on urban branding in Turin. *Cities, 25*(6), 370–382.

Walker, S. (2016). Urban agriculture and the sustainability fix in Vancouver and Detroit. *Urban Geography, 37*(2), 163–182. doi:10.1080/02723638.2015.1056606

Wendelin, M. (2014). Territorial equality in France: A historical perspective. In *metropolitiques. eu,* 4 June 2014. Available from www.metropolitiques.eu/spip.php?page=print&id_article=679&lang=fr, accessed 12 Dec. 2017.

White House. (2015). Administration announces new "smart cities" initiative to help communities tackle local challenges and improve city services. www.whitehouse.gov/the-press-office/2015/09/14/fact-sheet-administration-announces-new-smart-cities-initiative-help, accessed 13 Feb. 2016.

Wingfield. (2017). Amazon's living lab: Reimagining retail on Seattle streets. *New York Times,* 13 Feb., p. B1.

Wly, E. (2004). Commentary: The accidental relevance of American urban geography. *Urban Geography, 25*(8), 738–741. doi:10.2747/0272-3638.25.8.738

Yeates, M. (1990). *The North American city* (4th edn.). New York: Harper & Row.

Ziegler, E. H. (2010). Sustainable urban development and the next American landscape: Some thoughts on transportation, regionalism, and urban planning law reform in the 21st century. *The Urban Lawyer, 42/43*(4/1), 91–103.

6   Beyond post-authoritarian regimes

Smart city-regionalism in Eastern Europe and South Africa

Introduction: regime changes and smartness in city-regional governance

This chapter looks at the role of dynamically changing external conditions for the shaping of city-regional governance at the national and macro-regional level. The emergence and development of "transition regimes" (Fishman, 1990; Linz & Stepan, 1996) as changing "external" milieux has provided particular challenges, but also opportunities, for adopting and shaping smartness in city-regional governance as a local/regional ("internal") process of change. Both processes interact and thus combine different dynamics, as described earlier under the concept of "dual transition" (Chapter 4). Both scales of change – or transition – are characterized by extensive regime changes – albeit at a different pace and to a different extent, which result both in uncertainties, yet also new opportunities, to identify novel ways of doing things to boost the efficacy of policies vis-à-vis globalization and the pressures of economic competitiveness.

The phenomenon of "transition" has attracted a considerable amount of interest, both in political and academic debates (Altvater 1993; Gowan, 1995; Murrell, 1996). Arguments have revolved around the nature of change, whether this process would be ad hoc and complete, as suggested by Offe and Adler (1991), or more gradual like "transformational recession" (Kornai, 1993, 1994) or "learning on the job," what Elster et al. (1998) termed "rebuilding the boat in the open sea." The sudden and wholesale collapse of the communist regimes across Eastern Europe, marking the end of the post-war bipolar world order, focused attention much more generally on "regime change" as a process and conceptual object. This led to a plethora of publications on forms, processes, variations and mechanisms of "transitions" and whether there was an inherent tendency to "catch up" with the West and its "standard" democratic market liberalism (Kolodko, 2001).

Prior to the end of the communist regimes, the term of "transition" referred primarily to developing countries, and presumed a "standard" trajectory towards a Western-style market democracy (O'Donnell et al., 2013). Such a rather one-dimensional understanding of the outcome of societal development was strongly advocated during the 1980s. And so it did not really come as a surprise when the projected struggle between communism and liberal market democracies was considered "won" by the latter, as embodied in Fukuyama's boasting of an "end of history" (Fukuyama, 1992) and the ultimate pre-eminence of Western capitalism. This perspective has also been promoted by international organizations as part of the Washington Consensus of the early 1980s, then, for developing countries, with democratization, marketization and privatization as doctrinal *sine qua non* to qualify for support by the World Bank, for instance (see also Herrschel, 2007). And so it does not come as a surprise that there had been no interest in, or awareness of, a consideration of the underlying structural difference in "transition countries," which may affect the ways of doing things and thus the process of "transition" per se.

This hegemonic discourse projected onto the world the notion of a superior "West" as compared with non-Western regimes and, indeed, made it an integral part of the globalization agenda. The term "transition" *per se* thus points to a transformational process towards an envisaged "ultimate" stage of development. This may vary, of course, as has been argued in the past, such as between liberal market democracies on the one side, and Marxist communism, on the other. Getting there, it has been argued, requires certain formal, structural preconditions, be they economic development, to support democratization (see Rustow, 1970), or class struggle, as Marxists see it.

These external transitioning contexts thus vary in their complexity and extent, with those in former communist countries varying the most. This is because here in Central and Eastern Europe, for instance, all three main spheres of transition – economy, society and state – changed simultaneously (the so-called "triple transition"), often with an added fourth dimension of change, that of identity as part of nation and state building, that is, the so-called "quadruple transition." Kuzio (2001) thus speaks of a quadruple transition. In contrast, other forms of regime transition, such as that in South Africa, embrace just two major shifts: those in society and the nature and operation of the state, as the apartheid system got dismantled and a new democratic regime put in place. There were fewer of the fundamental economic shifts found under post-communism (Marias, 1998; McDonald, 2008).

These transformative changes have had major implications for the ways in which city-regions can function. In Central Europe, the main focus here within the post-communist world of Eastern Europe, the urban regions, especially those around the capital cities, have been at the forefront of the post-communist transition process towards a democratic market economy Western style. This has unearthed, and also reinforced, underlying inequalities in opportunities, yet also rendered as economically superfluous production systems guided by political, rather than economic considerations. Another legacy has been the somewhat volatile emphasis on the role of the state between neoliberalism, on the one hand, and étatism, on the other. There has also been engendered a strong sense of national self after regaining full sovereignty at the end of Soviet domination in 1991. Approximating "Western Europe," especially its free market model based on private consumption, has been a primary motivation of the changes, with democratization adopted as part of the bargain, and, because it was associated with the United States, as antidote to the confines of the Soviet Union. Such European "adjustment pressures" obviously have not played a key role in South Africa, where, instead, global and national dynamics of societal change have been paramount, especially claims to equality and civic rights as internationally recognized "standard." The inherited apartheid system was irreconcilable with that, and its formal abolition has had major implications for the socio-geographic and political-economic structuring of city-regions and their governance.

The case studies chosen seek to illustrate some of the key features of these two types of transitions of societal-political and also economic regimes and modi operandi. In the post-communist context of "Westernization," its impact on the formulation and implementation of the principles of "smart" city-regional governance will be examined for two cases from Central Europe – Berlin and Prague. Both are capital cities and therefore "special" in their respective national contexts of state structure (federalism versus centralism) and degree and nature of "transition." The two South African cases show the "external" impacts of common national policies and constitutional-legal structures – following the principles of Western "norms" of democracy, but also demonstrate how (internal) smartness discourses have varied considerably within the country as both city-regions reposition their space-economies in light of extant ecological limits and racial inequalities (OECD, 2008). This chapter therefore asks the fundamental question: How have these external (national) changes in inherited state structures, governing regimes and ways of policy-making affected scope and capacity, public discourses, as well as the agenda of city-regional governance to acquire "smartness"?

Beyond post-socialism: regime transition and metropolitan governance in Berlin-Brandenburg and Prague

The nature of post-communist regime change in Central Europe has impacted on the ways in which city-regional governance has developed. This includes the role of legacies of institutional practices, such as a strictly hierarchical order with top-down government with no scope for own local or regional policy choices, the absence of local decision-making capacities and the bureaucratic nature of administrative procedures kept out of view of the public. The two examples of city-regional governance under condition of post-communist transition, Berlin and Prague, illustrate the complexities resulting from a newly gained system that requires independent local and regional decision-making and government. There is thus greater responsibility for own decisions than under a hierarchical centralism, yet there was little experience with doing so and utilizing available policy measures, including inter-municipal cooperation.

Convention under socialism was for a strictly territorialized state, with clear allocation of administrative responsibilities, circumscribed by territorial boundaries. These boundaries became signatures of empowerment after post-communist, also under the influence of the EU's standards, meaning greater levels of self-governing at the local and regional level. Both cities are capital cities, which provides them with a particular dose of dynamism, as well as relevance as signifiers of the role of external regime change. Both cities share a clear administrative and functional-economic separateness from their hinterlands, with distinct own governmental capacities. In Berlin's case, a new focus on local self-responsibility after German unification in 1990 also meant an increase in inter-local and inter-regional competitiveness, encouraged by fiscal arrangements that reward non-cooperation through then likely increased local tax revenue (Hauswirth et al., 2003). Non-cooperation can also take on the meaning of individualist assertiveness on the basis of new powers – at last, one can make own decisions, rather than merely having to implement central orders handed down the political hierarchy.

It is here that novel and imaginative – "smart" – ways may be required, but also made possible, to reconcile reflexes based on historic systemic experiences and facing changing requirements as a result of far-reaching political-economic changes under the impact of regime transition. Responses to this conundrum by the two cities discussed here, Berlin and Prague, differ, especially with regards to adopting the image and label of "smart city" as a programmatic focus to imply creativity and shrewdness in governing the city-region. In Berlin, "Smart Berlin" has been developed into a distinct label with its own website and attachment to the leadership of the city. Indeed, much of Berlin's strategic planning revolves around this term and thus seeks to attach itself to high-tech economic development, including plans to turn the current main airport, Tegel, into a high-tech business park, after the airport's replacement by a new one further out of the city (www.berlintxl.de/en.html, accessed 18 July 2017). In Prague, by contrast, the term "smart" does not feature at all in official documents or websites of the city. Only in a small blog by a local NGO does the name "smart Prague" appear as a label for IT application-oriented development and thus adoption of a current trend in policy discourses.

In European polity, the claim and promise of "smartness" as driver of policy decisions has spread in political discourse and documents. Indeed, the adjective "smart" has become a label *de rigueur* for cities and regions; it seems to signal openness, innovativeness and trendiness as a place to live and work. And as such, it has become an increasingly universally adopted term to describe local and regional characteristics. But how does this impact on actual policies? Can it be more than a mere label to "keep up with the Joneses," as the saying is? Or does it mark changes in political processes, especially in city-regions and policy agendas, where policy learning allows identification of the link between individual local opportunities and the economic performance of the city-region as a whole. Yet political advantages are often tied closely to localist views and ways of action (Herrschel & Newman, 2002), Comparative studies suggest compelling reasons for better inter-governmental cooperation (Bolleyer, 2009; Sellers, 2002; Herrschel, 2014) between core cities and their environs: (1) the functional dispersal of urban activities that spread beyond central city boundaries requires institutional and policy coordination; (2) European Commission funding programmes require horizontal cooperation; and (3) competition driven by increasing economic globalization. Yet, these advantages need to be recognized and, importantly, understood by the public, so as to reward politicians venturing out onto the collaborative regional stage with political rewards (election). Effective regional governance should be able to concentrate expenditure on promoting the strengths and overcoming the weakness of city-regions, so that a "good return on investment," also from a political perspective, can be obtained.

Yet, generally it is also considered to require effective city-regional institutions to support such relationally, virtually "re-territorialized" economies (Brenner, 2004) "on the ground." It is just here, at the intersection of such policy spaces and the actually existing governmental structures that tensions and contradiction may occur and thus require innovative solutions. Established structures are reluctant to change and generally prefer the status quo as modus operandi. Concern about likely future implications, loss of local influence and established practices and expectations about "appropriate" ways of doing things all matter. Particularly in the former communist European East, newly won powers and policy-making capacities at the local level are guarded against perceived erosions through any resurgent supra-local layers of power. Such concern is the outcome of past experiences with top-down political centralism of authoritarian regimes, which embraced all aspects of political-economic and administrative-governmental conditions and developments (Kuzio, 2001). So, often it amounts to a challenge between trying to maintain the now familiar newly democratic and EU-conforming status quo of public administration and democratic legitimacy of governance, on the one hand, and the realization that changes may open up new opportunities through more effective and responsive ways of doing politics, including greater flexibility, even innovativeness in political practices and the range of policies and agendas pursued.

The dynamics of relationships between the multiple actors across scales of governance matter in their ability to respond to functional imperatives and overcome fragmented or spatially "mismatching" authority and possible intra-regional localist place wars with associated diseconomies through administrative inefficiency and obstructionism caused by politically motivated non-communication and non-cooperation/coordination within city-regions. Local advantages need not necessarily be gained through "going it alone," despite close functional interdependencies, even if such individualism may go down well as rhetoric with local electorates. Instead, collective action may ultimately offer greater local rewards by sharing a bigger (city-regional) "cake." The challenge, and political skill, is to identify and publicly "sell" such indirect manifestations of gains to the electorate in local elections with their often localist outlooks. It is here that the Berlin and Prague city-regions clearly illustrate the impact of divisive administrative arrangements, as well as the influence of wider structural (national) frameworks. At the national level, Berlin is part of a federalized system, while Prague is the centre of a centralized administrative structure. The regional level thus possesses very different functions in the two states, being represented by federal states in Germany, and being mere administrative entities, not at least in response to EU regional policies and support funding, in the Czech Republic.

Yet, both cities share the administrative arrangement of a "spatial doughnut," where the city sits within a surrounding separate region, with clearly divided responsibilities for spatial development, but close functional inter-dependencies between the two entities. In Berlin, the height of that division is greater, as it separates two federal states, than in Prague's case, where we are looking at merely administrative, not governmental-democratic, entities. The challenges for city-regional governance thus originate in both cases from a clear mismatch between administrative and functional geographies. Matching the two through territorial re-arrangements is unlikely as there has been political resistance to any re-bordering (Herrschel & Newman, 2005; Hauswirth et al., 2004), and so only soft ways forward are available to city-regional governance, requiring actors to communicate and negotiate in a "smart" way. Yet "smartness," as pointed out before, has many meanings and applications, and, indeed, degrees of adoption.

Berlin: "smart" as label for image-making and highlighting innovativeness

Berlin is an interesting example of the complex governance challenges for a city-region because of its multiple internal divisions through cross-cutting borders and boundaries. These reflect its history as "divided city" during the Cold War, with West Berlin a political-economic "Western" exclave within communist East Germany. German unification in 1990 brought together two very different political cultures and experiences which, up until this day, continue to make themselves felt, albeit less immediately evident in the centre. Greater differences can still be found between a growing and internationalizing metropolitan capital city and a surrounding, much less populated and economically productive hinterland of the federal state of Brandenburg. Both are separated by an important, relatively "high" administrative boundary between two federal states and their competing competencies. And this adds to an inter-municipal competition for residents and/or businesses to boost the local tax base which, in turn, determines scope for policy-making capacity of devolved local self-government (Herrschel,1997). Arrangements for local finance thus reward competitiveness, rather than collaboration, both at the local and state (*Land*) level (see Hauswirth et al., 2004; Herrschel & Newman, 2005). At the same time, growing suburbanization around Berlin produces increasing functional inter-relations and inter-dependencies, creating new spatial inclusions and exclusions between an "inner ring" of rapidly growing municipalities around Berlin and an outer, peripheralized part of the state of Brandenburg, with much lower growth dynamics (Zawatka-Gerlach, 2017).

Berlin with its 3.4 million inhabitants is an island in the middle of Brandenburg, far away from the Western European economic centres. Due to their history both East and West Berlin remained economically and administratively separated from their "natural" hinterland of the Brandenburg region. For West Berlin, surrounded by the Wall, any links to the GDR "*Umland*" had been impossible and in East Berlin suburbanization was politically unwanted as a sign of bourgeois lifestyle and weakening of East Berlin's presence as the GDR state capital. Most of the regional infrastructure circumvented West Berlin, establishing lengthy detours to the eastern half. It has taken up until now, more than a decade after the demolition of the Wall, to reconnect the western half of Berlin with its hinterland, that is, "core" with "hinterland." Administratively, however, if of a very different quality, the path of the old Wall continues its separating presence. The continued psychological impact of the former Wall gives the administrative boundaries between former West Berlin and the surrounding (formerly East German) Brandenburg quite a distinct quality compared with the similarly organized city states of Hamburg and Bremen. This is evident in today's relationship between Berlin and Brandenburg.

Not surprisingly, the separation between Berlin and Brandenburg has been perceived as "unnatural." Thus, the Brandenburg Prime Minister, Manfred Stolpe, described his state as "the *Land* with a hole in the middle" (Cochrane & Jonas, 1999, p. 155). Its economic structure and development depend on Berlin, yet there is no administrative or governmental access to this economic base. This is of particular importance, as there are no other major metropolitan areas in Brandenburg, giving Berlin a by far dominant position in its urban hierarchy. There are only four cities exceeding 50,000 inhabitants, less than 1/60th of Berlin's size. Even Brandenburg's capital, Postdam, can muster only 130,000 inhabitants, and it is an integral part of the Berlin conurbation. There is massive structural unevenness in the Berlin city-region between the urban core and the rural, sparsely populated "ring" of Brandenburg. This is the case especially in the outer areas with their much lower development potential than those parts closer to Berlin. These discrepancies, and thus policy requirements, are not reflected in the administrative arrangements. In some areas, like in northwest Brandenburg, local authorities joined together in self-help development policies.

Such unevenness produces formidable political challenges, as the current support found in Western countries for populist politicians promising inclusion and shared rewards from economic activity. Adopting "smartness" in framing policies may offer an opportunity to reconcile the conflicting agendas of internationally-focused (and driven) metropolitan competitiveness to boost local revenue, and core-periphery cooperation to address functional inter-dependencies, especially in transportation, and thus contribute to reducing spatial developmental and opportunity gaps both within and between city-regions.

Government within the wider Berlin city-region is fundamentally shaped by the fact that a state boundary runs through that region, separating two administrative-governmental and institutional regimes with considerable powers and responsibilities within the federated German state. Each possesses its own electoral considerations – such as controlling sprawling suburbanization in Berlin, versus seeking to attract inward investment in the surrounding, much less populated and economically developed municipalities of Brandenburg. But even here there are differences that follow a clear distance decay model – the further away from Berlin, the less growth there tends to be. The result is a concentric division of Brandenburg into a suburbanizing inner ring around Berlin, and a more struggling, rural and often stagnating or shrinking range of municipalities in the outer ring (Figure 6.1).

Quite evidently, such contrasting development has not only brought clashes between economic aspirations and environmental concerns for preservation and planned development, but also vivid clashes between "winners" and "losers" at the local level. For Berlin, Brandenburg serves primarily as back-up and recreational space (such as through Country Parks), where low development is seen as a welcome antidote to the hustle and bustle of the city. For the municipalities of Brandenburg, however, and the state, the opposite is true: while environmental protection and restriction of sprawl is all very well, it does not generate immediate revenue and thus a fiscal basis for genuine self-government. Nor does it produce politically useful evidence of economic growth and thus improved qualities of life for the residents. Interests are thus diametrically opposed. Such improvement is crucial, as we can now see in the

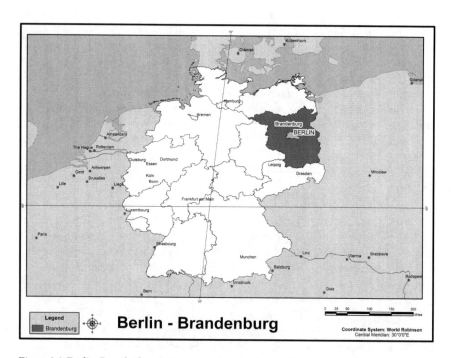

Figure 6.1 Berlin-Brandenburg city-region among the 16 federal states in Germany.

current political climate of populist clashes between a stylized "metropolitan elite" (seen simultaneously as political elite; Glaser, 2016) and a decoupled "left behind" rural population and places, especially in the former communist East. Maintaining, or even generating, support for the new liberal democratic, post-communist market society requires support among the population at large; the alternative may be a shift in support for a paternalistic authoritarian regime with cradle to grave care by the state, such as the communist state had promised.

Brandenburg's policy-makers thus face very contrasting conditions and thus policy requirements and expectations among the population in different parts, and they need to straddle and reconcile these competing or even conflicting agendas/ requirements. And this requires innovativeness and also a degree of experimentalism in framing and implementing governance for the whole of the city-region across the administrative, political, historical and social-economic boundaries. Both the regional states (*Länder*) and local governments face considerable financial pressures and, as part of fiscal arrangements, need to raise significant parts of own revenue individually through taxation to balance the books. There is thus a fiscal incentive to attract residents and businesses, as both are important sources for local and state revenue.

For hinterland municipalities, seeking to become a commuter village may well be a financially more rewarding (and, possibly, realistic) policy goal than trying to attract substantial new business. The local income situation thus clearly encourages competitive rather than cooperative thinking. New sub-urban residential or business developments also offer politically useful signs of achievement and "progress." Legacies matter in the form of accepted and pursued principles of governing at city-regional level. In former communist Eastern Europe, the region was an important level for relaying orders from the top down in the strictly hierarchical political and economic system. The region was thus the primary level of control of local developments and administrative procedures (and production processes) by the central state which was symbolized by its capital city.

Residential development in the Berlin city-region is driven by considerable suburbanization. This reinforces a stark contrast between the economically well-to-do places on those development axes, and the rather rural, economically backward and often shrinking communities away from these and further out from Berlin. By the end of the 1990s, there were more than 109,000 commuters coming from the Brandenburg hinterland and many more using Berlin's services. These figures were counterbalanced by the some 51,000 Berliners commuting into Brandenburg (*DerTagesspiegel*, 13 July 1999). Today, the figures are: 277,424 in-commuters and 166,350 out-commuters (www. rbb-online.de/wirtschaft/thema/2016/pendleratlas/beitraege/pendleratlas. html, accessed 26 Jan 2017).

"Smartness," as an explicit policy, has only recently made it into the discourse of Berlin's politics, when it was formally adopted in 2015 in the shape of the Smart Berlin Strategy. Much of its focus takes a rather "conventional" ICT-oriented approach through a technology-focused primary concern with high-tech "start-ups" or e-mobility (www.stadtentwicklung.berlin.de/planen/foren_initiativen/smart-city/download/Strategie_Smart_City_Berlin_en.pdf, accessed 14 July 2017). "Smart" is thus closely associated with ICT-supported efficiency gains in infrastructure provision. "to maintain their performance capabilities even in the face of increasing or changing demands, to improve the quality of their services for their customers and to achieve a sustainable reduction in their consumption of resources" (SDUDE, 2015, p. 3).

Officially launched by the city council in April 2015, the Smart City Berlin strategy, however, also seeks to take the agenda further with more innovative ways of policy-making, especially collaborative engagement across types of actors, territories and interests in the city-region – reaching well beyond Berlin city limits. In this way, the Berlin admnistration's understanding of "smart" goes beyond an ICT focus and adds organizational and governance aspects:

> But what actually makes cities "smart" and therefore viable for the future? As Berlin sees it, cities which are viable are those which achieve a significantly higher or stable quality of life while using the same or a lower level of resources. This can only be achieved by means of an urban management which, by using innovative information and communication technologies.
>
> (Ibid., p. 5)

Overall, the Smart City Berlin strategy seems a project still in progress, or in "transition," rather than being a fixed roadmap. Thus, it ventures to meet, and engage with, diverse circumstances and thus policy requirements in recognition of the variety of answers required. A potentially effective way of addressing that, and also squaring the circle between competing and, possibly, conflicting interests which make finding solutions more challenging, is seen in network-building to reach out to stakeholders, while also promoting the city-region's openness, creativity and innovativeness as a place-quality to an international audience. Such collaborative approach is deemed more promising than seeking to re-organize the state through administrative reforms including, as "grand solution," a merger between the two federal states, Berlin and Brandenburg. After the failure to do so, stopped by a plebiscite (Herrschel & Newman, 2002; Hauswirth et al., 2004), there is little political currency or, indeed, appetite for, trying again.

The primary rationale behind restructuring the state through the merger was projected savings through reduced administrative duplication and greater economies of scale. These included jointly created and managed infrastructure, environmental management, water supply, etc., rendering obsolete an otherwise complex administrative "jungle" of more than two hundred inter-*Land* contracts. Also, the joint population of some six million was deemed the necessary minimum for adequate administrative capacity of a *Land* government. The rationalization-driven proposed merger of city and hinterland region, however, faced considerable political and institutional obstacles as a result of political legacies – opposition to historic dominance of Berlin – as well as new admin-istrative arrangement under local "self-government." This applied in particular in the face of the dominant role of Berlin as capital of the GDR and thus seat of the former totalitarian government – and national (German/Prussian) capital before that (Benz & Koenig, 1995). These underlying animosities and resent-ments, inherited from the days of the Cold War and the East–West divisions in and around Berlin, have largely been held responsible for the popular rejection of the proposed merger between the two *Länder* of Berlin and Brandenburg in the referendum in 1996. Despite support by the two *Land* (state) govern-ments and other organizations, issues of identity and political self-government proved paramount. The result highlighted the importance of legacies, with a "merger-friendly" West Berlin and their more hostile eastern counterparts where a substantial majority rejected the proposal.

Instead, other ways of reducing the dividing effect of boundaries and lines of responsibility needed to be found. And the network relations seem the trend. The Smart City Berlin Network consists of some one hundred businesses, university and other research entities based in Berlin, including such global companies as Bosch, SAP and Siemens, which push for greater a international profile for Berlin as an attractive place to live and work. It is thus an arrange-ment as suggested by the triple helix model (Etzkowitz, 2008). The strategy as a whole seems to be largely borrowed from "smart" strategies elsewhere, add-ing Berlin-specific characteristics here and there as part of its tailoring to the city-region's specifics. The Network is intended to serve as platform for differ-ent actors and political interests and agendas to meet and negotiate – and thus help develop – the Charta Smart City Berlin and the strategic plan (vision) for developing Smart City Berlin (www.berlin-partner.de/standort-berlin/smart-city-berlin/netzwerk, accessed 18 January 2017). The plan makes some general references to the "common good" and the needs of citizens, as well as to the universities and their "spin-off companies," again a feature of the triple helix model. But there are also references to quality of life and citizen involvement.

> The Smart City Berlin Network is committed to making Berlin a city of the future for citizens as well as the private and public sectors, which will work together in a new, smart urban culture / society to make Berlin a national and international innovation leader. Berlin will be seen as an urban laboratory, showcase and reference city for products and services of the future.
>
> (www.berlin-partner.de/fileadmin/
> user_upload/01_chefredaktion/02_pdf/
> 02_navi/21/Charta_Netzwerk_Smart_City_Berlin.pdf)

Smart City Strategy Berlin "sets out an innovative strategic policy approach aimed at serving the common good by expanding and ensuring the future sus-tainability of Berlin" (SDUDE, 2015, p. 3). The strategy's focus is clearly on urban competitiveness and optimizing the organization of transport and other basic functions of the city to provide an attractive quality of life – in itself part of competitiveness. Indeed, "quality of life" is a key parameter, or surrogate variable, for "smartness." In effect, doing things the "smart" way is to produce greater quality of life as main justification of such an approach.

The goals of "Smart City Berlin" clearly revolve around topics that have become synonymous with "smart": reduced use of resources and environmental stress, enhanced international competitiveness in conjunction with innovativeness, enhanced infrastructure and, with reference to governance qualities, networking at regional to international level and stronger decision-making capacity in public administration (ibid., p. 5). It is here, when referring to city-region, that the multiple challenges become evident of fragmented territories of governing rights, and stark differences in prospects between shrinking and growing municipalities. The strategy is thus, in essence, still a work in progress, evolving out of a continuing process of identifying policy answers to changing challenges. Transition as a process of change, and policy learning are thus part of finding answers to a complex, internally divided city-region by administration, economic dynamics, population trends and ways of life.

Yet, perhaps an indication of the delicacy of the issue in the city-region, nothing much is said about governance as a way of reaching these sketched-out goals. Instead, the particularly complex governance and administrative arrangements seem somewhat untouched by this. Much of the strategy focuses on technology and "big data" aspects, and thus is, in its essence, a rather conventional approach to, and understanding of, "smart." In particular, not much is made of mentioning the wider region of Berlin-Brandenburg and its complex set of competing, interloping and even contradicting agendas/features. But it would be just here where some smart solutions/approaches/ideas would be useful to address the inefficiencies, etc. Some words are said on "smart administration," whereby they aim primarily at the technocratic aspect of "faster and simplified procedures through IT use" (ibid., p. 11), including e-government. Equally, reference is made to the need for addressing the "political challenges" arising from the "complexity of administrative processes" for businesses – in the interest of greater competitiveness (ibid.). So, it comes as a bit of a surprise that there is very little said about smart governance as a way to address the complex and mutually contesting agendas of competitiveness and cohesiveness (especially for Brandenburg). At the virtual level, such joint representation of an agenda seems less cumbersome, with references made to a "capital city-region" as part of a digitalization agenda which reaches across boundaries to connect the two states Berlin and Brandenburg.

The business community, perhaps not surprisingly, favours the broader, governance perspective as part of improving working conditions vis-à-vis the challenges of heightened competitiveness. A study by the Berlin Chamber of Commerce (IHK, 2015), for instance, points to the diverse demands placed on a "smart city" as a programmatic agenda. The Chamber thus advocates a "smart growth strategy" encompassing the securing of growth, both physically as well as in its political-economic and cultural manifestation, in the interests of envisaged enhanced prosperity, livability, sustainability and social balance. Smartness thus refers to more than the challenge of governance to reconcile diverse, even competing and/or conflicting, demands and expectations from urban development. Such may include lessons from "good practice" elsewhere as positively welcome triggers of learning processes and innovation in policy-making, such as through digitalization in economic processes and ways of life (UVB, 2016). Vogt (2016) speaks of a jittery start to the first year for turning Berlin into a smart city.

Indeed, business seems to view data (as processed information) as basis of Smart-City applications. Smart cities are understood in this context as bringing together "efficiency and sustainability, offering a higher quality of life and an excellent infrastructure for the economy" (UVB, 2016). This is to provide the opportunity for innovation and economic growth. But effective information flows are undermined by a multitude of territorially-based responsibilities and actor-ness. And here the Berlin city-region's many internal divisions and boundaries pose a major challenge to acting "smart." The stark differences in economic prospects and development paths between Berlin and the surrounding state of Brandenburg, especially the latter's outer, peripheral "ring" and the inner, suburbanizing areas near to Berlin, make for difficult political decisions. Subdividing Brandenburg into sectoral plan-ning regions is one attempt to "mix" inner and outer areas and thus avoid simply following structural dynamics. While Brandenburg, too, talks about digitalization of its economy, etc., it acknowledges that "much is still to do," such as linking government departments and policy fields, which weaken the city-region's economic competitiveness. "Smartness" ought thus to embrace the need for a joint strategy for Berlin and Brandenburg (www.smartregion.eu/html/1747.0.html, accessed 14 July 2017).

Acting in a "smart" way in Berlin includes attempts to boost the city's international strategy through participation in collaborative networks, such as the recent be.Berlin campaign (IHK, 2015). Similar to its competitor cities, such as Turin or Lyon for instance, this seeks to "position Berlin internation-ally as testing and model location for urban technology and innovation in the field of research, development and applications" (City of Berlin, 2015, p. 24). Importantly, this strategy also aims to develop Berlin's image as "smart city," through supporting a "start-up scene" constituted of "collaboration, net-works, new ways of working together and communicating to exchange ideas etc., incl. on 'smart city events'." Such include such initiatives as Smart City Summit providing a platform for public and private investors to meet. Indeed, bringing diverse actors together as part of shaping a "Smart Berlin" agenda has become a central strategic plank in the shape of the Smart City Berlin Network. Accordingly, Smart City Berlin also serves as image-maker for the city in its international competition efforts. Presenting itself as "Partners for Business and Technology," the city's strategy aims at emphasizing innovativeness and future orientation in its outlook, open for change and doing things differently, if and when required and deemed opportune in the face of changing circumstances and their challenges and opportunities. It is interesting that there is an explicit link drawn between the virtual and imagined nature of much of innovation and technological experimentation, and the structural and institutional framework of governance and thus the enabling of the "creative space."

> Smart City is the integrated approach to all the future topics with which we, as a city, will be dealing with in the decades to come. It is about anticipating trends and developments in all areas that affect life in a big city. The idea is to use ICT to develop concrete solutions to make our city more efficient, healthier, more sustainable, more livable and cleaner. In addition to benefiting citizens, climate protection, resource conservation and sustainability are of particular importance. It is necessary to create an organizational framework and network decision-making processes in the cities in order to establish smart technologies.
>
> (Smart City Berlin – Berlin Partner, www.berlin-partner.de/
> en/the-berlin-location/smart-city-berlin/, accessed 13 July 17)

Creativity and experimentalism are thus high on the agenda in Berlin's "take" on Smart-ness as political and policy-making agenda, including policy learning, but also quality of life as something people, that is voters, can experience first-hand. This is an important aspect in promoting smartness as an adjective to public policy, as also evident in Vancouver, Seattle, Lyon and Turin (see Chapter 5). Berlin's administration thus projects "smart" as being "also a laboratory for efficient infrastructure, informational networking, sustainable mobility, creativity and combining high productivity with high quality of life" (ibid.). Indeed, Smart City Berlin sees itself as a project of learning and experimenting with new approaches to "test the waters" for finding novel answers/ solutions to changing demands and expectations from policy-making. As such, the project sees itself as being about collaborative engagement through network between multiple actors, spaces and expectations, and part of a journey, a transition: "Network Smart City Berlin – Integrator of Urban Transformation Process (Smart City Berlin, 2017) (Figure 6.2).

While proclaiming smartness in policy documents and plans is the relatively easy bit, the realities of fiscal arrangements and sources democratic legitimacies make collaborative governing across state borders, even if essentially "smart" in terms of efficiency and efficacy, much more difficult. While there were early attempts to establish communication and coordination in the form of the joint Berlin-Brandenburg planning body (Gemeinsame Landesplanungsabteilung Berlin-Brandenburg, GLBB), this has more the hallmark of a "soft" institution in the form of a "round table" with mere consultative competencies, which sits outside the main administrative hierarchies and represents the city-region as virtual, "soft" strategy space (Hauswirth et al., 2003; Herrschel & Newman, 2005). GLBB is, in effect, a second-best solution to the popularly rejected full merger of the two state administrations and territories. The failed merger triggered a sense of missed opportunity, as a merged Berlin-Brandenburg was

Network Smart City Berlin – organisation

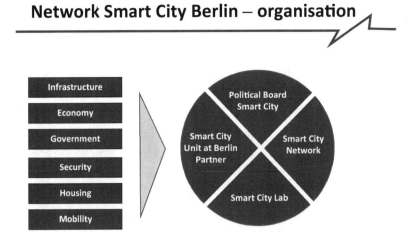

Figure 6.2 Smart City Berlin Network: example of network governance.

considered to be in a much better position to compete as a "global region" more effectively for new investment (*Berliner Zeitung*, 10 June 1999). Yet, political particularism and short-term self-interest stood in the way. Thus, while

> energy and climate policies in Berlin and Brandenburg continue so far to be focused on their own respective territories, strictly separated from each other, and they scarcely reflect the economic and functional inter-dependencies in the region. The challenge is therefore to come to an agreement on common political aims and strategies via the establishment of inter-*Länder* coordinating bodies, and to expand the project-oriented cooperation of the two *Länder* in the promotion of socio-technological innovation.
>
> (Monstadt, 2007, p. 339)

The location of the joint body in Potsdam, the capital of Brandenburg, just outside Berlin city limits, matters as a concession to Brandenburg's status as federal state, and its capital is thus formally positioned in the state hierarchy at the same level as Berlin, even if the economic and reputational differences are considerable: Potsdam is a small historic town on the outskirts of the Berlin metropolis, after all. The emphasis on representational parity and equality also serves to enhance prospects of acceptance of agreed policies by both administrations and also the public, as Berlin is not appearing – as usually suspected – as the senior partner. With different underlying political interests between the two governments, scope for agreements is difficult, not at least owing to inherent deep suspicions about the planning body's impartiality. In the absence of any statutory powers to implement policies, both parties modify agreements

188 *Beyond post-authoritarian regimes*

to their own advantage. Coordination may thus be seen as a "smart" move to suggest adoption of (sensible) coordinated public policy response to the growing functional city-region-wide interconnections, while maintaining governmental separateness and independence. Some additional "soft" cooperation without any formal commitments developed around tourism marketing. So it is not so surprising that in cases with greater financial consequences, cooperation has been less evident (Herrschel & Newman, 2005). A degree of distrust and competitiveness is never really far away, however, as the rather shambolic nature of building the new "capital city airport" Berlin Brandenburg illustrates, where competing government ambitions counteract each other. Its location just outside Berlin and the joint project development by both state governments has been highly politicized, with Brandenburg striving to not appear as the junior partner of Berlin. Competition and non-communication between political actors and administrations have led to the now six-year-late opening, with a definitive opening date still not set (Posaner, 2017)

Economic circumstances have changed fundamentally over the last ten or so years. At first there was a lagging behind high expectations of a rapid economic boom, which raised questions about the likely development scenarios of an only gradually developing city. Since the mid-2000s, however, such concerns have been turned on their head – Berlin is now a globally recognized city with considerable "sex appeal" as trendy city of clubbing, urban lifestyle and economic and cultural creativity. World city aspirations are now shaping the Berlin government's development agenda, something that looked somewhat far-fetched and unrealistic in the 1990s and early 2000s, when the city seemed to settle for a more regionally confined role (Cochrane & Jonas, 1999; Heeg, 1998, 2001; Lenhardt, 1998; Krätke, 2000). Of course, Brandenburg, despite its administrative and political separateness, seeks to benefit from this trend. The label of "Capital City-Region" is vague enough to transcend the state border and include Berlin and the surrounding municipalities of Brandenburg, without requiring any surrender of actual powers and responsibilities to any shared body of governance.

Economic development and opportunity is one important "gap" in opportunities and perceived benefit from regime change. After communism, while Berlin and its immediate hinterland were growing, the more out-lying parts of the region struggled or even declined. An increasingly evident speculative housing bubble in Berlin adds to developmental and policy challenges (Hung, 2012). Reconciling over-heating and struggling development is not easy, just as underlying localist interests of municipalities. "Smart" solutions are thus required to reconcile the diverse interests. And here Berlin illustrates well the two main ideas about "smartness": the administration focuses on a more technocratic, technology-oriented understanding of efficient public management (e-governance and transportation). The city seems somewhat of a late-comer in terms of adopting "smartness" as a development agenda, focusing still primarily on such conventional things as "big data" – related transportation schemes, as well as "innovation-focused" business. There seems, however, a move towards more policy innovation and "smart" ways of governing as a changing way of doing things, rather than more data-supported efficiency and fantasies about mini-Silicon Valleys, such as had been planned for the area of the to-be-closed airport Tegel (www.berlintxl.de/en.html, accessed 18 July 2017).

The culture of mistrust between the city and its hinterland, and between local and higher level governments, has its roots in the post-war history of the city-region. The new structures of government imposed on the "East" following the fall of the Wall, divided local and regional interests, at times continuing animosities inherited from the socialist period. This institutionalized prescription for localism, coupled with the economic pressures felt by the wider hinterland of Berlin in the separate state of Brandenburg has continued undermined the logic of regional cooperation in favour of competitive concern of equal status. History and institutional structures thus appear to map out a path for development likely to "lock in" policy-making in sub-optimal, rather than "smart" decisions, with genuinely new policy agendas and approaches not in evidence, as the fiasco around the joint airport illustrates. "Smart" seems a label for innovation-oriented economic activities, seeking to point to new opportunities in the future, in Berlin only. There is very little evidence of a broader adoption of "smartness" as a more widely policy-defining narrative. The locking out of such "novelty" from the Joint Planning Body's website points to a continued focus on clearly defined and agreed planning tasks of a more technocratic, administrative kind. The smartness agenda is separate and more economic development oriented and thus inherently more likely driven by competition, rather than cooperation.

Summary Berlin-Brandenburg

The case of Berlin has illustrated the fundamental difficulties of regional governance when based around strong local government. The inherent institutionalized focus on locally-based policy-making, including fiscal dependence on local economic performance and population counts, in the interest of greater autonomy in local decision-making, encourages localist views in policy-making. In the Berlin case, such competitive and essentially anti-cooperative thinking appears to embrace particularly those local authorities with inherently fewer development opportunities and thus scope for developing and implementing "voter friendly" policies. Such thinking also seems to influence policies at *Land* level, following similar institutional interconnectedness between economic and population growth, fiscal revenue and thus democratic policy-making capacity. Any form of cooperation will inevitably have to address the financial implications. A shift towards "co-operative localism" seems to require facilitating institutional arrangements to address these issues, but also a distinctly long-term view of potential benefits of any such cooperation, and this is not easy to maintain in an election and policy success-driven four-yearly timeframe. Any cooperation would have to succeed in a cost–benefit assessment, assessing in particular the implications of cooperation on the local political and fiscal capital.

So, where does that locate Berlin in our analytical matrix? Quite clearly, Berlin's development and political agenda are shared by its particular history as a divided city during the Cold War, with added challenges through its post-1990 status as a city-state as one of the 16 federal states in Germany. The city-region is divided by a number of different borders, and ideational, administrative and developmental differences. Accordingly, interests and priorities vary between different parts and actors within the city-region. The new independence of local governments in Brandenburg after the end of communism helped strengthen new identities and engendered a strong desire for autonomy that stood in sharp contrast to the powerless role of local administration at the bottom of the political-administrative hierarchy of the communist authoritarian state. But this has also favoured a degree of new localism on the back of a feeling of autonomy in managing local matters. So it does not really come as a surprise that debates in 1997 about merging the two states – Berlin and Brandenburg – were met with resistance from the Berlin hinterland (Brandenburg). Memories of the traditionally dominant role of Berlin as capital of the GDR and national capital before that played a part (Benz & Koenig, 1995).

Prague as *"laggard"*– what smartness?

The main challenges in the Prague and Berlin metropolises are similar: reconciling the need for collaboration on the basis of functional interdependencies, and competitiveness to generate politically useful job opportunities and revenue. The necessary political balancing act and requirement of linkages and communication between actors would suggest a certain degree of "smartness" necessary. On the contrary, however, this adjective barely features in the city's or region's strategic documents. Instead, "Smart Prague" as a name appears merely as a low-key NGO with an equally low-key website.

The Prague city-region, just like Berlin, exhibits a doughnut structure, with the city administratively separated from its surrounding region (see Figure 6.2). The "height" of these boundaries, however, varies, as state German *Lander* (states) have a greater range of powers and a direct democratic legitimacy, while Czech Regions act as both regional agents for the central state and independent representatives of a limited range of self-governed responsibilities, circumscribed by statute and fiscal provisions, especially own-revenue raising (Brusis, 2003). The main tasks revolve around economic development and strategic planning, and are thus more conventionally technocratic than political in nature. Regional bodies include the Regional Assembly, Regional Council, President and Regional Office. So, there is a clear element of democratic representation and legitimacy to policy-making (Herrschel, 2015). The 14 regions partake in a joint body, the Association of Regions of the Czech Republic. This serves as a platform for meetings between the regional presidents and the Lord Mayor of the City of Prague as members.

Prague dominates the Czech Republic economically and politically. The city accounts for 12% of the country's population, 15% of jobs and over 25%

of GDP (Ferry, 2014). Similar to Berlin, the city is administratively separated from its immediate surroundings and possesses a powerful status as a municipality enclosed by the region of Central Bohemia, like a doughnut. When, in 1989, the communist centrally administered and governed state system gave way to a stronger local government level, regions no longer were merely relay stations for top-down orders; instead they gained a dual role as agents of the centre and collective expressions of locally-based interests. This collective role was further strengthened in 2000 in the run-up to joining the European Union in 2004 to meet EU requirements for managing EU-funded regional policies. Greater autonomy at the local level meant that, just as in the Berlin case, localist agendas found favour as an expression of self-government, rather than top-down control. By the same token, the regional level is also an expression of development strategy by the state to support indigenous development potential in regions, while counteracting inequalities. And this is also taking on board EU cohesion policy agendas (Ferry, 2014).

So it is the national government that holds primary responsibility for managing and coordinating regional development, which is a clear reflection of the, in essence, continued existence of a centralized state. By the same token, the 14 regions also have self-governing responsibilities as collective municipal interests represented through directly elected local politicians. Fiscal provision with independent sources of local revenue provide the scope for exercising intended local policy-making capacity, although this varies according to the size and economic well-being of municipalities. The regional level is thus the level where local and national interests and agendas meet, whereby EU membership has pushed the balance in favour of the collective "bottom-up" role (ibid.). There is thus a compromise need between providing for the plurality of local conditions through greater flexibility in defining policies, and maintaining a degree of certainty and predictability as offered by national policies, especially where larger investment projects are concerned. The Prague region illustrates this duality: it combines local and regional powers and responsibilities, subdivided into 57 autonomous city municipalities with their own elected authorities (ibid.).

The inherent asymmetry between the position of Prague as a local actor and the surrounding municipalities of Central Bohemia region has resulted in the smaller municipalities around Prague having mostly failed to use the opportunity to strengthen their voices vis-à-vis the dominant city of Prague, as doing so "would require a view beyond local horizons" (A Strategy for Prague), and that is often missing (CDA, 2009, see also Hammersley and Westlake, 1996). It is a situation similar to the one in Berlin. Prague has a unique status within this system: it is a town, district and cohesion region and a NUTS II and III statistical unit within the EU. Prague is autonomously governed by the Prague City Assembly and other authorities. From the point of view of the execution of state administration, it is divided into 22 administrative districts and from the point of view of local administration, into 57 autonomous city municipalities with their own elected authorities. As a result of these changes together with some devolved policy-making responsibilities, Central Bohemia became Prague's partner for cooperation on the same scalar political level, making for a less asymmetric bargaining position than between the metropolis and the surrounding small municipalities. While collaboration or development of new policy solutions should have improved, this never materialized. Some of this has to do with legacies from the communist era command politics, similar to the situation in Berlin, where a lingering resentment at being talked down to by the capital city has remained evident.

Just as in the Berlin case, Prague city-region's fragmented administrative structure contradicts the needs of city-region-wide policy-making, as a multitude of small municipalities makes collaboration and coordination challenging. In addition, the city or Prague is itself divided into 57 self-governing local entities (with their own elective bodies), ranging in population from more than 100,000 to a mere 250 (Ferry, 2014), with equally varying policy-making capacities. The picture is similar in the Central Bohemia region, where responsibilities are sub-divided into 12 districts, each containing more than a thousand municipalities of varying size between 25 residents and 68,000 (ibid.). It is a structure that seems increasingly unviable in the face of shrinking population figures owing to out-migration and ageing. Institutional capacity and capability thus vary widely, making reaching a region-wide consensus a formidable task. This small-scale structure is not too dissimilar to the situation in Berlin

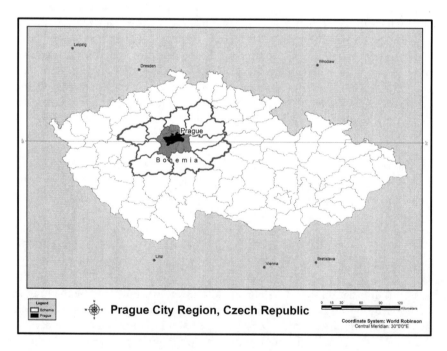

Figure 6.3 The Prague-Bohemian city-region in the Czech Republic.

prior to the administrative reform of 2001 (Engelniederhammer, 1999; Harms, 2006; Hauswirth et al., 2004), when Berlin's number of boroughs was near-halved to create larger entities with increased capacity. Such re-arrangements are contested, however, especially in former communist Europe with its legacy of a highly centralized top-down government with no local input at all. Local government with a degree of autonomy was considered not only an expression, but also a laboratory, of newly established democratic principles, and a clear break with the authoritarian past. Just as in the failed attempt at joining together Berlin and the Brandenburg states (discussed see above), people reject attempts at altering their grown foci of local identity, as also evident in the past two reforms in Brandenburg and so, again, for the one proposed in 2018 (Metzner, 2015).

Given its fragmented structure, it may be at first surprising that coordination of administrative and policy-making processes "in the Prague metropolitan region has not been sufficiently developed" (IPRP Prague Strategic Plan, 2008). Just as underpinning the resistance to changing the small-scale structure in the Berlin city-region, a strong sense of localist self-determination, as well as silo thinking among territorially-based actors, prevails in the Prague city-region. A concern with protecting and demonstrating local policy-making competencies, municipal agendas focus on administrative procedures, responsibilities and governmental powers, rather than pragmatic strategic, technocratic considerations of joint action to tackle challenges of cross-border developments. Instead, competitive thinking is widespread. This may also explain why policies seem little "trendy" in terms of terminology – no references to "smart" as indication of seeking novel ways and agendas in dealing with the city-region's development and governance. Instead, "there is [an] absence of a stable organizational structure" (ibid.) shaping inter-municipal inter-regional policy-making, as a formal mechanism of communication and negotiation between local interests. Informal "soft" governance seems to be struggling. Legacies of hierarchical government with topically separated columns of top-down flows of orders and control from the communist days have their legacy in a seeming dependency on clearly evident structure. Interviews with planning and development officials of both the Central Bohemia Region and the City of Prague confirmed this (Turba, PMR, 2014).

An unwillingness to engage between municipalities across boundaries reflects the tradition of state centralism and a top-down practice of coordinating lower tier plans at the regional scale. Thus, national government is the primary actor in strategic regional planning, including the programming of EU-funded regional policies. Coordinating policies is thus primarily a vertical, rather than a collaborative, horizontal, mode of governing. And this is despite possessing coordination vehicles, such as seminar or working groups, "coordination of strategic programming and management in the Czech Republic is a major challenge" (Ferry, 2014, p. 8).

Prague is by far the economic hub of the city-region, reflected in the high productivity of the city as national capital of high international standing.

As a result, any agreements with the surrounding municipalities are made out of a position of strength (see OECD, 2013), similarly to Berlin, which is likely to heighten the situation among these municipalities as to whether to engage at all, fearing a raw deal. Administrative structures are out of step with the dynamic functional relationships and interconnections across administrative boundaries. Continuing economic strength pushed administrative arrangements which increasingly show their mismatch with the functional realities within the city-region, especially the suburban ring around the core city. It is a situation similar to the one in Berlin. Yet, administrative reforms after the end of centrally-organized state under communism with a strict top-down implementation of policies and investment, Greater local powers and also regional competencies as part of democratization have also meant a reinforcement of localist thinking, where territorially-based powers have led to a self-centred focus on policy-making and planning, that ends at the respective administrative boundaries. Non-cooperation is not so much the outcome of an inherent hostility, but, rather, disinterest for want of political rewards for such engagement, as well as the desire to boast about new powers that did traditionally not exist. It is here, therefore, where the difference between a historically federal versus centralized structure lies: experience with necessary cross-boundary collaboration. When central directives were the norm, new found administrative freedoms may readily result in a degree of exuberance in the use and enjoyment of new powers gained. It is something also observed in Eastern Germany, for instance, when federal structures were introduced in the aftermath of the end of the centralized communist state (Herrschel, 1997).

So it may come as no surprise that, following Turba (Turba, PMR, 2014), the main challenges in the Prague city-region involve insufficient coordination of policies among municipalities owing to generally a limited interest in engagement across municipal boundaries by actors, despite growing functional interdependencies. Varying political interests, especially when governed by different parties, contribute to this non-communication/cooperation. This includes even such potentially financially and economically attractive activities as tourism, where there is a complete absence of a common voice and strategy to promotion (p. 13).

This stand-off has been "softened up" only gradually as a result of EU policies and associated incentives. The EU 2014–2020 programming period introduced a new instrument for tying together separate thematic objectives and programmes to an integrated development strategy of a specific territory. Such Integrated Territorial Investment (ITI) thus offers a new opportunity for changing the fragmented, localist way of policy-making in the Prague metropolitan region. One first result of such financially incentivized coordination is the formally agreed cooperation in 2013 between Prague and the Central Bohemia region, signed by the city's mayor and region's president. This established a working group comprising political leaders and technocrats to consider strategic objectives and also their possible implementation. Yet old habits die hard, and so there is also an attempt at limiting coordination to the absolute minimum necessary to gain advantage but surrender as little autonomy as possible. This suggests that the availability of funding has not really opened up a readiness to experiment with new policies as a way of innovative policy-making, but, rather, merely adopt a pragmatic, opportunistic rationale of raising additional income.

Different funding regimes under the EU's Regional Policy also contribute to continuing divisions in the region between the city of Prague enjoying Objective 2 status, and Central Bohemia that of Objective 1. By keeping the two regions apart, Central Bohemia can qualify for EU funding support to address seeming below EU average economic performance. Such would no longer be available for a combined region, as the EU average would be exceeded. Given the differences in funding available under the two schemes, the majority of the projects will most likely be implemented in the hinterland of Prague, that is, the Central Bohemia region, while Prague will be the main driving force in using ITI as a way of gaining in influence on the city-region's strategic development (see Turba, PMR, 2014).

Such new collaboration may suggest a change in strategic approach, at least among some municipalities, towards cooperation, even if for no other reason than obtaining some additional funds which could allow the realization of some local "pet projects." As the OECD (2013) report suggests, it is the smaller municipalities of the city-region outside of Prague that need to seek to boost their collaborative appeal, as they are in a weaker bargaining provision vis-à-vis the capital city. So far, however, such efforts have been somewhat limited (OECD, 2013). For them, it still needs to be evident that collaboration brings rewards, so they can achieve better bargaining outcomes. This is a widespread problem with collaborative approaches, especially in a competitive setting like the Prague region. For the smaller municipalities, a stronger regional voice could help reduce the asymmetry in city-hinterland relationships. But such recalibration needs to involve the central state in the Czech Republic, given the strong centralized administrative arrangement of the state. Re-organizing the administrative structures is, however, more contested now as a result of re-awakened localism, making such top-down changes to existing territorial arrangements, as imposed under communism, much more difficult to push through politically. Then, in 1968 and 1974, a large number of neighbouring municipalities were incorporated into Prague (Prague Metropolitan Region, provided by Prague 9 City Council, 18 June 2014).

Yet, a change in leadership seems to have triggered a new impetus for tackling Prague's somewhat bureaucratically-shaped approach to strategic policy-making with a particular focus on innovation policy to support the city's innovative capacity (EC, 2013; BRIS, 2004) – importantly not just at the city, but also regional level (Blažek & Uhlíř, 2007): "the Mayor initiated the establishment of Prague Innovation Council as a partnership platform for development of the regional innovation system and representation of regional interests in national R&D&I policy, and includes of representatives of business and academia, government agencies as well as the City of Prague" – quite evidently the type of cooperation as subsumed under the "triple helix" idea. The main task, quite evidently, at least in terminological terms, clearly relating to the idea of "smartness," is to develop and update the Regional Innovation Strategy in collaboration with relevant experts in the field outside the administration, and help develop new measures and projects as part of formulating "smart specialization domains; establish and supervise the work of innovation platforms" (ibid.).

As a further sign of seeking to open up deeply engrained administrative structures and ways of doing things, including encouraging a more open, collaborative "outreaching" approach in policy-making, is the transformation of the City Development Authority Prague, the city's well established development agency, into the Prague Institute of Planning and Development. By bringing together "structure" and "agency," the Institute, as an arm's-length institution owned and funded by the City of Prague, is to combine formal planning with design and strategic development and policy considerations. This includes reaching beyond city limits and engaging with the wider city-region through updating the Regional Innovation Strategy and participating in operational programmes, such as the EU-funded Triangulum programme. Both the City of Prague and the Prague Institute of Planning and Development (IPR) are participating in a living lab project – the Morgenstadt City Lab – as a research project coordinated by the Fraunhofer-Institute, to develop a complex sustainable city profile and related strategic recommendations in the context of the Smart Cities agenda in Europe. In 2014, Prague launched preparations for the concept Smart Prague as *primary vision* for energy, environment, education, culture entrepreneurship and communication infrastructure. And so, in November 2016, the IPR announced that it would jointly with Central Bohemia Region seek to obtain CZK 4.6 billion from the EU under the new ITI programme until 2020 to pay for infrastructure and educational projects as key policy agendas in the regional strategy (http://en.iprpraha. cz/clanek/1407/prague-and-central-bohemia-will-draw-European-money-together, accessed 17 July 2017).

So, looking at very recent developments within the last couple of years or so, there are signs on the city's side of seeking to push for inter-regional and inter-municipal collaborative policy-making in the spirit of the "smartness narrative." It is too early, however, to establish the success of these new initiatives. In fact, "smartness" as a descriptor of policy-making or programmatic agenda does not (yet) feature in official documents of Prague, let alone the city-region as a whole. Instead, the combination of "Prague" and "smart" is represented by an NGO "Smart Prague" (www.smartprague.eu). This small, low-key organization, with a limited, simple website, aims at imagining the nature of the city in 2030 as a "smart" city in terms of both "smart technological solutions" (that is, "big data"), such as traffic management, but also improving economic potential. Beyond this platform, however, Prague has not as yet claimed the attribute "smart" to characterize its policy agendas.

The lack in progress with city-region-wide perspectives and agendas has been one of the reasons Prague became involved in several international projects over the past decade, focused on cooperation in city-regions. Probably the most beneficial was the project IM-PLAN (co-operative planning processes in European metropolitan regions) implemented at the beginning of the past decade in cooperation with Berlin, Budapest, Prague, Sofia and Vienna. Yet, this did not go much beyond more general statements about the need and intent to collaborate (IM-PLAN, Common Statements, 2001, quoted in Turba, PMR, 2014, pp. 25–26).

More recently, in 2009, a wish to develop collaboration within the city-regions was affirmed in the then revised Strategic Plan for Prague – the first version dated from 2000, in which "formalization of collaborative arrangements to enhance scope for likely success" was one of the main declared objectives (Metaxas, 2008). This included a proposed joint advisory body – perhaps similar in nature to the one in Berlin, for the interaction between Prague and the region. The Prague Development Plan (CDA, 2000, 2009) involved bottom-up consultation of key actors to establish priorities. Part of this openness was to demonstrate a break from the secretive, dictatorial past of the communist years, by showing openness, rather than closed-to-the-public decision-making. There was an attempt to include a wider area than the administrative area of the city, but they are decidedly two separate entities, the City of Prague and Central Bohemia Region (Prague Development Agency, interview, 16 June 2003). The boundary between the two entities cuts through a functionally closely interconnected area. Yet, so far, only tentative progress has been made with establishing communication across administrative boundaries, let alone applying cooperation, between Prague and the surrounding municipalities. So, merely a third of the surrounding municipalities engage with Prague at all to either agree formally to the city's development goals as far as relevant for the region or at least give an informal "nod." At the time the first development plan for Prague (Prague 2010) was prepared, only a small number of municipalities accepted the invitation to voice their views and collaborate in planning procedures. By contrast, some 70 per cent rejected such collaborative planning out of a fear of a quiet attempt by the city to "take over" and reduce their new-found autonomy.

Strict localism and non-cooperation is viewed as a sign of local power and self-determination, as a form of "standing up" to the city's dynamic. Regional leaders may also see political capital in showing their commitment to promoting regional interests "under threat" from Prague's overarching dominance. And not appearing to be "soft" seems to be one of the profiling strategies followed (Prague RDA, interview, 16 June 2003). As a result, nothing much happens in terms of strategic cooperation. But loss of city-region-wide influence is also a concern for Prague, as suburbanization is one of the main challenges faced by the city-region because of the associated shifts in fiscal revenue, as tax revenue follows residents. Similar to the situation in Berlin-Brandenburg (Hauswirth et al., 2004), non-cooperation produces financial rewards by the design of the fiscal system. It is not surprising, therefore, that Central Bohemia region is quite happy with the effects of suburbanization and shows little inclination to collaborate with Prague in addressing the city's financial losses.

A visit to the offices of Central Bohemia Region on the borders of Prague City in 2003 gave a stark visual impression of that policy of détente: the development plan of the region showed a white spot in the centre, where Prague is located. Upon asking why Prague, despite its functional relevance to Bohemia Region's development, was not acknowledged as a neighbour, the answer was "why should we care, it is nothing to do with our planning, except where there are direct physical connectors through infrastructure." The legacy of Prague's dominance clearly manifested itself here: at last, Prague did not interfere and set the agenda. The role of past ways of doing things also manifested itself in another way: when asking for a copy of the planning map showing the regional administrative territories (and localities) in Central Bohemia – and a white spot in the middle, depicting Prague municipality – the answer was that a formal letter needed to be received requesting such information, so that an administrative process could be set in train to formally and officially permit the issuing of a copy of the map. One got the clear impression that there was little interest by the regional body in the goals of the city's strategy, because there was no formal mechanism requiring such engagement. Only technical necessities, such as the continuity of a road, seem to justify coordinative, let alone collaborative, interest. Otherwise, Prague remains a literally a white spot on the elusive map. Just to underline this disconnection, Central Bohemia Region adopts a distinctly outward-looking perceptive, proverbially "turning its back" on Prague, by seeking to engage internationally, with such as China and Southeast Asia (*Prague Daily Monitor*, 2017). Nevertheless, in the face of shared challenges, such as the 2013 floods of the river Moldova, both regions feel the need to solve their problems and challenges in coordination and mutual cooperation (Scholze, 2014). This experience gave an impulse to following up the strategic development opportunities offered under the EU's ITI (see above) to help facilitate and develop cooperation across administrative borders. The ITI tool may open a new avenue to more communication about, and, perhaps collaboration in, common projects between the city of Prague and the Central Bohemian Region. Such collaboration was given a high profile start by a formal agreement between the leaders of bothentities, the Prague mayor and the Central Bohemia Region's president. This established a joint working group to explore options and avenues for collaboration. Perhaps not surprisingly, this focused on conventional technical issues, such as the inter-regional transport system of Prague and Central Bohemia Region, as well as environmental questions (flood-prevention measures) and a regional education system embracing schooling capacities in the suburban ring of Prague city-region (ibid.).

In summary, what does the Prague example say about the adoption of "smart" city-regional governance? Just as in Berlin's case, the legacies of the *ancien regime* of communist era centralism and bureaucracy have influenced the way in which city-region-wide thinking among policy-makers has developed since the beginning of the 1990s. Newly established local policy arenas with associated responsibilities and resources, which replaced a previous role as mere recipients of centrally-defined orders handed down the hierarchy, generated a sense of local pride and a tendency to defend and utilize these to their limits. Just as in Berlin, the legacy of the capital city as former origin of power over, and control of, the rest of the state engenders distrust among those actors outside the capital city as to the real objectives of its policies: are they aimed at re-imposing political domination thus becomes the question? In Prague, unlike in Berlin's recent development agenda, traditional, politically less sensitive and essentially technocratic topics for collaboration have been chosen as politically "safe" to establish a degree of trust and rapport between the city and its surrounding hinterland. And so, it is interesting that "smartness," at least as far as in its "big data" meaning, has not (yet?) been adopted by policy-makers as a label to signify the city-region's openness to novel ideas and learning both at institutional as policy-making levels (Turba, PMR, 2014).

Cape Town and Johannesburg as *"stalled movers"*: beyond post-apartheid in the city-region?

The formal demise of apartheid in 1994 ushered in a post-apartheid period of history that arguably "ended," in turn, somewhere between the police massacre of striking Marikana mine workers in August, 2012, and the death of Nelson Mandela in December 2013. Or at least that is an expedient analytical departure. For history rarely creates such simple breaks. The core of apartheid was crumbling long before the mid-1990s. Moreover, its appalling social legacies and the uneven and inchoate impacts of post-apartheid policies – urban, economic, social, etc. – remain significant challenges today (Bond, 2000; Maylam, 1995; Robinson, 1998a, 1998b; Rogerson, 1989, 1997). So in truth, contemporary South Africa is shaped by the "inter-currence" of multiple institutional stories – "ancient," recent, embryonic – working themselves out in different "political times" across various scales and spaces (Orren & Skowronek, 1996).

Still, the relatively comprehensive replacement of the apartheid system with a new post-apartheid polity constitutes, with the parallel collapse of state socialism in Eastern Europe, one of the seminal political, constitutional and legal developments of the late 20th century (Pallotti & Engel, 2016). Albeit similarly concerned with new questions of ICT infrastructure in the search for competitiveness and sustainability, South Africa has indeed produced its own particular geographies of urban smartness. The transition from the authoritarian imperatives of territorial apartheid, in particular, has shaped the internal transition to smartness in both Johannesburg and Cape Town, even as local variances are equally important to emphasize (Figure 6.3). We explore the specificities of this dual transition here, ultimately highlighting both similarities and differences with the post-authoritarian transition in the cases of Berlin and Prague.

South African transitions: new state structures and (smart) policy discourses

Conceived as a geopolitical-economy, the apartheid system infamously operated at three spatial scales: the national, the urban and the individual. In the wake of the 1950 Group Areas Act (as reconstituted and amended multiple times), major urban areas like Cape Town and Johannesburg (Figure 6.4) were subject to racial zoning. This required forced removals from mixed-race neighbourhoods (e.g. Sophiatown in Johannesburg, Cato Manor in Durban, District 6 in Cape Town), which occasioned profound social injustices, deep structural contradictions, and persistent systemic inefficiencies that ultimately exhausted the entire project (Western, 1981; Worger & Clark, 2011). In apartheid theory, races developed separately, although the space-economy in practice required constant interactions to secure steady accumulation: in homes, in factories, in mines, in businesses, along the rails, on the docks, etc. (Maylam, 1990; Rogerson, 1989).

The National Party won the election in 1948 promising white voters a future of apartheid (or "separateness"), and then aggressively expanded the country's colonial and early post-colonial legal apparatus: for example, the Native (Urban Areas) Act of 1923; the Native Laws Amendment Act of 1937; the Native (Urban Areas) Consolidation Act of 1945. In addition to the foundational "Group Areas" and "Population Registration" Acts (1950),

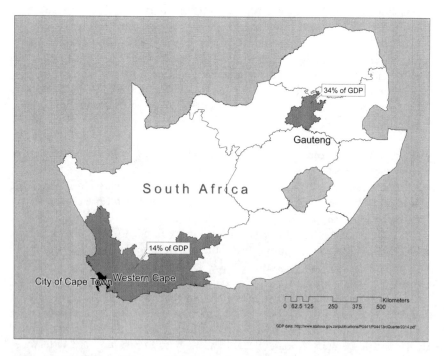

Figure 6.4 Cape Town (Western Cape) and Johannesburg (Gauteng).

the apartheid state steadily reconstructed (urban) society through, *inter alia*: separate amenities (1953); "bantu" education (1953); the prohibition of mixed marriages (1949); the prevention of illegal squatting (1951); pass laws and influx control (1951, 1954), and many other laws. Taken together, these laws and the administrative routines they set in motion merged place, race and power in ways that tightened the state's grip on the meaning and overall purpose of African urban labour in the national political economy (Robinson, 1997). Permanent African urbanization across South Africa was only allowed *de jure* in 1979; even then, "influx control" policies from African rural areas ("homelands") ostensibly still regulated both residential and labour choices (Dierwechter, 2004). Anti-apartheid resistance was thus constant, and often violently and ruthlessly suppressed. Teetering between martial law and civil war in the late 1980s, South Africa's "negotiated revolution" (Sparks, 1995) finally inaugurated black majority rule under Mandela in 1994, and the attendant politico-constitutional reconstruction of state–society relations thereafter. Much of the political-economy literature on South Africa since 1994 is essentially a debate about the accomplishments and disappointments associated with this conjectured "reconstruction" (Bond, 2000; Jenkins & Du Plessis, 2014; Marais, 1998).

For our purposes, the most important changes in South Africa since 1994 relate to the new "developmental" role of larger cities like Johannesburg and Cape Town that, as stated first in Chapter 3, have arguably experienced one of the most far-reaching periods of administrative and policy reform in the entire metropolitan world. Constitutionally, South African cities since 1994 – unlike in the United States, France or Canada, for example – enjoy autonomous status; in other words, their powers are not delegated politically by higher scales of state authority but enunciated legally within the new constitution itself (in the United States, by contrast, unmentioned cities are mere "creatures of the state"). Specifically, the South African Constitution provides for three categories of municipality: local, district and, of special interest here, "metropolitan municipalities," including Cape Town, Johannesburg and six other major urban areas in the country. The Municipal Demarcation Act and the Metropolitan Structures Act, both passed in 1998, significantly empowered from a legal perspective the elected councils of subsequently amalgamated Metropolitan Municipalities (merging the highly-fragmented apartheid system of local government) after 2000 to develop *single* metropolitan budgets, *common* property ratings and service-tariff systems, and *single* employer bodies.

This state-structural change, much more profound than most "New Regionalist" experiments in other world regions, was meant to help redress nearly unparalleled levels of spatial and social inequality, especially between races. As the new century opened, then, what was now called "developmental local governance" implemented through "integrated development plans" (IDPs) meant that, as articulated in the early though ultimately ill-fated Reconstruction and Development Programme (RDP), "development is not about the delivery of goods to a passive citizenry. It is about active involvement and growing empowerment" (cited in Binns and Nel, 2002, p. 922). We consider this sentiment significant to our themes here. To be sure, the post-apartheid policy emphasis on "integrated" planning, formally *re*-launched with passage of the Municipal Systems Act in 2000, was hardly novel from a global perspective (ibid.); but it did potentially up-end how local planning and policy development was now officially conceived, especially when contrasted with apartheid planning. Moving away from top-down, paternalistic, sectoral- and project-oriented practices towards, in principle, bottom-up, consultative, comprehensive and "joined-up" policy delivery implied not only the political *willingness* of citizens to do so, but no less importantly the fiscal-systemic *capacity* of the local state to do so. It was soon clear, however, that both assumptions proved difficult – and this helps to explain, we argue, the parallel rise of "smartness" discourses and cognate initiatives.

Early on, perhaps up until 1996 or so, the imagined spatialities of "post-apartheid" meant incorporating and then implementing a normative urban spatial policy that, as Alison Todes (2006) notes, emphasized a locally-developed "compaction-integration" model of city-regional (re)development with strong social justice expectations. Like the North American smart growth models discussed in Chapter 1, this specific South African model of planning called for aggressively reducing sprawl, prioritizing key transit corridors, imploding growth inwards and remixing *in loco* land uses – although with far greater attention than in North America to the contingent problems of economic and physical "informality" (Dewar, 1979, 1995; Dewar & Todeschini, 1998; Dewar & Watson, 1991). However, the profound political pressure to "deliver," particularly low-income housing, as well as extant market forces that still favoured low-density decentralization, eventually eroded the importance of "space" in favour of "speed." Housing projects built on cheap land, for example, paradoxically reinforced rather reformed the urban geography of apartheid. Moreover, local capacity problems, even in the relatively well-resourced metropolitan municipalities, reduced many early IDP efforts from strategic and long-range visions of development to "shopping lists" (van Donk & Pieterse, 2006, p. 122). Vanessa Watson (2002) has further suggested that the early IDPs increasingly conceptualized urban integration through technically managing policy budgets, not significantly restructuring material space, while Phil Harrison (2006) has charted how the late 1990s convergence of international policy discourses increasingly "circumscribed" IDPs through hegemonic claims around New Public Management: "a huge, interlinked global policy network influenced and significantly shaped the outcome of post-apartheid policy and practice," he concluded (p. 188).

As discussed in Chapter 2, since the early 1990s, no objective has been more central to this "huge, interlinked global policy network" of urban and regional development practice than enhancing the global competitiveness of local economies. Arguably, that paramount objective quickly overwhelmed other objectives in the post-apartheid macro-economic policy environment

(Gelb, 2006). The aforementioned Reconstruction and Development Program (RDP), for example, was discarded in 1996 for the Growth, Employment and Redevelopment programme (GEAR) – signalling for many observers a clear switch to neoliberal rather than social-democratic policy commitments (Marais, 1998). In 2007, however, the GEAR framework was itself reformed in favour of a new macro-economic and social policy approach called ASGISA (Accelerated and Shared Growth Initiative in South Africa). Considered "more of the same" by some, ASGISA nonetheless emerged in response to concerns that GEAR over relied on the credibility of policy to woo investors (Gelb, 2006, p. 5). While renewed emphasis on shared growth was certainly welcome, the obstacles in key economic sectors with global comparative advantages – such as urban tourism – have remained challenging (Rogerson, 2008).

Challenging, too, have been efforts to weave broad sustainability concerns into the daily fabric of developmental local governance, in general, and IDPs, in particular. In Chapter 2 we discussed how smart growth emerged in the United States as a pragmatic way to interpret and localize Agenda 21 goals associated with the Rio Earth Summit policy agenda (Roberts & Diederichs, 2002). As elsewhere in the world, the language of Agenda 21 has been visible in South Africa, but it has also required translation within the specific context of post-apartheid policy goals and institutional instruments. In their recent survey of local progress, Rumanza and Shackleton (2016) argue that IDPs in particular present an opportunity for "participatory mainstreaming of environmental issues and sustainable development in general"; unfortunately, they lament, "this opportunity is being missed" (p. 37). In principle, this is not for lack of formal national policy commitment, even as meaningful sustainability values are hardly endemic across all ministries, key policy frameworks or national investment priorities. Launched in 2008, the National Framework for Sustainable Development – predicated on a systems approach to sustainability – sought explicitly to "green up" local level IDPs. This in turn promulgated, in 2011, a National Strategy for Sustainable Development and Action Plan. The strategy and plan continued to emphasize the overall need to enhance "systems for integrated planning and implementation" that could strategically support improved natural resource efficiency, help coordinate a green economy, build sustainable communities and address climate change (Republic of South Africa, 2011). To ensure the "integration" of sustainable development into processes of government, though, meant building "a monitoring and evaluation system to facilitate the ongoing assessment of progress" (ibid., p. 16).

That has not occurred in most places (Swilling, 2010). Signalling the normative importance of integration within the context of developmental local governance, the Agenda 21 programme in Durban, as one example of these challenges on the ground, focused early on building an environmental management system that could enrich planning and development processes with social, economic and ecological concerns. But it was quickly evident that "lack of information" was a key obstacle (Roberts & Diederichs, 2002, p. 191). In addition, as Crane and Swilling (2008) report, the National Industrial Policy, the National Framework for Local Economic Development, ASGISA, and even national housing policy, "do not reflect an understanding of the need to decouple material economic growth from rising rates of resource consumption" (p. 264). They make the case for the promises of "dematerialization," but also draw attention to the now badly breached boundaries of most ecological systems, using Cape Town within the Western Cape as an illustrative case study. More generally, others have pointed out how the broader leitmotifs of restitution and rapid service delivery have too often rendered sustainability concerns "subservient" (Harrison, Todes, & Watson, 2008, p. 62).

In sum, much of the immediate "post-apartheid" period, from the early 1990s into the early 2010s, has been an effort to build new state structures and promulgate new public policies. Of particular importance, in our view, has been the expected role of administratively reconstituted metropolitan regions – and especially the key city-regional economies of Cape Town-Western Cape and Johannesburg-Gauteng. Through constitutionally-assigned institutions, local governments were now increasingly expected to drive "development," in large part by "integrating" the design and delivery of long siloed plans and parallel policies. While the core meaning of development itself arguably focused too narrowly on "growth" after the demise of the more socially redistributive, neo-Keynesian RDP in 1996, the shift to ASGISA in turn reflected a concern that neoliberal expansion under GEAR had paid insufficient attention to the quality of governance in attacking the multitude of apartheid legacies, notably economic and spatial inequality. At the same time, the mounting crisis of unsustainability – and especially climate change – challenged policy-makers to consider not only different kinds of development but also how institutions might be used pragmatically to facilitate that shift (Swilling, 2010).

Given the intensity of this broader attempted transition away from apartheid authoritarianism – and particularly the struggle to integrate institutional planning and policy-making through participatory information and indicators – it is relatively easy, then, to understand the specific allure in South Africa of the wider "smart turn" in urban and regional affairs. Indeed, as we have argued earlier in this book, smartness everywhere appears to provide a *re-defining context* for extant forms of city-regionalism – a central development in South Africa – in an attempt to reconcile competing, even conflicting, but certainly dynamic, ambitions and agendas. Or to put it more simply still: smartness has suggested, in South Africa, one possible way to get "beyond" post-apartheid, to re-energize cities, city-networks and local democracy, and thus to maximize institutional choices in the search for new ways of doing governance.

Case study: a smart(er) Cape?

Widely regarded as one of the most beautifully situated cities in the world, cosmopolitan and globalized Cape Town, founded originally by the Dutch in 1652, was paradoxically disfigured by British colonial (1795–1910), early national (1910–1948) and, especially, apartheid-era (1948–1994) socio-spatial policies and racial-legal regimes (McDonald, 2008). Though today considered internationally trendy, attractive to both domestic and foreign tourists, and blessed by still expanding economic competencies, including classic strengths in tourism, agro-food processing, and port and trans-shipment logistics, more than half of Cape Town's residents are nonetheless either abjectly poor or hovering just above poverty (Crankshaw, 2012); nearly half the overall metropolitan budget accordingly goes to mundane "brown agenda" needs like building and operating energy, water, waste and sewerage systems (Swilling, 2010). Other major challenges across the city-region include violence and social control issues, particularly in the "Cape Flats" area (Vigneswaran, 2013), as well as public health/HIV needs and aforementioned green concerns with ecological degradation in multiple socio-natural systems (e.g. air quality, groundwater, biodiversity) (Cartwright et al., 2012).

In their comprehensive, multi-sectoral "territorial review" of the Cape Town city-region in 2008, the OECD (2008, pp. 17–18) argued that, despite improvements in the development of public policy in Cape Town up to that point, a "second generation" of reforms was now needed.

> The extensive government reforms after apartheid left many serious problems unresolved, including congestion, lack of housing and a shortage of skilled labor. Grappling with problems of immigration, poverty, and the need to improve global competitiveness and foster inclusive economic development is not made easy by South Africa's adoption of strict public spending restrictions, the entrenched legacy of racial inequality, ecological fragility and the volatile political environment. Reforms are needed to respond to these challenges, primary to i) stimulate intergovernmental collaboration between municipalities and the province, ii) mainstream frameworks for regional planning, iii) improve public finance tools for economic development, iv) build and retain capacity in the national civil service, and v) strengthen civic engagements to improve governance and foster a more inclusive economy.
>
> (Ibid.)

Although the OECD suggested continued changes in the "hardware" of the state – including the creation of a strong planning authority for the "functional" city-region (Figure 6.5) similar to the one advanced by the Vancouver Agreement – many of the "second generation" policy measures it identified, such as those just listed, arguably reflected concerns with the "software" running through (and beyond) the new state structures and policy frameworks.

The OECD's strong focus on the ongoing need to strengthen (even further) the sub-national state at the city-regional scale of policy design and programme activity, albeit without necessary formalizing new institutional spaces *per se*, likely reflected then growing arguments – "post-ASGISA" – about the central importance of a "developmental state" rather than the increasingly threadbare

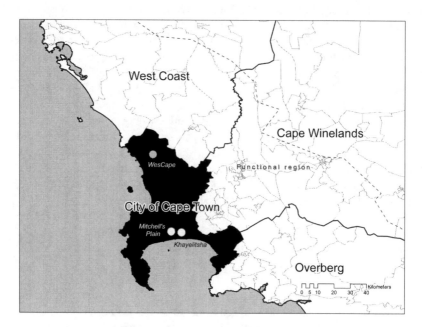

Figure 6.5 Cape Town functional region in the Western Cape.

assurances of neoliberal individualism and the freedom of global capital to invest wherever it might be "wooed" (Gelb, 2006). Interestingly, Parnell and Peiterse (2010), who did much to shape the OECD report, subsequently linked "stronger state capacity" at *the urban scale* to the creative enlargement of human rights beyond the "first generation" goals of early post-apartheid like universal suffrage and freedom from discrimination – as normatively foundational as these rights may be to any conception of a just society (pp. 147–150). While the neoliberal approach to human rights is typically "what the poor can do for themselves," they specifically posited, household- and neighbourhood-based problems like affordable urban services are "second-generation" rights; moreover, practical everyday problems such as pro-poor (im)mobility and quality public spaces are "third-generation" rights, while arguably the ultimate urban challenge – climate-resilient cities – is actually a "fourth-generation" right (ibid.).

As the 1990s shaded into the 2000s, global discourses of "smartness" evolved locally in ways that provide an interesting complement to these wider transitions. Odendaal (2016) notes that before the conceptual language of "smart cities" appeared clearly in Cape Town, local administrators and other key development actors, including foreign donors, were initially focused on then ascendant themes like "e-governance" and the "digital divide" (Bridges.org, 2001). Importantly, this was not only about creating new web portals for rapid information dissemination; nor only about virtually structuring citizen involvement into policy conception, delivery and billing. (Certainly, such initiatives were significant.) But early smartness *avant la lettre* was also about confronting the ongoing, indeed *obdurate*, challenges posed by the "soft" side of social transformation and territorial development, especially improving the efficiency and efficacy of "interdepartmental coordination" within the multi-scaled, now *re*-scaled, multi-sectoral state apparatus (Odendaal, 2016), for example efforts to improve cooperation between the police, the justice system and correctional services (City of Cape Town, 2006). In other words, it was about the many actually-existing problems that integrated development planning for developmental local governance discussed earlier was now actually experiencing on the ground; about the tendency for "shopping lists" (op cit.) to substitute for joined-up, multi-sectoral, area-based governance and social engagement capable of helping to transition from "first" to "second," "third" and indeed "fourth-generation" rights. In this sense, the smart turn in Cape Town was quickly subsumed within – and by – the broader, external project of a socio-spatial transition constantly struggling for sufficient oxygen.

As elsewhere in the world, then, the steady shift away from strictly "digital" and ICT-heavy themes to now somewhat wider "smart city" efforts within the overall Cape Town city-region emerged incrementally in the early- to mid-2000s. These efforts also focused mainly on discrete pilot projects or enhancement programmes that typically involved both state and non-state actors, including non-governmental organizations as well as corporations. While "state-building" through ICT infrastructure and e-governance training continued to be important, once again national, provincial and urban actors also experimented with various self-styled "smart" innovations central to the wider challenge posed by developmental local governance and integrated development planning (Sharif, 2007). Thus, the "Ukuntinga" project, for instance, focused on digitally-improved administrative controls and revenue management, even as new "Digital Business Centres" attempted to strengthen existing policy goals for stimulating entrepreneurship and small-, medium and micro-enterprise (SMME) development, while the "Kulisa Project" in turn especially targeted youth development and job creation. Finally, the "Smart Cape Access Project" was explicitly concerned early on with redressing directly the then profound digital divide across the region by providing free public access to computers and the Internet, principally in various community libraries; experimenting with open source software; and increasing new opportunities in historically disadvantaged communities (Valentine, 2004). While this seems quite basic, it is worth noting that, according to one report, as late as 2002 about 67 per cent of the region's residents had "never" used a computer (Bridges.org, 2001); this figure was a staggering 83 per cent in Cape Town's fast-growing informal settlements (Infomatics South Africa, 2003).

The Smart Cape Access project is especially interesting for several reasons. First, earlier efforts to expand access in historically disadvantaged areas through entirely private sector initiatives had failed, prompting one official to argue later that:

> If the city wants to succeed by offering people Internet access, it must be offered free. Citizens, especially previously disadvantaged citizens, are not going to spend [money] for 30 minutes at an Internet café when that money is needed to put bread on the table.
>
> (Cited in Valentine, 2004)

Second, the pilot phase was widely considered successful, attracting international acclaim (e.g. from the Bill and Melinda Gates Foundation in Seattle); so, it was subsequently "rolled into almost all the libraries in the city" by the end of the decade (Chigona et al., 2009, p. 13). Third, to use Parnell and Pieterse's language of rights broached earlier, the territorial expansion of this particular pilot project also suggested a developmental attempt to move *beyond* neoliberal rationalities of self-empowerment to "second-" and even "third-generation" rights. Indeed, seeing "digital access" as a human right – like voting, free expression, clean air or reliable transit – not a consumer taste, and, no less importantly, re-imaging libraries as *public spaces for smartness* – all this suggests a particular urban cartography not easily folded into techno-utopian models that over-sell the promises of sensors, apps and software. What is really "smart" here, in other words, is not the technology; it is the socio-political effort to deploy technology in ways that innovatively address improved labour market competitiveness and socially-just sustainability in a traumatized city-region. In so far as these efforts also strengthen open data efforts, as evidenced by advocacy organizations like Code for South Africa and the VPUU (Violence Prevention through Urban Upgrading), further potential remains (Shay, pers. comm.).

Yet as Vanessa Watson (2014) shows, such progressive initiatives must now compete with more recent and quite powerful discourses and practices of "smart" city development across much of Africa, including Cape Town and Johannesburg, that are often based on design fantasies of green urbanism arguably as energized by global circuits of property development as by local circles of social transformation. Watson's study is a critical survey of master plans for new "satellite cities" and/or large-scale urban renewal projects in cities like Nairobi, Dar es Salaam, Kigali, Luanda and Accra. But Cape Town's inability to reverse sprawl, leapfrog development and fragmentation over the past 20 years has led to similar dynamics (Watson, 2002, 2016).

Rather than the "compaction-integration" dynamic broadly consistent with smart growth/compact city theory discussed earlier, new satellite developments – and the prospects of whole new towns – now impend upon Cape Town's search *for a more progressive city-regionalism* embedded within the post-apartheid dream of spatial integration and social justice. Although inward investment and economic regeneration remain most needed in the "southeast" quadrant of the city-region, near predominately African Khayelitsha and predominantly Cape Colored Mitchell's Plain, the Minister of Local Government, Environmental Affairs and Development Planning nonetheless approved in 2014 a provisional scheme to develop "WesCape," located some 20 kilometres north-by-northwest of the Cape Town central business district. At full build-out in the late 2030s, WesCape would theoretically include 800,000 people, 200,000 homes, 400 schools, a university and 90 community facilities – while generating 300,000 jobs (though many temporary). This is rather like placing the entire city of Seattle outside of Cape Town rather than within it. For its advocates, WesCape represents sustainability and social opportunity through private-sector led self-containment and innovative/ smart urbanism. Watson, Odendaal and many others, however, have critiqued WesCape, in part because it abrogates key principles of the Cape Town Spatial Development Framework, adopted officially after extensive public consultation in 2012 as part of the city's overall Integrated Development Plan. For them, it is not smart at all but instead "a complete planning disaster" that betrays democratically and organically developed visions of the just and sustainable post-apartheid city (quoted in Davis, 2013).

While spatial planning critiques of Cape Town's un-smart post-apartheid development emphasize the unjust unsustainability of low-density, disconnected, segregated, oil-dependent landscapes, local discourses of a "smarter future" suggest more broadly that "data is the new oil" (City of Cape Town, 2016, p. 12). Here Cape Town is now on an exciting if difficult "digital journey," guided somewhat ironically by the Constitution and the same (partially abrogated) Integrated Development Plan discussed earlier, to build "digital institutions … driven by data and evidence, focusing relentlessly on [its] customers," according to the Executive Mayor (ibid.). Smartness, so conceptualized, is a multi-dimensional effort to move largely corporate sector innovations in digitization, illustrated best by Amazon, Netflix, Uber and AirBnB, to public sector values and modes of "business" (p. 9). Interestingly, the origins of Cape Town's digital journey largely coincide with the national creation of formal unicity authorities to redress the pernicious legacies of apartheid planning and racialized administration, merging pressing questions of city-regionalism with parallel concerns around smart governance, smart economies, smart infrastructure, smart citizens and so on. Steady "digitization" has meant, however, that smart governance, for example, is not simply about maximizing the number of permit, license and service applications issued *electronically*, but also about urban-political efforts "to lobby for changes to national legislation and regulation which stifle local innovation" (p. 14). What we are calling in this book the "internal" transition to smartness, in other words, bleeds inevitably to an "external" transition in post-apartheid South Africa that, in many ways, is too often seen as an obstacle rather than enabler to urban efficacy and innovation. The dual transition of smartness in Cape Town – as in Johannesburg – thus suggests two key city-regions in Africa insufficiently supported by higher-scale dynamics and effective modalities of political change. The smart city, in other words, is not supported sufficiently by "a smart state," a point we develop even further below (Dierwechter, 2017).

Case study: Gauteng as the "smart hub" of Africa?

While Cape Town contested the wisdom of WesCape as a new (South) African form of smart (ex)urbanism, a heavily market-driven, entirely

Chinese-financed, self-styled "smart city" located on 1,600 hectares of land broke ground in 2013 near Modderfontein within Johannesburg-Gauteng between Sandton and the international airport (Figure 6.6). Its precise form and function, according to one its early boosters, putatively would have less to do with public consultation or regional spatial development frameworks and much more with "what our clients or developers want, the sky is the limit" (SAPA, 2015). In his view, "Modderfontein New City" was set to become a "hub for Chinese firms investing in sub-Saharan Africa" (SouthAfrica info, 2015). From a wider geo-political perspective, this sort of vision aptly captures Johannesburg's longer-standing aspirations to become the "smart hub" not only of South Africa but of the African continent as a whole – a launching platform for Africa's emerging articulation with the global economy (and especially natural-resource-hungry China, which has recently replaced the United States as South Africa's largest trading partner). Such geo-political and geo-economic aspirations are perhaps still fantastic for African cities like Kigali, Luanda, Accra, Dar se Salaam or even Nairobi and massive Lagos; they are entirely plausible for "the most economically powerful urban centre in Sub-Saharan Africa" – a city that "has a continent to itself" (Rogerson & Rogerson, 2015, pp. 348–349). Yet as Watson might ask: are Gauteng's "smart hub" aspirations more dreams or nightmares – and for whom?

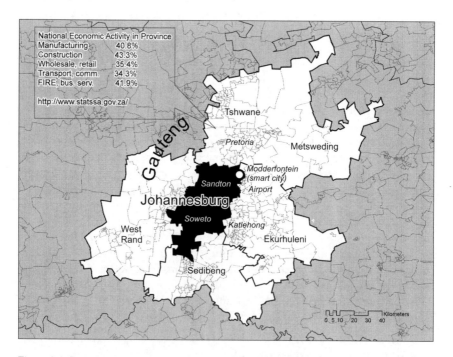

Figure 6.6 Gauteng city-region as smart hub of (South) Africa.

Johannesburg was one of the great shock cities of the 19th century. Cape Town emerged slowly; Johannesburg did not. Rather like Chicago in the heartland of the United States, Johannesburg transformed its wider region around new industrial competencies with few antecedents. In particular, Johannesburg emerged to excavate, finance and manage the new mining economy of South Africa after the local discovery of gold reefs in the 1880s (and an earlier discovery of diamonds in Kimberly). As pits deepened and inevitably grew more complex, massive African labour demands stimulated overall demographic and economic growth in the area – and new geographies of racialized accumulation. Large-scale capital requirements in turn led to industrial consolidation and a new stock exchange. By the 1920s, Johannesburg was easily South Africa's largest city. Growth continued throughout the 20th century, structured by the mining economy, carbon-based suburbanization and apartheid-enforced segregation. Race/class divides were predictably stark, from wealthy subdivisions in Sandton to challenged townships like Katlehong. But the agglomeration forces at work were impressive.

Since the end of apartheid especially, the wider Johannesburg-Gauteng city-region – unequal, unfair, but also undoubtedly dynamic – has emerged as a crucial "linking city in the global economy" shaped by the impacts of several large-scale strategic policy interventions "mediated through the metropolitan prism" (Rogerson & Rogerson, 2015, p. 349). Like Cape Town, and elsewhere, Johannesburg has also implemented a series of "smart" project and programme initiatives, often in partnership to address, *inter alia*: the digital divide (REF); the integration of ICT infrastructure into public service provision (REF); and, of course, the development of corporate smart cities like Modderfontein New City. Most interesting, though, are its strategic efforts to leverage and build upon its national and continental role as "a linking global city" across the regional space-economy of Gauteng. This space-economy – relational and territorial; formal and informal; firm-based and labour-oriented – has received limited scholarly attention (Dierwechter, 2004; Grant, 2010; Rogerson & Rogerson, 2015), a problem in Cape Town and urban South Africa as well (van Huyssteen et al., 2009). Yet public officials and urban practitioners across Gauteng, charged with managing what is today well over 40 per cent of the country's total gross valued added (Parnell & Crankshaw, 2013), nonetheless have focused for the past two decades on targeting key sectors and leveraging territorial assets that support a specific kind of global city-regionalism.

Some observers argue, for instance, that Gauteng's economic governance efforts since at least 2001 not only have been "quite imaginative" but evidence also of an emerging "smart entrepreneurial state" apparatus, *albeit at the urban-provincial scale of authority* (Bbenkele & Madikiza, 2016, p. 102). Such governance efforts include, as Bbenkele and Madikiza interpret regional policy developments, the Gauteng Industrial Policy Framework (2010-2-14), the Gauteng Small, Medium, and Micro-Enterprise Policy Framework (2010–2014) and, especially, the Gauteng Employment, Growth and Development Strategy (2009–2014).

These strategies evolved out of the mid-1990s Spatial Development Initiatives (SDIs) discussed earlier in Chapter 2, and especially out of what was instituted from 2001–2012 as the "Blue IQ" agenda (BlueIQ, 2002).

BlueIQ is worth highlighting here as an exemplar of city-regional smartness in the Johannesburg-Gauteng context. Originating in Gauteng Province's Department of Finance and Economic Affairs' Infrastructure Development Programme, BlueIQ was a provincial public entity that nonetheless operated as a limited private company. (In 2012 it merged with the Gauteng Economic Development Agency to form what is today known as the Gauteng Growth and Development Agency.) For most of the 2000s, BlueIQ was arguably the key institutional agent in the development of strategic economic infrastructure across the entire city-region, including: support for the automotive sector, the Innovation Hub, the Walter Sisulu Square of Dedication in Kliptown, the "Cradle of Humankind" and "Dinokeng" projects, as well as Newtown and Constitution Hill – all projects contributing in different ways to regional economic growth, inner city regeneration, community development, tourism and even rural development. Through both project and asset management services, in other words, BlueIQ focused mainly on "mega projects" in so-called "sunrise" sectors: financial and business services, smart industries, high value-added manufacturing and tourism. As a "catalyst," BlueIQ thus either created spinoff subsidiaries or eventually handed off projects to appropriate service agencies. For example, the Supplier Park Development Company, ltd. – "the first of its kind in Africa" (Blue IQ, 2011, p. 33) – aided component suppliers in the automobile industry by providing enabling infrastructure, logistics and services. A second example, the Gauteng Department of Public Transport, Roads and Works now manages "Gautrain," the rapid rail link initiated by BlueIQ that connects Johannesburg, Tshwane (Pretoria) and the airport. Gautrain, which passes through Modderfontein, is interesting not only because it is a growth management tool for planned densification along two regional axes of urban development, but also because it was conceived from the start as "a key element in improving economies of urbanization, increasing productivity and improving the conduciveness of the local economy" (BlueIQ, 2009).

In sum, Gauteng's territorial programmes have sought to balance global competitiveness and regional sustainability with the wider national policy agenda for social transformation and especially economic empowerment. The focus has been on the green economy and sustainable energy use, innovation and the knowledge economy, infrastructure, green jobs, community-led local economic development, skills development and capacity-building and spatial planning (Bbenkele & Madikiza, 2016). Again, these programmes relate to earlier efforts to reconfigure the industrial path-dependencies of Johannesburg's global city-regional economy into a self-styled "smart centre" or hub (Pillay, 2004). In his review of sub-national economic policy-making in Johannesburg-Gauteng, Rogerson (2004) notes the multiple and relatively early manifestations of "smart" discourses in the local governance agenda: *viz.*, the sectoral target-ing of smart activities, high value added manufacturing, transport and business tourism. For Rogerson, such targeted developments recognized that "globali-zation makes territorial production systems and not just firms compete with each other" (p. 74). That is to say, firms rely on regions that are "well-endowed with specialized infrastructures and institutions to assist them in their restructur-ing for competitiveness." In his judgement, too, the shift from national SDIs to sub-national programmes – and particularly Gauteng's Blue IQ – injected "a real spatial component" into economic governance. In this sense, Johannesburg has anticipated as much as followed the global smart turn. Indeed, as Rogerson (2001) has specifically shown, Johannesburg should be seen as a global pioneer in city-*regional* thinking about smartness, a scalar dimension often missing from smart city discourses (Morandi, Rolando, & Di Vita, 2015). As one report noted in 1998 (CSRC [1998] cited in, Rogerson, 2004, p. 89):

> Although Gauteng suffers from some impediments or disadvantages, nota-bly a lack of mobility of people, parts and products due to the high density development of the province, on the one hand, and some degree of lack of competitiveness of industry, the province can in fact be turned around and can become the smart hub of South Africa.

"State capture" and the external limits of smart city-regional transitions

The on-the-ground examples of specific projects, programmes and policy shifts within both Cape Town and Johannesburg – for example, *Ukutinga*, Smart Cape Access, Wescape, Modderfontien and BlueIQ, amongst many others – strongly suggest the "internal" transition to urban smartness is both varied and increasingly central to how we should conceive of developmental dynamics and overall territorial management in South Africa. The results are inchoate, uneven and debatable – particularly in regard to deepening urban sustainability – but they are, in our view, each important nonetheless in mapping and understand-ing the contingent geographies of post-apartheid governance. Yet, as we have suggested throughout this book, city-regional governance *per se* is multi-scalar and relational, shaped strongly by "external" stories involving wider societal changes and politico-economic forces and structural challenges.

Since the dénouement of the post-apartheid era somewhere between 2011 and 2013, and especially over the past few years, the most important of these challenges has been a growing and increasingly strident recognition among academics, practitioners, business leaders, activists and millions of ordinary citizens that the transformative socio-economic and ecological potential of South Africa's new state structures, policy frameworks and variegated urban experiments have been stunted by the corruptive weight and corrosive poison of what several observers now call a "shadow state" characterized by naked neo-patrimonialism and rent-seeking dysfunction (Johnson, 2015). In a recent analysis, prominent scholars working on the State Capacity Research Project (2017) argue that South Africa under the disastrous presidency of Jacob Zuma has essentially experienced a "silent coup." The ANC's ideological discourse of "radical economic transformation" – modernist-sounding and even "20th century" in its discursive confidence to occasion desired change – has acted mainly as a "smokescreen" to hide widespread and highly concentrated private accumulation from public governance through specific patron–client relationships that siphon-off local, national and, indeed, global circuits of capital. Instead of a "smart state" (Dierwechter, 2017) capable of exercising creative and enabling authority and targeted technical and financial support for the variegated and still-experimental smart transitions within and across both the Cape Town and Johannesburg space-economies and built-territories, this new shadow state "repurposes" the constitutional state to stunt the policy and political possibilities of city-regional change ostensibly seeking socio-spatial sustainability and economic competitiveness (State Capacity Research Project, 2017). The vast new world "beyond" the post-apartheid era – the world of the 2010s and soon enough the 2020s – is, it now seems to many informed critics, increasingly dominated by a "captured state" that is politically unwilling (and administratively unable) to edify local transitions in smartness radical enough to meet the promises of the immediate post-apartheid dispensation.

Conclusions

How have external differences in state structures, policy-making and public discourses in the four cases of what we have conceptualized in this chapter as "post-authoritarian" transition shaped the adoption of "smartness" in city-regional governance?

Like most city-regions around the world – and certainly like the four cases discussed previously in Chapter 5 – post-socialist Berlin and Prague and post-apartheid Cape Town and Johannesburg predictably each struggle to address "mismatch" problems of various kinds between their formal administrative and variegated functional geographies. Prague's struggles are, we have suggested here, relatively more profound, while the two South Africa cases arguably still benefit from a dramatic reterritorialization of local government in the 1990s that led to the innovative creation of so-called "unicity authorities" with independent constitutional authority to drive developmental local governance through integrated development planning. As much of the scholarly and practitioner community debates the merits of "new regionalism," the South Africans have actually contributed one of the more significant examples of governance reform in many decades (while the city of Prague, in contrast, still remains fragmented into 57 entities). Compared with Prague, too, Berlin benefits from the federal structure of the German state, yet the cultural-psychological legacies of top-down communism work against progressively regionalizing what we specifically called the "newly won powers" of local municipal control and policy-making, with East-West differences in legacies with the city having added uncertainty and also a degree of distrust and institutional competition. In addition, this chapter has suggested that extant arrangements for local finance incentivize competitiveness more than collaboration. Although dramatically different from Cape Town and Johannesburg, Berlin's Cold War experience as the world's most famous "divided city," in addition, has interesting parallels with the profound fragmentation and polarization that characterized the multi-scaled apartheid project. Having spent half a century purposefully divided through the ideological impresses of different kinds of authoritarian state power and territorial engineering, all four city-regions now collectively face the fundamental challenges of socio-spatial and institutional integration – a challenge which various smartness projects, initiatives and political reforms ostensibly seek to ameliorate. At least, they want to insinuate new approaches, novel perspectives and ways of doing things so as to overcome legacies of division, suspicion and inequality, as well as lack of political power and experience. This is a lot of historical weight to load on to urban smartness – certainly going well beyond apps, sensors and algorithms that target efficient parking, low energy budgets and smart buildings.

In key respects, smartness practices in Cape Town, in particular, are conceived as methods to modernize and expand the local state's policy and management efficacy through the imagined wizardry of ICT-led data integration. Indeed, South Africa's strong policy emphasis on integrated development planning – and the synoptic "plans" for urban transformation they invariably produce – face the common institutional "siloes" that bedevil all forms of strategic regional planning nearly everywhere *en face* of well established local/municipal interests and traditions. . We noted, for example, that problems of inter-departmental coordination between key state service providers still tend to generate "shopping lists", rather than joined-up, multi-sectoral, area-based governance and social engagement. Urban smartness in Cape Town pulses through the local state, as it seeks to ensure not simply the most basic of human rights, but as it seeks more generally to *transition towards* what Parnell and Pieterse (op cit.) once again provocatively call "second," "third" and indeed "fourth-generation" rights, the last of which is conceived as the right to urban climate-resiliency itself.

Interestingly, each of these city-regions sees smartness as a pragmatic and cost-effective strategy to deepen environmental sustainability while concomitantly advancing economic competitiveness, yet parallel efforts to create new regimes of city-regionalism are more advanced in some cases than others. Noteworthy here, we conclude, are Johannesburg's policy efforts over the past several years to embed itself within (and to some extent *as*) the wider and economically dynamic Gauteng Province. Various projects and programmes that have tried to construct this city-region as a "smart hub" not only for South Africa but for Africa as a whole essentially amount to an important world case study in smartness, highlighting both sub-national experiments that seek a "smart entrepreneurial state" (op cit.) along with the many contradictions and tensions that pervade such an effort. Chief among these are the political pathologies associated with a central government increasingly pervaded by neo-patrimonial rent-seeking. This simultaneously retards the full development and ironically amplifies the inequalities of Gauteng's nascent aspirations to become a global smart hub. Although the rise of "post-Westphalian" spaces of new urban networks is progressively significant (Herrschel & Newman, 2017), *national context also still matters*: city-scale managers must be able to identify both "threats and opportunities" associated with their respective national institutions (Berrone & Ricart, 2015).

In the case of Berlin and Prague (as well Lyon and Turin discussed in Chapter 5) these include regulatory, political and fiscal dynamics associated with the European Union too. That there are (real-and-imagined) "threats" as well as "opportunities" – that working together even within the same cultural-national environment – underscores the wider structural realities dramatically shaping urban smartness in various city-regions around the world. And it is these underlying tensions between internal dynamics and external state structures and institutional legacies and governance practices that have contributed to the somewhat delayed and hesitant adoption of "smartness" as expression of novel institutional and policy-making approaches that seek to reach through stagnant structures and power relations that increasingly fall behind the rapid dynamic changes in the challenges and tasks affecting city-regional governance. So, in our conceptual diagram above (Figure 4.3), all four "transition cities" show the clear impact of the respective states on the ways in which they practice city-regional governance, although different internal dynamics have allowed South African cities take greater strides in recognizing the need for collaborative action within the city-region, than in the two Eastern European cities, Berlin and Prague.

References

Altvater, E. (1993). *The future of the market: An essay on the regulation of money and Nature after the collapse of "actually existing socialism"*. London: Verso.

Altvater, E. (1998). Theoretical deliberations on time and space in post-socialist transformation. *Regional Studies, 32*(7), 591–605.

Bbenkele, E., & Madikiza, L. (2016). Envisioning public sector pathways: Gauteng as an entrepreneurial province in South Africa. *Journal of Entrepreneurship and Innovation in Emerging Economies, 2*(2), 91–108. doi:10.1177/2393957516654845

Benz, A., & Koenig, K. (1995). *Der aufbau einer region: Planung und verwaltung im verdichtungsraum Berlin-Brandenburg*. Baden-Baden: Nomos.

Berrone, P., & Ricart, J. (2015). *Cities in motion index*. Barcelona, Madrid: IESE: Navarro.

Binns, T., & Nel, E. (2002). Devolving development: Integrated development planning and developmental local government in post-apartheid South Africa. *Regional Studies, 36*(8), 921–932. doi:10.1080/0034340022000012342

Blažek, J., & Uhlíř, D. (2007). Regional innovation policies in the Czech Republic and the case of Prague: An emerging role of a regional level? *European Planning Studies, 15*(7), 871–888.

BlueIQ. (2002). *Blue IQ: The plan for a smart province – Gauteng*. Johannesburg.

BlueIQ. (2009). *Anual report 2008/09.* Johannesburg: BlueIQ Investment Holdings Ltd.

Bolleyer, N. (2009). *Intergovernmental cooperation: Rational choices in federal systems and beyond.* Oxford: Oxford University Press.

Bond, P. (2000). *Elite transition: From apartheid to neoliberalism.* London: Pluto Press.

Brenner, N. (2004). *New state spaces.* Oxford: Oxford University Press.

Bridges.org. (2001). *Spanning the digital divide: Understanding and tackling the issues.* Retrieved from www.itu.int/net/wsis/docs/background/general/reports/26092001_bridges.htm, accessed 2 Sept. 2016.

Brusis, M. (2003). Regionalisation in the Czech and Slovak republics: Comparing the influence of the European Union. In M. Keating, & J. Hughes (Eds.), *The regional challenge in Central and Eastern Europe: Territorial restructuring and European integration* (pp. 89–105). Paris: Presses interuniversitaires européennes/Peter Lang.

Cartwright, A., Parnell, S., Oelofse, G., & Ward, S. (2012). *Climate change at the city scale: Impacts, mitigation and adaptation in Cape Town.* New York: Earthscan.

CDA (City Development Authority of Prague) (2000). *Strategic plan for Prague.* City of Prague: CDA (unpublished).

CDA (City Development Authority of Prague) (2009). *Strategic plan for Prague 2009–2015.* Prague: CDA (unpublished).

Chigona, W., Roode, D., Nazeer, N., & Pinnock, B. (2009). *Investigating the impact of stakeholder management on the implementation of a public access project: Case of Smart Cape.* Paper presented at the Proto CIRN Community Informatics Conference, Monash University, 4–8 November.

City of Berlin (Senate Department for Urban Development and the Environment) (2015). Smart City Strategy Berlin, as of 21 April 2015. *Unpublished.* Retrieved from www.stadtentwicklung.berlin.de/planen/foren_initiativen/smart-city/download/Strategie_Smart_City_Berlin_en.pdf, accessed 1 Dec. 2017.

City of Cape Town. (2006). Cape Town's "smart city" strategy in South Africa. Retrieved from http://unpan1.un.org/intradoc/groups/public/documents/cpsi/unpan033820.pdf

City of Cape Town. (2016). The city of Cape Town's digital journey: Towards a smarter future. *Cape Town.* Retrieved from http://acceleratecapetown.co.za/wp/wp-content/uploads/2016/11/The-City-of-Cape-Towns-Digital-Journey-Towards-a-Smarter-Future-Rudy-Abrahams-CoCT.pdf, accessed 3 Sept. 2016.

Cochrane, A., & Jonas, A. E. G. (1999). Reimagining Berlin: World city, national capital or ordinary place? *European Urban and Regional Studies, 6*(2), 145–164.

Crane, W., & Swilling, M. (2008). Environment, sustainable resource use and the Cape Town functional region: An overview. *Urban Forum, 19*(3), 263–287. doi:10.1007/s12132-008-9032-y

Crankshaw, O. (2012). Deindustrialization, professionalization and racial inequality in Cape Town. *Urban Affairs Review, 48*(6), 836–862.

Davis, R. (2013, May 17). Is the future of Cape Town 25km from Cape Town? *Daily Maverick.* Retrieved from www.dailymaverick.co.za/article/2013-05-17-is-the-future-of-cape-town-25km-from-cape-town/#.WEMsweYrJWJ, accessed 4 Sept. 2016.

Dewar, D. (1979). *Low income housing policy in South Africa: With particular reference to the Western Cape / David Dewar, George Ellis.* Cape Town: Urban Problems Research Unit, University of Cape Town.

Dewar, D. (1995). The urban question in South Africa: The need for a planning paradigm shift. *Third World Planning Review, 17*(4), 407–419.

Dewar, D., & Todeschini, F. (1998). *Urban integration and economic development.* Cape Town: Frankolin.

218 *Beyond post-authoritarian regimes*

Dewar, D., & Watson, V. (1991). Urban planning and the informal sector. In Preston-Whyte, & C. Rogerson (Eds.), *South Africa's informal economy.* Cape Town: Oxford University Press.

Dierwechter, Y. (2004). Dreams, bricks, and bodies: Mapping "neglected spatialities" in African Cape Town. *Environment and Planning A, 36*(1), 959–981.

Dierwechter, Y. (2017). The smart state as utopian space for urban politics. In A. E. G. Jonas, B. Miller, K. Ward, & D. Wilson (Eds.), *The Routledge handbook on spaces of urban politics.* London: Routledge.

EC. (2013). *Innovation support takes centre stage in Prague's governance and growth strategy.* Retrieved from https://ec.europa.eu/growth/tools-databases/regional-innovation-monitor/news/innovation-support-takes-centre-stage-prague%E2%80%99s-governance-and-growth-strategy, accessed 18 Nov. 2016.

Elster, J., Offe, C., & Preuss, U. K. (1998). *Institutional design in post-communist societies: Rebuilding the ship at sea.* Cambridge: Cambridge University Press.

Engelniederhammer, S. (1999). *Berliner verwaltung auf modernisierungskurs: Bausteine-Umsetzungsstrategien-Hindernisse.* Berlin: Edition Sigma.

Etzkowitz, H. (2008). *The triple helix: University-industry-government innovation in action.* London: Routledge.

Ferry, M. (2014). Case study report. Prague metropolitan region. Working Paper Series. *GRINCH – growth – innovation – competitiveness: Fostering cohesion in Central and Eastern Europe.* Series 6, *Spaces, territories and regions.* European Policies Research Centre, University of Strathclyde. www.grincoh.eu, Paper No. 6.06.03.

Fishman, R. M. (1990). Rethinking state and regime: Southern Europe's transition to democracy. *World Politics, 42*(3), 422–440.

Fukuyama, F. (2006 [1992 reprint]). *The end of history and the last man.* London: Free Press.

Gauteng Province – Economic Development (Blue IQ) (2011). *Blueprints for a greener future.* Annual Report 2010–2011.

Gelb, S. (2006). The RDP, GEAR and all that: Reflections ten years later. *Transformation: Critical Perspectives on Southern Africa, 62*(1), 1–8.

Glaser, E. (2016). In defence of the metropolitan elite, in: New Statesman, 20 Oct 16.

Gowan, P. (1995). Neoliberal theory and practice for Eastern Europe. *New Left Review,* 213, p. 3.

Grant, R. (2010). Working it out: Labour geographies of the poor in Soweto, South Africa. *Development Southern Africa, 27*(4), 595–612.

Hammersley, R., & Westlake, T. (1996). Planning in the Prague region: Past, present and future. *Cities, 13*(4), 247–256.

Harms, J. (2006). Die Verwaltungsreform in Berlin -eine Zwischenbilanz. In *Public management-Grundlagen, wirkungen, kritik* (pp. 335–350). Nomos Verlagsgesellschaft mbH & Co. KG.

Harrison, P. (2006). Integrated development plans and Third Way politics. In U. Pillay, R. Tomlinson, & J. Du Toit (Eds.), *Democracy and delivery: Urban policy in South Africa.* Cape Town: HSRC Press.

Harrison, P., Todes, A., & Watson, V. (2008). *Planning and transformation: Learning from the post-aparthied experience.* London: Routledge.

Hauswirth, I., Herrschel, T., & Newman, P. (2003). Incentives and disincentives to city-regional cooperation in the Berlin-Brandenburg conurbation. *European Urban and Regional Studies, 10*(2), 119–134. doi.org/10.1177/0969776403010002002

Heeg, S. (1998). Vom ende der stadt als staatliche Veranstaltung: Reformulierung städischer politikformen am Beispiel Berlins. *PROKLA, 28*(0), 5–23.

Heeg, S. (2001). *Politische regulation des Raumes: Metropolen – regionen – nationalstaat.* Berlin: edition sigma.

Herrschel, T. (2007). Between difference and adjustment: The re-/presentation and implementation of post-socialist (communist) transformation. *Geoforum, 38*(3), 439–444.

Herrschel, T. (2014). *Cities, state and globalisation: City-regional governance in Europe and North America* (Regions and Cities Series). London: Routledge.

Herrschel, T. (2015). Migration and urban governance: Challenges for democratic legitimacy? In B. G. Peters, P. von Maravic, & E. Schröter (Eds.), *Politics of representative bureaucracy: Power, legitimacy and performance* (pp. 122–140). London: Edward Elgar.

Herrschel, T., & Newman, P. (2002). *Governance of Europe's city regions: Planning, policy and politics.* London: Routledge.

Herrschel, T., & Newman, P. (2003) Die Governance europäischer Stadtregionen. *Informationen zur Raumentwicklung, 8/9*, 543–555.

Herrschel, T., & Newman, P. (2005). Continued division through obstructionist institutionalism. *DISP 156, 40*(1), "Berlin – 15 Jahre ohne Mauer" special issue, 98–105.

Herrschel, T., & Newman, P. (2017). *Cities as international actors.* London: Palgrave.

Hung, J. (2012). Berlin's housing bubble and the backlash against hipster tourists. *The Guardian*, 18 Sept. 2012.

IHK (Berlin Chamber of Commerce). (2015). Smart governance: A study by the Berlin Chamber of Commerce. Retrieved from www.ihk-berlin.de/politische-positionen-und-statistiken_channel

Infomatics South Africa. (2003). *Evaluation of the Smart Cape Access Pilot Project: A City of Cape Town digital divide initiative.* Western Cape Province, Cape Town. Retrieved from www.westerncape.gov.za/text/2003/12/smart_cape_access_project_-_evaluation_final_report.pdf, accessed 5 Sept. 2016.

IPR Praha (Prague Institute of Planning and Development). (2014). PRAGUE Regional Innovation Strategy (PRAGUE ris3). [September 2014]. Available from www.rishmp.cz/public/d0/b3/33/2039316_587039_Prague_RIS3.pdf, accessed 30 Nov. 2017.

IPRP Prague Strategic Plan (2008). www.iprpraha.cz/uploads/assets/soubory/data/strategicky_plan/angl2008_web.pdf, accessed 4 Aug 2017.

Jenkins, C., & Du Plessis, M. (2014). *Law, nation-building and transformation: The South African experience in perspective.* Cambridge: Intersentia.

Johnson, R. W. (2015). *How long will South Africa survive?* London: Hurst & Co.

Kolodko, G. W. (2001). Globalization and catching-up: From recession to growth in transition economies. *Communist and Post-Communist Studies, 34*(3), 279–322.

Krätke, S. (2000) Berlin: The metropolis as a production space. *European Planning Studies 8*(1), 7–27.

Kuzio, T. (2001). Transition in post-communist states: Triple or quadruple? *Politics, 21*(3), 168–177.

Lenhardt, K. (1998). Bubble-politics in Berlin. *PROKLA, 28*(0), 41–66.

Linz, J., & Stepan, A. (1996). *Problems of democratic transition and consolidation: Southern Europe, South America, and post-communist Europe.* Baltimore, MD: JHU Press.

Marais, H. (1998). *South Africa limits to change: The political economy of transition.* Cape Town: University of Cape Town Press.

Maylam, P. (1990). The rise and decline of urban apartheid in South Africa. *African Affairs, 89*(354), 57–84.

Maylam, P. (1995). Explaining the apartheid city: 20 years of South African historiography. *Journal of Southern African Studies, 21*(1), 19–38.

McDonald, D. (2008). *World city syndrome: Neoliberalism and inequality in Cape Town.* New York: Routledge.

Metzner, T. (2015). Gebietsreform: Acht statt achtzehn Landkreise. *Der Tagesspiegel*, 27 Feb. 2015.

Monstadt, J. (2007). Urban governance and the transition of energy systems: Institutional change and shifting energy and climate policies in Berlin. *IJURR, 31*(2), 326–343.

Morandi, C., Rolando, A., & Di Vita, S. (2015). *From smart city to smart region: Digital services for an Internet of Places.* Cham, Switz.: Springer.

Murrell, P. (1996). How far has the transition progressed? *The Journal of Economic Perspectives, 10*(2), 25–44.

Odendaal, N. (2016). Getting smart about smart cities in Cape Town. In S. Marvin, A. Luque-Ayala, & C. McFarlane (Eds.), *Smart urbanism.* London: Routledge.

O'Donnell, G., & Schmitter, P. (2013). *Transitions from authoritarian rule: Tentative conclusions about uncertain democracies.* Baltimore, MD: JHU Press.

OECD. (2008). *Territorial review: Cape Town metropolitan review.* Paris: OECD.

OECD. (2013). *Rural–urban partnerships: An integrated approach to economic development.* Paris: OECD Publishing. http://dx.doi.org/10.1787/9789264204812-en

Offe, C., & Adler, P. (1991). Capitalism by democratic design? Democratic theory facing the triple transition in East Central Europe. *Social Research, 58* (4), 865–892.

Orren, K., & Skowronek, S. (1996). Instituions and intercurrence: Theory building in the fullness of time. *Nomos, 38,* 111–146. Retrieved from www.jstor.org/stable/24219548

Pallotti, A., & Engel, U. (2016). *South Africa after apartheid: Policies and challenges of the democratic transition.* Leiden: Brill.

Parnell, S., & Crankshaw, O. (2013). The politics of "race" and the transformation of the post-apartheid space economy. *Journal of Housing and the Built Environment, 28*(4), 589–603. doi:10.1007/s10901-013-9345-6

Parnell, S., & Pieterse, E. (2010). The "right to the city": Institutional imperatives of a developmental state. *International Journal of Urban and Regional Research, 34*(1), 146–162.

Pillay, U. (2004). Are globally competitive "city-regions" developing in South Africa? Formulaic aspirations or new imaginations? *Urban Forum, 15*(4), 340–364.

Posaner, J. (2017): Berlin airport opening delayed to 2018. *Politico,* 28 Dec. 16. Retrieved from www.politico.eu/article/berlin-airport-opening-delayed-to-2018/, accessed 15 Feb. 2017.

Prague Daily Monitor (2017): Central Bohemia to cooperate with China, other Asian countries, 4 Jan. 2017. *Copyright 2015 by the Czech News Agency (ČTK).* Available from http://praguemonitor.com/2017/01/04/central-bohemia-cooperate-china-other-asian-countries, accessed 10 Jan. 2017.

Republic of South Africa. (2011). *National strategy for sustainable development and action plan.* Pretoria: Department of Environmental Affairs.

Roberts, D., & Diederichs, N. (2002). Durban's Local Agenda 21 programme: Tackling sustainable development in a post-apartheid city. *Environment and Urbanization, 14*(1), 189–201.

Robinson, J. (1997). The geopolitics of South African cities: States, citizens, territory. *Political Geography, 16*(5), 365–386.

Robinson, J. (1998a). *Planning the post-apartheid city: Comments on the metropolitan spatial development framework – MSDF (Cape Town).* Unpublished paper.

Robinson, J. (1998b). Spaces of democracy: Remapping the apartheid city. *Environment and Planning D: Society and Space, 16*(5), 533–548.

Rogerson, C. (1989). Urbanisation and urban change under late apartheid: A commentary. *African Urban Quarterly, 4*(3/4), 203–205.

Rogerson, C. (1997). The changing post-apartheid city: Emergent Black-owned small enterprise in Johannesburg. *Urban Studies, 34*(1), 85–103.

Rogerson, C. (2001). Knowledge-based or smart regions in South Africa. *South African Geographical Journal, 83*(1), 34–47.

Rogerson, C. (2004). From spatial development initiative to Blue IQ: Sub-national economic planning in Gauteng. *Urban Forum, 15*(1), 74–101.

Rogerson, C. (2008). Shared growth in urban tourism: Evidence from Soweto, South Africa. *Urban Forum, 19*(4), 395–411. doi:10.1007/s12132-008-9042-9

Rogerson, C., & Rogerson, J. (2015). Johannesburg 2030: The economic contours of a "linking global city". *American Behavioral Scientist, 59*(3), 347–368. doi:10.1177/0002764214550303

Rustow, D. A. (1970). Transitions to democracy: Toward a dynamic model. *Comparative politics, 2*(3), 337–363.

Ruwanza, S., & Shackleton, C. (2016). Incorporation of environmental issues in South Africa's municipal integrated development plans. *Sustainable Development and World Ecology, 23*(1), 28–39.

SAPA. (2015). Gauteng's R84 billion smart city is coming. *BusinessTech*, 8 January. Retrieved from https://businesstech.co.za/news/general/76811/gautengs-r84-billion-smart-city-is-coming/, accessed 12 Sept. 2017.

Scholze, J. (2014). *Comparative policy analysis. City-regions. The possibilities of using EU structural funds for the development of urban – rural partnership in the 2014 – 2020 funding period.* German Association for Housing, Urban and Spatial Development.

SDUDE (Senate Department for Urban Development and the Environment) (2015), *Smart City Strategy Berlin.* Unpublished policy document. Status: 21 April 2015 (online) Available from www.stadtentwicklung.berlin.de/planen/foren_initiativen/smart-city/download/Strategie_Smart_City_Berlin_en.pdf, accessed 14 July 2017.

Sellers, J. (2002). Federalism and metropolitan governance in cross-national perspective: The case of urban sprawl. *Environment and Planning C: Government and Policy, 20*(1), 95–112.

Sharif, M. (2007). City of Cape Town's smart city strategy. In G. Misuraca (Ed.), *E-governance in Africa: From theory to action.* Trenton, NJ: Africa World Press.

Smart City Berlin. (2017). *The future starts here (1 June).* Available from www.urbanlearning.eu/fileadmin/user_upload/smart_city_berlin.pdf, accessed 14 July 2017.

SouthAfrica info. (2015). Work begins on South Africa's R84bn smart city (January 2015). Retrieved from www.brandsouthafrica.com/investments-immigration/business/investing/work-begins-on-south-africas-r84bn-smart-city, accessed 21 Nov. 2017.

Sparks, A. (1995). *Tomorrow is another country: The inside story of South Africa's negotiated revolution.* Sandton: Struik Book Distributors.

State Capacity Research Project. (2017). *Betrayal of the promise: How South Africa is being stolen.* Retrieved from http://polity.org.za/article/betrayal-of-a-promise-2017-05-26, accessed 3 June 2017.

Swilling, M. (2010). Sustainability, poverty and municipal services: The case of Cape Town, South Africa. *Sustainable Development, 18*(4), 194–201. doi:10.1002/sd.489

Todes, A. (2006). Urban spatial policy. In U. Pillay, R. Tomlinson, & J. Du Toit (Eds.), *Democracy and delivery: Urban policy in South Africa.* Cape Town: HSRC Press.

Turba, M. (2014). Prague metropolitan region. Regional Work Paper 5.1.3, Prague 9 City Council, 18 June 2014. Available from www.leipzig.de/fachanwendungen/city-regions/fileadmin/user_upload/Downloads/CiRe_5.3.1_Regional%20work%20paper%20Prague.pdf, accessed 30 Nov. 2017.

UVB (Unternehmensverbände Berlin-Brandenburg) and Prognos AG (2016). *Die Digitale Hauptstadtregion. Wie Wirtschaft, Wissenschaft und Politik den digitalen Wandel getalten koennen.* May 2016. Available from www.prognos.com/uploads/tx_atwpubdb/20160500_Prognos_Die_digitale_Hauptstadtregion_Ver.1.0.pdf, accessed 18 July 2017.

Valentine, S. (2004). *E-powering the people: South Africa's Smart Cape Access project.* Washington, DC: Council on Library and Information Resources.

van Donk, M., & Pieterse, E. (2006). Reflections of the design of a post-aprthied system of (urban) local development. In U. Pillay, R. Tomlinson, & J. Du Toit (Eds.), *Democracy and Delivery: Urban policy in South Africa*. Cape Town: HSRC Press.

van Huyssteen, E., Biermann, S., Naudé, A., & le Roux, A. (2009). Advances in spatial analysis to support a more nuanced reading of the South African space economy. *Urban Forum, 20*(2), 195–214. doi:10.1007/s12132-009-9061-1

Vigneswaran, D. (2013). Cape Town after apartheid: Crime and governance in the divided city. *International Journal of Urban and Regional Research, 37*(3), 1109–1110. doi:10.1111/1468-2427.12072_6

Vogt, M. (2016). *Der holprige Weg der Hauptstadt zur Smart City Berlin*. www.management-circle.de/blog/smart-city-berlin/, accessed 3 Nov. 2016.

Watson, V. (2002). *Change and continuity in spatial planning: Metropolitan planning in Cape Town under political transition*. London: Routledge.

Watson, V. (2014). African urban fantasies: Dreams or nightmares? *Environment and Urbanization, 26*(1), 215–231. doi:10.1177/0956247813513705

Watson, V. (2016). 10 reasons Cape Town's new city "Wescape" would be a disaster. Retrieved from http://futurecapetown.com/2016/06/10-reasons-cape-towns-new-city-wescape-would-be-a-disaster-future-cape-town/#.WECqp-YrJWK, accessed 3 June 2017.

Western, J. (1981). *Outcast Cape Town*. Minneapolis MN: University of Minnesota Press.

Worger, W. H., & Clark, N. L. (2011). *South Africa: The rise and fall of apartheid* (2nd edn.). New York: Longman.

Zawatka-Gerlach, U. (2017): Berlin wächst in alle Richtungen. In *Der Tagesspiegel*, 20 June 2017. Available from www.tagesspiegel.de/berlin/hauptstadtregion-berlin-brandenburg-berlin-waechst-in-alle-richtungen/19918110.html, accessed 1 Dec. 2017.

7 Conclusions

Smart transitions in city-regionalism

Reprise

In his famous book *The Condition of Postmodernity*, David Harvey (1989) frankly admitted he could not quite recall when he had first heard the term "postmodernism." He had imagined it would soon fade from view, like a flamboyant fashion from the 1970s. (It did not, so he wrote a book to explain why.) Similarly, neither of us can remember when we first encountered the term "smart" in urban affairs and regional studies. No doubt somewhere in the late 1990s, just as the new possibilities offered by digital communication and the still new Internet seemed to provide new ways of interacting and obtaining information on almost all aspects of the human and natural environments. It has not gone away either. Yet, while smartness is today "all the rage" in both theory and practice, rather like postmodernism, it too has splintered, morphed and grown diverse. So, as a result, it invariably now means different things to different people focused on different problems in different disciplines and, one might now add, at different times too.

In popular discussions, and, especially in journalism and corporate circles, the moniker "smart" often has a narrow, "hard," almost *architectonic* meaning, insinuating something inherently positive. Cities – especially larger core cities and national capitals, such as Paris, Budapest, Buenos Aires, Seoul or New York – are read as structurally outdated and bureaucratically encrusted places, just waiting to enjoy fully the presumed efficiencies of ICT-infused infrastructures and digitized modes of governance; their socially-related urban objects, sufficiently networked and virtually integrated through the "everyware" of technological novelty, could be the building blocks of truly "smart cities." If/when rolled out by sufficiently bold leaders, such cities might also someday (cheaply) have it all: dynamic green economies; reduced ecological impacts; and engaged (rather than uninvolved or disaffected) citizens. It almost sounds too good to be a likely scenario. In fact, in some accounts, smart cities become smart as digitally-savvy citizens steadily re-invent "from below" accepted modes of governance and urban (re)development through continuous citizenship (Townsend, 2013), thus infusing "smartness" with an "activist" dimension of innovation in governing.

It may be that some of the many themes now resonant globally in the smart cities literature emerged originally from (North) America's smart growth paradigm. In that paradigm, the long controversial politics of urban growth – "no growth, slow growth, go growth" (Knaap, 2001) – were theoretically *resolved*. So, "smartness" is linked to complex political challenges to address conflicting/competing agendas simultaneously. Planners, communities and development professionals (once again) re-scaled key development dynamics to the wider city-region, shifting a somewhat stale, repetitious and, in terms of innovation and novel ideas, threadbare conversation from a focus on the quantitative amount of growth in particular communities to the more broadly defined qualitative location of growth across metropolitan space-economies. Here comparative "performance" and "success" now included much more than mere quantitative economic criteria. As many have noted, for example, smart growth was, in part, an American response to the post-Rio Agenda 21 project of global sustainable development (Dierwechter, 2017), giving extra impetus to a lingering unease about the loss of open land, and more practically the cost of providing services to sprawling suburbs and exurbs that were growing at the direct expense of city centres. This mattered, as it directly reflected the more parochial politics of the United States, also found at the local level, and, not least, ongoing concerns there with lucrative economic bases and the use of locally-raised "tax dollars" required to fund public services that state-skeptical voters demand. If properly located and imaginatively designed, the US smart growth narrative claimed, urban growth could perhaps help to deliver everything at once: *inter alia*, urban sustainability, economic competitiveness *and* neighbourhood livability. As a further advocated advantage, it could also lower service costs and thus reduce necessary public outlays for bulk infrastructure. And this, in turn, could address the expanding problem, even the crisis in some places, of local public insolvency, such as symbolically epitomized by the years of fiscal crisis in New York in late 1970s (and Detroit, more recently). The austerity years after the 2008 financial crisis accelerated that narrative.

Yet, all this seemed, at critical times, too normative and unquestioned in its underlying assumptions – too "post-political" (MacLeod, 2013) for its own good. The argument lingers that the solutions offered are so *obvious*, so *rational*, so *self-evident*, that no one ("in their right mind") could reasonably oppose the proposed plans, policies and projects of mixed-use, public transit, design flexibility, community economies, etc. without appearing "dumb." In contrast, being "smart" seems also being avant garde, while eschewing this may suggest the opposite: being out of date, or worse still, irrational and racist, or, in fact, all the above.

Whether or not global work on smart cities emerged directly from – or, just as likely, in parallel with – the notion of smart growth, the popular smart cities literature soon adopted much of the same "post-political" romanticism of smart growth, even as it has (not yet) really engaged *in toto* with fast-re-scaling economics and politics. It is what Alan Scott (2001) and many others have charted in recent years as a new era of global city-regionalism (Harrison, 2012;

Jonas, 2013; Jonas & Moisio, 2016; Pezzoli, Hibbard, & Huttoon, 2006; Ward & Jonas, 2004). As first discussed in Chapter 2, the economic dimensions of city-regionalism, following Scott and other scholars, essentially foreground a novel spatial anatomy, a new developmental grammar, for global capitalism. It is not only that many cities in a now predominantly urbanized world have become regions, which is a longer-running story, but that key urban centres – key nodes like Los Angeles, the Pearl River Delta, Sao Paolo or Johannesburg, for instance – have really become "superclusters." Gaps within, and increasingly across, such superclusters and their rural "other" inside culturally shared national territories, have generated emerging political and social tensions between so-called "winners" and "losers," as manifested by the populist revolt of 2017 as well as the wider assault (now from the new populist Right) on the long familiar "devil" of neoliberal globalization.

These economic developments have created new challenges, complicating many older ones, for the *politics* of city-regions; for how dense, but often fragmented agglomerations of firms, workers and infrastructures might be more effectively managed to address global challenges, such as ecological unsustainability and the intensifying pressures on local economic competitiveness. In Chapter 3, we emphasized that, when seen comparatively, a series of diverse *political transitions* are also now occurring – and not only within city-regions but, increasingly, across them; new spaces of "clubbing together" are being imagined and built at multiple spatial scales (Herrschel & Newman, 2017). As often as not, these new spaces are "virtual" in that they are merely "softly" institutionalized (or "thinly" constituted) to give them variability and thus responsiveness to changing circumstances and "task profiles," while allowing members to join and depart as befitting their local self-interests and own agendas. And while such spaces might well depend on formal institutions for implementation, they seek flexibility and, increasingly, correspond with the opportunistic, time-dependent and goal-oriented nature of their overall rationale. They are, we specifically reasoned, of central importance to more recent "smart" transitions in city-regionalism, trying to be both organizing and implementation principle while also still "light" on institutionalization (and coercion) to allow membership with minimal infringement on local scope to pursue localized interests. Understanding the remarkable rise of smartness, in our view, thus requires us all to understand, better than we probably do, the various smart developments in the *new city-regionalism*, as economies, polities and societies at various territorial scales struggle to manage the emerging forces reshaping early 21st century urban life. Accordingly, we have been interested throughout this book in all those variegated efforts to manage competing and also conflicting agendas, such as the goals of sustainability and competitiveness in a historic era when, it appears, growing social divides are steadily enervating social cohesion, and even the taken-for-granted institutions of democracy itself (Barber, 2013), such as we can witness with the rise of populist leaders in Europe, the United States and also South Africa, who all challenge democratic principles.

Once again, the central theoretical approach advanced through this book to understand these empirical changes a bit better in their complexity and underlying dynamics, and, hopefully, to advance the critical literature on the geographies of smartness in its varying thematic references, has been through the synoptic concept of "dual transition." This has been explored through the lenses of diverse cases of rationalizing and implementing city-regionalism ("internal transition") in different socio-economic and cultural contexts in their underlying changes ("external transition"), a project that has unearthed an uneven world of dual transitions and manifestations of smartness in governance along the way.

An uneven world of dual transitions

Thinking empirically about the variegated economics and politics of smart city-regionalism as a series of dual transitions, we have tried to show in the preceding chapters how *internal* efforts to balance competing interests and agendas, such as sustainability and competitiveness, shape (and are shaped by) *external* changes – or transitions – in the wider context within which these city-regions are nominally embedded.

Much has been said already in the expanding literature on how local governments increasingly consider the promises and practices of smart city innovations in their struggles to balance the fundamental conceptual and ideational competition between sustainability and competitiveness (Albino, Berardi, & Dangelico, 2015; Hollands, 2015; Shelton, Zook, & Wiig., 2015; Wiig, 2015b). Some of this literature, in turn, relates directly to what was called in Chapter 2 the "hard" end of the smart city question, wherein important and, to some extent legitimate, new questions are posed about sensors, digital infrastructures, the internet of things and so on (Kylili & Fokaides, 2015; Perera et al., 2014; Zanella et al., 2014). In our view, however, as we suggest in Chapter 4, smartness reflects a larger willingness and capacity for creativity in territorial governance. While this dimension of smartness might be considered the "soft" end of the smart city question, paradoxically it is much harder to do. We suggest that the internal transition to smartness can be opened up theoretically, and interrogated empirically, around the synoptic problem of regionalism vs localism, wherein new city-regional governing structures and shifting economic conditions conjoin with focused policy-making capacity and, ultimately, local leadership to facilitate, or occlude, effective collaborations in particular places.

However, what we see as the *propensity* for policy innovation and collaboration – for "internal" smartness – is constantly shaped and conditioned by wider, or "external," transitions in political-economies and state–society–market relationships. We thus join many other critical scholars of cities and regions, who also see the influence of what we called in Chapters 4, 5 and 6 a "neoliberal market order." This we take to be largely business-oriented and set in a free-market, corporate-driven understanding of individualism, globalization and associated uneven opportunities between inevitable "winners" and "losers"

(Hollands, 2015; Rossi, 2016; Shelton et al., 2015; Söderström, Paasche, & Klauser, 2014; Wiig, 2015a, 2015b; Wiig & Wyly, 2016). But as geographers located in different world regions, we also see far more than that. As detailed in Chapter 4, we have drawn attention to other types of external "orders" *in transition*, including the many different legacies and territorial-institutional impacts of a "social market order," shaped especially in Western Europe by greater socio-spatial equity, democratic accountability and social justice and, indeed, a "statist-*dirigist* order" driven more by the state apparatus in a neo-mercantilist tradition. Especially the post-war consensus, embodied in the (German) concept of a social market economy, gave the emerging 20th century state a major role in maintaining a social component in a market economy, aimed at maintaining social equity also geographically to foster (or maintain) national cohesion on the back of democratization. Our sense is that smartness in key city-regions re-discovers the underlying virtues of that concept in relation to democratic legitimacy and, importantly, justification of a liberal order in which with competitiveness can, indeed, go together with collective responsibility. So, there is increasingly an effort to look not only "beyond post-Fordism," then, but also "beyond neoliberalism" and, in many societies, as in post-socialist Eastern Europe and post-apartheid South Africa, still (re)building and rolling out key state institutions "beyond post-authoritarianism" as part of imagining a new democratic order. Against this, it is important to understand what neoliberal globalization is doing *to* cities (Toly, 2008), then, by stressing individual opportunity and, thus, be no less critical to look "beyond neoliber-alism" (Parnell & Robinson, 2012). This is to provincialize all regions, while suggesting, instead, that multiple socio-spatial stories are now playing out as everyone deals differently with their own histories and geographies, their own path-dependencies, even as they take on common global challenges, such as the complex dualism of sustainably and competitiveness, both alone, yet also in new collective networks of learning and transformation (Bouteligier, 2012).

Such a *comparative provincialization* means, that, for instance, internal efforts to move "beyond" post-authoritarianism through smartness in Prague or Cape Town or Berlin or Johannesburg, are not the same as efforts in Seattle and Vancouver to build their own kinds of "smart city-regions" in ways that move beyond the heavier neoliberal strictures of North American political-economies, embedded societal values and institutional cultures. In fact, one of the main motivations for writing this book, detailed especially in the eight case studies in Chapters 5 and 6, has been to show the geographical diversity of these global experiences, as the *structuration* of smart policies and projects invariably reflect place-specific variables, or, what we have called in Chapter 4, *placeness*, being in constant motion through the interdependent and mutu-ally affecting duality of variably concurrent internal and external dynamics. While everyone is struggling with the so-called "smart turn," a comparatively more "neo-mercantalist" French state, eschewing an *Anglo-Amercianisme* of all-out neoliberalism, for instance, is not experiencing anything like the kind of legitimacy crisis now enveloping, say, the South African state. Meanwhile,

Canadian and American forms of (long-standing) federalism, for their part, have rather differently shaped internal city-regional dynamics in Vancouver and Seattle, respectively, embedded in the particular cultural narratives and histories of the Pacific Northwest. Berlin and Prague also differ in their respective capabilities to "throw off" the mentalities and governing habits of their previous systems of "stateness" as all-dominant *dirigisme* that controlled society as well as economy and their spatial manifestations. Quite evidently, then, there is not a single smart modernity, but likely many, just as there are many, and changing, variations of transitions in societal values and expressions of *regime*. Nevertheless, and important to point out, there are, just as with transition, a number of common features across otherwise diverse city-regions now engaging the trendy new concepts of, and discourses on, "smart" projects and "smart" policies that constitute "smart" cities. Smart projects *in* places often exhibit the same technological "DNA" and, perhaps, even comparable socio-spatial *effects*, just as telephones, railroads, cars, televisions and radios did in previous eras, and, in various ways, continue to do. The revolutionary diffusion of smart phones, for example, creates new uniformities across urban-global space, as texting, wayfinding and ambulatory surfing entangle with local cultures of interaction. And this may, indeed, produce a new form of "globalization" in the ways of doing things and value systems held. Yet, as Doreen Massey (1994) once argued, the real work of geography is to find out how general processes work themselves out in specific forms in response to, but also as shapers of, spaces and places, because, as she also observed almost stubbornly, despite the unifying and even universalizing effects of technologically-driven flows of information, *geography matters*.

Many of the concrete initiatives discussed throughout this book are, indeed, *general* experiments found everywhere, that are progressively important in the production of contemporary urban geographies and overall regional development patterns – raising interesting new questions for researchers embarking on moves forward. For example, we noted in Chapter 5 that the *city* of Seattle appears to have dominated (so far) in the local production of new spaces strongly associated with the smart, creative, green, sharing, innovative and hip "after" post-Fordist economy, exemplified by the rise of "coworking" facilities. While such facilities have become "commonplace within a highly individualised labour market in which urban professionals work as a casualised, project-based and freelance workforce" (Gandini, 2015, p. 193), the question arises to what extent their actual spatializations in particular places tend to favour core cities over suburbs or even edge cities? To what extent are the new "superstar cities" like Seattle (Florida, 2017), home to Amazon's retail-transforming innovations, now reversing urban decline – Seattle was once a "shrinking city" – but paradoxically, and often elsewhere, undermining established local *modi vivendi* and, thus, as a result, amplifying urban (and regional) inequalities, where the already deep rifts between what we called "winners" and "losers" grow even more intensive and consequential? Put another way, we need ask to what extent smartness as (economic, physical or political) space is now part and parcel of what Scott (2001) sees as the "beyond" post-Fordist city-region. Here, he reasons, the "digitization" of the global economy, the erosion of standardized (Fordist) labour and the rise of a new class of "cognitive-cultural" workers, such as those that populate Microsoft and Amazon in Seattle, are effecting inter-urban structures of production and work, and, concomitantly, increasingly challenge established core patterns of urban and regional growth and crystalize new forms of social stratification (p. 849). Digitized urban social spaces are now part and parcel of, it seems, "the colonization of former blue collar neighbourhoods ... by members of the cognitariat" (p. 855) and, indeed, the globalization of "hipster" culture (Coffey, 2017).

Yet again, though, given our concluding insistence on comparative provincialization, we might also ask how relevant these arguments are to, say, Berlin and Prague, or Turin and Lyon? Or to Cape Town and Johannesburg? Or even to Seattle's "distance neighbour" of Vancouver (MacDonald, 1987)? If they are relevant, as the evidence in this book suggests they are, how are they nonetheless *specifically modified* by, for example, stouter (if admittedly now weakened) traditions of social-market government in France or Italy or Germany, or the explicit legacies of post-authoritarian pathologies – now couched in nationalist-populist public discourses – and the specific institutional experiences in Eastern Europe and South Africa? Our theoretical insistence on the complex co-mingling and mutually affecting of internal and external transitions, of structures and agencies and places, suggests that we pay considerable attention in future to how "smart city" projects are embedded within both their unevenly endowed regions and their wider political-economies. And, moreover, there is a need to look into how geo-historical changes in these wider contexts shape the actual possibilities for policy innovation and city-regional collaborations.

In some cases, such as Prague, internal evidence of creative propensity for smart policy innovation in the form of cross-scalar governance collaborations, is still rather limited. This is due, in part, as we have argued in Chapter 6, to the counter effects that those wider structures and norms bequeathed from the socialist era have had on the nature and progress of such processes. Specifically, we have suggested that non-cooperation between Prague and adjacent authorities is not so much the outcome of an inherent hostility, but, rather, of simple disinterest for want of obvious and tangible political rewards for such engagements, as well as an understandable desire to protect, and practice, "new-found" powers long effaced under the previous *dirigiste*, strictly top-down, political regimes. Johannesburg, in contrast, has arguably done as much as any case discussed in this book to link its urban destiny to the wider theoretical concept of a smart city-region, or what South African policy-makers and scholars see as the African "Smart Hub" of Gauteng, easily the most important "supercluster" on the African continent. We emphasized evidence, for example, of an emerging "smart entrepreneurial state" apparatus there, albeit at the urban-provincial scale of authority (Bbenkele & Madikiza, 2016). If that is so, then, obviously, we have much to learn *from* Johannesburg about the novel territorialities and modalities of the "smart state," even as we also emphasized, more soberly, growing concerns in South Africa with long-familiar pathologies like deep rent-seeking, open corruption and patron–client tribalism.

Still, negative issues of clientilism, corruption and avoidance of responsibility through bureaucratization can also be found in post-communist transitions in Eastern Europe. Such problems hardly characterize, for instance, the Canadian state in the same ways, and so the dual transition to smartness in the Johannesburg-Gauteng city-region cannot be explained by simply importing theory from outside, but only by generated theory from within (Robinson, 2006). This implies that there is no need for "a" theory of "the" smart city-region, that is, something akin to a perfect new "garden city" model for the digital age. We need theories, emphasizing "duality" and/or other epistemologies, of how variously situated city-regions are now engaging smartness as they pragmatically transition towards a normatively desirable world located between the twin goals of competitiveness and sustainability, "squaring" the elusive circle of regional development and societal change.

Smart city-region(s) and our normative future

The framework we have deployed in this book, first introduced in Figure 4.1, emphasizes analytical tools to chart two related transitions in smartness, including the internal extent of local regionalism and the external nature of state–society–market dynamics, and especially large-scale shifts away from both post-Fordist and post-authoritarian geo-political economies. The book thus proposes that understanding smartness, particularly when expanded beyond questions of technology *per se* into the wider realm of territorial governance, requires researchers to understand better the emerging global role of city-regions both in economic and political terms. And this needs to be done within a context that appreciates the diverse transitions co-constituting the development and performance of these city-regions and their political and societal discourses on key values and the relative roles of individuals alongside more collective opportunities and responsibilities.

Accordingly, whether work on smartness in various forms grows in the coming years, or, eventually, fades from view – just another flamboyant fad of the moment, resembling a shiny disco ball eventually discarded for "the next great thing" – depends squarely on its role in illuminating, in its multiple facets, what is really at stake. As suggested in this book, the remarkable interest in all things "smart" has less to do with snazzy apps or convenient and efficient parking or even real-time citizen feedback on service provision to suggest a "listening" public administration; it has to do with whether or not, and how, the accepted dominant paradigm of competitiveness can also be made sustainable – to meet another rapidly rising global paradigm. In effect, this means asking how a globalized world of "superclusters" can generate future livelihoods *equitably*, and without significantly eroding the ecological foundations of the planet and thus future generations. As we stated in our opening chapter, but worth reiterating here in the light of our major findings, smartness increasingly signifies efforts to capture variegated changes in the way urban development both can, and should, be directed. Smartness as innovative and also experimental governance seeks to accommodate multiple, even conflicting aspirations and agendas (Herrschel, 2013) – including underlying theoretical claims and empirical meanings that vary from place to place, between publics and between scholars, but especially with strategic reference to city-regional dynamics (Jonas, 2012). Again, Shahrokni and Brandt (2013, p. 117) are (partly) correct in suggesting that the smart city is a broader "urban region," where new technologies "weave together" physical, social and business infrastructures to help facilitate "intelligent decision-making and efficient city dynamics in order to realize sustainable development goals through citizen empowerment and participatory democracy." They are (entirely) correct, though, to suggest the possibilities of integrating technocracy, democracy, urbanism and sustainability. Yet as shown in Chapters 5 and 6 in our eight different case studies, any given "inter-weaving" depends strongly on how agency and structure are shaped, interwoven and connected by the sheer *placeness* of particular circumstances, and that at multiple scales.

The overall attempt in this book to provide a new "global map" of experimenting *smart* city-regions, however incomplete and methodologically bound by the familiar horizons of time and space, thus supports other scholars working on the new geographies of global city-regionalism, and especially how these new geographies of change illuminate wider strategies to forge sustainable regional economies in an "actually-existing" world shaped by political-economies loaded with history and culture (Brenner, 2001; Deas & Ward, 2000; Harrison, 2012; Jonas, 2013; Perlman & Jimenez, 2010; Savitch & Adhikari, 2016; Swanstrom, 2006; Ward & Jonas, 2004; Zimmerbauer & Paasi, 2013). As with recent critiques of sustainable cities, our normative sense is that the pursuit of smart(er) city-regions requires us to move well beyond what Karvonen (2011, p. 187) neatly calls the "technomanagerial endeavor to upgrade existing infrastructure." Such infrastructural endeavours, however important, at least initially exciting, and certainly worthy of detailed attention, nonetheless depend, as the ultimate conclusion here, on collective capacities to produce creative innovations with existing structures and policy tools, and thus to respond to what are essentially the politico-economic dynamics of city-regions *in transition* across a still, and perhaps ever more so, heterogeneous world under the impacts of globalization.

References

Albino, V., Berardi, U., & Dangelico, R. M. (2015). Smart cities: Definitions, dimensions, performance, and initiatives. *Journal of Urban Technology, 22*(1), 3–21.

Barber, B. (2013). *If mayors ruled the world: Dysfunctional nations, rising cities.* New Haven, CT: Yale University Press.

Bbenkele, E., & Madikiza, L. (2016). Envisioning public sector pathways: Gauteng as an entrepreneurial province in South Africa. *Journal of Entrepreneurship and Innovation in Emerging Economies, 2*(2), 91–108.

Bouteligier, S. (2012). *Global cities and networks for global environmental governance*. Hoboken, NY: Taylor & Francis.

Brenner, N. (2001). Decoding the newest "metropolitan regionalism" in the USA: A critical overview. *European Planning Studies, 9*(7), 813–826.

Coffey, H. (2017). Why hipster culture is the new globalisation – and why it's taking over the world. *The Independent*, 2 Aug. 2017.

Deas, I., & Ward, K. (2000). From the "new localism" to the "new regionalism"? The implications of regional development agencies for city-regional relations. *Political Geography, 19*, 272–292.

Dierwechter, Y. (2017). *Urban Sustainability through smart growth: Intercurrence, planning, and geographies of regional development across Greater Seattle*. Cham, Switz.: Springer.

Florida, R. L. (2017). *The new urban crisis: How our cities are increasing inequality, deepening segregation, and failing the middle class – and what we can do about it*. New York: Basic Books.

Gandini, A. (2015). The rise of coworking spaces: A literature review. *Ephemera: Theory and Politics in Organisations, 15*(1), 193–205.

Harrison, J. (2012). Life after regions? The evolution of city-regionalism in England. *Regional Studies, 46*(9), 1243–1259.

Harvey, D. (1989). *The condition of postmodernity: An enquiry into the origins of cultural change*. Oxford: Blackwell.

Herrschel, T. (2013). Competitiveness and sustainability: Can "smart city regionalism" square the circle? *Urban Studies, 50*(11), 2332–2348. doi: 10.1177/0042098013478240

Herrschel, T., & Newman, P. (2017). *Cities as international actors*. London: Palgrave.

Hollands, R. (2015). Critical interventions into the corporate smart city. *Cambridge Journal of Regions Economy and Society, 8*(1), 61–77.

Jonas, A. E. G. (2012). Region and place: Regionalism in question. *Progress in Human Geography, 36*(2), 263–272.

Jonas, A. E. G. (2013). City-regionalism as a contingent "geopolitics of capitalism". *Geopolitics, 18*(2), 284–298.

Jonas, A. E. G., & Moisio, S. (2016). City regionalism as geopolitical processes: A new framework for analysis. *Progress in Human Geography*.

Karvonen, A. (2011). *Politics of urban runoff: Nature, technology, and the sustainable city*. Cambridge, MA: MIT Press.

Knaap, G. (2001). *Land market monitoring for smart urban growth*. Cambridge, MA: Lincoln Institute of Land Policy.

Kylili, A., & Fokaides, P. A. (2015). European smart cities: The role of zero energy buildings. *Sustainable Cities and Society, 15*, 8–-95.

MacDonald, N. (1987). *Distant neighbors: A comparative history of Seattle and Vancouver*. Seattle: University of Washington Press.

MacLeod, G. (2013). New urbanism/smart growth in the Scottish Highlands: Mobile policies and post-politics in local development planning. *Urban Studies, 50*(11), 2196–2221.

Massey, D. (1994). *Space, place and gender*. Cambridge: Polity Press.

Parnell, S., & Robinson, J. (2012). (Re)theorizing cities from the global south: Looking beyond neoliberalism. *Urban Geography, 33*(4), 593–617.

Perera, C., Zaslavsky, A., Christen, P., & Georgakopoulos, D. (2014). Sensing as a service model for smart cities supported by Internet of Things. *Transactions on Emerging Telecommunications Technologies, 25*(1), 81–93. doi:10.1002/ett.2704

Perlman, B. J., & Jimenez, J. (2010). Creative Regionalism: Governance for stressful times. *State and Local Government Review, 42*(2), 151–155.

Pezzoli, K., Hibbard, M., & Huntoon, L. (2006). Introduction to Symposium: Is progressive regionalism an actionable framework for critical planning theory and practice? *Journal of Planning Education and Research, 25*(4), 449–457.

Robinson, J. (2006). *Ordinary cities: Between modernity and development.* London: Routledge.

Rossi, U. (2016). The variegated economics and the potential politics of the smart city. *Territory, Politics, Governance, 4*(3), 337–353.

Savitch, H. V., & Adhikari, S. (2016). Fragmented regionalism. *Urban Affairs Review, 53*(2), 381–402.

Scott, A. (2001). Globalization and the rise of city regions. *European Planning Studies, 9*(7), 813–826.

Shahrokni, H., & Brandt, N. (2013). Making sense of smart city sensors. In C. Ellul, S. Zlatanova, M. Rumor, & R. Laurini (Eds.), *Urban and regional data management, UDMS annual 2013* (pp. 117–127). Boca Raton, FL: CRC Press.

Shelton, T., Zook, M., & Wiig, A. (2015). The "actually existing smart city". *Cambridge Journal of Regions Economy and Society, 8*(1), 13–25.

Söderström, O., Paasche, T., & Klauser, F. (2014). Smart cities as corporate storytelling. *City, Analysis of Urban Trends, Culture, Theory, Policy, Action, 18*(3), 307–320.

Swanstrom, T. (2006). Regionalism, equality, and democracy. *Urban Affairs Review, 42*(2), 249–257.

Toly, N. (2008). Transnational municipal networks in climate politics: From global governance to global politics. *Globalizations, 5*(3), 341–356.

Townsend, A. M. (2013). *Smart cities: Big data, civic hackers, and the quest for a new utopia* (First edn.). New York: W.W. Norton & Company.

Ward, K., & Jonas, A. E. G. (2004). Competitive city-regionalism as a politics of space: A critical reinterpretation of the new regionalism. *Environment and Planning A, 36*(12), 2119–2139.

Wiig, A. (2015a). The empty rhetoric of the smart city: From digital inclusion to economic promotion in Philadelphia. *Urban Geography,* 1–19.

Wiig, A. (2015b). IBM's smart city as techno-utopian policy mobility. *City, 19*(2–3), 258–273.

Wiig, A., & Wyly, E. (2016). Introduction: Thinking through the politics of the smart city. *Urban Geography, 37*(4), 485–493.

Zanella, A., Bui, N., Castellani, A., Vangelista, L., & Zorzi, M. (2014). Internet of Things for smart cities. *Ieee Internet of Things Journal, 1*(1), 22–32.

Zimmerbauer, K., & Paasi, A. (2013). When old and new regionalism collide: Deinstitutionalization of regions and resistance identity in municipality amalgamations. *Journal of Rural Studies, 30*, 31–40.

Index

Note: Page numbers in *italics* relate to figures; page numbers in **bold** relate to tables.